'Don't read this book if you don't have the courage a
lead change.'

Mark Cutifani, Chief Executive O

'A welcome complement to the first edition, this book should be the top-drawer practical text for all leaders. It reinforces the case for primacy of human over technical systems, and the importance of trust among employees as the outcome of an effective culture.'

David Murray, former Chief Executive Officer of Commonwealth Bank of Australia (during successful transition from government ownership)

'During my career at Southern California Edison, I have implemented many of the principles described in the Systems Leadership book and can attest to their value in bringing about organizational change and improving effectiveness. It is a must read for leaders wanting to make their organizations more innovative and customer responsive.'

John Fielder, retired President, Southern California Edison

'This is a timely and important book that contributes significantly to our understanding and development of positive organisations. Built on rock-solid theoretical foundations, this book offers much to both academics and practitioners and provides a rigorous and coherent approach which will support all those interested in helping organisations and individuals fulfil their potential.'

Professor Andy Adcroft, Deputy Dean, Surrey Business School

'Leadership of complex organisations like the NHS needs to marry people and systems thinking, sound theory and learning through application. They are here in one excellent book.'

Alan Willson, Associate Director, Aneurin Bevan Continuous Improvement, NHS Wales

'For school leaders who want to make a real difference, read this book and start using the concepts, models and tools of systems leadership. The best thing you could do for your work and your school.'

Clive Dixon, former Regional Director, Far North Queensland Department of Education

'People in complex organisations have a powerful need to understand what is expected of them to perform at their best. "Systems Leadership" provides a practical framework to describe and organise work, enabling team members to interact without fear or ambiguity.'

Steve Hodgson, Chief Executive Officer, Rusal Marketing GmbH

'A city manager faces constant demands for better services at lower cost (and lower taxes). Any mis-step can make headlines. Years of experience had given me a good intuitive understanding of what needed to be done in my city, but I found the language and theories of Systems Leadership and Stratified Systems clarified my experiences and allowed me to make changes to put the right people in the right roles and to improve our city's systems and services to our citizens. I recommend this book for City Managers and all public managers who can help themselves, their employees and their communities by applying these ideas in your public organization.'

Don F. McIntyre, former City Manager of Pasadena, CA

'There are few books that provide essential leadership theory, based in both organizational and human behavior, as well as practical guidelines and solutions to everyday leadership challenges the way Systems Leadership does. The theory presented in this book has been foundational to my understanding of organizations over the years. Systems Leadership is designed to provide spot on support for structuring routine leadership tasks along with easily accessible principles that offer insight for addressing difficult issues and people within the work of an organization. The novice as well as the seasoned leader will find Systems Leadership to be a rich resource for personal and professional development.'

Wilsie Bishop, Vice President for Health Affairs,
Eastern Tennessee State University

'The sound theory and ideas described in this latest version of the book remain highly applicable to the Higher Education sector and have influenced our approach to a series of challenging issues over the past 10 years with very beneficial outcomes.'

Paul R Thomas CBE; Chief Operating
Officer Brunel University London

FROM THE FIRST EDITION

'Like most leaders, I have initiated many changes in organisations – some were successful and others were disasters! While the changes may have been ultimately achieved, it was more trial and error, with loss of time, human capital and leadership trust. This book revolutionized my approach to leadership and cultural change. It is a "how-to", providing the requisite roadmap with many practical tools for the leadership tool belt to help transform efficiently any organisation. Having worked across several mining and metals industries and in countries from the United States, to Wales and Russia, these tools transcend all cultures providing common, practical people-based concepts that will stay with you for a life time. This material is not "rocket science" – it is a refreshing reinforcement of the common sense behaviors all leaders must have to be successful, but may have lost in their search for the 'quick fixes' or "silver bullets".'

Wayne R. Hale, Senior Vice President,
Upstream SUAL-Holding, Moscow, Russia

'I have been eagerly awaiting Systems Leadership (Macdonald, et al.). The theoretical under standings and tools developed by the authors have long been central to my work. Systems Leadership however exceeds my expectations. It greatly extends my understanding. While I will use system leaderships as a seminal text as a school leader, I realise anyone fair dinkum about leadership or organisational effectiveness, no matter the size or context of their organisation, will also benefit. I needed this book. I will use it, because I know the material works.'

Don Anderson, Tagai State College, Australia

'This work is based on a multitude of practical experiences where the sustainable benefits from implementing the methodology have been very significant. ... Experienced Leaders will recognise much of this material as a good fit with their intuitive understanding of how they have achieved success in the past. The value of this work is the ability to standardise this insight and to develop a new generation of leaders with confidence in a positive outcome both for them and the organisation.'

Oscar Groeneveld, Chief Executive, Rio Tinto Aluminium

'This book is a must read for those who want to attain sustain able competitive advantage as the world moves away from industrial relations systems to human relations models. It helps build the prerequisites for an organisation to link its human systems to the business model (and vice versa). CEO's, executives, boards, policy advisors and academics should read it if sustainable productivity improvement is on their agenda. After all, multi factor productivity is ultimately driven by labour productivity. Social process deserves the same degree of rigour that we traditionally apply to science, engineering, etc. if we are to achieve the most challenging and rewarding work through proper and ethical concepts of leadership.'

David Murray, retired CEO of Commonwealth Bank
and Chairman, Future Fund

'Systems Leadership is some of the most import ant work ever written with respect to understanding and improving organisations and their culture, irrespective of size or type. For those of us in the business of running companies, advising to executive teams or boards, Macdonald provides the ability to predict with absolute certainty the effect of management initiatives, well meaning or otherwise, on the organisation's culture and employee relations. It provides a framework for the design of your organisation and people systems. Virgin Blue Airlines, voted Worlds Best low cost airline in 2004 and 2005, continue to use Systems Leadership theories to guide the rapid growth of our business and maintain our unique guest service experience. I cannot recommend the practical importance of this work more highly to those serious about sustaining an effective executive career.'

Bruce Highfield, General Manager People and
founding executive team member, Virgin Blue Airlines Ltd

'Systems Leadership provides a unique perspective on the social building blocks that need to be put in place for businesses to be positioned to deliver success. It doesn't promise miracles, it provides a framework for leaders to create an environment in which people are encouraged to fully utilise their capabilities to deliver a successful organisation. Macdonald et al. have refreshingly acknowledged there are no shortcuts or silver bullets to delivering performance. Leaders must under stand the world in which they exist and provide appropriate context for the teams they lead.
... don't read this book if you don't have the courage and perseverance to lead change. Our business is people and we will ultimately be measured as leaders by the results people deliver.'

Mark Cutifani, Executive Vice President and
Chief Operating Officer – CVRD-Inco

Systems Leadership

The new edition of this influential and bestselling book is concerned with how people come together to achieve a productive purpose. Survival and success in business and social terms have always depended upon our ability to form and sustain social organisations. People have a deep need to be creative and to belong. By creating positive organisations, we can fulfil these needs and build a worthwhile society. One of the failures of organisations is precisely the lack of efficient and effective social organisation, which is what this whole book is about. Poor social organisation, including poor leadership, are major drivers of poor productivity and lead people to give up or retreat into a minimalist approach of just doing what is needed to get by and survive.

The authors provide a language for developing, discussing, thinking and working with propositions about organisations and management. They do not tell you what decision to make but rather present tools to help you consider, analyse and predict the consequences of your decisions.

This new edition is much broader in its application areas – public, private and not-for-profit sectors. It contains new models and propositions with regard to types of social organisation, domains of work and the nature and use of authority. It contains a range of new case studies, and throughout looks at how these ideas can be used to achieve an organisation's purpose while encouraging creative working. It is not a book about fads or fashion but an integrated approach that offers the user the benefit of foresight.

Dr Ian Macdonald is Founder and Director of Macdonald Associates, an international organisational consultancy. He is a director of BIOSS International Ltd. He is also an honorary fellow at Brunel University, teaches at Surrey Business School and works with NHS Wales and Welsh government.

Dr Catherine Burke was Associate Professor of Public Administration, University of Southern California. Her research focuses on organisation and systems design, management theory and leadership. She has been a consultant to Southern California Edison, the cities of Los Angeles and Pasadena, and the Congressional Office of Technology Assessment. Her publications include *Innovation and Public Policy*, and articles in various academic journals. She was a director at Commonwealth Aluminum.

Karl Stewart is a mining engineer spending most of his working life in leadership positions. He spent four years as an internal managerial consultant developing a thorough understanding of the theory underpinning the leadership of people in organisations and the systems that facilitate that activity. He implemented these ideas as Managing Director of Comalco Smelting.

Systems Leadership

Creating Positive Organisations

Second Edition

IAN MACDONALD
CATHERINE BURKE
KARL STEWART

 Routledge
Taylor & Francis Group

LONDON AND NEW YORK

Second edition published 2018
by Routledge
2 Park Square, Milton Park, Abingdon, Oxon, OX14 4RN

and by Routledge
711 Third Avenue, New York, NY 10017

Routledge is an imprint of the Taylor & Francis Group, an informa business

First edition published by Routledge in 2006

British Library Cataloguing-in-Publication Data
A catalogue record for this book is available from the British Library

Library of Congress Cataloging-in-Publication Data
Names: Macdonald, Ian, 1950 October 23– author. | Burke, Catherine G.,
    1939– author | Stewart, Karl, author.
Title: Systems leadership : creating positive organisations / Ian Macdonald,
    Catherine Burke and Karl Stewart.
Description: Second edition. | Abingdon, Oxon; New York, NY :
    Routledge, 2018. | Includes bibliographical references and index.
Identifiers: LCCN 2017059079 (print) | LCCN 2017061133 (ebook) |
    ISBN 9781315178486 (eBook) | ISBN 9781138036543 (hardback : alk.
    paper) | ISBN 9781138036574 (pbk. : alk. paper)
Subjects: LCSH: Organizational sociology. | Organizational effectiveness. |
    Leadership.
Classification: LCC HM791 (ebook) | LCC HM791. M33 2018 (print) |
    DDC 302.3/5—dc23 LC record available at https://lccn.loc.gov/
    2017059079

ISBN: 978-1-138-03654-3 (hbk)
ISBN: 978-1-138-03657-4 (pbk)
ISBN: 978-1-315-17848-6 (ebk)

Typeset in ITC Stone Serif
by RefineCatch Limited, Bungay, Suffolk

Visit the companion website: www.Routledge.com/cw/Macdonald

MIX
Paper from
responsible sources
FSC
www.fsc.org   FSC™ C013985

Printed in the United Kingdom
by Henry Ling Limited

This book is dedicated to our parents who were fine role models and influenced our thinking and behaviour more than they realised.

Contents

Figures

Tables

Tables

Preface to the Second Edition

Whenever another edition to an existing text comes out, there is always the question of 'why?' In this case it is over ten years since the first edition and in that time we have expanded the material, brought in new ideas and significantly refined and developed others. In addition, other ideas have emerged in the field of Organisational Behaviour.

As such this second edition contains new material as well as a refinement of the original material. We have also learnt much from further testing these ideas in an even broader range of organisations and received feedback from that work as well as from readers who have shared ideas and experiences and given us suggestions for improvement.

In particular we recognise the more general field of 'Systems Thinking' and the similarly titled 'System Leadership', which has become known especially in the UK Public Sector. There are similarities in that material but also significant differences.

So what's new in the second edition?

First of all this edition explains more fully what Systems Leadership is: its purpose, what is distinctive about it and why it is both unique and practical. This will be explained in Part 1.

Secondly we have reorganised the structure of the book to flow more easily and be of more help to potential users.

Thirdly there is new material including a new chapter on social, technical and commercial aspects of organisation, a new chapter on Social Process, and clarification of our ideas regarding authority and power. There is new material concerning different sources of authority and how that impacts upon organisations.

We discuss how the purpose of the organisation determines appropriate organisational structures and systems. Thus the book has relevance not just to the business sector but also to all sectors such as public and not for profit.

This material is based upon over fifty years of research, practice and testing in many different types of organisations in many different countries and cultures.

Fourthly there is expanded discussion and examples of material not only for business organisations but also for public agencies, charitable organisations, hospitals, educational institutions and others that have found our material useful. There is a related website that offers case studies and discussion. As such we have increased the practical relevance of the book.

Unlike many approaches we do not simply state the 'What'; e.g. 'it is important to build trust' but we actually describe 'how' to do that and how real organisations have applied our approach. This is something most books about organisation do not do.

As in the previous book we do not simply state 'best practice', or current fads but base our concepts on tried and tested theory. Like our definition of work we help 'turn intention into reality'.

We are concerned with developing Productive Social Cohesion by applying an integrated approach based on sound theory. That in itself is unusual.

We as authors and practitioners are still driven by the need to help create positive organisations: places where people can be creative, realise their potential while engaging in effective and productive work. Still today that is far from the reality for many people during their working life.

We believe this is still vital because our own observations, supported by new data from the Gallup Organisation, indicate that the problem that has concerned us – the development of Productive Social Cohesion – is still a serious problem in too many organisations. The damage done to people and the inefficiency in organisations are still too prevalent.

Gallup has been studying employee engagement for decades and by 2013 had reviewed more than 25 million responses to their employee engagement survey (Gallup, 2013: 4). They found 30% were 'engaged and inspired in work'. Thus good leadership and organisation is possible, though apparently not common. It is sometimes more by accident than design. The bad news is that only 35% of managers (who are of course also employees) are engaged in their work (Gallup, 2015: 22). Even worse, Gallup attributes 70% of the variance in employee engagement across business units to managers (ibid.: 8).

The size of the sample gives confidence that these numbers do, in fact, indicate the magnitude of the problem, whether or not they are precisely accurate. They indicate that when leaders fail to create working environments that allow and encourage people to maximise their contributions, maximise their human potential, and improve the quality of their working lives, there are major costs both to the organisations and the people who work within them. Human social processes and systems have a direct impact on whether the organisation can achieve its purpose.

To quote Jim Clifton, Chairman and CEO of Gallup:

Most CEOs I know honestly don't care about employees or take an interest in human resources. Sure, they know who their stars are and love them – but it ends there. Since CEOs don't care, they put little to no pressure on their HR departments to get their cultures right, which allows HR to unwittingly implement all kinds of development and succession strategies that don't work.

(Gallup, 2015: 2)

A bad CEO can destroy what has taken years to create (Witzel, 2015), so Boards take heed. 'Managerial incompetence is not consequence-free. It kills companies and sometimes too it kills people too' (Witzel, 2015:19). We argue in this book that creating the culture is the work of leadership and that starts at the top. HR departments are not accountable for the organisational culture; that is the work of management.

We have seen organisations and parts of organisations function well. Often this is due to the people there at the time. We are concerned about sustainability, not just temporary success, however spectacular.

This book is about how to create long-term, sustainable success. It is neither quick nor easy. Many others will present apparently more attractive, more popular solutions: single terms like 'Collaboration', 'Innovation' or catchy phrases that imply simple, even 'secret', solutions that like the latest diet will promise magically to solve the problem.

Finally we have, along with our publisher, created a website where case studies new and old can be found. If you have a case you would like to share, where things went either very well, very badly, or somewhere in between, we would like to see it, and perhaps include it on the website. The best cases analyse why things occurred as they did – what caused the successes and what caused the failures (and we all have failures from time to time), and how you dealt with each. The website also includes related papers comparing and contrasting approaches.

We will also be producing further 'how to do it' materials called the Work of Management Series to provide more detailed guidance on how a variety of managers have used this material to improve their own work situation. This series will also include more detailed examples of how these ideas apply in governmental and non-profit organisations, including the leadership of volunteers.

Positive organisations are essential to a healthy and just society. At an individual level they provide the means whereby we can be creative and justly feel that we 'have made a difference' whether that is nursing a child, cleaning a room, repairing a car, digging ore, restructuring a department, designing a new system, implementing a strategy or serving a customer. At a social level they provide the goods and services we all need and thus help build productive social cohesion that is part of an infrastructure that maintains a mutually supportive society.

The purpose of this book is to provide practical help, based on sound theory and principles, to those trying to build such a society.

The following websites may be useful:

Routledge: https://www.routledge.com/Systems-Leadership-Creating-Positive-Organisations/
    Macdonald-Burke-Burke-Stewart/p/book/9780566087004
MAC: www.maconsultancy.com
BIOSS: www.bioss.com
SLDA: www.sldassociation.com

Overview of the Book's Content

First, we should point out that this book is not intended to be a complete textbook on running an organisation. We focus on human social processes and relationships. We do not present a complete picture that includes financial, technical or legal elements of leadership and organisations. These are available in other publications. We do, however, try to show the links to these other important areas of organisational practice.

This book is written to help leaders create conditions that actively encourage people to use their capabilities in achieving constructive goals.

We argue that this is not a matter of applying a few simple rules. It is not easy because elements of an organisation are connected. The structure is influenced by systems and in turn influenced by the capability of people. The quality of leadership, clarity of work and role and the underlying nature of relationships all help to determine how an organisation runs. This is why understanding these relationships requires a coherent, overall, conceptual framework from which a set of tools can be fashioned to help understand and manage these relationships. There is no short cut. We have found that for many leaders of organisations understanding this material gives a structure and meaning to their experience. It gives 'common sense' a rationale. Many good leaders have told us how these ideas gave form to what they do intuitively and filled in the gaps, helping them understand why some actions worked and others didn't.

This book is about how to build and run a positive and successful organisation. Success is defined as:

- achieving the organisation's purpose;
- providing work to match and challenge the capabilities of employees/members;

- providing appropriate recognition and reward for that work;
- making a positive contribution to the society within which the organisation operates (or a range of societies in the case of multinational and international organisations).

Running a successful organisation over time cannot be done by charismatic leadership alone. There must be structures and systems that can survive individuals. Therefore this book is organised and written to build from very general statements and propositions about human behaviour to very specific examples of implementation in particular contexts.

Each part of the book builds on the previous part and will not make full sense without understanding the basic propositions made earlier.

Part 1 explains why we regard conceptual clarity as critical. We ask the simple question 'What is work?' from which flows a discussion of the importance of work to us as people and society. We look at how we come together to form social organisations and how different types of organisation need structures and systems appropriate to their purpose. We also discuss authority, where it comes from and how the way it is enacted impacts upon how we are likely to respond.

In Part 2 we propose six principles of behaviour that underpin all social interaction and influence all that we do and say in creating social cohesion.

In Part 3 we describe how we understand organisations: the nature of human capability and how that links to the underlying structure which in turn reflects different types of complexity and uncertainty.

In Part 4 we address the real work of leadership: how to build a productive culture, often required but rarely explained in terms of what must be done. We argue for the need for clarity and describe in practical terms how we can work together effectively. We describe not only the work of leaders but also the work of team members, rarely discussed in practical detail.

Part Five describes how to make change happen. We examine this as an ongoing process and go into depth about the nature, importance and effect of systems including their design. We look at actual cases; examples where Systems Leadership Theory (SLT) has been used to design, implement and reflect on organisational change. We then look at dangers in the process and what needs to be done to secure positive changes and Productive Social Cohesion.

The theory and practices presented provide analytical tools, a methodology and logic for good management and leadership practice. They can never, however, take the place of judgement that is the lifeblood of the organisation.

It is vital that this distinction be understood, as it is the common thread throughout the book. We emphasise the difference between necessary and sufficient conditions. Too often organisational texts suggest we can create systems that provide both the necessary and sufficient conditions for success. We believe this is a misguided quest that ends in the creation of organisations and systems that function as straitjackets. When such systems are implemented they lead to frustration and failure. Eventually, if the organisation is to survive, people will simply get round them.

Once again, theories and systems can only provide the necessary conditions; the sufficient conditions must be provided by human judgement. We will discuss the elements that properly set the limits on managerial judgement while at the same time allowing (and requiring) managers to exercise their judgement. We respect the right and necessity of each manager to make such judgements, and none of our propositions should be seen to conflict with that right and necessity.

Acknowledgements

As we said in the first edition, this book is not simply the result of our own work, including more than fifty years of experience, but many others have contributed to our ideas. Just after World War II, in England a small group of theorists and managers, led by the late Dr Elliott Jaques, began a concerted effort to bring the discipline of science to the practice of management. They sought to develop explicit theories with hypotheses (predictions) and to test their validity. Wilfred (later Lord) Brown was the managing director of Glacier Metals who collaborated with Jaques in developing the ideas and putting them into practice (see Jaques, 1951; Brown, 1960; Brown and Jaques, 1965; Brown, 1971; Gray, 1976; Jaques, 1976).

In the 1980s this body of knowledge became known as 'stratified systems theory'. In this book we draw on the early work of Jaques and Brown, especially the concepts of work, levels of work and organisational structure. We have, in the light of our experiences, modified their ideas but their work was seminal to our efforts.

In 1966, Jaques was a founder and first director of the Brunel Institute for Organisational and Social Studies (BIOSS) at Brunel University near London. Dr Ian Macdonald began working with Jaques at BIOSS in 1973. Dr Gillian P. Stamp, who became director of BIOSS after Dr Jaques, has done research on human capability and development that has informed our thinking. Other important research was conducted at Brunel by David Billis, R.O. Gibson, John Isaacs, Richard Joss, Lucy Lofting, B.M. O'Connor, Ralph Rowbottom, Stephen Cang and many others. A selection of their publications is listed in the Bibliography. This was a very creative time involving many staff at BIOSS contributing to stratified systems theory.

Sir Roderick Carnegie, who was then chairman and chief executive officer of CRA Ltd of Australia (now Rio Tinto), began introducing many of these ideas into the company in the 1980s. Sir Roderick and later Jack Brady of CRA Ltd led the implementation of these structural ideas in their organisations and provided major intellectual and material support as the work progressed. One of the present authors, Karl Stewart, had the privilege of working for Sir Roderick and Jack Brady, first as an internal group consultant to CRA from 1983 to 1986 and later as managing director of Comalco Smelting. While at Comalco Smelting, he had the opportunity of extending the concepts and applying them in practice. It was during this time that many of the theories and models in this book were conceived, developed and implemented.

As group consultant, Stewart was given the task of developing a plan to restructure Hamersley Iron (HI) Pty, a large mining complex in Western Australia. He was also to devise a set of theories that would allow the development of systems to underpin the restructuring. These systems were then to be used in other CRA business units. Members of the Hamersley Iron Organisation Development (OD) teams from 1984 to 1988 made significant contributions to this work. Terry Palmer took over from Stewart to lead the third and fourth HI OD teams. Later he became managing director of Hamersley Iron and then chief executive officer (CEO) of Comalco Ltd. He was a long-time friend and colleague who made major contributions to the work of the authors. Before his untimely death he put these ideas into practice and provided clear evidence of their usefulness in helping a manager to predict behaviour and deliver outcomes.

Ian Macdonald worked with Stewart and Palmer at CRA where they created the 'values model', theories of leadership, behaviour, systems and symbols and the ideas concerning teams and teamwork. Catherine Burke began working with Stewart and Macdonald in 1985 and contributed to the development of these ideas in the United States. She has been able to test these ideas in an academic setting over many years and encourage her students to carry out further research.

John Fielder moved from general manager to department head, to vice president, to senior vice president and then president of Southern California Edison (SCE) during the course of our mutual association. He had the courage and foresight to adopt many of these ideas, bringing them into his organisation. He was especially instrumental in demonstrating by application the value of the theories in a rapidly changing high technology environment of computing and communications.

The original, and crucial, support at SCE came through the efforts of Dr Dan Smith, Manager of Quality and Training in the Information Services Department who brought Burke in as a consultant. They enjoyed a close collaboration for nearly ten years. Other managers at SCE also made important contributions.

Brigadier Roderick Macdonald of the British Army (and brother to Ian) spent a year on a Defence Fellowship with Burke at the University of Southern California studying leadership processes (Macdonald, R., 1991). While still in the army, he spent significant parts of his leave time working with his brother and Stewart to develop the values model and theories of leadership. Brigadier Macdonald was able to bring the personal experience of combat leadership as a test of the concepts of leadership. Since leaving the British Army he has moved to the US, where he continues to work with us and to apply the theories in a wide range of settings.

Also in the 1980s and 1990s Ian Macdonald formed an international association of consultants, Macdonald Associates Consultancy Ltd (www.maconsultancy.com). All the consultants have contributed to our work. These include Revd David Dadswell, Dr Richard Joss, Geoff McGill, Tony Dunlop, Phillip Bartlett and the late Revd Michael Evers and Revd Philip Biggs. This work has now developed and expanded through the formation of the Systems Leadership Development Association (www.sldassociation.com); the work is further tested and refined through this association. In addition Ian has rejoined the organisation originated at Brunel University and now called BIOSS, another international consultancy (see bioss.com).

Steve Burke has worked as a consultant with Dr Burke since the early 1980s. He has made significant contributions to our thinking and especially to the systems of performance management.

Over the years, managers and scholars in Argentina, Australia, Canada, Denmark, Russia, Singapore, South Africa, Sweden and the United States as well as the UK contributed to the development of both theory and practice. We are deeply indebted to all of these people, many of whom we have worked closely with up to the present time: the late Dr Neils Busch-Jensen, Les Cupper, Kathy Gould, the late Colonel (and Dr) Larry Ingraham, Dr Harry Levinson, David Brewer, the late Dr Carlos Rigby, Mark Woffenden, and David Sadler who, as both a Managing Director and Associate, has developed and implemented these ideas particularly in the area of safety where his work and advice has without doubt saved many lives. There are of course many other managers and theorists who have contributed, perhaps more than they realise.

They and other members of the Social Analytic Learning Society, which was active from 1985 through the early 1990s, took time to listen, to argue and to illuminate ideas which would be far less well-developed were it not for their hard-edged analyses and criticisms.

In addition, we are indebted to the managers and employees of the organisations we have been associated with. The organisations include mines, smelters, city governments, voluntary organisations, churches, indigenous communities, housing associations, colleges, schools, banks, health authorities, the US Army and the British Army, rolling mills, computing organisations, utilities, an internet service provider, an airline and even a manufacturer of vitamins. They used and commented upon earlier versions of this book. They also gave their time to test, argue, criticise, develop and anguish over the application of the theories in practice. Without their perseverance, often in the face of real anger and frustration, this work would not have been possible.

There are many doctoral students who contributed by testing these ideas through their dissertation research with Dr Burke. Drs Wilsey Bishop, David Boals, Loren Goldman, Donald Gould Mu Dan Ping and Edward Pape, Jr have used these theories to study nursing, public libraries, police agencies, university libraries and cross-cultural relationships.

In more recent years we are indebted to those in the Far North Queensland Region of Education. This work, which is the subject of a separate book, has tested and refined the ideas in the education of young Australians, especially Aboriginal students and Torres Straits Islander students. Special mention goes to Tony Tiplady who has worked tirelessly with these ideas across many organisations since the 1980s and provided friendship and support as well as ideas. Clive Dixon introduced the ideas and tested them throughout the entire region.

We thank them all. This book represents their thinking as well as our own, though their interpretations and thinking may differ from ours. We hope we have not abused their ideas, and we accept full accountability for any errors, misinterpretations and omissions.

We acknowledged David Dadswell and Duncan Harvey's contribution to the preparation of the first edition. This time we must thank the invaluable work done by Deborah Ussher and Patricia Nolan in preparing, working on, reviewing and retyping manuscripts. Their patience and skill have been remarkable. We also thank Jonathan Norman, our previous editor, who, although moving to another role during the writing, generously continued to offer his skills and knowledge that have undoubtedly improved the quality of this book. We would also like to thank the graphic designer David Varley for his contribution and excellent advice with regard to cover design.

Finally we thank our long-suffering families who have put up with our seemingly never-ending rewrites instead of paying them the due attention that they deserve!

Systems Leadership: Why the Title?

Introduction to Part 1

Over the years we have observed that there are almost as many ideas about what makes a good organisation as there are people. We have said that organisational design is an area that is subject to fad and fashion almost as much as dieting or child rearing. There seems to be a strong attraction towards simple solutions often expressed in terms of one aspect. Whatever is assumed to be the 'answer' changes from year to year. One year it is 'leadership', next it is 'teamwork' or 'empowerment' or 'collaboration' or 'innovation'. There is a fashion to move away from 'hierarchy' or so-called 'command and control' towards an 'organic emergent network' or 'holacracy'. One problem with this is that such terms are never clearly defined. Like beauty they remain in the eye of the beholder and can eventually lead to a wide range of organisational arrangements where it is unclear what is contributing to or detracting from success or failure.

We argue that if we are to understand what contributes to the difference between success and failure we must have clarity about what we mean. We need shared definitions so as to be clear about what we mean by empowerment or innovation or even hierarchy.

Systems Leadership is a body of knowledge that helps not only to understand but also to predict the way that people behave and are likely to behave in organisations. Using Systems Leadership gives you the 'Benefit of Foresight'. It is about how to create, sustain and improve productive social cohesion that is it helps to create the conditions where people willingly work together and give of their best.

Systems Leadership (SL) is a coherent and integrated theory of organisational behaviour. It is based on over fifty years of research worldwide and across many organisations and cultures. Its uniqueness lies in the fact that it covers all aspects of organisation. It has a clear leadership model but that is also directly related to a theory of capability that in turn is related to structure and systems. The underlying theory of Productive Social Cohesion also includes a theory of what is specifically meant by culture and values based behaviour. Therefore the critical advantage is that fragmentation can be avoided by not having to use different approaches to these aspects of organisation. Using a range of approaches may mean that they are unrelated and can indeed be in conflict and contradictory. Other approaches often only cover one or two of these topics. There are other models of leadership and or teamwork but how they connect to the design of an organisation may not be specified. Models of culture maybe disconnected from ideas about systems design or the operation of an organisation.

Although analogies and metaphor can be simplistic, we can liken SL to the functioning of the body. Although there are specialists in fields such as the heart, brain or muscles and so on, none of these makes sense until we understand how they all function together as an overall system. The structure of an organisation (skeleton) only functions when operating through systems (muscles, blood flow) which in turn are integrated with the human elements of capability and values (vital organs). We should not isolate, study or change elements without knowing how this will impact on others.

We argue that it is not effective to introduce leadership training independent of examining the structure and systems of an organisation or the capability of people to do the work required.

Another metaphor would be a motor vehicle. We do not design a car without understanding as to how all the parts fit together and, in particular, function together according to engineering principles, theory and purpose. Yet we will work on 'bits' of organisations without reference to an overall predictive theory.

In SL we see an organisation as a social process. It requires a purpose and a design to turn that purpose into reality. SL describes the principles whereby people come together, interact, design, operate and review their organisation to create productive social cohesion.

Not all bodies are the same and not all cars are the same but they do function according to underlying principles which can predict how well or poorly they will function.

This book is about establishing leadership that can liberate people and organisations from stultifying systems and structure. It is about eliminating the waste caused by unclear objectives, arbitrary use of power, and the excessive levels of activity and effort (much of it wasted) found in the 'unorganised' organisation. The human and material costs of bad organisation are a disgrace to an enlightened society.

While the business outcomes are essential if the organisation is to survive, we agree with Elliott Jaques who wrote, '... the efficiency of one or other form of organisation cannot be assessed merely in terms of economic or material outcomes; it must be considered in the fullness of its impact on human feelings, on community, and on social relationships and the quality of life in society' (Jaques, 1976: 15). The concepts we set forth in this book, we believe, take into account the needs of the organisation, the needs of the people associated with it and the society it is embedded in.

Many managers we have spoken and worked with over the years have wanted to create such organisations. Some have succeeded. Yet despite the outpouring of books telling managers and leaders what to do very few offer a coherent reason or set of principles as why some approaches work or in what context they might or might not work. Many recognise an urgent need to improve. Global competition will destroy organisations that fail to provide the goods and services desired by their customers and clients. Governments will fall, and voluntary associations will fail to attract both money and volunteers if they do not serve their constituents effectively.

Systems Leadership is essentially about how to create, improve and sustain successful organisations.

This book is not a set of prescriptions; it contains a set of principles which, if we use them recognising the context and moderated by that context, will lead to improvements, sometimes very dramatic improvements. It is not a set of rigid rules, it is not simply 'best practice'. As such, if applied in a formulaic manner it will fail. It requires work and at heart a real desire to create not just control.

If we further use the analogy of medicine as a discipline we are now (after many years!) fairly confident that we know how the body functions and what helps or hinders its functioning. The fact that there are still many people who are unwell, unfit and may lead an unhealthy lifestyle does not prompt the question; 'So why doesn't medicine work?' Like SL, medicine is a predictive and holistic theory that evolves. So I can't reasonably say, 'Well I don't think this medical theory is any good because I am walking 10k a day and not losing weight! Obviously medicine doesn't work!' Of course I haven't added in that at the same time I am eating pizzas, burgers and drinking copious amounts of beer! The test of the theory is whether the outcomes are predictable using that approach and whether by changing the process the results will change predictably. There is a dearth of this sort of coherent approach about organisation and a reluctance at times to admit and to engage with the complexity and effort needed to improve the situation.

SL contributes to improvement across a variety of types of organisations. There is now considerable evidence to suggest that SL, if used appropriately, does indeed contribute to significant improvement. There is a bank of case studies and work to demonstrate this. Some are in the book, others on the related website.

Today's organisations provide for most of our needs as individuals and as a society. It is largely through our organisations that we take actions today that will influence and shape our future. In the industrialised democracies, the majority of citizens work in such organisations. The quality of our lives is dependent on the quality of work that we carry out in organisations, which in turn depends upon the quality of the workforce and its leadership.

The degree and rate of change in technology, global competition, process innovations that tightly link relationships among suppliers, producers and customers, and changing social and political relationships make leadership ever more important.

However, many leaders and commentators see those changes as being driven by technology, or 'markets'. While a great deal of money is poured into new technical processes and their development, the understanding of their impact and dependence upon social processes (that is, the way that people behave and work together) is underrated.

This book recognises that leadership and creating positive organisations is difficult and hard work, that people are complex and have opinions. It recognises that, if an organisation is to be successful, then understanding the social processes is just as important as understanding the technical or commercial processes (see Chapter 3).

If leaders *do not* understand people and how they view the world, they will fail. If they *do* understand people, they have a chance to engage the creativity embodied in everyone. Technology can be bought or sold. Two organisations can have the same technology. No two organisations have the same workforce or the same leaders. Having the right people in the right place at the right time doing the right work is difficult but immensely rewarding for both the organisation and the people in it.

Many leaders will say 'people are our most important asset'. Yet (as the Gallup results show) their behaviour contradicts this every day. Even describing people as an 'asset' or as 'human capital' shows a lack of understanding that people are living beings with a will of their own. This will be directed to the benefit or detriment of the organisation.

Creating a positive organisation is not easy; even for the more serious leader or student of organisations there are difficulties.

> There are three areas in life where people seem particularly vulnerable to fads and short cuts: dieting, parenting and leadership. We seem to want to hear about a magic, quick and easy solution. If that is your view about leadership, this book is not for you.

Leaders have found that too many management 'theories' are not really theories at all. They are presented as magic. They tell you what goes in and what comes out, but you don't know what happens in the 'black box' in the middle.

They make assertions, followed by stories of a few exemplars who have had success. There is no context, no linking of cause and effect. There is no statement as to how and why it works, nor is there a statement regarding conditions where it will succeed or where it is likely to fail. Too often managers find themselves in the position of the old Indian Chief in the movie *Little*

Big Man: when his prediction did not come true, he said, 'Sometimes the magic works and sometimes it doesn't.'

As a consequence members of the organisation just wait for each wave to pass. The workforce becomes more cynical and Dilbert becomes an international hero.

Micklethwait and Wooldridge (1996: 60) perhaps say it best:

> *from the management industry's viewpoint, the beauty of the system [where one management theory rapidly follows on from another] is that none of the formulas work – or at least they do not work completely as the anguished and greedy buyers hope. The result is enormous profits for the gurus but confusion for their clients.*

In one organisation that had pursued fad after managerial fad, the managing director said, 'We put a lot of planes in the air; we are very good at take offs, but not very good at landings.'

Such fads also leave behind real fear and anxiety, as well as considerable human wreckage. At the most basic level, managers and workers fear losing their jobs. Managers also find contradictory advice not only frightening but disorienting. As one recently promoted senior executive, with a highly successful 30-year career, put it, 'I don't know what my job is, and I'm afraid someone will find out.'

The ways we perceive the world, absorb information and turn it into useful knowledge still has much in common with our ancestors. We need safety and security, recognition and esteem. We hope to succeed, but we must live with the fear and insecurity of our imperfections. Working in today's social, political and economic environment takes great courage. It would be helpful to have some sound advice.

Purpose

The purpose of this book is to present a coherent approach that explains why people behave as they do in organisations. This in turn can guide leaders of such organisations along the path of creating the conditions that encourage genuinely constructive and productive behaviour.

1 *What Use is Theory?*

Relating Theory to Practice

Each of the authors has heard managers argue that *theory is for academics; experience is what counts*. Some managers seem to pride themselves on their disdain of theory. These same managers then go on to quote their own views of management, and that good leadership *is just common sense*, but what is *common sense* other than an implicit theory?

All capable managers use such implicit theories every day, often with success. When this is done exceptionally well, we may refer to the person as a charismatic leader, which always carries a hint of mystery.

On the other hand, some scholars articulate theories, but never put them to the test of practice. These are the academic theories often scorned by many managers. Even where such articulated theories are put to the test, the methods too often reflect a distorted view of science that eliminates human intentions and values, or are so conceptual they are unrealistic. See the many journal articles on social organisation that have no impact on real managers. It may sound good in theory, but it won't work in practice.

To get things right requires an understanding of the elements and relationships illustrated in Figure 1.1.

We argue that all human beings have beliefs, values, dreams and aspirations. Any valid theory of human behaviour must take these into account. All managers operate on the left side of the diagram, using cells A and B, some of the time. Their actions are guided by their intuition (gut feel). When the result they intended does not occur, the shock forces them back into their beliefs to consider what happened and how they might change their actions to reach their intended goal. Unfortunately, if their theories are implicit and unformulated, they are largely untestable. Therefore it is more difficult to replicate success and to avoid future failures.

Sometimes, it is impossible to articulate to others what we have actually learned. This can become quite serious as one of the authors observed in a meeting with Hewlett-Packard executives. Both Bill Hewlett and David Packard were long retired, but in this meeting to deal with several difficult issues, the question came up more than once, *What would Bill and Dave have done?*. Executives recognised these two founders had insights that others were struggling to grasp, but they had not been able (or perhaps even aware of the need) to pass their insights on to their successors.

Academics often get locked into A and C, caught in a loop that never makes contact with the real world. If people are locked into the relationship between B and C, the formulations and the tests are devoid of human meaning and intention. Some of this research may be useful, but it is difficult to apply when the human dimension is omitted, often on the claim of being *value free*. This leads to tragedy, as when scientists become so disconnected from their human values they are capable of inhuman experiments like those conducted at Tuskegee University or Auschwitz.

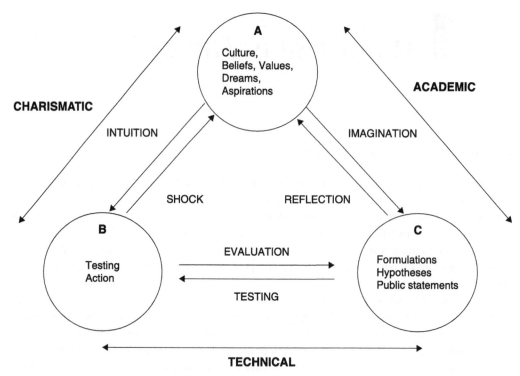

Figure 1.1   Human Decision-making Model

What is required, of course, is that all three elements be used together. This may be better done by a number of people working together. It is not that managers cannot articulate their hypotheses; it is that they are often too busy and time-pressured to take the time to define terms clearly and formulate clear hypotheses. In our experience, such formulations do not come easily or quickly. They require much hard work, and once articulated, they often have to be modified as they are tested in practice.

That is why the authors have found their joint working relationship so productive. We were continuously in touch with all three elements of the model. As you reflect on your work, keep in mind that *all* the elements, A, B and C, are essential.

Language – Social and Scientific

One difficulty that all writers and practitioners involved in organisational theory and behaviour confront is that unlike physics, chemistry, biology or engineering, there are no terms or concepts in our field with universally accepted definitions. In the sciences, key concepts such as mass, volume, acceleration, DNA, cell, tensile strength and stress are agreed upon, even where there are competing theories that incorporate them. Thus, it is possible to share meaning quite precisely. This is a difficulty that Elliott Jaques was highly aware of and described as a major problem in the field.

To study social processes such as management, two types of meaning need to be introduced. The first is *scientific* meaning, where an entity or term has an agreed meaning by which we can determine whether an entity is *one of those* or not. The second type we term *social*

> **Box 1.1   Social and scientific meanings**
>
> Social meaning: A term which is assumed to have similarity for the purpose of social interaction: you know what I mean?
>
> Scientific meaning: A precisely defined term with deliberately clear boundaries for the purpose of testing hypotheses: this is what I mean.

meaning. In our everyday lives we approximate and assume an overlap in understanding without worrying too much if we mean precisely the same thing.

Throughout our life we gradually learn increasingly sophisticated and more abstract discriminating (in the literal sense) categories. Thus, for a small child, all animals might be *dog*, but gradually the set of *animal* becomes superordinate to dog, cat, cow, kangaroo and so on (see Box 1.1).

One of the problems in the field of organisational behaviour is that language used to describe the concepts is often in the domain of social meaning. That is, we have a general understanding of terms such as manager, leader, authority, power, team or organisation, but there may be and often are significant differences. Is a manager also a leader? Is a leader a manager? Can one be a manager if one has no direct reports? Do you have a team if a manager appoints the leader or must a team select its own leader?

In everyday conversations such details usually do not matter. To emphasise such details would appear at best pedantic, at worst bizarre. For example, if friends get together for lunch and one asks another, *what do you do?*, a reply might be, *I am a supervisor*. It would be odd, indeed, if the first person then asked, *so what exactly is the extent of your authority; how does it differ from that of a manager?*

In the workplace, however, such issues of authority are of utmost importance, especially to the operator who may be asked to carry out a task. He or she needs to know if this person has the authority to tell him or her what to do, and within what limits. These are significant issues for both the operator and the supervisor, issues that may significantly change the response of the operator to the supervisor's direction. When trying to implement a new way of working, social meaning can cause considerable confusion.

The Practical Value of Good Theory

A good theory uses defined terms and specifies the relationships between and among them so that clear formulations can be made and tested. So often in books and journals on organisation we see terms undefined. Jaques often asked people to write down the definition of a manager. It is an interesting task. Critical terms such as *leader, culture, authority,* even *work* itself are just not defined but simply used, assuming a shared definition. Like Humpty Dumpty in *Alice in Wonderland,* words can mean what we want them to mean and as a consequence misunderstanding can be *your fault.* Terms then get recycled to sell new ideas: *change* becomes *transformation, detail* becomes *granular,* and *redundancy* becomes *down-sizing* or *right-sizing.* For an excellent treatise on this point see Don Watson's *Weasel Words* (2004).

We have confusing terms such as *self-directed teams* and *team pay.* Do such teams have no manager or leader? Does everyone in the team get the same pay? We have found that asking these questions is often regarded as pedantic or pretentious.

Michael Armstrong, in *Rewarding Teams* (2000), asserts 'There is no secret to success. It is never wise, it is never fair, it is never safe to generalise about team based pay.' If this is the case, then it raises questions about the quality of the underlying theory, or the lack thereof. To be valid, a theory must explain all the activity in the field it covers and allow users of the theory to predict outcomes under varying conditions.

Professionals in other fields are not so reluctant to be specific about, for example, the effect of smoking on the lungs, stress on a bridge, aerodynamic properties required to keep a plane in the sky, or the temperature in a reduction cell needed to produce aluminium. It is important to note, however, that all these propositions depend absolutely upon a base of shared definitions of entities and the clear description of properties, relationships and constraints. In turn such definitions and descriptions allow clear understanding of the relationships (or processes) that apply in given circumstances and allow prediction of the effects of changing the parameters or constraints of those processes.

Without clear concepts, generalisations are largely meaningless. For example, what can we say about *flatter organisations* or *performance-based pay*? Many argue that organisations need to be more *flexible*, able to *respond more quickly*, or should be *constantly re-organising, organic, fostering chaos, changing the culture, agile* and so on. What do these phrases mean in the social context, never mind the scientific context? They may generate the illusion of both meaning and significance but have little substance in reality.

While there is no argument in technical fields regarding the need for theory, definition and clear articulation of process, organisational behaviour and design fields remain theory deficient. Indeed, in these fields ideas and concepts are widely criticised for being too academic if they are specific. Worse, ideas and concepts are considered out of date or *at the end of their shelf life*, as new fads replace the old. The implication is that an organisational theory is allowed only a specific amount of time, regardless of its content. While this constant turnover of ideas is lucrative for consultants and opens the field for publication by academics, it does not further our understanding of why people behave as they do in organisations, or how to build a productive organisaton.

In the absence of real knowledge and testable theory, there seems to be a tacit assumption held by many that in leadership and management we cannot do a lot better than we are doing now. Better or worse leadership remains somewhat mysterious, even though recognised examples of both abound. We believe and argue in this book that leadership and management *can* be understood, that significant improvement is possible, and that the methods of implementation and the outcome can be predicted accurately from theory. As you can undoubtedly recognise, even with a good theory, good management is often not easy to put into practice; positive organisations do not grow by accident.

Buckminster Fuller (1969) noted that if we find ourselves on a sinking ocean liner and a piano lid floats by, we could use it as a lifeboat. On the other hand, were we to design a lifeboat, we would not create a piano lid. Too often in organisations we are operating with piano lids; what we need is better understanding of leadership processes, systems and organisational design so we can create more effective organisations to meet human, organisational and societal needs.

People and Science

There is a long, traditional argument about whether or what scientific method is valid for studying people. Science deals with things we can observe, either directly or with the aid of various instruments. People, on the other hand, have intentions: purposes that cannot be observed but can only be revealed in the course of dialogue with others. We can never see these intentions and we may not even be aware of them. People may or may not choose to reveal their intentions to an outside observer. Further, people have opinions about being observed, and this may influence their behaviour.

When we observe human behaviour, we interpret what we see in order to provide meaning for ourselves. This may or may not accurately reflect the meaning or intent of the person being observed. As we will discuss in later chapters, we make such interpretations all the time. Those who become good at observing social processes often make what appear to be quite accurate interpretations. Nonetheless, developing a scientific base for interpreting social phenomena remains difficult.

We grow up learning how to predict behaviour and our environment. We learn to read our mother's behaviour first, and over time we evolve internal theories that we may call rules of thumb, hypotheses or prejudices concerning why people behave as they do. We use these theories to shape our own behaviour and predict other's behaviour. Sometimes we are right, thus confirming our theories; sometimes we are wrong. When we are wrong, we must decide whether our failure to predict is because our theory is wrong or, if it is accurate, the event was a special case.

Thus, we develop our own ideas about what directs all human behaviour. Consequently, propositions made by others about organisations, (which are essentially about human behaviour), compete with our own – usually implicit – theories. This is very different from theoretical propositions in the natural sciences.

We don't have to grow up developing theories about aeronautical engineering, physics or chemistry. We can get by in life without having theories about smelting, open-heart surgery or nuclear physics. We *cannot* get by without theories (or at least working models) about human behaviour. We must have these predictive theories even if implicit, internalised and built on experience. If we didn't we would not be able to predict either how others will react to us, or how we might respond to others.

Developing a Common Language

The scientist Antoine-Laurent de Lavoisier developed the language of chemistry in the early eighteenth century, and it was only after his publication of a standard vocabulary that the science of chemistry began its rapid development. His statement of the importance of language to the development of knowledge applies as much today as in his own time:

> *We cannot improve the language of any science without at the same time improving the science itself; neither can we, on the other hand, improve a science, without improving the language or nomenclature which belongs to it. However certain the facts of any science may be, and, however just the ideas we may have formed of these facts, we can only communicate false impressions to others, while we want words by which these may be properly expressed.*
>
> (Lavoisier, 1789 in Bolles, 1997: 380)

In this book we provide a language for developing, discussing, thinking and working with propositions about organisations and management. Of necessity we use words that have a common social meaning, but we have defined them carefully for our purpose so that those who use them can have shared definitions. (See the Glossary). This does not mean that other definitions are wrong; they are simply less useful for our purpose, which is to advance knowledge in the fields of leadership and organisation. This will continue to be a contentious area until there is an acceptance that we need universal definitions in this field.

In part because there are alternative definitions, the specific language requires mental discipline to understand and apply. Initially, neither the shared definitions nor the methods are easy to learn, and as instructors we have found in using this material that the insistence on *correct* language is at first regarded as being pedantry. As they apply these ideas in the work setting, however, most people come to understand the value of a clear language to communicate organisational issues. This language allows you to ask questions and to think through answers, all with the discipline of shared definitions upon which the formation of testable propositions is dependent.

A number of the concepts we use were developed by Elliott Jaques and colleagues as the basis for stratified systems theory (Jaques, 1976; 1989). These concepts led him to a theory of organisational structure. Using (and in some cases modifying) the concepts as well as expanding on this theory we have developed a number of definitions of organisation and management terms that are far more precise than everyday social language. These precise definitions are emphasised to facilitate communication within an organisation and among students of management and organisational theory. Their precision also allows managers to make fine discriminations among phenomena that are often viewed as similar. Such fine discriminations make it far easier to detect error and correct problems early, as well as spotting and seizing opportunities. Peter Senge (1990) noted, 'The ability to learn faster than your competitors may be the only sustainable competitive advantage.' As we have argued and as Lavoisier demonstrated, it is impossible to learn in the absence of clear, shared terms and concepts.

We provide such terms and concepts, but members of the organisation will need to learn this language, or create a language of equal or greater precision, if they are to gain the advantages of clarity and accuracy in communication and analysis.

Caveat: The theories presented in this book may appear to be simple, even simplistic, on first encounter.

This apparent simplicity is, however, deceptive. As one gains experience with these ideas, the surface simplicity gives way to a deeper complexity. We believe, and many managers have confirmed, that this makes the theories more powerful for practising managers who must deal with complexity in human relations, new technologies and rapidly changing organisational environments. As one of our clients remarked during a workshop, 'This is hardly rocket science'; a comment came back from a participant, 'no, it's much more difficult'.

None of what we say replaces the decision-making of leaders. With all the advice in the world, a decision must still be made by someone with appropriate authority. It is not helpful to blame advisers for decisions. They are accountable for the quality of their advice. Any advice, including military intelligence, is just that. It does not absolve the person with executive authority for their poor judgement.

As such, the authors respect executive authority. We do not tell you what decision to make but rather present some tools to help you consider, analyse and predict the consequences of your decisions. We offer guidance in the form of principles, concepts and tools that will improve the systems and leadership of any organisation (see Chapter 10). Using this definition, all managers are leaders of people; they have no choice. Their only choice is whether to be a good or bad leader. In this we again agree with Drucker, 'one does not 'manage' people. The task is to lead people. And the goal is to make productive the specific strengths and knowledge of each individual' (1954: 21, 22).

Box 1.2   A note on managers and leaders

There is considerable confusion in the literature regarding the concepts of 'manager' and 'leader'. Often 'leader' is used as a positive term suggesting vision and charisma, while 'manager' is used in a slightly denigrating way indicating someone who is concerned only with efficiency or the stewarding of material resources.

We believe, with Drucker (1954: 9), that 'management is the specific and distinguishing organ of any and all organisations'. We define a manager as a person who is 'accountable for his or her own work and the work performance of people reporting to him or her over time' (see Chapter 10). Using this definition, all managers are leaders of people; they have no choice. Their only choice is whether to be a good or bad leader. In this we again agree with Drucker, 'one does not 'manage' people. The task is to lead people. And the goal is to make productive the specific strengths and knowledge of each individual' (1954: 21, 22).

There is no magic here and we use very few metaphors or analogies such as *Who Moved My Cheese* (Johnson, J., 1998). Used correctly, metaphor and analogy can be helpful. For example, there is a famous story of the scientist Kekule who in 1865 dreamt of a snake whirling in space biting its tail. This led him to the discovery of the cyclic formula of the benzene ring, a linchpin in the study of carbon chemistry. Used badly, metaphor and analogy can become an impediment to the development of knowledge. They become a justification for poorly formulated, half-baked ideas – in short, for stories masquerading as science (Church, 1999).

Conclusion

Our intent is to move beyond magic, metaphor and analogy. We seek to take the next step in the growth of knowledge – to define terms clearly, to state organisational relationships as hypotheses to be tested, to predict outcomes, and explain why particular outcomes do or do not occur. In other words, we are trying to move toward the sort of science described by Karl Popper (Munz, 1985).

Effective leaders must have clear statements of relationships that link action to outcome so they may test and learn from their actions. Without this it is difficult to know how to replicate success or avoid repeating failure.

Leaders also need a language that allows them to discuss their management and leadership process with accuracy and precision. As we have argued, we take this language facility for granted in the hard sciences. A legal or commercial document begins with a glossary of terms, yet the field of management is a linguistic free-for-all. It is impossible to pass on what one has learned if it cannot be articulated clearly. We may also communicate false impressions to others if we do not have a common language to express our observations and ideas. However as a leader it is not enough to know it, or say it. You must be able to *do* it, consistently and in real time.

People are not machines. Each of the authors has had the satisfaction of seeing people prosper when provided with the right leadership, organisational role, authorities and systems. Some members of Karl Stewart's workforce even testified in court about the improved quality of their working lives. (See Parts 3 and 4 and the Comalco/Rio Tinto case studies.)

We also recognise the high value people place on organisations, not only in order to accomplish personal goals and earn a living, but also to provide a means to use their capabilities to achieve larger social purposes. Ian Macdonald (1990) has shown how we develop our very identity through our work. Work is our connection to the world and reality. David Whyte (2001: 5) states, '... the consummation of work lies not only in what we have done, but who we have become while accomplishing the task.' On the cover of his book, Whyte notes, 'Work is an opportunity for discovering and shaping the place where the self meets the world. Work is difficulty and drama, a high-stakes game in which our identity, our esteem, and our ability to provide are mixed inside of us in volatile, sometimes explosive ways' (Whyte, 2001: 11).

Which provides a useful segue into Chapter 2 in which we explore the nature and purpose of work.

2 *What is Work?*

It is interesting to note that, although many books are written about work, it is rare to find a clear definition. The word *work* is used often and in many different ways. The *Oxford English Dictionary* affords the term considerable space referring to expenditure of effort, striving, exertion of force in overcoming resistance, tasks to be undertaken, achievement, employment, earning money and to have influence or effect – to mention only a few.

The definition of work in the physical sciences is, of course, very clear – work = force × distance. We are concerned with a different form of work. Despite the many social meanings of the term *work*, we have found it useful to define human work as follows:

Box 2.1   Definition of Work

Work: Turning intention into reality.

Work is the process by which an idea generated by a person becomes evident in the external world and open to recognition. While this undoubtedly requires effort, it is not simply the expenditure of effort. This definition we use is closely related to Jaques' definition and can be seen as such by reference to Jaques' explanation in his book *A General Theory of Bureaucracy* (1976: 100, 113), in which he says 'The term work refers to activity, to behaviour, to that human activity in which people exercise discretion, make decisions and act so as to transform the external physical and social world in accord with some predetermined goal in order to fulfil some need': in short, turning intention into reality (Jaques, 1976: 101).

Schutz (1972) also emphasises this transformation when he describes a person as working when that person is trying '… to produce an objective output which is the realisation of a subjective project'. One of the authors, Macdonald (1990), wrote about the concept and particularly emphasises the need for recognition of that process in his doctoral thesis: 'Identity Development of People with Learning Difficulties through the Recognition of Work'. The link with recognition is crucial because this is what provides confirmation from outside the mind of the worker.

As Macdonald wrote, 'The whole process allows the person to identify themselves as an active agent in the world' (Macdonald, 1990). Kegan (1982) in *The Evolving Self* also emphasises this by saying '(work) directs us to that most human of regions between an event and a reaction to it … to this zone of mediation where meaning is made'. Sigmund Freud also stressed the importance of work when he stated, 'no other technique attaches the individual so firmly to reality as laying emphasis on work; for work at least gives a secure place in a portion of reality'.

Like Jaques, Schutz, Kegan and Freud, the authors regard work and the recognition of it as essential to mental health and well-being; it is a fundamental part of our identity. This is in contrast to views of work as labour or toil. For example, Dahrendorf (1985), says that 'work in the simple everyday sense of the world, has never been regarded as a particularly agreeable dimension of life'. Marx in *Das Kapital* even argues that freedom begins where work ends; to paraphrase, 'instead of working, people are free to fish or write poetry as they please'. (An understandable view given the miserable working conditions of the time.)

This perspective of work as a burden has grown up, in our view, because of a separation of the process of articulating intention from the process of transforming reality. There is a qualitatively different experience between realising someone else's intention and realising one's own. This is seen, for example, when completing a specifically defined task assigned by someone else for someone else. Similarly, if the intention is mistakenly or deliberately attributed to someone else, then alienation results. This is why it is so important for a leader to engage with team members so that all of the team genuinely share the purpose (intention). They, therefore, identify with the transformation and have the opportunity to gain recognition for their contribution to the result.

To put it very simply, if in performing work:

1.   we are prevented from realising our intentions (either by others or ourselves), and/or
2.   we do not get recognition for our contribution to the process and result, then
3.   we will not only be alienated from our work but our identity will suffer.

Thus work is essential to our well-being. It is potentially a creative expression of ourselves, especially when recognition is given accurately and appropriately. This definition, 'turning intention into reality', clearly extends beyond the realm of employment work. We see small children working extremely hard (adults call it play), applying intense concentration and effort, experiencing immense frustration and joyful success – processes we continue throughout our lives if we are to enjoy a positive identity.

While the definition of work goes beyond employment it is also very relevant to it.

Jaques in *General Theory of Bureaucracy* uses a most helpful diagram, reproduced here as Figure 2.1, to highlight the process of work.

Thus in employment work we have activity that is directed towards achieving a goal which can be specified in advance. This activity will always be bounded by constraints or limits

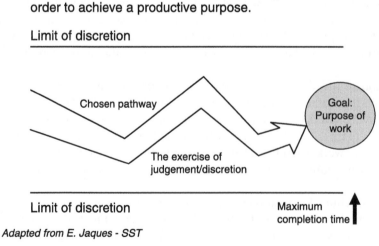

Work is the exercise of discretion in making decisions in order to achieve a productive purpose.

Limit of discretion

Chosen pathway

Goal: Purpose of work

The exercise of judgement/discretion

Limit of discretion

Maximum completion time

Adapted from E. Jaques - SST

Figure 2.1   The Process of Work (after Jaques)

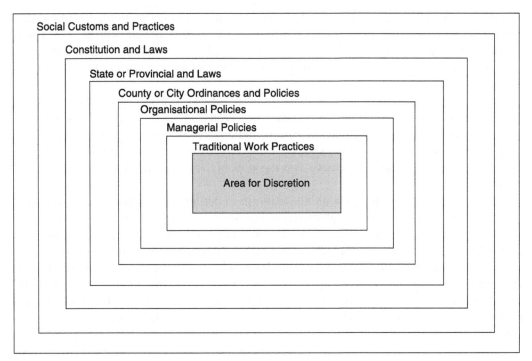

Social Customs and Practices

Constitution and Laws

State or Provincial and Laws

County or City Ordinances and Policies

Organisational Policies

Managerial Policies

Traditional Work Practices

Area for Discretion

Figure 2.2   Constraints or Limits Bounding Activities

(see Figure 2.2). These can be variously described in terms of the laws of society (written and unwritten), policies of the company, the specific authority of the role and more particularly, the resources available – materials, money, people and time.

The goal is set in a time context. It is never open-ended or is it merely a wish; there should always be a maximum completion time, which if not achieved devalues the goal. The person carrying out the work must devise a way to achieve the goal within all these constraints.

Human Work and Identity

The construction of a pathway towards the goal is at the heart of work. The person must make decisions and choices, overcoming obstacles presented by the context, while staying within the constraints. It is this decision-making that is essentially human. No two people will ever construct exactly the same pathway or method. The same person will rarely, if ever, construct exactly the same pathway twice, even if the goal is similar and the constraints remain the same.

The pathway is, thus, unique to the individual; it is like a signature and part of our identity. To a casual observer it may appear to be the same either for a number of individuals performing the same task or an individual repeating an activity, but close observation will always reveal some difference, even if very small.

Herein lies the opportunity for improvement. Human beings have a natural drive to improve methods. Think of an occasion when you have attempted a task for the first time. It is almost impossible to prevent reflection on how to do it better next time. Often in the way that we organise work or design and implement systems in organisations, we inhibit this process or even actively try to prevent it. Nonetheless, most people will at least think about improvement even if they cannot act on those ideas. Inhibiting a person's ideas for improvement not only frustrates the individual, it destroys an opportunity to advance the organisation's goals.

If we consider work to be a constructive and productive process that contributes to individual well-being, then it is important that the person carrying out the work is able to identify with the goal. This is not to say that the person would carry out this work whether employed or not, but rather to say the person should be able to see the goal as a worthwhile objective that he or she actively wants to achieve. It is the work of the leadership of the organisation to establish this condition.

The person who is to do the work needs also to understand the nature of and reason for the constraints. It is not good enough merely to be informed of them and instructed to achieve the goal. If the person is not aware of why the constraints exist and the nature of them, this lack of knowledge may lead to dangerous or illegal behaviour as the person sees no rationale for a constraint and therefore breaches it in an attempt to reach the goal. A lack of explanation will also lead to alienation and disengagement. We can find this situation in extreme form in forced labour camps and less extremely in poorly led organisations that use the rationale, *just do as I say*. That statement effectively replaces a person–person relationship with a person–object relationship (see Part 2).

Thus, when tasks are assigned, the leader assigning them should be clear about the context of the work (for example, the overall state of the market or business or the political or societal situation for government agencies or non-profit associations), the purpose, e.g., to satisfy an important potential customer, and the quality requirements of the output (goal) as well as the quantity requirements. In addition, the person performing the task needs to know what resources are available and what limits are operating. Last, but not least, the time to completion must be clear. None of this interferes with the work of determining how the work should be done (as will be discussed in more depth in Chapter 14).

Clearly, some work is more difficult than other work. Some tasks take more time to complete than others. The pathway needed to achieve the goal may be more or less difficult or complex; it may involve more or fewer abstract variables, in other words, elements that cannot be seen or touched. For example, designing a corporate remuneration system is more complex than photocopying a letter; constructing an effective business plan is more complex than cleaning an office, though both are necessary. These differences in complexity of work will be explored in more depth in Chapter 9.

Whatever the complexity, all these activities require work. They are all about turning intention into reality and they all require the person to work out the best way (the how) of achieving the goal. All of these types of work, in their own way, can be satisfying and creative.

The person in the process of working has to determine the relationship between what he or she is doing and the output. Each one of us has to recognise how our current behaviour impacts on, or is more or less likely to produce, the desired result. It is the understanding of this relationship between immediate process and end product that is critical to achieving our intention.

As such, work may involve an understanding of what is primarily a technical process such as aluminium smelting, electrical transmission, dressing a wound, internal combustion in an engine or digital arithmetic in a personal computer. Work may also require an understanding of what is primarily social a process – leading a team, interviewing or recruiting a potential new employee, providing customer service or communicating information. In employment work there is always an interaction between the technical and social processes and between these and the commercial process (see Chapter 3).

Throughout our lives, we continue to learn and refine our understanding of how process relates to outcome. As discussed in Part 2, we need to predict our environment. We also like to feel that we have an influence and effect on the world. It is essential for our sense of identity and mental health.

Importance of the Recognition of Work

The affirmation of our contribution to the process and outcome of work, especially when positive, recognises that we exist and that the output of our thinking has genuine worth; it encourages us to use and develop our capabilities. This is why recognition of work is so important. It is very significant for the leader to accurately recognise the different contributions of team members.

We have all had the experience of our work being wrongly attributed to, or even claimed by, others. We have also had the experience of our work being ignored. These are very demoralising experiences, causing disappointment, anger and resentment, and often a feeling of *why bother?*

We use the term *recognition* because it is a neutral term and does not presuppose a successful outcome, unlike *reward*. It is essential to understand why a process failed to produce the desired result, and this needs to be recognised in order to improve the process we use in the future. Recognition of apparent failure does not necessarily imply the negative aspect of blame as the person may have done everything she or he could or was supposed to do. Without proper recognition there can be very little learning.

Conclusion

We have argued that, while there are many, varied, definitions of work, the authors have found it most useful to define work as *turning intention into reality*. This is not an idiosyncratic definition; the development of it is consistent with others' definitions, notably those of Jaques and Schutz. Like Jaques we see work as essential to a valid sense of identity and productive relationship in the world.

Work is essentially about the *how*. It is concerned with the construction of a method, or pathway, in order to achieve a desired result. Work may differ in complexity but has the common feature of requiring human judgement and decision-making. Work (especially employment or paid work) inevitably involves constructing this pathway within limits. We cannot do whatever we wish. We do not have unlimited resources.

The final essential component of work is the accurate recognition by another or others (for example, team leader, fellow team members) of our contribution. Such recognition encourages us to use our capabilities to our full potential.

3 Social, Technical, Commercial (STC): Domains of Work

In the previous chapter we defined human work *as turning intention into reality*, a definition we have found to be essential to understanding and creating positive organisations. In the field of organisation and leadership, the lack of a clear definition has led to unnecessary confusion as managers and academics tried to understand the experience of people working in organisations and also to clarify the work to be accomplished in various work roles.

Similarly when we think about an organisation what do we mean by that? What actually is being organised? From our definition of work: *turning intention into reality* we can see that work and the purpose of an organisation are connected in that an organisation is a way of trying to bring an intention into reality. It is a social construction. Someone or some people (see Part 3) have to agree as to what sort of organisation is most likely to realise that intention. Then they must decide how work is to be categorised, distributed and what authority people will have to spend money, use resources, direct others, or be directed in order to achieve the purpose (intention) of the organisation.

One option would be just to list all the tasks that need to be done and then randomly give them to people or send them to people who work in the organisation. This might be fun for a while but it would not seem very well organised. However not all the work is the same and not all people are the same. So we can see that there are different kinds of work: teaching a class is different from running the whole school, cleaning a hospital corridor is very different from conducting a heart transplant. Nor is it simply a matter of apparent importance, all work should make a vital contribution to the overall purpose of the organisation. It is dangerous to conduct an operation in a theatre that has not been properly cleaned or with un-sterilised instruments.

However we need to be clear about the sort of work we are talking about. We have always argued the need for clarity about the difference in complexity of work (see Chapters 8, 9 and 10). What has become more evident to us in recent years, because it is of great practical help to those we work with, is to distinguish between three different domains of work. These domains help to categorise work into three critical areas and help to shed light upon crucial differences in areas that are all necessary in every organisation. No organisation can function unless all of these three domains are operating effectively. It is not a matter of determining which is more important but rather to understand the work that needs to be done in each domain and how it interacts with the other two interdependent domains. Understanding this interdependency is of critical importance.

The three fundamental domains are the Social, Technical and Commercial (see Figure 3.1).

Between them they cover all the work of an organisation. They can be used to help think about how the organisation is structured, roles designed and systems designed.

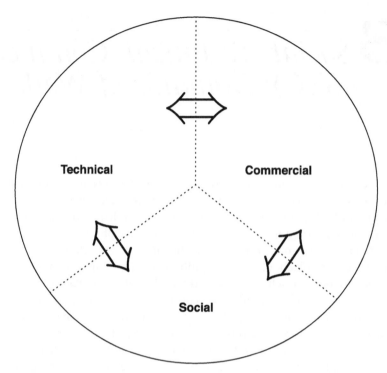

Figure 3.1   The Domains of Work

The TECHNICAL domain includes all the specialist activity. It is often associated with the core purpose of an organisation, For example, in a school it is educating, in a hospital it is curing and caring, in a civil engineering company it includes designing, engineering and constructing. It includes the specialised processes involved in manufacturing, mining, transporting – indeed all the verbs that describe the particular nature of the organisation. It includes the required, technical expertise that is needed to source, produce, sell and deliver whatever constitutes the business or purpose of the organisation. So this could be products, or services, tangible (manufacturing) or intangible (insurance). It requires knowledge, skill and training.

The COMMERCIAL domain includes an understanding and management of all costs, revenues, margins, capital and generally value for money. It includes all the systems associated with assets, cash flow, net present value, budgets, financial auditing and accounting; everything required to ensure that the organisation continues to be financially viable over time. This requires sound and accurate knowledge of what constitutes cost and revenue, sources and use of capital. This domain also includes an understanding of markets and hence price, competitors and contracts with suppliers and customers. In government it is the understanding of the politics regarding authorisations and budgets. It requires expertise in all aspects of finance including loans and interest. It requires sound expertise and knowledge in terms of book-keeping, accountancy and banking. This applies to non-commercial organisations. All charities, NGOs and voluntary organisations have cost and revenues.

The SOCIAL (or People) domain is concerned with all the ways in which people work together to achieve the purpose of the business including the structure. This includes all the *people systems*: recruitment, selection, appraisal, review, promotion, discipline and so on as well as all the systems that go to answer the *three questions at work*: *What am I meant to do? How am I doing?* and *What is my future?* This includes Role Descriptions, Task Assignment, Succession Planning, Career Development. It includes the daily social processes: how people interact, the quality of leadership and team members' behaviour and generally how people communicate directly and symbolically. It includes all the daily work scheduling systems such as meetings and working hours.

Any organisation needs to be effective in ALL three aspects. It is not sufficient to have a well-run and technically excellent organisation that cannot control its costs. Similarly we may have excellent technical and commercial arrangements but no one stays long or uses their capability because people are treated so poorly. We might have reasonable commercial arrangements and good people but we have no future because the technology is out of date and no longer wanted.

It is interesting to observe that when we talk about the Technical or Commercial domains we are used to being precise and clear about what is required. For example if someone applied to become a teacher she or he would be asked what qualifications they had. It would not be sufficient for the person simply to say, 'I think I get on very well with children and they seem to like me, so please give me a job.' Anyone would expect to be questioned about what skills and knowledge they had if they wanted to be a pilot, a nurse, a mining engineer or indeed fill any organisational role. Even so-called unskilled roles require clarity and training as to, for example, how to stack the shelves or deliver the pizza.

Similarly in the financial domain we expect precision. If you were a supplier you would expect to know how much and when you will be paid. If you were negotiating a loan you would expect a specific rate of interest to be agreed as well as a specific period of time or repayment. If you were an employee you would expect your salary to be clear and specific. If you ask: 'how much will I be paid?' and the reply was: 'don't worry, I think you will find it is enough' that would clearly not be satisfactory.

When we move to the Social domain, however, we find much less clarity; more importantly, the need for clarity is underestimated or even denied. We use terms such as manager, or supervisor, without having clear definitions. Even more significantly we use terms such as Leadership and Culture, without necessarily being clear what we mean; and sometimes there are many different, contradictory meanings for those terms.

We talk about a need for a cultural change without clarity about what that really means or more importantly how to achieve it. We talk about appointing somebody with *good leadership qualities* and yet what those qualities may be poorly defined. Even what we mean by *meetings* or the *work of the role* may be very different. We argue that it is just as important, to be clear as to what we mean in the Social domain as it is to be clear about what we mean in the Technical and Commercial domains. Misunderstandings, leading to lack of clarity around expectation and meaning in the Social domain are in our view a major cause of distress, inefficiency ineffectiveness and poor quality working relationships.

Of course this does not mean that everything can be precisely or exactly defined at any one time, nor does not mean that things, especially in the Social domain do not change. In fact our constant emphasis on *context* and *purpose* is precisely because we are aware that the situation changes all the time. When we speak of precision, however, we are referring to the terminology. At any one time people should share an understanding of what the terms in the Social domain mean. If words can mean whatever we want them to mean this undermines good working relationships and we remain trapped like Alice in Wonderland. All positive cultures and productive social cohesion have a foundation in a common language.

At the same time we are very aware of the nature of ambiguity, complexity and abstraction. Indeed the entire model of Levels of Work is a model of increasing complexity and abstraction. However, if people are to work together effectively they must have some shared terminology and language just as exists in the Technical and Commercial domains. Indeed, all professional work depends upon such shared understanding.

Part of this problem of lack of shared definition (or need for definition) in the Social domain is due to the fact that we all have our own ideas and experiences as to what makes for a good organisation or a good leader or indeed most of what is contained in this domain. We would not expect to turn up to work and be asked to fly a plane with little or no training. However we see in many instances people put into roles which have significant work in the social domain; such as large leadership roles, with little or no clarity of expectation or training. So we see good technical teachers, good technical doctors put into roles such as Principal of a school or Head of Department with little preparation. After all, surely all of this is just *common sense*; surely we should *just be able to get on with it* or at least rely on our experience whatever that might be?

Our view is that this is not sufficient. We all know of examples where the great salesperson becomes the terrible manager of salespeople; the great police officer becomes the dreadful sergeant who 'could not manage a one-car funeral,' as one police officer described his situation.

It is not sufficient to exhort people to *collaborate* or *innovate* or *empower* without explaining further what these terms actually mean in practice. They sound positive but do people understand what they are meant or even authorised to do?

We recently had the experience of a Head Teacher who was reprimanded for not being 'collaborative enough'. She asked what that meant and was told that she shouldn't make decisions without the approval of her team. She should not only consult them but also get 'buy in', and if they didn't agree she should not go ahead. The Head was left wondering how it was fair that she remain accountable for outcomes in the school but did not have the final say in decisions.

Interestingly in the same organisation others had interpreted collaboration differently: as meaning supporting the Head Teacher in decisions even if they didn't like it, a further interpretation was simply that people should work more in teams and look for opportunities to help and support each other. These three quite different views have very different expectations. There was no written or shared definition ... back to Alice!

The material in this book and the content of Systems Leadership is all about the Social domain and how, by being clear about what we mean and expect in that domain, we can significantly enhance the quality of work in the organisation and improve the chances of achieving the purpose of the organisation. We also improve the quality of life for the people who work in the organisation.

From the above discussion, however, we can see that when thinking about an organisation people can sometimes be captured by one aspect. They might over-emphasise one domain or another.

This is partly understandable because often the purpose of the organisation is to be found in the Technical domain. For example Health Services, Social Services, Educational Services and indeed all professional service organisations; lawyers, architects, engineers are there to deliver their expertise to society in the form of customers or clients. It can seem therefore that, this is *clearly the most important work* or even, *the only work of importance*. The other two aspects are either ignored or demeaned. When working at a university with a group of academics they clearly and explicitly thought their Technical work in the form of their academic specialty was all that mattered, and that the administrators were overpaid and an impediment to the *real* work.

When discussing the changes in finances, government grants and fees and the Vice Chancellor's requirement that they deliver *commercially viable* courses one professor commented angrily – 'This is a university not a business!' It was as if any consideration of cost and revenue was not relevant, and even worse, it was insulting. Another comment from another academic was – 'Changes are imposed on us, we do not get consulted'. When it was pointed out that there were meetings organised and academic representatives asked to attend and contribute, the response was 'I haven't got time to go to meetings!'. In this organisation it is as if the Social and especially the Commercial domains are lesser and almost unworthy topics.

In manufacturing businesses, there is often tension and conflict between the Technical and Commercial Domains. This was best expressed by Bob Lutz in his book, *Car Guys vs. Bean Counters: The Battle for the Soul of American Business* (2013). Interestingly the Social domain is rarely mentioned in this exposition unless there is a derogatory reference to HR.

Despite these issues, it is very clear that all aspects are necessary. There can be no university without income or expenditure; there can be no university without administration and social organisation. With Western governments trying to reduce public expenditure and the cost of services such as police, social services, education and health; there is the call not to reduce *front line services*. By this they mean the Technical domain. However, increasing regulation in health and safety, accounting and governance, child protection and so on, actually increases the work in the Social domain. Sometimes administrators are cast as parasites, backroom staff living off the organisation. Now we are not arguing against any particular regulation, nor against the need for efficiency, merely that all domains must be appreciated in terms of their necessity for the sustainability of the whole organisation.

We have found many of the problems in organisations are rooted in the lack of understanding of the Social domain. The lack of clear terminology has made shared understanding difficult, if not impossible in many situations. Our work; largely developing concepts and theory in the Social area, actually does provide clear approaches to reducing the negative aspects of bureaucracy and increasing productivity but it also appreciates the necessary work in all these domains. A simplistic cost cutting approach – 'reduce costs by 20%' – does not improve much unless the work necessary to achieve the organisation's purpose is clearly understood. Such approaches or short cuts are usually primarily about short-term cost issues not long-term objectives. Even worse, such across the board cuts punish the most efficient and reward those who over-staff either through inefficiency or, just in case there is a reduction in workplace.

Roles

We are emphasising the importance and interdependence of all three aspects – (STC) – but that is not to say they are always equivalent in terms of proportion or should always be equivalent at any particular time.

If we consider roles in an organisation, each role should be considered in terms of these domains and, depending upon the purpose of the role, work distributed appropriately amongst these aspects. For example, a classroom teacher or nurse should be focusing mainly on their technical expertise and social process. Most of their attention should be devoted to that. However it is useful to ask how much should they appreciate costs?

At a mine in Western Australia, a young electrician who was mending a large power supply cable for a jumbo drill was asked if he knew how much the cable cost. He replied with the exact cost per metre and said – 'That's why I'm being bloody careful!' We are not suggesting he should know the cost of everything but that knowledge helped him be more productive from the organisation's perspective.

Similarly, people in such roles should not spend a great amount of time in meetings. However, as work is a social process and an organisation a social structure, people should understand the purpose of their role, how it relates to the purpose of the organisation and other people in the organisation. One of the primary causes of failure of organisations is precisely the lack of efficient and effective social organisation. Poor social organisation, including poor leadership are major drivers of poor productivity and lead people to give up or retreat into a minimalist approach of just doing what is needed to get by and survive.

Box 3.1   Getting on With the Real Work

The All Wales (U.K.) Strategy was a policy statement concerning treatment of people with severe learning difficulties. The essential principles concerned the achievement of normal patterns of life, treatment of people as individuals and support from the community to help them realise their potential and included participation by service users themselves.

The central problem in achieving this purpose was to overcome uncoordinated service delivery to achieve the objective of providing an integrated service. People could receive services from a social worker, community nurse, teacher and volunteer as well as occupational therapy, music therapy, speech therapy, physiotherapy, clinical psychology and educational psychology. Families were faced with a bewildering range of talent, but the different professional backgrounds resulted in different methods of approach from people employed by different agencies.

The service users needed a point of contact – one where there was sufficient knowledge as to where they might get help. The individuals and their families needed a coordinated pattern of care centred upon their particular situation. Two questions arose for the providers of services.

• Who would manage unqualified staff providing basic services – Social Care workers (SCWs)?
• How would qualified staff from different professions and employing agencies work together?

What had been underestimated was the amount of work involved in answering the two questions. An analysis was put forward that identified three components of work:

Specialist work – requiring training and background in a specific technical expertise in methods and theory (Technical Domain).
Scheduling work – organising the work of oneself and others. Plan coordination (compiling an Individual Plan), gaining knowledge of relevant contributions, arranging meetings, venues and appointments (Social Domain).
Communicating work – exchanging information with colleagues or seniors, clearly explaining tasks, allocating work, discussing and reviewing progress (Social Domain).

The professionals were concerned their specialist work was being eroded. The need to manage SCWs and coordinate plans inevitably reduced the amount of time available to deliver specialist technical work.

What was found is that among the caring professions, scheduling and communicating work is often undervalued. It is not seen as *real work*, as compared to delivering direct care to a service user. The specialist work feels more like real work; doing something, taking action is what professionals are trained for. Scheduling work, on the other hand, feels like delay, which in one sense it is. Both scheduling and communicating work involve reflection, a case of look before your leap. This can be time-consuming, especially the arranging of meetings and appointments. It can also be frustrating and seen at times as an unnecessary waste of time, when you could be otherwise doing something else.

This research demonstrated, however, that a critical part of providing an integrated community service involves more than valuing or even carrying out direct service work. Although the direct delivery is sometimes seen as the only *real* work, other work, which is less immediately rewarding, is necessary if the service is to be delivered in a coherent way. Macdonald and others found that in order to enhance the actual service delivery great care and effort is required in the design of systems, which make sense to the service users, their families and the service providers.

Leadership

So who is meant to integrate these Domains? We argue that this is a key part of the work of leadership. It is the work of leaders at every level to understand and be able to explain how and why a role is constructed as it is and why all three domains are important.

The design of roles is critical. If someone's primary purpose is to be a technical expert, he or she should not be encumbered by having to run a large department and be required to carry out a large amount of Social or Commercial work. Similarly, a general manager or school principal/head teacher knows the role will require considerable amounts of leadership work (Social) and managing a budget (Commercial) and so it would not be reasonable to expect them (in the case of the school principal) to have a full teaching load.

Box 3.2   A Brilliant Geologist

One of the mining companies we worked with had an internationally recognised geologist – one of the best in the world. Because he was so good, the company promoted him to be a manager of geologists so he could be paid appropriately for the quality of his work. The only problem, as he expressed it, was that he 'couldn't find anything sitting in an office and the paperwork was pure waste'.

Thus he was put back into the field reporting to a manager in a role of IV complexity (see Chapter 9 on Levels of Work). At the time, no technical role in this organisation could be classified as higher than the third level of complexity. Because of his capability (see Chapter 8), he was highly paid so no competitor could steal him with a better offer. The problem for his manager was that he was *difficult*.

For example, his expense accounts were a mess. He would turn in an account that included $7.85 breakfast, $12.55 lunch, $54,000 miscellaneous. This last report was the final straw; his manager recommended he be fired. Fortunately the CEO learned of this at the same time he was changing the structure of the organisation. He recognised, not only the value of this geologist, but also his high level of capability.

In the restructured organisation, high-level technical work was recognised, and the geologist was placed in a role at Level V, reporting to a Senior Vice President at VI. The Vice President recognised that the geologist should not be worrying about paperwork; he was to find ore bodies, valuable commodities for the organisation. He arranged for an administrative assistant to take care of all the paper work. He also clarified the work of the role – to find ore bodies and to select what the geologist thought were the most promising young geologists who would be assigned to be his assistants and learn from him as he did his work and explained his methods. He was also told that if he needed to rent equipment (the $54,000 miscellaneous expenditure), he had a budget of $100,000. If he needed to spend more than that he was to call the Vice President who would decide if the company could afford such expenditure at that time.

The story has a powerful pay-off: the company had rights to an area for exploration. Two of their geologists had gone over it and found nothing of real value and recommended giving up the rights. This geologist had a different view and went out personally to check on the area before the company gave up its rights. He found one of the world's largest diamond mines.

The leader, therefore, integrates work across the social, technical and commercial domains (which in itself is work in the social aspect). The leader must be able to explain why each role has work and expectations in each of the domains and why that work is distributed as it is.

Use of the STC Model

We, and people we have worked with, have found this model has utility in several ways.

FIRST, AS AN ANALYTICAL TOOL

We can examine an organisation in terms of its relative strengths and weakness in each of these domains. Take a moment and reflect upon whether there is clarity in your own role concerning these domains of work.

Is the content clear and connected to the purpose? Is it balanced appropriately? Next consider a part or even the entire organisation. Are certain aspects over or under appreciated?

We mentioned earlier that it is easy and quite common to see the Technical as the only worthwhile work and so to denigrate the other aspects when all are essential. It is a little like arguing which of the heart, lungs or liver is most important. In using it as an analytical tool we must not jump to conclusions as to which domains(s) need(s) addressing.

For example, a manager might see a problem with production as Commercial. 'We can't produce enough because we need to buy new equipment'. In actual fact the lack of production may be poor maintenance perhaps due to the lack of skilled, technical expertise to keep the current equipment running. It may be a Social issue. Perhaps the leadership is poor or roles poorly defined or poor training leading to bad use of equipment. Similarly, problems of safety may again appear Technical or Commercial when in fact the root cause is Social – poor organisation and leadership.

SECONDLY, AS AN EXPLANATORY TOOL

For example some organisations are out of balance because one or two domains are valued more highly. Tony Dunlop (Macdonald Associates Consultancy internal paper April 1999) wrote of *missionaries* (people whose main driver is getting people to change), *mercenaries* (main driver is money) and *mechanics* (main driver is technical excellence for its own sake) as a useful categorisation of what influences people. If the organisation is dominated by mercenaries, the Commercial aspect will be relatively overvalued, mechanics will overvalue the Technical, and missionaries the Social. Further, those organisations that have been state or world monopolies have not had to pay much attention to the commercial, since they operated in an environment where they could fix price or supply. Sometimes the Social becomes distorted and over emphasised when the processes become more important than the purpose. (See Chapter 16 on System Design.)

THIRDLY, AS A PROBLEM-SOLVING TOOL

Any problem in the organisation can be looked at through these domains. So for example if we are considering a capital project, an acquisition, a significant restructure we can categorise issues in terms of these three domains. What are the Technical, Commercial and Social Critical issues we need to address if the work is to be successful? (See Chapter 15 on Teams and Teamwork.)

While it is standard practice to examine the commercial (financial) aspects in an acquisition, there are also environmental issues that may exist (and can be hugely costly in the future.) We would recommend that social issues be very seriously analysed in any acquisition. Are the cultures compatible or not, and what must be done if they are not compatible? One example is the issues between pilots of differing airlines who have different procedures that are very important to them. Following the merger of two companies, getting the pilots from each organisation to work together as one was a significant issue. While the problem appears to be Technical, it was in our opinion, largely Social (Sotham, 2015).

Conclusion

We find that many organisations are more conscious of how important it is to understand and manage the Technical and Commercial aspects with discipline and rigour based on sound principles and theory. There is less awareness that the Social or people aspect should be subject to similar rigour. We have developed Systems Leadership Theory to help redress the balance, not because the Social processes are the most important but because they are equally as important: successful and positive organisations need all three to be in balance.

This categorisation of aspects of work and organisational activity has some similarities with the work of Trist et al. (1990, 1993, 1997) and others from many years ago (Emery, 1969, 1981) That work and ours looks at work systems and the relationship between people and objects or the Technical processes that are used by people to achieve the purpose of the organisation. The work of Trist, Emery and others had origins at the Tavistock Institute and have the same roots as the thinking of Jaques who also worked there. We recommend the reader read these references (and compare similarities and differences).

The full appreciation of that work and discussion would take much more time and space than is possible here. Suffice it to say that our approach, like the socio-technical systems concept, pays great attention to the discretion within roles and the need to connect and enhance human decision-making rather than alienate people by reducing their choices and creativity. Also similar is our shared concern that too many levels of management, not only add bureaucracy, but also stifle creative opportunity. Both approaches look at organisations in terms of systems; from the entire organisation to parts of it and, as we explain, the Social, Technical and Commercial systems and how they interact.

4 *Social Process and Authority*

We have discussed the Three Domains that make up the work of an organisation: the Social, Technical and Commercial. They are distinct domains but all interact through the behaviour of people operating in those domains.

All organisations are social in that they involve people coming together to work to achieve a purpose. The way in which they then work together can have a profound effect on whether that purpose is achieved or not. As we have noted the impact of these organisational arrangements on behaviour can easily be underestimated. People working in organisations have very strong views about their organisations and how they are run, especially the quality of the leadership.

Everyone knows whether or not they like going to work and working with colleagues. People have strong feelings about whether they are being treated respectfully, whether anyone assigns work fairly and reviews that work honestly, whether anyone has the courage to make difficult decisions. We spend a significant proportion of our lives working, whether that be in the private sector, public sector organisations or voluntary organisations. These issues matter in community organisations, religious orders and anywhere where people come together to work to achieve a purpose. The way that an organisation is set up and run has a significant impact on people's lives and on their behaviour and whether or not they willingly give of their best.

We always begin with *the work*, and continue to concentrate on the work. By starting with the purpose of the organisation we can then try to find people who can do the work rather than start with the people and create an organisation around whatever they may be good at.

As we have argued, the unique advantage of Systems Leadership Theory is that it is comprehensive. All of the concepts are connected and so there is not a need to use separate, and perhaps contradictory, models to examine elements of organisation practice (e.g. leadership/capability/structure/system design.)

Systems Leadership provides a shared language with which to discuss organisational issues, essential for any coherent culture and as well a very clear model of Leadership and Team Membership.

Also, as we have said, one of the main features of Systems Leadership is that it not only articulates the WHAT, but more importantly the HOW. Simply ask of any other approach: does it explain how to put this into practice? Thus we see material that says *leaders must build trust … must build a committed team …* but with little or no explanation of how to do that.

In Chapter 3 we discussed the three domains including the Social domain. Here we examine two aspects to the Social domain, first the *content* and secondly the *enactment* of that content.

Content of the Social Domain

This book and Systems Leadership are all about the Social Domain. This includes the way that an organisation is structured; the working relationships, including authority; the design and implementation of systems; the creation and nature of culture, leadership and teamwork and the capability of people to do work.

The Social domain not only covers the elements listed above but also examines the Social Processes; that is the way in which people behave as that work is carried out. In other words it describes how people behave towards each other in ways that are more or less likely to result in a productive outcome. What we will refer to as Productive Social Cohesion.

Systems Leadership is based on the premise that clarity is fundamental for organisations to be effective. For example it is unfair to hold someone to account if you have not been clear about what is expected by when.

Systems Leadership principles also emphasise the need for clarity of purpose of the organisation, the content of roles and authorities. Confusion in these areas results in significant problems.

Systems Leadership proposes that an organisation is formed to achieve a purpose through the work of people, not simply serve the members' interests. Thus a school is there to educate students not just provide employment for teachers, an airline to fly passengers, a restaurant to serve meals to customers, a mining company to dig, process and deliver ore to customers. While this might seem obvious, many organisations (sometimes unconsciously) design their systems around the staff, not the clients, customers or service users.

In order for the people in any organisation to do work then those people must have the authority to carry out the work of the role. Indeed an organisational chart can be seen as a map of authority. Roles carry authority: to use resources and equipment, to spend money, to access information or physical space. Crucial authorities (in an employment organisation) are to assign and review work. If no one has clarity about the authority to assign work, the organisation cannot function in any predictable way and there can be no acceptance of accountability. If work cannot be assigned or reviewed people can do as they see fit or what they want, which may or may not accord with the purpose of the organisation. The only way, in such circumstances, that the organisation can get work done is by personal persuasion and/or by gaining what is sometimes described as *buy in* (even though staff are already being paid!).

However, it is evident in many organisations that leaders (and others) have become afraid of, or reluctant to use, authority.

In the last twenty years or so there has been a massive muddle between *authority* and *authoritarian*. There has been a rather loud argument against *hierarchy*, a fear of *command and control*; an anxiety about being too directive or even just being a *boss*. This anxiety is the result of confusing the very real and important authority that needs to be associated with a role and the WAY that that authority is enacted ... exactly what we describe as Social Process. That is the enactment of the intent of the organisation. The Social Process turns the organisational intent into reality.

We will discuss Social Process as it is used constructively while acknowledging that it can be used destructively, a means of exercising power.

Social Process can be likened to similar concepts such as *People Skills*, *Interpersonal Skills*, *Emotional Intelligence*, *Soft Skills* and more recently, and perhaps a little unnervingly, as *Soft Power*. While these terms are quite similar very few actually refer to the outcome but rather concentrate

---

Box 4.1   Social Process (constructive)

The ability to interact with others at work to produce a productive outcome.

on the process itself. In Systems Leadership we are clear that such skills need to be directed to achieve a productive purpose. This area of people skills is often wrongly assumed to be *the ability to get on with people*. It can be quite easy to get on with people if you don't ask them to do much or never give any honest feedback about performance, especially when it is below standard.

The emphasis purely on so-called people skills or interpersonal skills is leading in our view, to a highly unsatisfactory state in some organisations. Putting all the emphasis on social process skills has avoided the very important issue about the appropriate use of authority that should be associated with any role and enacted in any role relationship. Our current, apparent anxiety and ambivalence about that term authority has led to the situation where because of strong social process skills some people can get others to do almost anything, while the others with lesser skills are unable to get the people to do the work they are paid for even though it is central to their role and even though the person with the lesser skills is in a leadership position. This practice distributes leadership on the basis of social process skills not on the basis of the work that needs be done in each role.

Step One is to identify the appropriate authority associated with any role relationship.

Step Two is to ensure that this authority is mutually understood and Step Three is to help, where appropriate, to improve the social process skills needed to enact that authority in a way that is seen and felt to be fair and respectful of each person's dignity.

For good reason an employment contract embodies the acceptance of the authority of a role's manager, a position long supported in law. The effectiveness of the use of this authority is determined by the manager's demonstration of social process skills. It is not appropriate to ask people to rely on Social Process skills alone and neither is it appropriate to rely only on the authority as described in the role. The way a person uses Social Process skills has a significant bearing on whether the authority is experienced to be reasonable or not. It is largely the use of Social Process that determines whether or not a work relationship becomes a highly productive two-way interaction.

Systems Leadership identifies Social Process skills as one of the five core elements that define the capability of whether a person is competent to do the work of the role (see Chapter 8 on Human Capability).

Clearly not all roles carry the same authority (see Chapter 10); while one role may have the authority to assign work, another might have the authority to give advice or ask for a service. As such, the Social Process skills will differ accordingly. Take for example the role of a General Manager of a mine. Here the person will have to interact with many different people and groups inside and outside the mine. Not only employees of the organisation but members of the community and at times politicians and the local or even national or international media. The demand for highly developed Social Process skills, demonstrable by the role incumbent, is significant. But are those skills identified and made explicit say prior to an appointment, *other than must get along with a wide range of people?* The role may succeed or fail on these skills – having and using them effectively.

In Systems Leadership Theory, the Leadership and Team Membership Process (see Chapter 15) is described. It has been demonstrated clearly that if people use this approach it will result in a productive outcome. Further it leads to the acceptance of decisions without needing to resort to consensus (which assumes that everyone has equal authority) or voting (similar assumption). If people in an organisation do have equal authority then it must be assumed they are not only doing the same work (e.g. Members of Parliament), but also that they cannot be differentiated on the basis of their work role and as such should all be paid the same.

It seems that too often it is assumed (rather stereotypically) that authority only flows downwards in an organisation. Actually it can, and should flow in all directions since its purpose is to enable work and it is very important that there is clarity about this. Thus in Systems Leadership Theory the team member has the authority to require the leader to explain the context and purpose of work. She or he can *demand a review*. These are not simple authorities, but a means whereby a team member can call the leader to account for their work as a leader … *command and control* it certainly is not.

The other main area where people need to be clear about authority and Social Process is in the enactment of systems. For example a coach may be employed to offer advice as to the improvement of technical practice. It must be clear what authority he or she has. Can she choose which person to observe? When should she observe and advise? What are the consequences if any, positive or negative? This should be clear in the system design and implementation and thereby set a transparent context.

Many people avoid addressing difficult situations because they do not have confidence in their Social Process skills. If the organisation does not have clarity about roles, the authority of the role and systems to monitor the use of role as authority, this avoidance can go unchecked. Further if the organisation is avoiding *authority* because it has confused that with *authoritarian* then these issues will continue to remain unresolved. Social Process becomes the application of skills to avoid problems not face difficult issues. Problems are continually smoothed over in the hope that *no one will notice, it is necessary that no one be upset* or that the problem *will just go away*, meanwhile social cohesion actually crumbles and the quality of service and output drops or remains variable.

Authority and Power

Systems Leadership Theory is based on the proper use of authority in organisations. It is one of the most important concepts in creating positive organisations. We also recognise that power is used in organisations, sometimes for good, but more often to their detriment. While both these terms have been used primarily in the study of governments and politics, in organisations the issues with regard to authority and power are actually concerned with social process, relationships between people. Therefore we needed definitions that dealt with the reality of human relations within organisations (see Box 4.2).

Box 4.2   Authority and Power

Authority: the exertion of will in the context of the mutual acceptance of agreed limits.
Power: the exertion of will while breaking one of more limits of authority

A – – – – – – – – – – – → B

In an organisation if A wants B to do something that A wishes, then A is using authority when he or she is:

1.   Requiring B to act within the limits of his/her role description.
2.   Requiring B to act within the limits of role-relationships, i.e., that it is clear that A can require B to do something.
3.   That B is required to act within the existing policies of the organisation.

4. That B is required to act within the limits of the law.
5. That B is required to act within the ethical framework of the organisation or within custom and practice providing it does not breach 3 or 4 above.

Further, the context of the relationship assumes that B has freely entered into the role, i.e. B has not been coerced or appears to have no other choice. We will explore these elements below.

POWER

If A uses power without authority to influence B to do something, then in bringing that influence to bear, A breaks one or more of the five conditions above, or it is clear that B has unwillingly entered into the role. A has asked B to do something that is:

1. Outside the limits of his/her role description.
2. A does not have a role relationship that acknowledges the right to ask for this action.
3. Requires B to violate one or more of the existing policies of the organisation.
4. Requires B to break the law.
5. Requires B to act unethically or outside existing custom and practice.

Both power and authority, as defined above, can be (and are) used in work hierarchies. Both can be used, to achieve an objective but an organisation based on power takes a significant toll on its employees and is detrimental to psychological health. These are organisations with stressed employees. Power relationships may often be experienced by one party as being treated like an object.

Organisations based on power require a lot of energy to protect one's turf, to gain more turf, to manipulate others to act and avoid accountability. This drains energy from the productive work of the organisation and causes burnout in some employees (see discussion in the main text).

Power based systems also alienate a large portion of the work force. It is debilitating and demoralising to have to deal with *favouritism, power games, office politics,* unclear accountabilities, blame placing, and decisions made on the basis of who will gain power rather than their effects on the long-term viability of the enterprise.

The organisations that we propose provide conditions where clear systems of authority and accountability can be created and enforced. Such systems of authority and accountability show respect for human dignity, drive out unauthorised power networks and thus release tremendous energy for productive purposes.

Managers (and other employees) are empowered – more able to act – but they act through authority systems, within limits that are subject to review. Their ability to act derives from a clear grant of authority from the organisation, which holds role incumbents accountable for the proper exercise of that authority.

No matter what the laws or policies state, however, no one has authority unless the leader's direct reports accept it. What is required to be fully accepted as a leader is a good understanding of the universal values, mythologies and cultures. A new leader's behaviour will be observed and evaluated through the mythological lenses of his or her workforce. If that behaviour is placed at the negative ends of the scales of universal values, the leader is unlikely to gain full acceptance of his or her authority even though the workforce may go through the motions based on the authority of the role.

Box 4.3   Royal Court or Meritocracy

ROYAL COURTS AND POSITIVE ORGANISATIONS

We have observed that organisations that run on power often function like a Royal Court. At Court the only thing that matters is what the King or Queen wants. It is critical to be 'in favour', 'have the ear of the Monarch'. This encourages in-fighting, cliques and elites that become more concerned with power than achieving productive results. People advance on the basis of holding onto knowledge, manipulating others, starting and spreading rumours that denigrate rivals. Whilst this can be fascinating (see Game of Thrones), it is hugely wasteful and damaging to many people.

Contrast this with the *Positive Organisation*: here people identify with the purpose of the organisation. Capability to do the work is paramount and working relationships and authority are explicit and mutually understood. The overall purpose of the organisation and purpose of the roles are more important than status and personal standing.

Our experience is that whilst the Royal Court produces much more intrigue, gossip and content suitable for television and film, it can be a most destructive place to work. The Positive Organisation is both productive and a healthy place to work and actually makes a real contribution to society.

Conclusion

The Social Domain consists of all the behaviours and arrangements whereby people work together. Part of that includes the Social Process Skills required to carry out the work of the role and enact the authorities associated with that role. The recent anxiety about confusing authority with authoritarian has blurred the clarity needed to design the appropriate authority into any role and its proper use in a role relationship. Unless a role has the appropriate authority to carry out the work of the role, with regard to both people and resources, it is unfair to hold the person in the role to account.

The avoidance of clarity around authority has also blurred the nature of accountability and certainly felt fair accountability. This avoidance of authority is also due to a very simplistic view that authority only flows in one direction and that *hierarchy* is also somehow out of date and to be avoided. We know of no organisations that can run without both authority and some form of hierarchy. That does not make them authoritarian. Rather, authoritarian approaches are due to poor Social Process Skills and thus poor leadership. Substituting authority with the need to exercise brilliant Social Process Skills is no answer either ... we need both. The absence of clarity around authority and Social Process skills leads to organisations run on power; the basis of cliques, fragmented cultures, internal rivalry and favouritism. All are enemies of meritocracy and positive organisations.

5 Types of Social Organisation

For society or any organisation to prosper there must be social cohesion; agreed arrangements about what is acceptable and/or productive behaviour. However, clearly not all people do behave in constructive or productive ways. So why might that be the case? Often when we see people behaving in ways that we do not understand. A simple, and rather lazy, way of explaining, or perhaps dismissing that behaviour, is to categorise it as Mad, Bad or Stupid (MBS) or a combination of those. Why would a person be working at a height of 50 metres on a construction site with no safety harness or safety equipment? Why would someone keep silent in a meeting implying agreement and then criticise the outcome outside the meeting? Why would someone not maintain his/her equipment properly? Why would someone only do a small part of the work that is needed? All of these questions can be answered or perhaps more accurately dismissed by saying they are Mad, Bad and/or Stupid.

When we are applying Systems Leadership in an organisation we ask people to try and explain such behaviours (and of course many other similar behaviours) without recourse to MB or S. These are explanations of last resort and before we come to such conclusions we need to have a deeper understanding of what might be causing or driving those behaviours.

We argue that the way in which we organise: the structures, the systems, the way we appoint people to roles and the way in which we assign work, have a great impact on behaviour. Indeed if we use the principles of Systems Leadership to understand the way that an organisation is set up and run we can, within limits, predict the sorts of behaviour that such arrangements will encourage or discourage. This in turn can determine the extent to which the organisation can achieve the purpose it has been set up to accomplish.

Our experience is that the relationship between organisational arrangements and human behaviour is not as well understood as it might be. Consequently the reason why a positive organisation is not achieved is also not understood, and therefore the remedies put in place are most often inappropriate and/or irrelevant. This is one reason why organisational change is subject to so many fads and fashions.

So is there one type of organisation that is better than any other? Can we come up with an ideal way of organising? Again we see the influence of fashion: *hierarchy is out of date, we don't really need leaders* rather, we should have; *consensus and buy-in*, we need *innovation. We are in a post-industrial, post-modern world when none of the old rules apply*. People assert that there is much more complexity and uncertainty today than ever before. Some claim that we don't need rigid structures but networks. However, many of these apparent solutions are unclear in what they actually mean and tend to be universal statements rather than addressing specific issues and specific behaviours. It is as if regular exercise was being promoted as a cure for all illness. It's not that regular exercise is wrong it just may not be the solution to this particular problem.

In the 1980s in the United Kingdom, and probably elsewhere in the Western world the model of private industry was idealised. All public sector problems would be solved if only they could be run like a business. Such thinking was even applied to academic institutions, voluntary organisations, and even religious organisations. It is no wonder that such a simplistic approach gave hierarchy a bad name. Just as today, some people will avoid concepts of hierarchy and authority altogether.

We very specifically argue that one size does not fit all. We argue there is a need to understand the purpose of the organisation, the current and desired culture of the organisation and how the current arrangements are helping or hindering the achievement of that purpose. Systems Leadership provides a set of principles, concepts and tools that can not only provide a deeper understanding of organisational issues, but also help to contribute to how they might be addressed. This is not a simple process.

We stress that people are social; the key to our survival and success lies in the way that we work together to achieve our purpose: turning intention into reality. As the social fabric changes we do develop changes to the way we work together, for example the gender or race of people that we work with but those ways are not independent of the purpose. A private sector model rigidly applied to a church organisation will not work and over time hinder the purpose of the Church. There may well be aspects and qualities of private sector organisation, however, that could be very beneficially adopted by such an organisation. The Church is not a business but it does have to manage cost and gain revenue and provide an appropriate set of systems for its clergy and congregations. We need to understand what specific approaches are relevant and why.

Types of Organisation and Associated Authority

FAMILY, CLAN OR TRIBE (GERONTOCRACY)

In order to work together we must make arrangements about who is to do what. We need arrangements concerning authority such as who can direct whom, who can advise, what consequences are there, if any, around the achievement or lack of? We have, of course, been doing this throughout history. If we look at social organisations over time we can see that the oldest form of social organisation is the family group. Whether we call that a clan, a tribe or family the basic organising principle is that relationships and authority are based upon blood relations. We are not claiming to be expert anthropologists and we do not imply that all organisations based primarily around blood relations are the same.

Patriarchal and matriarchal societies are obviously significantly different; however, their similarity lies in the fact that such rules, social customs and practices are constructed around direct and indirect family relationships. Rules around those relationships determine what behaviour is allowed, disallowed, required or forbidden. Who can marry whom? Even who can talk to whom or be in the same room, and particularly who has authority over whom and how that authority is passed on.

Authority in such social organisations is usually vested in the elders and based on seniority; it is sometimes vested in one or a small group of families who are deemed to be the most significant (Max Weber (1922b; 1978) termed these traditional forms of rule.) Patriarchal societies are often ruled by a king with key positions in the authority structure held by family members.

The most obvious and current examples of Gerontocracy are royal families. In Saudi Arabia, the rule is patriarchal with the King and his family as heads of the government. There is also a more modern version as found in the United Kingdom. The head of the current royal family is the Head of the Executive of the UK Government and even though that title is essentially symbolic, as we will discuss later, symbolism has a very strong influence on behaviour. The Queen (or King) is the Head of State.

It is significant that the British Armed Forces swear allegiance to the Monarch and have pictures of the reigning Monarch in their headquarters whilst the United States Armed Forces the pictures are of the current President who could change every four years.

When we look at the purpose of the family, clan or tribe it is to continue the line. It is about making sure of the survival of the next and subsequent generations. Therefore the main celebrations in a family concern time passing, especially birthdays and significant anniversaries.

RELIGION (THEOCRACY)

Another common and ancient form of organisation is that associated with religions. Most if not all societies have some form of organised worship to God or gods. Their organisational forms differ but have common features and commonality of purpose. Their purpose is to form organisational arrangements including rules, rituals and norms in order to worship God or gods. The underlying common belief is in some all-powerful force or will that transcends human and material reality and that can have positive or negative (sometimes catastrophic) impact on people.

Beyond specific religious organisations, there is something called a theocracy. For example: Iran, Saudi Arabia and other Middle Eastern countries governed by Sharia law. The point about the organisational structure is that authority is vested in the person or persons deemed to be the most holy in terms of closeness to God and/or has the potential to influence God. Religious leaders have the authority to prescribe or proscribe certain behaviours on the basis of religious teaching and scripture. Failure to behave in accordance with these teachings may well lead to the exclusion from the society and organisation with varying consequences, some extremely severe. Thus the purpose of a religious organisation is not the same as that of a family and as such we should not be surprised that they adopt different organisational arrangements.

DEMOCRACY

Once societies have grown beyond the possibility to manage on the basis of blood relations or religion, new forms of organisation must be found in order to create productive, social cohesion. This may be because the group has grown in size and family relationships are unclear in terms of kinship, which may be because of intermarriage with other groups and families. It may be because there is not one single religion or because of the need to trade beyond kinship or religious boundaries. There are of course many different forms that community and government organisation could take, but perhaps the most dominant, currently, is democracy. Authority within a democracy resides with the members of a society, or at least those who are enfranchised. The point about democracy now is that there is no differentiation between members. (In earlier forms this has not always been the case.)

The purpose of a democracy, we argue, is to bring about productive social cohesion across a disparate group of people so that they can live peaceably together. As such no one person's vote has any more or less weight than any other. The purpose of the vote is to elect a legislature (and in some democracies an executive), such that the members of the legislature also have equal authority. The biggest threat to democracy occurs with any attempts to undermine the equality of member authority, such that one particular group, perhaps family, ethnic group, the wealthy, a religious group or a demagogue has dominance. There are of course many different forms of democracy, which are beyond the remit of this book, but the point here is simply to recognise another completely different form of social organisation with a different purpose and consequently appropriately different forms of organisation.

MERITOCRACY

The fourth type of organisational structure identified here is that of a meritocracy. The core of the definition here is that the organisation is based upon capability to do the work of a role in the organisation. Like the three previous forms of social organisation mentioned, meritocracy has a very specific and deliberate purpose – it is an organisation that is set up to produce goods and services. Or to put it the other way round, if you want to build an organisation that is particularly set up to produce goods and services, then a meritocracy is the most effective way of doing that. Later in this book (see Chapter 7), we will discuss meritocracies in more depth.

For now, however, we are defining meritocracy as an organisation where people are appointed to a given role, and given the authority to perform the work of the role on the basis of their capability to do that work, and to exercise that authority appropriately (see prior discussion on social process). That is, people are not appointed on the basis of other influences such as nepotism, favouritism, seniority, gender, race, religion or election. The advantage of meritocracies is the speed of decision-making and the speed at which resources can be deployed, and issues of varying complexity can be addressed.

This, of course, depends upon the purpose of the organisation and roles being clear and the people in those roles being genuinely capable of doing the work of their respective roles. That is people are recruited, selected and promoted on the basis of their capability. We will discuss other aspects of meritocracies in the chapter dedicated to that topic. The point here is that the organisational structures and systems appropriate to a meritocracy are quite different to those appropriate to the other three forms of social organisation mentioned here.

Of course there are many other forms of social organisation; we have identified the main ones that we believe are designed to attempt to create productive social cohesion. Other types of organisation are prevalent in the world such as oligarchies and dictatorships. Such organisations are more concerned with oppressive social cohesion, and the forms of organisation are primarily directed to keeping a small elite in power at the expense of the many. Whilst we recognise that these organisations are significant and potentially extremely destructive, discussion of such organisations is not the primary purpose of this book.

We also recognise that within the field of meritocracy there are many different forms that can be made to work such as co-operatives, partnerships, as well as public and the private manifestations.

Muddles

We have described, albeit briefly, these different types of organisation to demonstrate that there are very legitimate and different ways of creating productive and socially cohesive organisations depending upon the purpose of the organisation. We have also distinguished these as general types to argue that certain systems may be relevant in one type of organisation but not in another. However, we also see that people transfer organisational concepts relevant to one type of organisation to another without recognising the consequence of what they might be doing.

For example, because we may regard democracy as a *good thing* that does not mean to say that meritocracies would be improved or more effective if everybody voted for their leaders or if all decisions were put to a vote. This is because authority is not distributed equally in a meritocracy. It is deliberately distributed in accordance with the requirements of the role. In a legislature, committees are relevant because the members have equal authority and as such, if they are to work together, they need a decision-making mechanism that is consistent with this equality. Voting here is an appropriate system. Committees are therefore not appropriate structures and voting not an appropriate decision-making system in a meritocracy.

It would surely seem absurd to suggest that if people wanted to have children that they should be required to advertise, write a role description, carry out interviews and then select accordingly (although some people might consider it preferable at times). Similarly it is counter-productive and not appropriate to differentiate love towards family members on the basis of their capability. We do not *let one of our children go* because they have not performed adequately.

To do so would be to muddle structures and systems appropriate in one context with another. However, we do see such muddles occurring when we import family, religious or democratic processes into meritocracies. These muddles undermine productive social cohesion. It is like putting petrol into a diesel engine. It is not because only one is fuel; it is because one *type* of fuel is designed for a particular *type* of engine.

Conclusion

We are arguing here that there are appropriately different types of organisational structures and systems according to the purpose of the organisation. We are also arguing that to muddle up those structures and systems across different types of organisation causes not only inefficiency, but potentially may threaten the purpose of the organisation and undermine productive social cohesion. We're clearly saying that there is no one perfect way of building an organisation to achieve any particular purpose. Instead Systems Leadership identifies principles, systems models and practices that can be used to identify what is relevant in the particular context. Some of our models are relevant to all types of organisation; see for example values, myths and culture. Others are specific to one type or another; see for example, specific systems appropriate to meritocracies. Being clear about the nature and purpose of an organisation is critical. We can see very serious and destructive consequences if we superimpose one type of organisation on another. For example, consider the current conflict in the Middle East. Here we see societies where the dominant authority is distributed primarily according to kinship and religion. Superimposed on these traditional structures is a Western view that authority with regard to democracy and meritocracy should be dominant. While some view the Middle East as a problem that can be solved by the imposition of a democratic government and meritocratic organisations, this is to misunderstand the current nature of authority in most of those societies. It completely underestimates the time and processes it takes to build such organisations.

So whilst some muddles may not cause too much harm and, in some cases, even be quite amusing, others can be devastating causing massive human suffering and disruption.

2 *The Six Principles of Behaviour: Core Concepts of Systems Leadership*

Introduction to Part 2

This part of the book contains the central propositions of Systems Leadership. It is the heart of the book. Our propositions about behaviour and especially universal values underpin everything else that follows. As such if this material is to be used constructively, these concepts must be fully understood. It is not about any particular type of organisation, it is about how and why people associate and come together to achieve a purpose. It explains why associations succeed and why they fail.

As we have said, Systems Leadership is essentially about how to create, improve and sustain positive organisations through creating productive social cohesion. While we do not underestimate the critical issues in creating commercial and technically viable organisations, all are built on the social process of human relationships.

There are qualities and principles in human relationships that are not limited to work organisations but are relevant to all relationships. Although human beings are adaptable, they are not chameleons. We do not completely transform as we move from one relationship, say work; to another, say family. Of course there are important and significant differences but there are also similarities. Indeed, the ability to transform totally and be a completely different person in different situations is regarded as socio- or psychopathic. The formation of stable social relationships and entities, essential for our survival, is not possible if people generally behave psycho- or sociopathically.

This part of the book proposes a set of general principles about human behaviour relevant to all relationships including work organisations. Like the outer layers of an onion, these principles form the context that surrounds the more specific relationships we have found in organisations. If we are unable to develop an understanding of these general principles, then the deeper meaning of specific relationships will remain hidden. Behaviour will seem either more mystical or technical than it is, and the ability to change our own behaviour and to influence others' behaviour will be diminished.

In this section we look at how we try to order our social environment, make sense of it, and make decisions about whom we can or want to associate with. We look at how and why we try to change our own and/or other peoples' behaviour. All of these principles apply in an organisation, but we explain here how they apply more generally as well. As we move through the book, we gradually move the focus from the general to the specific. If we started with the detail, we would lose the sense and depth of structure underlying these relations and end up with a more shallow and descriptive account rather than a set of propositions that allow us to understand and predict more effectively.

As a concentrated summary of our approach we outline it first in the form of 6 core principles. It has been suggested to us that these are sufficient for a book in itself, certainly the 6 core principles are the foundation on which Systems Leadership is built.

We start with our fundamental need to predict our environment in order to feel safe. We cannot focus on work or be creative if we do not know what might happen next. We need a context that is neither distracting nor threatening. We then examine how important it is to recognise other people's view of the world so that we see people as people rather than as objects to be manipulated. This may seem obvious but the objectification of 'the other' is the most common cause of conflict and abuse. We then argue that all of our behaviour is value based. Not only that but, perhaps most radically, those values are universal. All people share the same set of values against which we judge behaviour.

Thus we argue that we are fundamentally connected with all others and what binds us is far more important than what separates us as people. This unusual proposition leads us to look at how we form cultures and social cohesion. How we are drawn to people who share the same views (mythologies) as to what constitutes positive behaviour. Whilst this is understandable it can also be dangerous if we only reinforce our views and never challenge them. We argue that behavioural change is based upon an experience of dissonance. By dissonance we mean how we feel when what we expect is confounded and our predictions fail. The experience of dissonance may be a positive or negative one depending upon the nature of our expectations.

We then argue that there are three main tools that can be used in behavioural change: Systems, Symbols and Behaviour. We examine the difference between relationships that are built on authority rather than power and finally, strongly argue for the need for clarity if we are to create productive social cohesion.

6 *The Six Principles of Behaviour*

Principle 1: People Need to be Able to Predict their Environments

Most of the time we are in environments that are relatively familiar, and at such times we are not aware of how we are scanning the environment and testing it against our expectations. We often only become aware of this process when there is an exception or surprise. We can underestimate how important it is to predict and monitor precisely because we are not fully conscious of doing so. Indeed, if we were fully conscious of the process all the time, we could not easily concentrate on the task at hand. Whenever we see or experience an unusual event or failure of prediction, we cannot ignore it. We cannot simply note an exception; we must explain it, so that we do not get surprised again.

For example, a colleague who is usually friendly and courteous cuts us short. Why? We must have an explanation and if we can't find one we will invent one. We are very inventive. So our colleague may be (a) very busy, (b) upset, (c) angry at a work related task or (d) some other reason. Most people are primarily concerned to discover 'is it anything I have said or done?' We need to know what reactions we provoke by our own behaviour or the world becomes an unpredictable and potentially threatening place. Some explanations may mean that we do not have to change our predictive model: 'His mother has recently died.' Others may imply that we do: 'He is fed up with you constantly asking how he is.'

From virtually the moment we are born, we embark on the quest of observing and classifying behaviour so that we may understand it and learn how to predict it. This heuristic process helps us figure out from our earliest experience what makes someone come to feed us, what makes someone laugh, what makes someone angry. We learn to predict what encourages generosity, what encourages love, what causes indifference, what leads to friendship, what to bullying and so on. We learn from our immediate family and friends, then from school, the community, the media and the organisations in which we work.

We do not have to be taught to do this. It is an essential, natural, human process. This heuristic methodology results in a set of models and rules for predicting behaviour of people and the physical world around us. In doing so we are all developing our own theory of human behaviour as well as a theory of the material world. It is not only important to us; it is essential to our sense of well-being and even survival. In certain circumstances, if we 'read' the situation wrongly, it may put us in serious danger.

Think for a moment about what makes you nervous or anxious. It is most often caused when you are about to go into a situation where prediction is difficult, but the outcome is critical. For example, many people become anxious before having a job interview, a final exam, a public presentation, a negotiation or, at the extreme, combat. What eases that anxiety is the reassurance of preparation – the work of anticipating and rehearsing the *what-ifs*. What if I am asked this? What if she gets angry? What if they find the presentation boring? (These are Critical Issues: see Chapter 15 Teams and Teamwork.)

If we are to avoid constant stress and are to feel comfortable, we must be in an environment where, in general terms, the situation and people's behaviour are predictable. Now, of course, this does not mean we need or want to predict exactly what someone is about to do or say.

Nonetheless, to avoid anxiety we do want people to behave in a way that stays within predictable boundaries. This means we can operate in a stable environment and consequently focus our attention on what we have to do – operate the machine, discuss a business deal, write a report.

When one of the authors, Ian Macdonald, first started working in a large psychiatric hospital in 1975, he made his first visit to a locked ward. On entering, some of the residents immediately rushed up to him. One put his face a few centimetres from his; another touched his arm; another circled him, staring. In ordinary life such behaviour would have been extremely threatening. It is not benign for strangers to behave in such a way unless there is a threat or intention of sex or violence, or both. Macdonald very quickly had to learn a different set of predictive rules, to ascertain in this context what was a real threat and what was simply a different normality.

In a less dramatic way we all have to learn these new rules or norms when we visit countries overseas, move to a different community, move to a new organisation or simply visit someone's home for the first time. Most people can remember instances from childhood when such visits led to surprises. *This family does/does not eat together. They argue a lot. They don't talk to each other. They let/don't let their children watch certain TV programmes. They do or don't allow mobile phones or limit 'screen-time' for children. They do/do not take off their shoes in the living room.* We learn not to blurt out our surprise, but to observe, learn and increase the scope of our predictive models. Some we find can be comfortably accommodated, others not so.

Similarly, think about visiting or starting work in a new company. Induction is not simply about work and safety processes. You must learn how to address people. Do you use first names? Where do you find facilities, for example, the canteen or toilets? What is a reasonable break time? And so on. It is at times like this our heuristic process becomes more conscious and so we are more aware of the process we have used and continue to use all our lives.

It is important to state here that predictability gives a sense of stability and reassurance even if the situation appears to be counter-productive. Again, Ian Macdonald has worked with families that may be described as dysfunctional but are in another sense stable. Children learn to see the patterns of behaviour and avoid at least the worst excesses. They learn what triggers violence, how differently an adult behaves when drunk or drug affected. These may be very unhappy relationships, but they endure because the participants have learned the dance of survival by predicting behaviour.

If we look at industry, certain companies are characterised by dreadful workplace relations, but they are predictable. The workers know the management are bastards and out to get them. The management knows the workers are lazy, out for what they can take with the least amount of work. Each side plays its predictable role, keeps to the script and enters a regular ritual of protracted, tough negotiations trying to win points from each other. It may be economically wasteful, even disastrous, but it is predictable. Everyone knows their place and hangs on to their correct view of the world. *We all know where we stand.* Historically in many societies, class and caste systems may bestow privilege on some and oppress others. However they may be stable due to their predictability at least until the excesses become unbearable.

Thus predictability is critical. One extreme public example of this happened on 11 September 2001 (aka '9/11'). Worldwide, many people had that date imprinted in their minds forever. The loss of life was appalling. However, the deeper shock was the unpredictability of the event. Worse, unlike an earthquake, it was a deliberate, indeed meticulously planned, human act that was not foreseen.

In the media interviews, people used revealing comments. It was not a *normal* hijacking. Now hijackings are not normal in one sense, but we had come to expect that hijackers don't want to die. They make demands: they threaten; they do not deliberately fly planeloads of innocent people into buildings. Why? For what purpose? What on earth had we done to deserve this? What sort of people are the hijackers?

Enormous amounts of energy have necessarily been expended trying to answer these questions. Until we can answer them, we cannot feel safe. When we board a plane or work in a skyscraper, we cannot help wondering and considering what we would do if ... What could we do? Why do some people hate us? Why do some love us? It is intolerable to leave these questions unanswered, or we would live in a random universe, a world of uncertainty where we have little or no sense of influencing our own destiny.

Now, sadly we are much more familiar with suicide bombings and they no longer produce the level of shock to the outside world although their victims are no less damaged or killed.

So we must learn to predict, to have an effective model that does not result in constant surprises, especially shocks. People who have great difficulty heuristically constructing such models, for example, people with autism, suffer great anxiety and express a great need for control. In short, we must understand social processes in such a way that we can generally predict behaviour around us.

We must also understand the difference between prediction of a population's behaviour and the prediction of an individual's behaviour.

Understanding social processes involves not just explaining why someone behaved as they did but also predicting likely behaviour. However, it is important to distinguish between predicting behaviour in general and predicting an individual response. For example, if a person is working and producing an output, it is a general principle to say that, if that person receives valid feedback and due recognition, he or she is more likely to continue to work hard, giving care and attention to the quality and quantity of what is produced compared with someone who receives little or no feedback or recognition. This will not, however, be true in every single case. Some individuals will work hard despite poor leadership. Others will find it difficult to work hard even with good leadership. Thus, we can work from general principles about people in general but we need to consider the individual case and exceptions, bearing in mind that an exception does not necessarily invalidate the principle. If we confuse the general and the particular we can make some serious mistakes. For example, a person who smokes may well cite an elderly relative 'who smoked all their life and never got cancer' as a means of denying the dangers of smoking. In effect, this technique is a way of avoiding dissonance.

It is impossible to predict in minute detail any individual's behaviour (including our own). This does not, however, differentiate natural science from social science. No theory can predict exactly the behaviour of a single entity, be it a person or atomic particle. Paradoxically we can make a general prediction (in social science) that people will actually resist prediction if it is felt to be manipulation. People *in general* do not like to be labelled, categorised or put in boxes because it appears to deny our unique individuality. We need to be very aware that a general prediction will not account for every person's behaviour. We are unique but we also know that we are extraordinarily similar in terms of biological makeup and our need for food, shelter and companionship. We respond similarly to perceived threat, cold, lack of sleep and lack of food. In our everyday lives we depend on the general predictability of behaviour of those around us in the street, on trains and in our workplace or home, but we resist the notion that therefore we are totally predictable as individuals.

Whilst there are always differences, there are also common characteristics. The problem with using statistical models and probability statements lies with the reality that probabilities are about populations while personal experience is by definition singular. Therefore, whereas it may be both true and accurate to predict that a company will reduce the workforce by 10% over the next year, at the end of the workforce reduction employees do not experience a 90% role. Either I keep my job or I do not, zero or one. When we look at safety statistics by plane, train or car, we may know the statistical safety figures. However, for each of us we either have an accident or we don't, again zero or one. Many of us choose to behave unsafely at work because 'we will get away with it', gambling on the zero not the one. Thus, experientially, we are not overly impressed or influenced by statistical evidence even when it is true because the basic gamble for the individual is win or lose. Even when we lose, we may fool ourselves that we *nearly* won because our raffle ticket was the number above or below the winning ticket.

Leaders seeking to influence behaviour will not be very successful if their main or only argument is quoting statistics. The examples must be taken through to personal experience, so that the person links the statement to personal experience. We do not particularly like to be normal, average, or accept the implication that we are effectively indistinguishable from others. This lack of recognition of individual difference reduces us to apparent objects. In understanding the detail of social process we must work from general principles about people to specific hypotheses about particular groups or cultures and then to individual need. It is important to work at all three levels at once and not exclusively at any one or two. That is, we must move carefully from the general to the particular, shaping our explanation and behaviour as we do. For example, at work I may start with a general assumption that people require feedback and recognition. I, then, may make a specific statement about a particular group, say a crew of underground miners, a team of young Aboriginal Australians, a troupe of actors in a theatre company. This will involve *how* that recognition and feedback is most appropriately given. In our experience it is not helpful to publicly single out miners or Aboriginal people. Better to give such recognition quietly and with little fanfare. An actor, however, may require public individual praise, applause and so on. One final important step, however, is to take into account individual differences. Not all miners, indigenous Australians or actors are the same (see Box 6.1).

We are very keen on exceptions, because it appeals to our individuality and a sense that we are not victims of predetermined fate. There are huge industries that exploit our need to do this: smoking, drinking and gambling. The gambling industry and particularly lotteries are dependent upon our belief that we might beat the odds. Some of the most dangerous behaviour at work and socially is founded on the notion that *it won't happen to me*, exactly the opposite of the gambler who hopes, against the odds, *it could be me*. Thus we have the contradictory, but absolutely human, behaviour of running across a busy street to buy a lottery ticket.

Box 6.1   Individuals – Statistics

In a mining company in Australia the leadership were about to offer staff conditions including a salary structure to supervisors who were at the time on hourly rates of pay with overtime. As part of the consideration an analysis was done to see what percentage of supervisors' pay was due to overtime. The overall figure came out as just over 15%. Therefore it seemed logical to think about *buying out* the overtime by adding a figure around 15% to the salary.

On closer analysis, however, a very small proportion of supervisors covered a significant amount of overtime (some up to 40% of base pay). Further, we found that those supervisors who earned these large amounts were disliked by their crews and fellow supervisors. Their crews saw them as dishonest, since they fixed the system so that they came in on weekends, outside the normal shift, for the slightest of reasons. They also saw this as unfair. Very few were even moderately trusted. Taking this small group out of the equation reduced the overtime loading to below 10%. Therefore, the leadership built in a loading to the salary of 10%, paid to all supervisors irrespective of time worked, which was seen as fair and honest by the productive supervisors and highly punitive by the poor supervisors, most of whom left. Thus, by using an analysis at all three levels – general, group and individual, the organisation retained effective workers; lost people who were exploiting it and reduced cost from the first analysis. This example also works if it is seen as using the trio of leadership tools: systems, symbols and behaviour: the systems being the employment and overtime systems, the behaviour being the leadership's efforts to carry out a detailed analysis (perceived as fair and honest) and the symbolism of rewarding effective supervisors and not rewarding poor performers.

Building general, predictive models with attached statistical probabilities is not demeaning to individuals. We do it throughout our lives. However, a leader must not impose this model on either a specific group of people or an individual since it objectifies the person. Instead, it is a starting point to be able to identify groups and, within groups, specific individuals.

Nevertheless, it is not simply a matter of having predictive models. We also imbue these models with value and morality. They are infused with a sense of right and wrong, good or bad, and all the shades of grey in between.

This brings us to the next principle.

Principle 2: People are not Machines

This common sense statement that people are not machines is central to understanding change processes. It is one that, despite its appearing obvious, is easily forgotten.

Change processes are often described as *organisational change, culture change, re-engineering*. We look for *efficiency improvement, performance enhancement* and *productivity gains*. What all of these have in common is that people have to change their behaviour in order to achieve them. Without behavioural change there can be no improvement. Thus all change processes, whether technically or commercially driven, depend upon people doing things differently. Therefore any discussion of organisational change needs to address how behaviour is influenced. Anyone who wants to bring about behaviour change needs to consider their assumptions about behaviour and how and why it changes.

This does not mean that everyone, or even those leading an organisation, has to be a professional psychologist. These chapters explore the core principles about behaviour that have significant impact on the success or otherwise of any social process.

Many change processes are initially driven by technological change, the availability of equipment, resources and materials that can potentially lead to improvement in effectiveness and efficiency. This should not obscure the essential social process (see Box 6.3).

PERSON–OBJECT

In the relationship shown in Figure 6.1, we do not have to worry about the object's will or intent. What matters is the person's will. The object will react to any action on it in a predictable way, according to the laws of physics. Thus if I throw a cup on the floor and it breaks, it will break according to the force applied to it, the hardness of the floor, the angle that it hits the floor, and so on, and will depend on what the cup is made of. In this process I do not have to worry about what the cup *thinks* about being thrown to the floor. It will not *try* to break neither will it *try not* to break. It will not consider my intent as cruel or unjustified or reasonable. Neither does it have any notion of its own value or the value I attribute to it. Thus I can experiment quite freely on physical objects and entities.

Figure 6.1   Person–Object Relationship

PERSON–PERSON

Look at Figure 6.2. You can see that when it comes to my action on people there are (at least) two wills operating. If I try to throw a person on the floor, he or she will certainly have a view about it. The context as well as intent will influence behaviour. For example, is the person a wrestling partner or a complete stranger? A person will presumably try not to break; will try to make sense of my behaviour. Why did I do that? Was it accidental? Was it typical? If I announce my intent that will also influence the event, unlike the relationship with the cup, which will behave no differently whatever warning I give it. Further, this event will not end at impact. The person will try to make sense of what happened after the event, which in turn will influence future relationships. Any person will have a sense of both their own personal value and a judgement about how I value them.

Box 6.2   Different Types of Relationships

In our relationship with the world there are basically two fundamentally different types of relationship. The first is our relationship with other people; the second is our relationship with objects.

For an in-depth analysis and discussion of these relationships and their differences, see D.J. Isaac and B.M. O'Connor, 'A Discontinuity Theory of Psychological Development' in *Levels of Abstraction in Logic and Human Action* (1978), ed. E. Jaques, Heinemann educational books.

Figure 6.2   Person–Person Relationship

The distinction between people and object relations may seem very simple and obvious. However, despite this simplicity we all sometimes muddle them up. The authors have heard leaders describe people as *units* (of labour) or numbers. In one organisation workers had their employment number instead of their names on their overalls. We hear about *cost reduction* and *efficiency improvement*, meaning that people will lose their employment. The phrases used to describe change often do not mention people specifically, for example, *cultural change*. We have all heard discussions that assume that people have no will or that their will is a nuisance. It can easily be experienced as hypocritical when the leadership extols vision and mission statements about the apparent value of people, customers and being *the chosen supplier, employer* when at the same time people are being treated as objects. Planning the change process can reduce people to statistical events. Treating people in this way may not even be deliberate but it has the effect of objectification. It can be comforting for the leadership to assume the people–object relationship because it gives the illusion that people can be controlled. We can control objects; we can only influence people. Treating people as objects breeds cynicism and malicious compliance. It is always worthwhile to examine if and how in high-level discussions, the current language used and the systems reduce people to objects. In our view, one of the worst examples but one that is very common is the phrase *human capital*.

Of course we can also get confused the other way round. We sometimes behave towards objects as if they did have will and intent. We plead with a car to start, curse a computer for crashing. We try to persuade machines to keep going, encourage them to work faster or stop. What do we think we are doing at such times? We have projected the qualities of people (at least will) onto the object. If we can do this, we have a chance of persuading the printer to work. Every now and then such persuasion coincides with a restart of the machine. This only encourages us to continue with the illusion that objects are temperamental and have human qualities.

While it may be amusing to reflect on our own or others' attempts to persuade objects to act reasonably; it is less amusing to reflect on people being treated as objects. In extreme form this constitutes oppression and abuse. The irony is that attempts to control people completely are essentially self-defeating. Not only is there a question of morality but the energy required to maintain such a controlling regime will not, over time, produce an efficient outcome since by definition it stifles initiative, creativity and enthusiasm. The energy put into control will exceed the energy produced from the 'controlled' person or group (this occurred, for example, in pre-1989 Eastern European economies). Confusion between people and objects often occurs without deliberate intent, for example, when introducing a new IT business-wide system, or during technological production process improvement. The discussion often focuses on the benefits of the new 'objects' while the role of people who must implement, run and improve these systems are effectively ignored or discounted. The case for the change may be judged to be obvious, in terms of rational, economic argument, so we expect people to comply. If people based all their behaviour on purely objective logic why would anyone smoke, not wear safety equipment or drive too fast?

> **Box 6.3   Consider Relationships**
>
> Thus, if we are serious in accepting that people are not machines then each relationship needs to be considered in the following terms:
>
> - What is the other person's view of an event?
> - How does the other person view you?
> - Can you predict accurately how the other person is likely to react now and over time?

Certainly many projects are started, or relationships entered into, without due consideration of people's views or without articulating the hypothesised answers to the three questions below.

If we really can be disciplined about not treating people as machines or objects, then we can try to understand how people view the world. We need to understand not only what 'the organisation' needs, but also what people need and what they assess as worthy or unworthy. Only then can we be really effective in introducing change and begin building a positive organisation (see Box 6.3).

Next we will examine and define what we mean by values and culture. Values and culture are both terms that are used widely but often with different meanings. We find such terms are often vague and only give the illusion of meaning. We define culture very specifically. We also make a central proposition which is contentious: that all people share the same values. This counter-intuitive notion actually forms the basis for understanding productive social cohesion and is perhaps the most radical proposition in the book. In short we argue that our behaviour and decisions are value based.

Principle 3: People's Behaviour is Based on Six Universal Values

We have explained that we need to predict our environment, both in terms of how others behave and how others react to us. This stems from a very basic need not only for security and survival, but also for association. We are social, and our survival depends upon others. So upon whom can we depend? Who is on 'our side', who is friend, who is foe? Our fundamental proposition is that we answer these questions by judging, or evaluating, behaviour against a set of universal values (see Box 6.4).

Part of the problem with the word *value* is that it can be used as an abstract or concrete noun, an adjective in terms of a quality and a verb in terms of an activity.

With the frictions that are causing so much mayhem and commentary around the globe at present, it seems that 'values' and their variability are at the core of every problem and conflict.

To quote from Donald's 'Origins of the Modern Mind': 'we are social animals, we have evolved as such and our brains are uniquely developed to process social signals. Our continued survival as a species is dependent upon our ability to build and maintain cohesion in our social group' (Donald, 1991, President and Fellows of Harvard College).

This confusion of language can be seen in many settings. For example, when talking to workers and their managers about difficulties in their working relationships, we often hear, *the problem is they have different values from us*. When we talk to these same people in the context

Box 6.4   Common Language and Definitions

Before we examine this issue of values and culture in more depth it is important to define our terms. As mentioned earlier we have to use language that is in common usage and has social meaning. We are not saying these other meanings are invalid, only that we need to be precise about what words mean in this context. Here we define and discuss the way some terms are used.

VALUE

Defined as behaviours which, when assessed positively, strengthen social group cohesion; when assessed as a negative, weaken it.

UNIVERSAL VALUES

This is a set of six 'values' that are essential properties of constructive social relationships that result in productive social cohesion. They are adjectives describing behaviour: loving, trust-worthy, dignifying, courageous, honest, fair; or they can be abstract nouns: love, honesty, trust, respect for human dignity, courage, fairness.

HEURISTICS

Defined as *a method or process of discovery from experience.*

It refers to how we find out and learn from a range of experiences as to what is of positive value and what is not. It is how we generate the rules by which we can judge situations and behaviour.

MYTHOLOGY

Defined as *the underlying assumption and current belief as to what is positively valued behaviour and what behaviour is negatively valued and why it is so.*

These are the rules that we have learnt heuristically, for example *don't trust strangers.* This statement is the tip of the iceberg; again heuristically formed. We do not trust strangers because we cannot predict their behaviour and they may hurt us. We build mythologies unconsciously and consciously from, amongst other things, tales of morality, films, lessons from family, friends; the media; observation of others. They form our belief system about how to interpret behaviour.

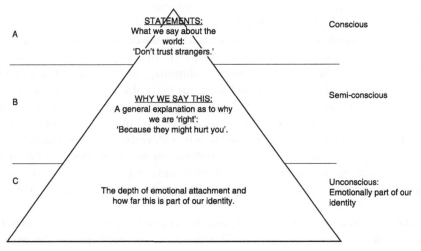

Figure 6.3   Mythologies

We call these assumptions or beliefs Mythologies because:

1.   They are linked to the core values.
2.   They are a mixture of mythos (stories with emotional content) and logos (rationality).
3.   Mythologies, myths in common usage are stories that contain a fundamental truth, even if the facts are not true, for example, the story of Daedalus and his son Icarus: Icarus ignored his father's warning not to fly too close to the sun or the wax holding his wings would melt and he would fall and die. Icarus ignored his father's warning and did fall into the sea and die. Thus the fundamental truth – the need to show respect for your father and family by listening to and thinking about advice.

As people we do not operate either entirely rationally or entirely emotionally.

In our experience People use the term *value* in many different ways to describe very different concepts. People mix the concepts of *value*, heuristics, mythology and behaviour and call them all *values*. For example the quote, 'People don't value the old values anymore.'

•   It is our contention that values, in terms of the universal values do not change. Neither are they a matter of choice.
•   The way we learn what behaviour is valued and how, negative or positive, is a heuristic process.
•   Our current assumptions concerning how behaviour is valued (positively and negatively) is determined by our mythologies: stories of explanation. These can and do develop as we learn and gain more experience. This development is often referred to as erroneously, as *changing, new or different values.*

Finally, we also acknowledge that people value material objects, goods and services. Whilst we recognise this as an emotional and important part of society it refers to the person–object relationship. I may value a house but it has no mythology about me. What we are discussing here is the content of social relationships, that is, person(s)–person(s) relationships where values and valuing occur from both parties.

of their communities, churches and sports teams and ask why they can work together so constructively there, they say, 'Here we have the same values.' Often these are the same people. We do not believe people change their values with their work shirts. It is clear that something is different, but it cannot be their values if values are at the core of our social existence.

It is our argument that these universal values form the deep bonds that connect human beings one to another. When we examine our evolutionary history, it is obvious that humans would not have survived as a species had they not been able to form and maintain social groups. The other species which co-existed with our earliest ancestors all had sharper teeth, longer claws, were faster, could jump higher and in general physically outmatch the earliest humans. Newborn human babies are extraordinarily vulnerable and dependent. They require a social group – a family or clan – to support them for years, or they will die. If this had happened too often, we would have become extinct and our present discussion would not be occurring. Therefore, we believe, that to survive humans had no choice but to evolve as social animals.

As social animals we needed (and still need today) a methodology to allow us to function as productive members of a social group. This is true of all social species. For example, the social insects have specific, complex chemicals that allow individual insects to function as productive members of a very coherent social group, for example, a beehive or an ant colony. These chemicals are their operating methodology and function as their heuristics and mythologies.

Central Proposition

We propose that all people, societies and organisations actually share the same set of universal values. We have articulated this proposition and the six universal values in various publications and articles, and they have been tested in commercial, public and not-for-profit organisations, and in a wide variety of communities and countries around the world by the authors and their associates.

Working with both the Hamersley Iron Organisational Development teams and Roderick Macdonald, we have identified six values which we believe make up the set of shared values which are necessary for the continuing existence of human social groups. Each of these can be thought of as forming a continuum from positive to negative. Behaviour at the positive end of the continuum strengthens the social group; behaviour at the negative end weakens and will eventually destroy it.

Most of a member's behaviour must be at the positive end of the scale in order for him or her to be accepted and relied upon by others. Without such positive, reliable behaviour social groups must fail. Simply predicting behaviour is not enough. It is possible to predict that an individual will behave in a cowardly way, but such behaviour will weaken the group.

Figure 6.4 shows the values upon which we argue that all societies are based. These are the fundamental social qualities that underpin relationships.

The basic propositions are:

1. If a group of people is to maintain a productive social cohesion that lasts, then the members of that group must demonstrate behaviour that will be rated at the positive end of the continua of the core values by the other group members.

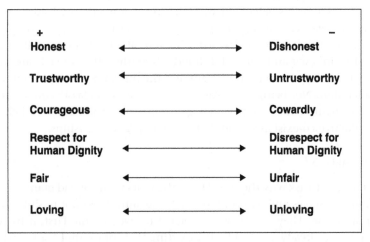

Figure 6.4   Universal Values

2.　If a member of that group demonstrates behaviour that is judged by the other group members to be at the negative end of one or more of the continua of universal values, the person will eventually be excluded (although attempts to change the behaviour may be made prior to exclusion).

3.　If several people exhibit behaviours that are similar, but judged by the rest of the group to be at the negative end of one or more of the continua of universal values, then the group will break into separate groups. This often happens with political organisations and religious organisations whose members break into 'factions' or 'sects'.

Values, per se, cannot be observed. We can and do observe what people say and how they behave. All of us interpret behaviour and draw conclusions about the values that an individual's behaviour demonstrates. Sometimes we have to wait for confirmation that our conclusions are correct, and sometimes we may be left in doubt. In some cases we may disagree with others as to how particular behaviour should be interpreted. In general, however, within a coherent social group, agreement is gained in time, often very quickly.

In essence, values are the criteria against which we assess our own worth and the worth of others. We argue that all people use these values as the basis for judging their own and others worth as they observe and interpret behaviour.

Consider a situation that might happen in any group. Imagine a group of people of which you are a member. You believe one of the other members has behaved in at least one of the following ways: told lies, stolen something, made fun of a less capable member, been indifferent to another's serious misfortune, regularly failed to keep promises, demanded more than his or her share, or consistently avoided difficult situations. Is it possible for this person to maintain membership of the group if he or she fails to change their behaviour?

We cannot maintain a productive relationship with someone we cannot trust, or who is dishonest, cowardly, does not respect others' dignity, and is indifferent to our feelings or unfair. It is likely that we and other members of the group will point out the negative behaviour, but if it persists, the person will be actively excluded from the group. This reflects the basic need of any group or society for predictable behaviour that mutually reinforces social cohesion.

However, specific rating of behaviour cannot be set in stone if the group is going to exist over time. We not only judge but also ask; if Josh has taken the last cake, why? For example, why would Josh think that his behaviour was fair? In other words any leader of a group and the other members must demonstrate their ability to understand *the other*, that is, be able to see the world from another's point of view. This differentiates the mature adult world from the egocentric world of infancy and early childhood where the other's needs are not seriously considered except to satisfy the self. It differentiates the fundamentalist position from that of reflective consideration. Not being concerned for the other is a classic condition of psychopathy. Others are manipulated for personal gain with no regard for well-being. It is the antithesis of productive co-existence, and destroys working relationships.

WHY THE SIX VALUES?

It is, of course, relevant to ask why these six? Over the years we have had many debates on this topic, both among ourselves and with others. First, the authors do not posit these as immutable and unquestionable. They are, however, related to two criteria. First, if there are other, similar words, are they already covered by the existing six? For example, integrity is a similar term but already covered by honesty and trust. Fairness and justice are very similar, but we prefer fairness because of the possible legalistic implication of the term justice. We have tested these core values in different societies including with indigenous groups, in different continents and in very different types of organisations – multi-nationals, churches, schools, voluntary organisations, local authorities, manufacturing, services, finance – and they have survived so far.

The second criterion is that a person's behaviour may be judged to be positive in terms of one value but at the same time be judged negative in another. A manager may admonish a team member publicly for his or her poor work performance. The manager may be at the same time being honest, but showing lack of respect for human dignity. A soldier may admit fear and run away in the battle. The soldier is again honest, but may be cowardly and not to be trusted in combat. Another person may insist on the exact distribution of resources as authorised, believing they are acting fairly, but at the same time be indifferent to the greater or special needs of some individual or group. Thus, no two values ever (or should ever) correlate perfectly. If they did, they could be combined.

Thus we are saying that these values demonstrated positively are the defining properties of a cohesive social group. If members behave in a way that is perceived to demonstrate those positive values, then the group will remain cohesive. If members do not demonstrate such behaviour, that is, the other members regard their behaviour as a negative expression of values; the group will fragment and fracture. It is all but impossible to achieve any productive purpose over time if the group is not socially cohesive.

Some people are uncomfortable with the word love and prefer care. Of course in English we have one term to cover many meanings of *a loving relationship*. However, love is chosen because it is different from care. It is love that causes parents to sacrifice themselves for a child or a soldier to go out under enemy fire to bring back a wounded mate. As a corporate organisational development team member once said, 'the difference between love and care is passion, good leadership is always passionate' (Donna Loon, Comalco employee verbal comment 1991).

Sometimes we attribute these values directly to people; for example, *he is a loving person. She is trustworthy. He is fair. She is courageous*. What we are really doing is making a judgement about the likely behaviour of an individual. This may be based on direct experience, another's report or reputation. What we are essentially saying is, 'I expect that person to behave honestly.' 'I expect that person to behave courageously.' 'I expect that person to treat other people with dignity', and so on. It is actually dangerous to infer that values are inherent properties of people, or that people inherently lack values. This false assumption leads us then to either idealise or objectify people, as is the case with racism and sexism. The only way of reducing these six values is merely to replace them with *good* or *bad*, *right* or *wrong*. That, we have found, is just too simplistic.

The values continua form part of our predictive model. They help to categorise behaviour and allow judgements to be made very quickly.

At the heart of these propositions, and any society, is the need to understand how others perceive the world and, hence, will judge behaviour. We do not *choose* to have these values. We argue that they are properties of relationships whether we like it or not. We *cannot* pick or choose. We cannot say 'I will adopt these as our new corporate values.' You are already being judged by them! This also means that should you adopt four, perhaps because honesty and courage are too difficult, tough luck! We might want to leave them out but others will not let us. These universal values are as oxygen to social groups. We cannot choose to function without them nor can we avoid demonstrating them through our behaviour. It is their very unavoidability that is cause for careful consideration by, in particular, all those who lead others.

> **Box 6.5**
>
> When Ian Macdonald was working in northern Canada with a First Nation community he presented the Values Continua and members of the community laughed. 'Where did you get those?' he was asked. They then went on to explain that they almost exactly represented their *Grandfather Principles* which have been (orally) handed down from earliest times and which guided their lives.
>
> In another instance in Oman, the same author was thanked for including *Islamic Values* in the presentation.

Next we look at culture:

Principle 4: People Form Cultures based upon Mythologies

There is a wealth of literature today around culture: *cross-cultural, multicultural, culturally sensitive.* Culture is defined in terms of geography, religion, ethnicity, food, traditional dress, language, institutions, currency or behaviours (often called tradition), all of which can be both interesting and confusing at the same time (see Box 6.6).

Such differences can make discussion difficult. We have a simple definition of culture that is not limited by any of the usual boundaries. Indeed it transcends the usual categories. It is simply that people who share mythologies will cohere together in a social group forming a culture. We argue that mythologies form a stronger bond than the categories mentioned. For example the 2016 US Presidential election and the UK vote on membership of the European Union (Brexit) divided each country almost exactly in two. Each side having strong, emotionally driven mythologies not just about the issues but even more strongly about each other. A book by Joe Bageant (*Deer Hunting with Jesus*) examines the mythologies underpinning the cultures in the USA and articulates the process we are describing.

A very obvious ability of people is the speed at which we make judgements, especially judgements about behaviour. For example, a manager has very clearly explained to her department that absenteeism and lateness are unacceptable and that in future people taking days off sick without proper cause will be disciplined. A week later one of her team is late and then takes an unauthorised sick day. On return to work she reprimands him but after a one-to-one discussion, she does not take any disciplinary action. What do we make of this? Is the manager honest? Is it fair to the rest of the team? Is it loving towards the individual? Is it cowardly? Is she likely to increase or decrease trust? We might like to know more. Was there a special reason?

Although we often say that we would like more evidence, a common characteristic is that we often form an opinion on the basis of very little evidence. Two classic examples of this are (1) the remarkable ability of sports fans to be able to judge the accuracy of a referee or umpire's decisions instantly, even from remote positions in the stadium and (2) the speed at which we make decisions about people at first meeting, the well-known *first impression* (Gladwell, 2005).

Although these examples stand out, think how quickly we all form views about the behaviour of politicians, celebrities or the police. There is now a huge business built around this in the form of TV reality shows where people are voted out of the house or off the island by the public. Why and how do we do this? A basic survival mechanism suggests that from the

---

Box 6.6   Definition of Culture

A *culture* is a group of people who share a common set of mythologies. That is, they share assumptions about behaviours demonstrating values positively or negatively. Essentially the more mythologies people have in common, the stronger the culture.

---

earliest times we had to quickly decide who was and who was not a threat. We had to judge whether the behaviour of a person makes them one of us or one of them, friend or foe.

This is not to argue that all judgements are made this quickly or that, once made, they are irreversible. We merely make the point that human beings not only have the capacity but also the tendency to make judgements about behaviour very quickly, even if they are later reconsidered. *How do we do this?* The terminology that we use here is that we judge through our *mythological lens* (see Figure 6.5). In effect we all wear a pair of perceptual glasses. We see the world through a lens that refracts what we see onto the continua of shared values. That is, we observe behaviour and the lens directs that behaviour to be seen as fair or unfair, honest or dishonest, loving or unloving, and so on. Clearly this is not a simple bipolar rating, but the behaviour is placed somewhere along the continuum of one or more of the core values. If it is not, then it has no value and we are literally disinterested in it.

How is this lens formed? Our experience and research is consistent with other psychological research and common sense that suggests this lens through which we view the world is formed by our experience. It is formed as we are growing up and expands as we change. We learn from every experience, that is, heuristically: first from our immediate and extended family experiences; from our school, fellow students and teachers; from our community; from our workmates and bosses; from the media.

It is interesting to note that in biology there are very similar theories used to explain the development of perception and hearing. This is now seen as a very active process based on heuristically learned patterns. Essentially, mythologies are based upon perceived patterns. For example, a manager assigns a task. It is completed but he gives no feedback, thanks or recognition. This happens again. A pattern has started, it happens a third time and it is virtually a law. *This person never gives any thanks.* The mythology now is building that this manager's behaviour is indifferent, undignifying and maybe even unfair. Now we have established a mythology, we have an unconscious tendency to do two things:

1. reinforce the mythology and
2. form a culture.

Box 6.7

Since the first edition of the book there has been a growth in research and development in what is called *cognitive bias*. This field of psychology reinforces our findings and propositions and articles give evidence of influences on decision making (Bless, H., Fielder, K. & Strack, F., 2004; Baron, J., 2007; Haselton, M.G., Nettle, D. & Andrews, P.W., 2005). *Cognitive bias* tends to look at *errors* in judgement and how we *fool* ourselves.

Our view is that these *errors* are in fact a natural process, the heuristics of creating mythologies by which we interpret the world. Our view is that the *error* lies in not questioning the judgement; but rather taking a fundamentalist or closed view.

This failure to remain open to other possibilities is disastrous in a leadership role despite our fantasy to idealise leaders as being decisive and unswerving.

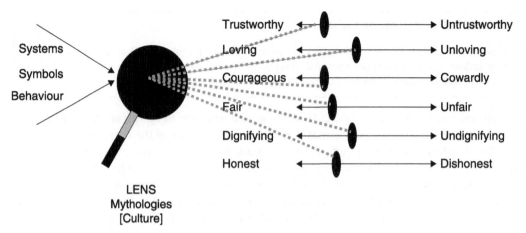

Figure 6.5   Making Sense of the World through the Mythological Lens

We will now be sensitive to this manager's behaviour and note every instance that confirms the pattern. We are also likely to discuss it with other colleagues and be most at ease with people who have the same view. There is great comfort in the phrase 'yes, you're right, I agree with you'. If we find someone who has received praise or recognition we can put this aside as a special case or the boss's favourite.

This specific relationship and associated mythology can now, with reinforcement from others (the embryonic culture), become generalised. Now we build a mythology about managers at this company. This can grow to managers as a class and all sorts of evidence from history can be used to strengthen the culture and build mythologies. Now we know that 'all managers are bastards'.

Although some people have argued that the term *mythology* implies the assumption or belief is untrue, this is a limited view of mythology. We have pointed to the combination of mythos and logos. We should also recognise that historically myths are stories that have a fundamental truth embedded in them (Campbell, 1949). Stories and myths have been told throughout the centuries to inspire people and to tell us how good people behave and how 'bad' people behave. They help to set and reinforce behavioural norms. It is not a question of true or false that would be used as evidence in a court of law, which attempts to be pure logos.

Children love stories; they demand that their favourite stories be read or told over and over again. In adulthood, the film industry and a large amount of television and entertainment are based on telling stories. Some of the most popular films, such as the *Star Wars* series, and books, such as *Harry Potter* and *Lord of the Rings*, are based on ancient myths that have been retold for generations. Even computer games have story lines with heroes and villains. All the major religions are based on books that essentially tell stories about what is acceptable and unacceptable behaviour.

Our mythologies give us a framework within which we can begin to organise our world and behaviour. They combine the story with its essential emotional component together with the logical, rational, scientific element. Thus our lenses are a combination of the two, neither wholly one nor the other.

This is of particular relevance in relationships when some behaviour or opinion is dismissed as illogical or emotional, as if rationality is the only, or, at least, the superior element.

Underneath this dismissal is actually an admission of the failure to empathise with the other or to understand how they view the world. We ignore other people's mythologies at our peril.

Thus we all have a unique pair of mental glasses with mythological lenses. One wonderful quality of such lenses is that we each have a pair that, apparently, accurately sees the world, while, sadly, everyone else's lenses are slightly or significantly distorted. While all lenses are unique to the individual, they do have similarities with other people's lenses. We all have experiences both of sharing opinions and of coming into conflict with others with different opinions. No one exactly matches our worldview.

Thus over time people seek out and form relationships most easily with people who share their mythologies, that is, share a view about how to interpret specific behaviour as positive or negative on the values continua. That is, they form *cultures*.

This definition of culture is quite liberating since it is free from many assumptions of what constitutes a culture.

The strength of the culture will depend upon:

1. the extent of shared mythologies – how much overlap there is among individuals;
2. the relative importance of these mythologies to those concerned; and
3. the context and significance of the issue/behaviour being judged.

Thus *cultures*, in this definition may well cross-geographical boundaries, ethnic association, organisational or professional boundaries. We would argue that not being precise as to the definition of culture leads to dangerous, even racist assumptions. For example, is there an African-American culture? Do all African-Americans share mythologies and to what extent? Do some African-Americans have more in common with people outside this category than inside it, and how do we express that? We often read or hear about 'The Muslim Community' or 'The LGBTQ Community' as if all in these categories share the same mythologies. They may not form a cohesive group at all and may actually have a range of mythologies some quite contradictory.

Many groups of people do have common stories, especially if they have experienced oppression. Mythologies created from oppression are rich in heroes and villains, and they have great strength and depth. It may be a false assumption, however, that later generations will necessarily internalise such mythologies in the same way as their earlier relatives. In fact, history is constantly being rewritten and re-evaluated based on contemporary issues and concerns (Becker, 1958). See also Joseph Campbell's book *The Hero with a Thousand Faces* (Princeton University Press, second edition 1972).

There may be many different cultures within an organisation or ethnic group or country or age group. It is important to ask the same basic question: 'What is similar about the ways in which these people rate behaviour?' We must be careful about assuming there will be significant similarities just because a person is *working class* or *male* or *first generation* or *Italian* or *in sales* or whatever general and perhaps too-convenient label can be stuck to them. This is simple stereotyping that is a crude and often inaccurate grouping of people on the basis of one or two variables that may have nothing to do with mythologies.

Culture is subtler than that. Cultures may or may not be long lasting. Recently single-issue politics have produced an apparently diverse group of people who join together to resist an urban development or campaign for animal rights or against genetically modified foods and so on. At the other end of the spectrum there is a current anxiety with regard to what is termed globalisation, that international capitalism is creating a dominant culture that rides rough-shod over less powerful and localised cultures.

Such concerns have been expressed, for example, in *The McDonaldization of Society*, by George Ritzer (1993). It is interesting to note that Ritzer explains some of the attraction for this process in terms of expanding predictability, for example, McDonald's, Holiday Inn and other similar organisations that are almost identical wherever in the world they are located; including controlled internal climates, furnishings and services. This appeal is understandable in terms of the need for predictability discussed earlier.

We have stressed the importance of mythologies in creating culture. Indeed, we argue they are what generates a culture. We continue to argue for the need for clear definition, hence the choice and explanation of the term *mythology*. Essentially we are influenced from birth not just by what we observe but by the way we make sense and categorise these observations. This sense is a combination of the stories we are told and the rational, logical application of reason.

From this we are able to categorise and rate behaviour along the values continua. We are naturally attracted to people who rate behaviour similarly. Another part of the entertainment industry is based on this. *Oprah, Jeremy Kyle, Question Time, Jerry Springer* and other TV shows where opinions are sought and commented upon are highly popular. What you may notice is that such shows rarely produce any change in view. Their main function appears to be to reinforce views and assumptions and draw even clearer boundaries around cultures.

So far we have looked generally at these concepts. The next step is to look more specifically at how such cultures are shaped and changed.

We look at how behaviour can change, why we change our behaviour and what sustains that change.

Principle 5: Change is a Result of Dissonance

Through the use of our mythological lenses, which develops with experience, we learn to predict and how to interact with people and the world around us. Gradually, for most people a relatively stable worldview develops that is, for the most part, accurate in its predictions of how people and objects are likely to behave in their usual environment.

This does not mean that a stable or predictable world is necessarily pleasant or productive. As mentioned, children in abusive families learn to discern with necessary accuracy the patterns of abusive behaviour so that they might avoid them as far as possible. For most people a predictable, stable environment, even a relatively unhappy one, is actually preferable to an unpredictable one. It may seem odd to an outsider that a violent relationship continues, that adversarial industrial relations continue, that people repeat dysfunctional relationships. However, that is to underestimate the strength of the need for predictability, summed up in such phrases as 'better the devil you know', 'out of the frying pan into the fire'. Habitual patterns of behaviour are hard to break, especially if they appear to be underpinned by economic necessity. So does this mean we are therefore captives of our mythologies caught in a repetitive cycle of behaviour where change is an almost hopeless uphill struggle? No.

There is, however, an essential ingredient that is necessary for change to occur and that is *dissonance*. Dissonance, a term which we use in the same way as Festinger (1957), is an experience where our expectations or predictions are challenged. To put it simply, the data does not fit. This could be a minor experience. For example, a recipe, apparently followed as before produces a sponge cake like a brick. More seriously, it could be when a trusted friend is deceitful. This is a challenge, major or minor, to our worldview. We have several ways of dealing with this depending upon the strength of our attachment to the worldview:

1. *Denial*. In this case we simply ignore the data. It is cast aside. It may be described by others that we are *blind to his faults*. Essentially we try to pretend it hasn't happened. Denial is never completely successful and requires more and more energy to sustain, becoming more and more dysfunctional over time. Conspiracy theories are driven by the need to explain events that generate dissonance and require denial of the generally accepted explanation.
2. *The exception that proves the rule*. Here we move from denial but wish to maintain the original view. Therefore we need to explain it in terms of a *one-off*. There were unusual circumstances. The person didn't realise what they were doing, didn't mean it, didn't see the consequences. If the person is a member of a group, for example, in an instance of police corruption, we might say that they are *bad apples*, or an *unrepresentative minority*.

If instances persist, these methods of defending our mythologies become ever more difficult and more disturbing. We reach a point where the difference between what we predicted and reality simply cannot be reconciled. This is the state of dissonance and we cannot tolerate dissonance for long. If the strategies of denial and exception fail we need a new explanation, a new predictive model. The manager really has changed and consequently we need to behave differently towards them. Paradoxically, once the balance has shifted, and a new mythology has been established, we may well then reconstruct the past to justify the shift. We remember other instances, which viewed with hindsight or more commonly with the new lens, did give us a clue. We now listen to others who tell us 'I never thought he was that bad.'. Thus the new mythology is established and nurtured as carefully as the previous mythology.

THE THREE DATA POINTS: (BOX)

Dissonance can be positive or negative; it may be a 'pleasant surprise' or a 'nasty shock'. Either way something unpredicted has happened. As mentioned the first instance may be denied or explained away as an exception. The second may be explained away as a coincidence, but a third occurrence is very difficult to deny. It actually implies a system change and therefore three data points will almost inevitably result in a new mythology. (See also below and Chapter 12)

It is very important to note that mythologies are not changed; new myths have to be built and prove useful but the old ones are always there to be called upon.

ORGANISATION-WIDE MYTHOLOGY

Perhaps one of the most significant examples of the process of mythology has been the revelations of sexual abuse of children in the Catholic Church (and other institutions). We take the example of the Church because it follows the process described above. First there is denial. The accusations are so contrary to the entire purpose and espoused intent of the Church, especially its leadership. Next we explain it away as *bad apples* or *exceptions*. Finally the evidence is so overwhelming that the dissonant views cannot both be held and we have to adjust our opinions and new mythologies are created.

There is a common assumption that people (especially in organisations) are resistant to change. Further, that this resistance is inherent. In fact, we have found people are remarkably interested in change. From an early age we are experimenting, trying new approaches, learning, testing. However, we are doing this in order to build a predictive model of the world. Apparent resistance to change is characterised by three factors:

1. There is no dissonance. Our predictive models still appear to work.
2. There is no association between the change and benefit to the individual. *Why should I adopt this new approach when it appears more difficult and does not appear to result in any improvement for me?*
3. There is a sense of helplessness. *Although I do not like the situation, I feel that there is nothing I can do about it.* For example, the demise of a business through market changes or a pattern of delinquent behaviour or addiction.

There is in fact a very good reason for this resistance to change. Without it society would become unstable through the failure of social cohesion and our continued existence as a species would be at grave risk.

Changing Behaviour: Systems, Symbols and Behaviour

From our experience and work over the last thirty years, we have argued that building a new culture and changing behaviour is the essential work of a leader. It is a key part of the work of management. Although many discussions of organisation assert the need to change an organisation's culture, very little is said about how this is to be done in terms of specifics. We have argued that most of the material on this issue overemphasises the *what* but has very little detail on the *how*.

We identified that to bring about such change, the leader has three tools: *Systems, Symbols* and *Behaviour*.

1. The SYSTEMS of the organisation – designing and implementing systems with a constructive, productive purpose that are seen to be so by others.
2. SYMBOLS – described as the currency of leadership including badges, insignia, clothing, voice tone and so on to signify change or consistency.
3. Their own BEHAVIOUR – leading by personal example.

We note that this trilogy has become popular and has been used by others (Taylor, 2005).

In this section we deal primarily with the leader's behaviour. Systems and symbols will be discussed later (see chapters on The Work of Leadership and The Process of Successful Change).

From the discussion above, the work of the leader is to:

1. Identify the mythology and the associated behaviour: you (the manager) are unfair and unloving because you never give us feedback.
2. Create dissonance: face up to the mythology and associated behaviour as if it is true (this can be painful). Don't try to argue. Well, I know I do sometimes. Then create dissonance by behaving differently.
3. Continue with consistency: do not expect to build a new mythology on the basis of one new behaviour. Keep at it, and then keep at it again, and again.
4. Don't expect behaviour change for some time: there will be a lag between the manager's new behaviour and the building of a new mythology and new behaviours. Don't be discouraged.

Dissonance is at the heart of all behaviour change (see Box 6.8). There is an old saying that *insanity is continuing to do the same thing whilst expecting a different result.* The work of anyone involved in changing behaviour is to demonstrate actual contradictions between expectation and reality.

Box 6.8   Factors Influencing Behaviour Change

In order for a person to change their behaviour, a person:

- must experience dissonance;
- must have a sense that the new behaviour will improve the situation (for the individual or social group);
- must have a sense that he or she is an active player in the process, that he or she can influence the process.

Until a new myth is established, even a single instance of behaviour that reinforces the old myth may destroy your efforts at change. Once a new myth is established, occasional deviations will be interpreted as that, deviations, not as instances of the old myth.

During the process others may not perceive the situation as you do. This too can cause them to interpret your behaviour in a way that is different from your own interpretation. You may believe you are demonstrating respect for dignity by your behaviour but your team may perceive your behaviour as demonstrating their dignity is only important when it is convenient for you, not when the chips are down. Therefore they perceive you as dishonest, lacking courage and not to be trusted.

We emphasise the importance of understanding other mythological lenses so that your behaviour will be seen at the positive ends of the continua of values through *their* eyes, not simply your own. One of the best ways to learn this is to come up through the ranks, to have experience at the lower levels of organisation and have learned how your friends and peers at those levels see the world. Another way to learn this is to spend time with your colleagues and/ or employees, get to know them and talk about their views. A third way is used by the military, where sergeant majors have the role of interpreting the needs and beliefs (mythologies) of the troops to the officers. Whatever the method used, such understanding is essential for effective leadership that is able to build new mythologies, organisational cultures and behaviour.

We argue that a further element of the work of leadership is to turn dissonance into hypotheses, creating questions and possible answers where there is now uncertainty. Be aware, however, that the attempt to build mythologies carries significant risk. In fact as mentioned, mythologies do not really change; the old mythologies may recede into the background, may even be apparently forgotten, but they are likely to be present for many years. If behaviour slips so it can be seen to be on the negative side of the scales of shared values, the old negative mythologies will be stirred up and be more powerful than ever, since the newer mythology proved to be false and the old myth reinforced: *We have been let down, it was a trick.*

Some have suggested to us that knowledge of this model of leadership processes could make it easier for dishonest managers to fool their direct reports. Any manager, who believes they could do this, might like to try it. The process is subtle and unforgiving, requires constancy and consistency, people will spot a dishonest manipulator every time.

Behaviour alone, however, will not change the culture of the organisation as a whole. It can change the relationships between leaders and team members, but for overall change, the other tools of leadership – systems and symbols – must be engaged. These tools will be explained in more detail in later chapters. In the West we place an unfair burden and expectation on leaders to build a culture on the basis of their own behaviour alone. We idealise individuals then become disillusioned when they 'fail'. We look too much for charismatic personalities. Without the use of all three tools of leadership culture cannot be built or sustained.

It is both a behavioural example and a symbol if a leader does not pick up litter, or, worse still, causes it, while at the same time extolling the virtues of *good housekeeping*. The leader may or may not be in a position of authority to change systems, but he or she can certainly try to improve them, if only by suggestion. Finally words of praise, a small gift/presentation/ award, contacting or visiting a sick worker may be symbolic examples which, if rated positively on the values continua, can support more substantive change.

Obviously some changes are more difficult to bring about than others. Years of industrial conflict may have undermined trust between workers and leaders to such an extent that a great deal of hard and consistent work may be needed to rebuild it. We have all seen in the past few years a growing cynicism around politics and politicians, an expressed lack of trust in *the establishment*. Mythologies have developed that we cannot trust politicians, they don't respect people, they are dishonest and generally their behaviour is seen towards the negative end of the values continua. This has created huge divisions in society; these views are not based on rational argument but are visceral and deeply held. Such mythologies have driven the UK's exit from the EU (Brexit) and the vitriolic US Presidential campaign (2016) where there was no dialogue, no considered argument, respect or compromise between the entrenched cultures. The extent and emotional depth of the mythologies, reinforced and refined through stories of events past, was strongly influenced by the process.

If people have already seen the contradiction (for example waste, poor practice, poor behaviour) but have not been in a position to do much about it, the promise of change may well be applauded. Change is more difficult where habitual behaviour has become entrenched – *we've always done it like this, it is running to its full capacity, bosses are just like that*. Nonetheless, change is always possible if there is both an understanding of how to bring it about and the will to do it.

Finally, there is no point in change if it can't be maintained. Regaining trust only to be let down again results in an even worse situation than we started with. The negative mythologies will be reinforced.

In summary if we want to change our own or others' behaviour, there are several key steps:

1. Understand the mythologies: why do people think that behaving as they do now is justified in terms of the values continua?
2. Understand the strength of the culture: how well reinforced are the mythologies in terms of stories and past events.
3. Identify how dissonance can be created. What behaviour, systems and symbols would be useful to demonstrate a contradiction between expectation (prediction) and actual events now? It is important to state that this cannot be based on trickery. There really has to be a demonstrable contradiction, say, between an old method of working and with safety; or smoking and good health; a mythology about leaders not telling the truth (dishonesty) and a genuine change that makes real information available that can be verified to be truthful.
4. Sustain the change with consistency. If the process has been successful, if changing behaviour has succeeded, it needs to be constantly and consistently reinforced or the old, habitual behaviour will return. It is crucial to remember that while in the change process new mythologies can be created, the old ones never die; they lie like silt on a riverbed ready to be stirred up again.

Dissonance need not always be negative. The positive aspect of a shift of balance can be summed up in the phrase *the penny dropped*, or *the light went on*. Change of behaviour occurs when our expectation changes as a result of changing our internal predictive model, but this is often not an easy task.

As we argued in Chapter 3, when considering behaviour change, it is as important to understand social process in detail, as it is to understand the detail of technical process.

If someone wanted to build a road bridge across a river, make aeroplane engines, prescribe drugs for the sick, run a railway or drill for oil, there would be no doubt that the person would be required to demonstrate a detailed knowledge of the technical process to be used and the theory behind it. Considerable alarm would be generated if, when discussing the safety of a nuclear power plant, a group of people with little experience and less technical knowledge claimed that they would decide what was safe by using common sense. 'Oh', says one, 'I think we should put the waste in big, secure containers.' 'Yes', says another, 'and I think those containers should be metal, perhaps steel with some good locks.' 'Yes', says a third, 'my experience is that some good steel should be fine.' After a while a member of the group who has been silent says, 'Perhaps we should be more specific? What sort of waste will this create? Will steel be protective enough?' Then the person has the temerity to start discussing isotopes, half-life, contamination and degradation of crystal structure and strength by radiation.

He is told not to be so pedantic and so theoretical. This is, we hope, an absurd scenario but, when translated into a discussion about social process, it is not quite so unrealistic.

'We need someone to head up the new marketing division for the UK.' 'Yes, we need someone with experience, and good leadership qualities.' 'Yes, someone who can get real results. Those marketing types can be difficult. There are some real prima-donnas in the marketing department.' 'What about Johnson from head office?' 'Not a bad idea, she's really bright and has had some experience in Japan'. 'Yes, but she's a bit young. Will she be able to impose herself?' And so the discussion goes on. Terms are used with little definition. There is an assumption about shared meaning, but it is not tested in any rigorous way. Critical decisions are often made on the basis of such common sense and pragmatism, which is so highly prized over theory. Why is this so, especially when compared with the value of theory and detail in technical areas? There are three main reasons for this:

PEOPLE–PEOPLE RELATIONS ARE ACTUALLY MORE COMPLEX

Although there are references to people–people relationships as the *soft* areas and technical issues as *hard*, this is misleading. These *soft* areas are often highly complex and difficult to explain. Unlike objects, we cannot effectively ignore people's purpose, will, mythologies and culture. These are all less easy to observe and manage than objects'.

THERE IS A LACK OF A SHARED LANGUAGE

While there are universally accepted definitions in many of the so-called hard sciences, this is not the case in social science. There are no generally accepted theories in the sense of clear expositions of principles with predictive validity.

Instead of a rigorous and agreed set of terms and definitions, social science and perhaps, particularly organisational theory, is subject to fads and jargon. All disciplines have scientific language, which may not be easily understandable from outside. However, in the area of organisational literature there is a suspicion that jargon is used in a deliberate attempt to make something that seems to be simple appear more complex and technical than it seems. Another suspicion is that jargon is used to make something that is unpleasant more palatable or acceptable. In the military, killing your own troops is *friendly fire*; killing civilians is *collateral damage*. As George Orwell and others have written, language can be used to clarify or confuse or simply mislead. Many politicians have used language to deny reality or reinvent it. We are now told we live in a 'post truth' time where 'alternative facts' (lies) are insisted upon as truth. As someone once said 'are you going to believe me or your own eyes?' We believe this process has always been present and is an essential part of the demagogue's use of power.

WE ALREADY HAVE OUR OWN THEORIES ABOUT SOCIAL PROCESSES

As we have said previously, we all have our own theories about people. We do not start with a blank sheet when considering social processes. Thus, any outside theory of social process will be judged against our own theory, any predictive statement is compared with our own. As explained in the discussion of values these theories may be deeply embedded and very emotionally charged. To propose an alternative is not an innocent or even purely rational process.

If a change process is to be managed, it is critical that there is a shared understanding of how to analyse social process and how it can be influenced effectively.

Many of the criticisms of business process re-engineering can be seen as pointing to a failure to take into account the need for a detailed understanding of social process.

In an issue of *People Management* (2 May 1996), an article entitled 'Business Process Re-engineering RIP', by Enid Mumford and Rick Hendricks argues that 'the corporate panacea of the early 1990s is widely seen as a disastrous experiment'. Yet earlier, the books *Process Innovation* by Tom Davenport (1993) and Hammer and Champy's *Reengineering the Corporation* (1993) had become obligatory additions to managers' bookshelves, superseding *In Search of Excellence* (Peters and Waterman, 1982), *The One Minute Manager* (Blanchard and Johnson, 1982) and others. In the Nov/December 1993 edition of *The Harvard Business Review* Hall, Rosenthal and Wade (1993) examined why process improvements had not resulted in bottom-line improvement and argued it was because the difficulty of planning and implementing a redesign was underestimated.

Hammer and Champy's response was to explain that *re-engineering* had been interpreted to mean *downsizing* (dysfunctional issues) and that 'management isn't aligned behind the change' (process issues). Results showed only '16% of senior executives were fully satisfied with their re-engineering programmes'.

Tom Davenport (one of the original re-engineering gurus) stated 'The rock that re- engineering foundered on is simple: people'. As transpired in the cases quoted in books such as *In Search of Excellence*, the success stories of re-engineering are no longer such success stories (Capital Holding, Hallmark and Mutual Benefit Life).

In their article, Mumford and Hendricks identify one of the main reasons for failure as the absence of theory. In fact both Davenport and Hammer put this absence forward as a positive aspect. As Mumford says 'This was a message that attracted the macho-manager who had never believed all that soft, look after the people stuff … This may be a viable strategy for a company on the verge of bankruptcy where fast action is essential. It is not a safe strategy for a company that is doing quite well but wants to do better'.

In recent years the term *emotional intelligence* has become popular. This has some similarities with what we have always referred to as social process in that both concepts refer to people–people relationships. However, we prefer *social process* as it focuses on the relationship,

---

Box 6.9   Social Processes

We are saying that:

1. Social processes have as significant an impact on the output of human endeavours as do commercial and technical processes.
2. Social process is, however, treated differently, partly because we all have our own 'theories' and because we lack a universal theory and we lack a shared language to discuss it.
3. It is often underestimated because it is classified as 'soft' whereas we say *this is the hard part*!

---

whereas a term such as emotional intelligence can imply a quality of an individual with all the problems of the nature/nurture argument and direct comparisons with other *types* of intelligence.

We analyse social process by applying a general set of tools such as mythologies, values and culture (See Box 6.9). However, social process is also impacted by elements other than individual behaviour. It includes understanding the effect of systems, symbols and behaviour. How the organisation is structured is also a vital part of social process. We do recognise the importance of the individual's ability to understand and influence social process and that is discussed in subsequent chapters especially Part 4.

We argue here that, until leaders devote significant time and resources to improving their detailed understanding of social processes, they will remain confused as to why some apparently excellent technical and commercial processes fail. Safety is a leadership issue; as is quality, waste reduction and improved effectiveness. This cannot simply be left to common sense.

Principle 6: It is Better to Build Relationships on the Basis of Authority Rather than Power

There are many different definitions of authority and power in the literature. Some overlap. The way that the terms are used here is as follows. They are both concerned with changing behaviour. A person can exercise authority or power in order to direct another person's behaviour towards achieving a particular purpose. If a person uses authority then he or she will be acting within limits known and agreed by the other person. The use of power will breach one or more of these limits.

For example, if I come to work and start an activity without the proper safety equipment, say, hard hat and glasses, and I am seen by a supervisor, then I know there may be some disciplinary procedure to follow. Let us assume that I know both the policy and the consequence of non-compliance. The supervisor has been *authorised* to carry out this procedure. Let us say that he offers to turn a blind eye for a favour in return (say covering for his absence). This is classic *power*.

Person A exercises authority or power in relation to person B when A is able to direct B's behaviour towards achieving a particular purpose. Authority always operates within the limits of the law, the policy and rules of the organisation and accepted social custom and practice. Power breaches one or more of these limits. If B does not behave in a way directed towards achieving the articulated purpose neither authority nor power are functional and a third party becomes involved and another process ensues.

A supervisor may assign a task to one of his or her direct reports that is within the law and company policy and which the direct report is competent to perform safely, but if the social process he or she adopts in doing so is demeaning and unfair the supervisor is exercising power. The boundary of acceptable social custom and practice has been breached. A supervisor who turns a blind eye to safety breaches by his or her direct reports in exchange for favours such as covering for his sleeping on the job is a classical example of the exercise of power.

This may be obvious but sometimes it is difficult to tell the difference between authority and power due to:

1. Lack of Knowledge. In particular circumstances the person may be using authority but I experience it as power because I am unaware of his or her limits and my own.
2. Lack of Acceptance. Although I know the person has been authorised by his or her organ- isation I do not accept it, as authority for example, being reprimanded by another manager for a behaviour that is common although technically against the rules such as leaving a few minutes early on a Friday, I see it as power.
3. Lack of Clarity. A situation occurs where neither side has clear knowledge of the bound- aries of their authority. There the problem may lie in the fact that there is actually no policy or role description. This is not unusual in organisations.

The basis of healthy and productive relationships is authorisation, where authority is exer- cised, in both directions, within mutually agreed and understood boundaries. The use of power is the main source of mythologies that place the behaviour at the negative end of the Values Continua and demonstrate that the leader is *not one of us*. Organisations are rife with stories of people and situations where power has been used. We discuss this in more depth later (particularly in Parts 4 and 5.) However, it is important to point out that it is not simply a matter of authority being *good* and power being *bad*.

It takes a great deal of work to construct and operate effective, authorised relationships. Our work and Jaques's work among others do not claim this is easy but that over time it is much more effective. Other approaches and some current fads argue that *authorising* relation- ships is *hierarchical and bureaucratic* and by implication old-fashioned and inefficient. Metaphors and analogies abound about organic, flexible, liberated organisations that are unrestricted by rules and therefore more creative; leaderless teams and unclear authority abound. Anyone who has worked in such organisations is aware of how quickly they degen- erate into power and politics with dominant so-called charismatic individuals manipulating the organisation and people overtly or covertly taking advantage of the confusion. Such organisations are toxic for all but those exercising power (see Chapter 23).

COHERENCE

An insightful analysis of order within an organisation or social group has been made by Mike Church. In his paper *Organising Simply for Complexity: Beyond Metaphor Towards Theory* he refers to an important continuum of control and order.

The information in Table 6.1 forms the core of his argument. *Coherence* is what is being sought. At any time, because it is in a changing environment and made up of people, an organisation is moving towards more order or disorder (to the right or left on the continuum). It is the work of the leader to try to achieve and maintain coherence.

Table 6.1   Order and Chaos

Description of control	No control	Strange attractors	Control without controlling	Command/ control	Total control
System type	Random	Chaotic	Coherent	Top-down command	Mechanistic or rigid
Relationships	Independent random relationships	Randomness within underlying regularities	Highly ordered interdependent relationships in which the costs of achieving order are minimised, that is, 'order for free'	Predominantly dependent relationships; order is controlled from above with signi-ficant added costs	Fully dependent, fixed and immutable relationships. Very high cost to sustain

In our view, consistent with Church, the leadership of an organisation should maintain the organisation so that it achieves its purpose with the minimum number of rules (structure and systems). Higher order thinking is consistent with generating a simple set of interrelated rules (*epigenetic*) which can help the organisation cohere without, so-called, bureaucracy and red tape, we do not suggest this is a simple exercise however (see Levels of Complexity Chapter 9 and System Design Chapter 17).

We argue strongly that clarity of boundaries is the basis of freedom.

We can see that if the rules are designed at the appropriate level of complexity (that is, they are effective, efficient and interrelated), they do not produce complicated and wasteful procedures and outputs. Indeed bureaucracy, in the negative sense, is produced precisely because systems and procedures have been designed at too low a level (see also Chapter 17, How to Design Systems). The result is an obstructive, clumsy process that wastes time and energy, causes frustration and invites people to cut corners and work out ways to get round the system. Thus, an over complication invites the use of power.

There is another way of inviting power and that is to be unclear as where the boundaries lie. Thus power is associated with too many or too few boundaries with people left wondering where the boundaries are or why they are set in such a way.

Power is inevitable where there is a lack of clarity. It is a classic methodology manipulative people use to blur boundaries. In organisations people will intimidate or sexually harass others and claim it was only a joke, an accident, unintentional, and so on. Racism, too, falls into this category and is most effective when boundaries are unclear. Lack of boundaries or rules does not lead to creativity; it leads to power. It causes anxiety because behaviour breaches the stated rules and there is severe doubt as to who is justified to do what.

However, when boundaries are clear, we can work creatively and safely. Creativity occurs most effectively when a person is not under immediate threat. Despite the romantic notion of the creative artist living in a garret producing works of genius, the reality is quite different. Many great works have been produced under patronage (Michelangelo, Da Vinci, Tchaikovsky, being three.) The creator is left to grapple with their creation (work) without constant anxiety about their environment.

Box 6.10   Clarity

It is a constant theme in this book to strive for clarity:

- clarity in the definition of terms and meanings;
- clarity in relationships and authority;
- clarity in purpose.

An essential element in a positive organisation is clarity.

Similarly, a good leader or manager should work to reduce anxiety and uncertainty in their team so that the team members can concentrate on their work. This is done by establishing clarity in roles, expectations, goals, tasks, resources, limits and sound social process. If the team members are constantly concerned about lay-offs or a plant closure, or who is going to be screamed at next, it is difficult for them to concentrate on their work.

We believe that these are the conditions that build trust and will result in behaviours which are likely to be experienced positively and so valued. It is hard work but worth it. Finally Church, in his paper, argues a similar point when he criticises pseudo-science. He quotes from Sokal and Bricmont (1997) the accusation that many people in this field are, 'displaying a superficial erudition by shamelessly throwing around technical terms in a context where they are completely irrelevant. The goal is, no doubt, to impress and above all, intimidate the non-scientist reader' (see Box 6.10).

Church refers to an excellent example of the use of power, accompanied by mysticism and magic. It is the antithesis of this book, which attempts a more difficult path of clarity, openness and dialogue.

Conclusion

It is not possible to bring about and sustain change; and create productive social cohesion, unless we understand both the current situation and what we want to achieve. This understanding must be clear, shareable and testable. It is not sufficient to stay with general (often vague even vacuous) statements: 'we must build trust' – 'we must change the culture'. We argue, sometimes against current trends, that we should be specific and have a detailed plan. We have described the principles above; we know they are not easy to act on. They require a genuine desire to bring about change that brings mutual benefit, a genuine desire to see the world from another's perspective without denigrating that view: a genuine desire to reflect on how we are seen by others and consider the validity of that view. Then there are tools that can be used, principles that can be understood to create a more positive organisation and contribute to a more productive and just society.

3 *Understanding Organisations*

Introduction to Part 3

In this part of the book we look at how we might understand organisations, why and how they are structured the way that they are and why and how authorities flow through the organisation. We put forward some clear propositions concerning human capability and how they relate to different types of work in terms of complexity.

Currently there is a lot written about the rate of change; whether it is increasing or not, also there is a lot written about complexity in organisations and whether it is increasing or not (Obolensky, 2014). We will discuss those points in more detail later in the book, however we concentrate here on how we might understand the way in which people construct their worlds, identify work and organise to achieve their purpose. We assume that there is always change occurring and always complexity and uncertainty to address and always has been. Much of what is argued to be increasing complexity and/or rate of change is in our view rather an increasing volume of noise, not information to deal with. It is interesting to consider whether it is more complex or less complex to run an international organisation now, with all our electronic devices and instant access to information, or in Roman times to organise an empire without any such resources.

We begin by examining the nature of organisations that are set up to provide goods or services. We have already mentioned Meritocracies in Chapter 5, here we look in much more detail about what this means and indeed whether it is possible to build one. When we look at work, that is 'turning intention into reality'; there are clearly different ways in which this can be done. It is much more difficult to turn some intentions into reality than others. For example it is much more difficult to create peaceful coexistence in the Middle East than it is to paint a room in the house. It is not simply a question of difficulty but relates to the implicit complexity and uncertainty vested in the tasks and in our imaginations as to how we might address such problems and achieve our goals. We will look at the capability of people to do work and a clear model of capability that proposes that some elements are much more fixed than others. We will then look at how those differences in capability are reflected in the different types of work to be done in an organisation. We then look at how these elements influence the way that organisations are structured and the way that authority is distributed in the organisation.

We have found that while many books describe different types of organisation and authority few, apart from Jaques (and related works), hypothesise why organisations are structured as they are and how this relates to human capability to do work of different kinds. We recognise that some of this material is contentious in that we clearly propose that not everyone can do any type of the work even if they have the opportunity and training. Our work over the years has included working with people at both ends of the spectrum. That is on the one hand people who need help and support simply to function effectively on a daily basis, to, on the other hand, those people who run very large and complex organisations whether that be in the public, private or not-for-profit sectors. We have found qualitative differences in the capability to handle uncertainty and complexity and correspondingly a good sense in each of us to recognise when we have reached our limit. Our and related research indicate that if you are clear enough about the nature of work that is required then people have a good sense as to whether that work is enjoyably challenging, overly demanding or indeed boring.

We also look at the importance of giving people the authority to do their work and how lack of clarity in this area is a major impediment even if the capability is there to do the work.

7 *Meritocracy*

We, like others, begin with the observation that now most goods and services are provided through organisations, more so than at any time in history. Prior to the industrial revolution agriculture was dominant over manufacturing and people worked and lived in the same communities, primarily in family groups or collections of family groups. We have discussed different types of social organisations in Chapter 5 emphasising the particular nature of a meritocracy.

Organisations beget bureaucracy, but the phenomenon of bureaucracy is not new in itself. In pre-industrial times bureaucracies were more limited to government or religious spheres (see, for example, Shafritz and Ott, 1996). Although in China, Assyria, Egypt and Rome they were for a time quite effective, they did not have all the characteristics of what we think of today as bureaucracy. They were more patriarchal or patrimonial, rather than the legal-rational organisations they became in the nineteenth century, continuing up to the present time (Weber, 1921–22b; 1978). Weber wrote largely in the nineteenth century, though a compilation of his work was published posthumously. Most of the writings on organisation became significant as the industrial revolution led to large non-governmental institutions, and most of the writings are products of the twentieth century Taylor (1997; 1911), Weber (Gerth and Mills, 1946; 1922), Fayol (1930), Gulick (1937), Barnard (1938), Roethlisberger and Dickson (1939), Blau (1956), Emery and Trist (1960), Burns and Stalker (1966), Drucker (1954, 1969), Mouzelis (1967) Jaques (1976), Mintzberg (1989). Bureaucracies and organisations on this scale then are a relatively recent development. As a widespread social phenomenon, they have come to dominate in most developed human societies.

We argue throughout this book that a meritocracy is the most efficient way of producing goods and services. We do not say that a meritocracy has to be large, international or publicly owned. We are not confusing it with a bureaucracy, which may or may not have some of the characteristics of a meritocracy (see Box 7.1).

In a meritocracy, people are rewarded on the basis of merit and people can ask, without irony, 'what have I done to deserve this recognition?' A meritocracy is possible when the organisation has:

- the right people
- in the right roles
- doing the right work.

Box 7.1   Definition of a Meritocratic Organisation

Meritocratic organisation: a social organisation where those selected and appointed to work to produce goods and services are chosen on the basis of their capability to do the work required.

The reward, promotion and disciplinary systems are operated on the basis of demonstrated work performance and work behaviour that has been, or could be, articulated.

This may seem obvious, but true meritocracies are quite rare. Most organisations, in spite of what they claim, are hybrids involving other systems that are not based on merit.

Tony Dunlop, a psychologist who has contributed to these ideas and was a Principal of Macdonald Associates, clearly expressed the significance of a meritocracy and the difficulty in creating and sustaining it when he wrote:

> For a meritocracy to function effectively the key requirements are quite specific. Meeting these requirements is difficult, in that it requires good system design and implementation, and consistent and effective leadership behaviour.

(Dunlop, 1999)

See Table 7.1 for a clear explanation of Dunlop's theory of meritocracy.

When people are employed in a meritocracy, they need a clear explanation of how their work fits into the overall purpose of the business. They need the opportunity to appreciate the business goals and believe that the organisation is worth working for. They must be clear about what they need to do in order to be judged to be performing work successfully, and must trust that the processes in place to determine merit will actually reflect the contribution they are making through their work, taking into account their opportunity to do so from where they are placed in the organisation.

Ambiguity of purpose and multiple purposes about which there are political conflicts, must be dealt with. The disputes and conflicting political demands make working in public agencies often more challenging than in businesses, although no organisation is free from politics.

Table 7.1   Towards Meritocracy: Aligning System and Leadership

Basic Requirements	Implications for People Systems (Systems, Structure, Staff, Style)	Implications for Leadership (Staff, Style, Skills, Shared Values)
Organisation viewed positively by staff. Cultural alignment. Competency in role. Capability matches work complexity. Clear expectations. ('What is expected of me?') Performance review and feedback. ('How am I doing?') Merit-based reward. Development of potential ('What is my future?') Managing unacceptable performance.	Comprehensive set of systems backed up by Fair Treatment System to promote appropriate behaviour. Recruitment based on capability. Clear role descriptions. Requisite structure. Standard task assignment approach. Work performance review system. Performance pay system. Career assessment system. Due process exit system.	All leadership behaviour, systems and symbols aligned with organisational goals. Assessment of capability in current roles. Judgements on role capabilities. Providing context and purpose. Accepting accountability and exercising appropriate authority. Team process management. Monitoring, coaching and counselling skills. Making and delivering judgements of work performance. Capability for assessing potential. Mentoring. Confronting and counselling skills.

Whether in business or government, employees must be given work that is within their capability, which is sufficiently challenging to provide an opportunity for them to add value by contributing. They must be clear about what is specifically expected of them, be given feedback on how they are doing, in a timely manner, so that any problems can be addressed, and receive recognition and reward that is related to their contribution to success. Over the longer term they must see that the organisation is willing to support them and provide opportunities for them to develop the potential they have, so they may make an even greater contribution in the future.

In cases where the person is not performing well-assigned tasks to the required standard, where they are not meeting the manager's reasonable expectations of the role, the organisation must address this in an effective way. Systems must be available to order and control the activity required to resolve issues of unacceptable performance fairly with respect for human dignity. In a meritocracy, based as it is on the merit of work performed, it is untenable to accept poor work performance. Such acceptance gives the lie to the concept of meritocracy. It is unfair to other employees not to take action to redress it, even if this does require the dismissal of an employee from the organisation.

Leadership in itself will not build and maintain a meritocracy. Irrespective of an individual leader's ability, humans are prone to error and, in every organisation, leaders change over time. Good performance may vanish when people change roles unless leadership is underpinned by sound systems. Each factor that contributes to a credible meritocracy places specific requirement on leaders, and these requirements should be supported and reinforced by effective systems. The appropriate systems need to be in place to drive and support the appropriate leadership behaviour. The system designs need to include control and audit processes, which provide a flow of data on the behaviour of leaders, and on the effectiveness of systems in achieving the business goals (Dunlop, 1999).

Dunlop goes on to explain the critical nature of specific systems and organisation structure, including the need for a fair treatment system (to appeal against felt poor judgement), systems for correct task assignment and review, clear performance indicators, differential reward, potential assessment and development and systems to deal with unacceptable performance (all of which are discussed in Parts 3 and 4 of this book). Perhaps most importantly Dunlop emphasises the role of leadership in a meritocracy. He writes:

> The implications of a meritocracy for leadership capability and performance are enormous. As most outcomes for individuals in a meritocracy depend on leadership judgement, all employees need to have leaders whose judgement they can trust. This means that all leaders must be capable of their role, and must be appropriate in their behaviour. They must be able to understand their manager's work and their own context, so as to add value and provide the context for their teams' work. They must have a good understanding of their individual team members' capability, effective task assignment skills, and pay appropriate attention to monitoring and coaching. They must demonstrate the standards themselves, that they wish others to meet, so must be effective schedulers, and meet the reasonable expectations of all team members.
>
> All leaders need to have adequate coaching, counselling and confronting skills in order to deal with issues that arise. They also need to be able to manage social processes within the team, so that the teams' capabilities are harnessed effectively, for problem solving and in taking action to achieve objectives.

(Dunlop, 1999)

We argue that a meritocracy, if built properly, is the most effective way to deliver goods and services. In order to do this we must distinguish appointment and reward and recognition based on merit from other approaches such as seniority or nepotism. We must also be clear about the differences between a meritocracy, a democracy, and other sorts of human organisation like a gerontocracy or even a theocracy as we have discussed in Chapter 5.

This is not to say there is no room in a meritocracy for acknowledging birthdays, religious holidays or years of service; merely that these are distinguished from the work of the role and recognition for that work. Meritocracies are difficult to build and maintain since they require robust structure and systems and, perhaps most importantly, good judgement by the leadership. Output measures are not sufficient; the measures must be related to how people achieved the output: their work performance (see Box 7.2).

While many people complain of hierarchy as 'bureaucratic and slow', in fact, if capable people are in the right roles and they have clear and accepted authority, such an organisation can, because of the clarity about authority, make decisions without long processes of discussion, voting, consensus and so on. Similarly, authority can be given in a moment to redistribute resources to where they are needed. Clearly the quality of the decisions will depend upon the capability of the people in every role. An organisation with incapable people in roles with ambiguous authority can very quickly implode, especially in a highly competitive environment.

Capability is important because an organisation can so quickly either advance or go backwards. An obvious example of the need for fast distribution of resources and decision-making is an army in combat (a very rigorous form of direct competition). The huge territorial gains made initially by the German army in World War II were based upon clear authority at every level, which allowed for competent fast decision-making whilst the context was changing. It took the Allies several years to match this (Van Crevald, 1982; 2007).

One frequent mistake in organisational theory is to confuse authority and decision-making with information. The explosion of information technology and systems has seduced some people to think it is enough just to give people information. Without clear purpose, authority and capability, however, this flood of data may overload people or simply allow poor decisions to be made by the wrong people.

Information systems (including information technology) can be a major help to a meritocracy but only if the information is used at the right level, because it is organised on the basis of work complexity, and has a clear and fast operating authority structure. A meritocracy has the best chance of recognising the importance of specific and pertinent data from the information systems and utilising it to inform sound decisions.

Note: We believe it is helpful to recognise that what are referred to widely as information systems, are in fact, data systems. Information is generated by human capability being applied to work with the data.

Box 7.2   Why Is Meritocratic Hierarchy Potentially So Effective?

In producing goods and services in the context of competition then the three most significant attributes that give advantage are:

1. The relative quality of the good or service – how does it compare with your competitors?
2. The speed at which decisions can be made.
3. The speed, effectiveness and efficiency with which resources can be deployed.

Finally, a further danger lies in the very strength of meritocracies as they interact and sometimes compete with other forms of organisations. If a large multinational corporation is a meritocracy and does not have to worry about specified terms of office as does an elected government, the leadership has the potential to plan well into the future and to commit huge resources to achieve its objectives. This can bring it into conflict with governments and other forms of civil structure.

Often these same civil systems, by their nature, appropriately take significant amounts of time to arrive at decisions – understanding opinion, canvassing, discussing, voting, reviewing and so on – and they may take even longer to deploy resources. It is the lack of appreciation of the relative time horizons of the two different forms of organisation, both functioning as they were designed to function, that can lead to frustration, and at times, muted conflict.

Indigenous groups that Macdonald and Stewart worked with needed to combine a system of family relationship with consensus decision-making which could take weeks, months or even years depending upon the issue in question. It is a current concern that organisations of very different types need to develop and improve ways of interrelating with each other. There is a general social concern that 'globalisation', in the form of large international and multinational companies, has led to unfair and uncontrolled distribution of wealth. That such organisations have made the rich richer and have politicians in their pockets. This is producing a nationalistic backlash.

The process has been for businesses to lobby politicians in order to cause the democratic-ally elected governments to change the rules in their favour, under the guise of building a more productive and fairer economic environment for the electors. Modern communication technology has aided and abetted this process but is not the cause of it.

The realisation that the economic circumstances for the majority of electors are not improving is leading to the current backlash and the understandable, if very unfortunate, belief in the simplistic 'solutions' of false prophets. These 'solutions' are in the emotive language of the myths of the oppressed electors but, nonetheless, provide no real or lasting solution.

Piketty's book *Capital in the Twenty First Century* (2013 Éditions du Seuil, 2014, President and Fellows of Harvard College) has a chilling articulation of the numbers.

While meritocracies can be described we have never found one in its pure form. That is where everyone has been selected, appointed and promoted on merit. We have already seen in Chapter 5 there are different types of social organisation appropriate to different purposes. When looking at organisations that are not pure meritocracies we have found that they include one or more organisational principles that are different.

Organisational Principles Alternative to Merit

SENIORITY

A common form of organisation is based on seniority. That is, people are rewarded and/or promoted on the basis of either age or length of time in role or employment. Experience is highly valued. This form has been popular for two reasons. First, it appears to be more objective and fairer than using a system that relies on judgement for determination of work performance. However, this contention of fairness is, in fact, an admission that either the organisation cannot differentiate between the performance of individuals or that the method of judgement is inaccurate or unfair. Second, it more obviously relates to family life or agriculture where rewards and celebrations are based upon the passing of time (birthdays and anniversaries) or seasons passing in a cyclical way. A system of seniority applied to the assessment of the work performance of people is based on the presumption that any judgement about the worth of work performance is inferior. It also assumes that something that can be measured and about which there is no disagreement can be put in its place. In a seniority system this is time.

The assertion that capability to perform work is related to experience provides support for a seniority system, the evidence is lacking. Repetition of an activity through time does not necessarily improve skill, even technical skill. As one of Catie Burke's students who was a Director of Training for a large police department stated, 'There is a difference between 15 years' experience and 1 year's experience 15 times.' Still, for occupations that do require a high level of technical skill, such as that of a silversmith, there can be no doubt that experience is vital. However, there are clearly evident differences between the works of experienced silversmiths.

Time to learn the systems and work methods applying in the organisation is essential for every new employee, and the opportunity to do so needs to be provided. This is not, however, a justification for a seniority system applying to work performance assessment across all or part of the organisation. The improvement in skill is rapid initially, but the gain in skill falls off over time.

A seniority system applying to people and work in an organisation effectively treats people as if they are unable to use judgement about work but are, instead, essentially extensions to machines but, unlike machines, improve as they age. Given the disadvantages of seniority systems applying to people working in organisations, it is interesting they persist so strongly.

Where seniority systems are used, the people to whom they apply are usually aware of the disadvantages of the system for them. Seniority systems were introduced as part of industrial action to curb managerial decisions perceived by the workforce to be unfair – arbitrary dismissal because of race, religion, ethnicity, family membership, political persuasion or personal prejudice – almost any excuse other than work performance. A seniority system is far preferable to such arbitrary managerial actions.

The mythologies about such dishonest behaviour by managers remain strong in many industries and organisations. These are very effectively refreshed by every poor decision about work performance or promotion that a manager in these environments makes.

NEPOTISM

Under Nepotism, position and reward are based upon kinship. This is still clearly evident in large global organisations such as Fox (which is owned by the Murdoch family), the Trump family businesses or the 2005, Glazer take-over of the UK football club Manchester United where the three Glazer sons were appointed to significant roles by their father, the owner. This is not to say that these people are automatically incapable of the work; rather that their appointment is primarily based on family relationships. This is a system of favouritism where family relationship is a significant factor. We see, even in apparently democratic political organisations, family members look to succeed others e.g. Kennedy, Bush and Clinton.

Societies have historically used such systems in governance. With the circumstance of a royal family, and an aristocracy with inherited wealth, good governance of the country is totally reliant on chance factors that a son or daughter will have the capability to carry out the work of the role. History has documented the consequences of such systems in the form of the English Civil War and the French and Russian Revolutions. The potential of harm with this system of leadership selection is compounded when other sources of authority are assumed, such as God's will. The theory of the divine right of kings in Europe and Japan not only perpetuated a family dynasty but also underpinned that authority by claiming a divine authority for the system. (See speech by Charles I of England defending himself at his trial before his beheading.)

DEMOCRACY

With this system, when properly applied, the appointment to positions of authority is by majority vote. As a system of governance this is now put forward as the most effective so far devised and is argued to be *a good thing* for everyone especially by the current Western governments. The passion with which democracy as a form of governance and authority distribution is defended can be compared with the missionary zeal and governmental support for Christianity and missionary work during British colonial rule, though it lacks the cachet of divine guidance. However, recent events in the West have cast doubt on politicians and their connection with the people. The underlying principle of the universal right to vote is not under question.

We can see that publicly owned businesses do include a democratic process. Here the right to vote is obtained by owning a share. This, in turn, gives the authority to elect board members who in turn appoint an executive. The difference in democratic societies is that, by being a member of society (a citizen, social *shareholder*), an adult has the right to vote for a government, which then appoints an executive that in turn is supported by an appointed civil/public service. This is discussed in more depth in Chapter 3.

FAVOURITISM

The fourth principle operating in many organisations is simply that some people are favoured above others for reasons other than merit. This gives rise to the common phrase: 'it's not what you know but who you know that counts'. Thus people are favoured because of friendship or association ('old boys' club') or because of race, ethnicity, gender or sexual preference. Societies that depend economically on organisations that provide goods and services have sought to limit such discrimination. They have enacted legislation that embeds merit and capability as the most important criterion. Of course this also gives rise to debates about how to rebalance opportunity and include groups who have been historically discriminated against. One advantage of our propositions about the distribution of mental processing ability is that we have no evidence to suggest that such a distribution is related to race, gender, ethnicity or sexual orientation.

Conclusion

We are saying that a meritocracy is potentially the most efficient and effective way to organise to produce goods and services. We also note that it requires considered effort and courage to build one and that often other forms of organisation are woven into meritocracies making them hybrids (nepotism, seniority, democracy). This muddle makes the establishment of a meritocracy doubly difficult because the 'others' are a constant demonstration that the claim to be a meritocracy is a lie.

Box 7.3

Three Questions: A Simple Test: (See also Chapter 18)

We have found that in organisations that are functioning well there are three questions that people can answer with confidence:

1. What is my work? That is people know what the purpose of their role is, what tasks and projects they are meant to be working on and how this fits with the work of other people and the purpose of the organisation.
2. How well am I doing? People receive regular and specific feedback from their leader; also from colleagues and information from systems and processes they are operating or involved in. These should be underlying systems of recognition and reward that are connected to the work.
3. What is my future? Here the person knows about what opportunities there are for advancement and also the real state of the organisation and its future in the context of demand and competition.

We use these three questions regularly when working with organisations (see also Chapter 18 Systems and Symbols Audit).

---

8 *Human Capability*

Elements of Individual Capability

We have explained that all organisations require people to work in order to achieve their purpose. That work differs in kind: from designing a new product, to developing a long-term business plan, to stacking shelves or maintaining equipment. Some of this work requires significant leadership work with people; other work requires more technical knowledge and skill. It is fairly obvious that not everyone can carry out all of the tasks equally successfully. This is not just a question of volume of work but the nature of the work itself. People's skills and ability differ. A positive organisation is one where each person's skills and ability matches the work they are required to do. In order to consider assigning work appropriately so this matching can be achieved it is necessary to have a concept of human capability.

We have found it remarkable that many organisations do not have a shared concept of human capability. They will talk of experience, education, training, interpersonal skills but do not have a coherent articulation of capability. There is little agreement about what elements of capability can be influenced or learned, and how this might be done, apart from having people attend training courses. One hears comments to the effect that 'so and so is quite bright', but there is often no real consideration of what this might mean (unless perhaps based on the results of psychometric tests).

Unless we have a view that every person can perform any nominated work if they have the interest and training to do so, we do need an understanding of human capability, how it may vary from person to person and how it may, and may not, be changed. Our concept of human capability has been developed and refined by experience and practice. In this chapter we will explain it and then raise some questions of comparison and why we have not incorporated some of the more popular concepts of human capability.

When selecting a person for a role or considering a person for a particular project or task, the following elements are critical. We will define and discuss each in turn. All of these elements should be examined when making the selection, although some are more open to influence than others (see Box 8.1). The object is to identify the attributes an individual needs to bring to the task so he or she is able to perform it effectively and efficiently. Each of these is defined later in this chapter, while the specifics and subtleties of task assignment are discussed in Chapter 14.

Box 8.1   Elements of Individual Capability

- knowledge
- technical skills
- social process skills
- mental processing ability application – desire, energy and drive applied to work

---

KNOWLEDGE

Knowledge here consists of two categories: first, part or all of an accepted body of knowledge; and second, knowledge that has been produced as a largely self-generated body.

Knowing all or part of a body of knowledge is what we have referred to before as scientific meaning. It is concerned with knowledge of currently agreed-upon definitions, theories or facts, for example, nuclear physics, the periodic table, algebra, calculus and/or other scientific disciplines with current but not necessarily uncontested inter-relationships. In the arts there are also bodies of knowledge covering facts (Who wrote *Great Expectations* and who are the main characters?) and knowledge about opinions (Do you know Christopher Hill's analysis of the English Civil War? How does he critique this conflict?). Essentially this element is about what we learn in schools, colleges and universities and from our own researches. Employers and educationalists may differ as to what is important to learn but it is about learning subjects from an established curriculum. We make assumptions about the knowledge an individual has in specific disciplines from the shorthand of qualifications, even though there are debates about the value of degrees from certain universities or institutions.

Another type of knowledge is self-generated – heuristics. Thus a person may have knowledge gained as a result of their experience of people with mental illness, living in a large family or travelling internationally. The point about this self-generated knowledge is that it may not be organised into disciplines or accepted structures. It is more difficult to test but can be elicited by careful questioning and listening.

All roles and all tasks require some prior knowledge and it is important to be clear what knowledge is required and to what extent the person being considered for the work has such knowledge.

TECHNICAL SKILLS

This element refers to a proficiency in the *use* of knowledge. It includes learned routines that reduce the complexity of work required to complete a task.

It has been recognised that having a skill makes a task easier. It essentially reduces the complexity of a task because you do not have to think through or work out the process being considered to carry out the work. This emphasises the difference between knowledge and skill. I may have a significant amount of knowledge about the internal combustion engine, but can I change a piston? I may know all the letters on a keyboard, but can I type?

The need for skill and the difference between knowledge and skill is most apparent when we learn a new skill: driving, playing tennis, golf, skiing and touch-typing. At first it is very difficult to steer, change gear and keep an eye on the road at the same time. Gradually the processes become less conscious until it is internalised and second nature. This allows us to concentrate on what is really important. In the case of driving, not having to think about steering, breaking or changing gear allows us to concentrate on the road, other traffic and pedestrians. This is most apparent when we suddenly have to consciously re-engage with the process because of an unexpected event such as a sudden flat tyre, poor brakes or loss of steering.

In effect, technical skills once acquired do not require much cortical brain activity. This effectively allows more room for the cortical activity to be applied to real and current problem solving (see Mental Processing Ability below). The more pressing the immediate problem, the more important the embedding of the skill. A fire fighter does not want to be working out how breathing apparatus works whilst in a burning building. A combat soldier does not want to try and remember how to load a rifle in the middle of a battle.

We recognise that certain skills appear to be learned or acquired more easily by some people than others. We recognise that some people have what is usually referred to as a *natural aptitude*. Others appear to have no aptitude at all: they are *all fingers and thumbs*, or more technically, they suffer from *dyspraxia*. We do not intend to discuss this in depth here as our experience is that technical skills in organisations can be taught to most people if they are sufficiently interested. Those organisations where the key staff are employed first and foremost for their extraordinary technical skills, are not usually traditional employment hierarchies, for example, professional athletes and artists.

Whatever the work, as we have said about knowledge, it is critical to identify what skills are required and make an assessment as to whether and to what extent a person has, or could quickly acquire, the skills required to perform the work successfully.

SOCIAL PROCESS SKILLS

Work is an activity with a powerful social element. Our survival requires social cohesion. Values are embedded deeply in the process of all human relationships. Recognition of the central significance of social process is evident throughout this book. Understanding and managing social process is critical. Thus for many years we have given significant attention to the development of a deep understanding of social process (see Box 8.2).

This element is at the heart of leadership. Too often in organisations we have seen leadership roles given to people who are very technically skilled and/or intellectually very able but who have poor social process skills. The result is usually damaging, if not disastrous, and at times tragic if the person involved is lost as to why he or she is failing as a leader. Poor leadership also damages the people subject to it.

By social process skills we do not mean the ability to *be nice* or *get on with people*. Social process skill is required for handling confrontations, disciplinary issues or poor performance. In the Church and many voluntary organisations people often equate good relations and social process with being friendly or not upsetting people, whereas we are referring to the ability to get work done.

As discussed throughout this book, relationships with people are not *soft science*. This area can be highly complex and sensitive. Brute force, oppression or intimidation will not only fail over time but will not release capability. If we are not to objectify people we must understand how they see the world. We must understand their mythologies, how they view themselves, each other and us. In addition we must work out ways of influencing relationships so that they are directed to a productive purpose, not simply to building the harmony of the group. In short, if we put too much emphasis on output and thereby ignore social process, that output will not be sustained over time. If we put too much emphasis on social processes designed to generate person-to-person harmony, we will degrade our ability to achieve the output required.

This highlights a fundamental difference between work relationships and friendships. Work relationships exist to produce a good or service that is valued by others. Friendships exist

---

Box 8.2   Definition of Social Process Skills

Social process skills are those skills that give the ability to observe social behaviour, comprehend the embedded social information and to respond in a way that influences subsequent behaviour productively (see definition in Chapters 3 and 4).

for the sake of the relationship. A friendship does not have to be productive or even particularly valued by others outside the friendship. Friends can just be with one other. Confusing these different types of relationship will lead to problems. It is not necessary for people at work to be friends as long as they behave towards each other positively according to the values continua. It is not necessary for friends to engage in highly productive work. This does not mean that work colleagues cannot be friends, or that friends cannot be actively engaged in making or doing things, merely that the social processes are different. You may have experience of, or know of, friends who have embarked on a business venture or turned a hobby into a business who have become disillusioned. You may have experience of, or know of, colleagues who believe they have been let down by people at work: 'I thought you were my friend – why did you apply for that job?'

The authors have long been wary of companies that promote a lot of social events, bonding, inviting spouses and partners to events and talking about work being like a family. It is not that these are inherently bad, but they can cause confusion and cynicism when the invitation is really a requirement and the social, bonding event is really a covert assessment centre.

In this book, we are referring to a person's ability to establish good, productive working relationships both directly and indirectly through teamwork and delegation. It requires an interest in and genuine regard for people, an appreciation of people not as production units but as creative and curious individuals who have their own unique way of seeing and being in the world.

This element, that for many years we have termed social process skills, has some similarities with the more recent term *emotional intelligence* (Goleman, 1996). While we have detailed differences and concerns with that concept, we do agree that this element has been underestimated by many organisations as an essential part of successful working relationships.

MENTAL PROCESSING ABILITY

Perhaps the least familiar of the elements that make up our formulation of human capability is mental processing ability (often referred to as MPA). We begin with Elliott Jaques' definition of cognitive processes: '… the mental processes by which a person takes information; picks it over; plays with it; analyses it; puts it together; reorganises it; judges and reasons with it; and makes conclusions, plans and decisions, and takes action.' (Jaques, 1989: 33). These mental processes are the way an individual organises his or her thinking when working (attempting to turn intention into reality) (see Box 8.3).

The richness and diversity of the world that each person creates is indicative of the complexity of the mental process that a person can apply to make sense out of their experience of the world. Because our environment is constantly changing, this effort to make sense of it is a continuous process. It requires constant work – turning intention into reality.

From our own experience we know that people are more able or less able to comprehend the information available to them in a given situation, its relevance to the work at hand and to formulate cause and effect relationships between events they experience in the world. People show differences in their ability to generate and test hypotheses about relationships and to predict the outcome of a course of action. All of us have differing abilities to do work.

Each of us perceives the world in our own way. Some people will see the world as it presents itself in front of them; they are most comfortable with what they can directly see and even touch. They like direct links between the action they take and the result they get. Their

---

Box 8.3   Definition of Mental Processing Ability (MPA)

Mental processing ability: the ability to make order out of the chaotic environment in which humans live out their lives. It is the ability to pattern and construe the world in terms of scale and time. The level of our MPA will determine the amount and complexity of information that we can process in doing so. (This definition draws in part from I. Macdonald (1984: 2) and also from Jaques (1989: 33). Also see his definition of cognitive power, above.)

By 'chaos', we refer not to random disorder, but to the patterns of complexity and the multiple scales of complexity that are now being studied as part of a general theory of chaos (see Gleick, 1987; 2008; Strogatz, 2014, if you wish to pursue this topic). Classical science and much theory of organisation have searched for deterministic relationships in the observable patterns that will that allow prediction: if this, then that.

Chaos theory studies non deterministic relationships where prediction becomes more and more difficult the further you move out into the future, a situation which covers virtually all significant organisational and policy problems today (see Zimm, 2003). A minute change in one variable may cause profound changes out into the future. Chaos theorists refer to this as the Butterfly Effect. The idea that a butterfly fluttering its wings in Beijing in January disturbs the air and this perturbation may be one of many causal links for a thunderstorm in New Jersey in June.

The recognition of chaotic relationships forces us to confront the fact that no matter how much experience we have and how well we understand the present, the predictions we make about the future will become progressively less accurate as they extend forward in time. Our mental processing ability is the facility to make order of this chaos, to perceive the universe and to discover or create order which we can then use as we take action.

---

solution will deal with what is immediately present. Other people will see that the results they want cannot be achieved directly, that many different systems and outside influences will have to be changed, if there is to be a successful outcome. The difference is in the way different individuals take in and organise information, how broadly they see the inter-relationships of what is going on, and how much they can encompass in their formulation of their world.

For example, there is a truck with a broken gearbox. To one person that is the problem and it can be fixed today. Another person realises that while the damaged gearbox can be replaced today and the truck put back in action, he or she appreciates that driver behaviour may have been part of the cause and considers how it might be rectified. A third mechanic considers that the original design of the gearbox could have a part to play and thinks through how this might be corrected. Finally, a fourth person might question the use of trucks for this type of transport and proposes an alternative. All of these views are valid and helpful. We need to ask: what is the work required by whom?

Like Jaques, Gibson and Isaac (1978) and Stamp (1978), we agree that these different ways of seeing the world are divided into distinct groupings. Rather than MPA being seen as a gradual, continuous line along which the whole population is spread, what Jaques originally found was a series of types of processing. Because each approach to the world and problem solving is discrete, someone with Type II MPA will see a problem and its potential solutions in a completely different way from someone with Type IV MPA. The person with Type II MPA will simply not see the problem with the same range of variables, relationships and consequences. These differing approaches are neither right nor wrong, but their appropriateness depends upon the context and the inherent complexity of the particular task to be accomplished.

The concept of discrete orders of complexity is discussed at length in the following chapter. What we believe requires emphasis here is the importance of these discrete orders to what follows. Their effect is pervasive. Our argument is that the chaos itself is not formulated with discrete levels of complexity, but is chaotic. It is our observation that it is human work, making order of the chaos, that has discrete, and therefore discontinuous, levels of complexity. It is the discontinuous nature of the human mental processing ability that generates order from the chaos to bring work to fruition, turning intention into reality and in so doing generates the discontinuity in work complexity.

We do appreciate that the notion of discontinuity is at odds with many of the popular concepts of the distribution of mental processing ability in the population. As to the mechanism that leads to mental processing ability, there is, at present, no certainty. Recent research suggests the element of brain functionality referred to as working memory may be relevant (Baddeley and Hitch, 1974: Baddeley, 2000; McLeod, 2012).

There have been many attempts to describe this intellectual or cognitive element of capability. This ranges from the classic IQ to new and different forms of intelligence such as *crystallised and fluid* (Cattell, 1971, 1987; Belsky, 1990). What is common about all of these attempts, including ours and Jaques', is that all concentrate on problem solving and all are concerned with moving from the concrete to the abstract as part of the higher complexity problem solving.

APPLICATION

People may be very able in terms of mental processing, very skilled in managing social processes. They may have great general knowledge and technical skill, but unless they actually apply it in the workplace it is of only latent value. Practising managers value this attribute of application for its obvious practical relevance.

When one of the authors (Ian Macdonald) worked for the British Civil Service Selection Board, this element was divided into *drive* and *determination*. Kolbe (1991) refers to it as *conation*, a term we like, which is defined as the desire to perform an action. Essentially this is the element that affects not whether a problem *can* be solved (by someone) but whether it *will* be solved. A person with high application has the drive to see a task through to completion, providing they have the MPA and skills to resolve the inherent complexity of the task.

Box 8.4   Definition of Application

Application: The effort and energy that a person puts into applying the other elements of capability to their work.

So Why not Include Experience, Competencies or Personality/ temperament?

Many models of capability include experience as an element; we do not. Rather, we incorporate what is usually meant by experience in our concepts of knowledge (especially self-generated knowledge) and technical and social process skills. We deliberately do not use it as a separate element because we have found it often leads to a trap. This trap is to ask for experience which translates to years or time doing something, rather than what has been learned from doing it. For example, 'Oh good, she has three years' experience in sales' or 'Oh dear, he has no experience of working in another culture.'

Concentrating on knowledge leads to specific questions directed towards the extent and specific content of the experience.

We do not use the extremely popular term *competency*. This is for two reasons. First, at a more general level, *competency* is not sufficiently specific. Competency fits well when unpacking other elements. For example, in technical skills, we need to ask in what process should a person be competent for this role? We regard competencies as related more to specific skills in the technical, commercial and social areas. The second reason for avoiding competency is that it is poor at discriminating different levels of work and complexity. For example, is a person competent in terms of leadership? Does this mean at any level of work? *Planning* is another word that floats from level to level but, as with other competencies, can be delivered at one level and undeliverable at another. Drawing up a long-term business plan for a multi-national corporation is quite different from a departmental plan or shift plan.

With regard to personality or temperament, like Jaques, we see this as a possible negative distraction. We agree with Jaques that a role can be filled and successfully operated by people of very different personality. Only at the extremes, virtual mental illness or psychopathy, does personality have a significant bearing. We can fall into traps of assuming that sales people should be extroverts, and that leaders should be charismatic. One of the most effective leaders in the British Army in recent times, Sir Peter de la Billière (commander of the British Forces in the first Gulf War and head of the SAS), is a quiet, compactly built, introverted man who certainly does not fit the stereotypical, macho leader but he is very highly regarded and has been decorated by his country for his capability as a leader.

We have seen Myers-Briggs type indicators used creatively to understand team dynamics and individual differences in working style better, but we are very wary of associating any specific personality type with a role type.

Nature or Nurture?

When discussing any human attribute, there is usually a debate about what is inherited, what is constitutional, what is innate, learned, acquired and so on. Many people have devoted a great deal of time and effort to such questions over millennia, and they cannot be resolved here in a few paragraphs. When it comes to the issue of leadership of an organisation, providing the opportunity for people to improve their capability requires us to address the nature/nurture debate because it is important to determine where it is worth expending the resources required to provide this opportunity and what changes may be expected. In doing so we exercise care about any proposition that makes absolute statements, especially about human attributes that are supposed to be unalterable. In this we have been influenced by the work of Stephen Jay Gould, *The Mismeasure of Man* (1996) and Stephan Chorover, *From Genesis to Genocide* (1979). Here Gould quotes the early twentieth century psychologist Goddard from his book *Psychology of the Normal and Subnormal* (1919) to demonstrate the kind of statement that we believe must be avoided:

We must next learn that there are great groups of men, labourers, who are but little above the
child, who must be told what to do and shown how to do it; and if we would avoid disaster,
must not be put into positions where they will have to act upon their own initiative or their own
judgement.

(pp. 243–244)

MENTAL PROCESSING ABILITY

Despite these caveats, we cannot ignore the reality of the differences between people as demonstrated in their performance of work, especially with regard to mental processing ability. We see the way in which a person makes sense of the world (making order of the complexity of the chaos) as essentially fixed by the time a person reaches early adulthood. We have not seen successful examples of adults learning entirely new mental processes and being able to solve original problems of a type that previously they were unable to resolve. We accept absolutely that people can learn techniques and methods that enhance their current abilities or help realise potential. In other words, their capability to carry out work through time can increase, while *their mental processing ability* remains constant.

TECHNICAL SKILLS

While we have experienced many examples of the inability of people to improve their mental processing ability in adulthood, we have seen plenty of evidence for the acquisition of skills, even late in life. While, some people appear to have more aptitude than others (hand–eye co-ordination, for example, or balance or dexterity), most skills are teachable to the level of organisational requirement. Some aspects of very fine craftwork or sporting prowess may be more difficult to learn and are either due to aptitude or life-long learning (child apprentice-ships). For the purposes of this book and the range of activities covered by most organisations, the technical, mechanical and other skills required to work effectively are, from our observa-tion, possible to teach to the great majority of people.

SOCIAL PROCESS SKILLS

Again, we believe these can be taught. We do not subscribe to the simple *born leader* theory. It is inevitable that early experiences and opportunities can strongly affect this area. A person brought up and encouraged to engage in social processes is more likely to be adept and skilful than someone brought up either in a more isolated milieu or someone who has been encour-aged to develop relationships with objects rather than people.

It is interesting to note here the general, but not exclusive, nature of socialisation for boys and girls. While this has been changing in recent decades, girls are still more often encouraged to engage in social process (talking, discussing, analysing relationships) and playing social games (including families, dolls and nurses) than boys. Boys are likely to be socialised into interest with mechanics, technical, electronic games.

The analogy for social process would be more like learning a language. If it happens early in life, it is easy, natural and the facility is both acquired and used with apparently little effort. Learning a language later in life is not only physically more difficult; it requires more deter-mination, effort and desire. It is not, however, impossible. It can also be likened to musical ability. Some people have an 'ear' for music. They can hear a piece of music and then just play it on an instrument. Such people are rare as indeed are people who are truly, totally tone deaf.

Most of us fall somewhere in between. We do have musical ability and it can be enhanced by training and practice.

This should come as no surprise. The social process skills are the first learned and most often practiced. Consider the effort a mother puts into establishing person-to-person bonds with her child and the joy of receiving the child's first smile of recognition in response. It is to be expected that one's social process skills are not easy to change and in fact universal plasticity of social process would result in a highly unstable society, not supportive of continued species survival.

KNOWLEDGE

Clearly, knowledge can be more readily and easily acquired than skills and can be expanded throughout life. It is, by definition, learned. Even self-generated knowledge acquisition continues. People, however apparently fixed in their ways, will not be able to prevent learning even if it is uncomfortable. However the rate of learning and hence the amount that can be learned will vary, and will also vary from person to person. This rate of learning, or building the knowledge base, will depend to an extent upon the knowledge already held about a subject and the interest and attention paid during the opportunity to learn. One very important determinant of learning rate, however, is often not appreciated is a person's mental processing ability. A person who can order high levels of complexity, construe and understand complex patterns and derive the relationships that exist between the variables in play, will build and acquire knowledge at a faster rate than another person who is unable to do this but may be presented with the same opportunity to learn. This ability to build knowledge rapidly from the experience of the chaos is sometimes described as learning from first principles.

Thus while we all continue to acquire knowledge, the rate at which we do so, its inherent intricacy and our subsequent use of it to perform work are dependent upon our mental processing ability.

APPLICATION

In accord with Kolbe's concept of conation, we recognise that some people appear to have more energy, drive and determination than others. Whether this is innate or strongly influenced by early experience, we do not know. What we do know is that application in the workplace is very strongly influenced by the context. This includes in order of influence:

- The quality (that is, behaviour) of the person's immediate leader including how well, or poorly, the leader clarifies expectations and gives feedback.
- The structure and systems of the organisation: is the work of the role clear? Does it have proper authority? Are the work systems helpful in achieving goals or are they layered in red tape? Are the resources necessary for the work readily available?
- The general quality of relationships. This includes other leaders, the manager-once-removed and work colleagues.
- Symbols: the quality of the equipment, plant, housekeeping and the attention to safe practice.

So while some people do give up before others, and few of us have the drive and determination of the explorer Ernest Shackleton, this element, for most people, is strongly influenced by their environment. In Gallup and other work surveys there is a consistent message that the main reason for people leaving an organisation (for negative reasons) is poor leadership in the form of the person's immediate manager.

One of the authors (Macdonald and Couchman, 1980 and Macdonald, 1990) observed and documented significant changes in behaviour, especially in 'application', when the context changed for people with learning difficulties.

Caveats

We have already warned of the dangers of labelling so clearly stated in Gould's work, *The Mismeasure of Man* (1996) and in Chorover's *From Genesis to Genocide (1979)*. There are other dangers: two significant traps await a leader in the work of selecting a person to fill a role in the organisation.

1. ASSESSING THE PERSON, NOT THE ROLE

We have found it to be common practice for leaders to assess and rank people against each other rather than being clear about *what the work is that needs to be done*. Before we look at capability we must be clear about capability for what? This question does not answer itself, of course, it drives a discipline of developing a clear answer. Too often people are assigned to poorly designed roles, given poorly defined tasks in the hope, sometimes realised, that they will work out what to do.

Apart from leading to circumstances wherein it is most unfair to expect people to accept accountability for their work. *You did not tell me you wanted me to do that; I did the best I could at the time*. It also leads to the use of power and chance achievement. A leader who behaves in this way is simply passing the buck or asking someone else to do the work for which he or she is paid. In all fairness, such leaders should pass on some of their salary with the buck.

The pertinent issue for a leader assessing someone for a role is whether or not he or she has the capability to do the work of the role and not how they compare to Fred or Anne.

2. BE CAREFUL NOT TO ELEVATE ONE ELEMENT ABOVE OTHERS

Certain roles or tasks will appropriately emphasise one or more of the elements of capability. For example, a leadership role may require stronger social process skills than those required for a technical maintenance role, which in turn will require more specific knowledge and technical skills. However, it is dangerous to emphasise one element at the expense of another. For example, while mental processing ability is necessary, it is not sufficient and will not compensate for poor application or social process skills.

Box 8.5   Working – Under Pressure by Roderick Macdonald

In 1982 I was commanding 59 Independent Commando Squadron Royal Engineers as a young (34-year-old) major in the Royal Engineers. We had just sailed 8,000 miles from the United Kingdom and audaciously landed a force of 3,000 Royal Marine and Army Commandos and Parachute troops on the Falkland Islands. The Falkland Islands, close to the Antarctic continent and the coastline of Argentina, had recently been invaded by 11, 000 Argentine troops covered by combat air patrols flying from Argentina. They had plenty of time to establish strong defensive positions.

The history of amphibious landings is not glorious. Many thousands of soldiers died at failed landings in World War I, such as Gallipoli, and in World War II on the beaches of Normandy. Even when landings were successful, such as during the American war in the Pacific against the Japanese or Allied landings in Sicily and Normandy, they all had one thing in common; yet again thousands of soldiers died. Another defining issue in all successful landings was overwhelming air superiority in support of the amphibious forces. For the first time, an amphibious landing was to be undertaken by Western forces without air superiority. The British paid heavily. Warships, logistic ships and civilian ships taken up from trade were sunk by the Argentine air force with impunity. I was part of the small British force that landed in San Carlos, 75 miles away from the capital Stanley. We were without consistent supply of ammunition, food, clothing or helicopters. This occurred in the midst of an Antarctic winter where temperatures regularly dropped well below zero centigrade and wind, snow and rain blew continuously in excess of 30 miles an hour. There was no shelter because there are no trees. In order to regain air superiority from the Argentines it was essential that a landing and re-fuelling strip be built on the island, and this was one of my tasks.

The combat and Commando Royal Engineers supporting 3 Commando Brigade had some experience of doing this work; however, there was need for technical expertise to give guidance on the intricacies of both the design and construction process. Design started quickly but ran into trouble when we discovered that most of the equipment for the task was sitting at the bottom of the South Atlantic Ocean. The stores had been loaded on a supply ship, *Atlantic Conveyor*, which had been sunk by Argentine aircraft. We did manage to unload some equipment that had been transported on another ship specifically for repairing the airfield at Stanley when it was eventually taken by British forces. Even the fuel supply, pumping and rafting equipment was not fully intact. This posed considerable problems for the young troop commander who had been given this task. He turned to the technical expert who had been given to him to do this design work and the answer was swiftly given.

'We can't do it, this is not possible. We don't have enough equipment to build this installation!'

The technical expert was correct. According to the book, which he knew in detail, the work could not be done. However, this was not the answer I needed to hear. Soldiers and sailors were dying because we did not have air superiority and we needed to build this installation regardless of what the book said. The technical expert did not have the mental processing ability to adopt a different strategy. It was now up to the troop commander.

This young officer did have engineering knowledge. This was a combination of theoretical engineering knowledge from his degree course at Cambridge University and down-to-earth practical training from Army engineering school and training exercises. His higher level of mental processing ability allowed him to come up with a unique design to complete and build this installation with the equipment available. This was accomplished in very difficult circumstances. As a result the British achieved air superiority with their Harrier aircraft. It was a small but important step in helping achieve overall victory in the campaign. The young troop commander was mentioned in dispatches (bronze oak leaf medal) for this and, later, for bravery under fire.

So what do we learn from this? We certainly do not learn that technical knowledge is not important. It is. It is equally dangerous to come up with a theoretical design that does not work because there is a lack of understanding of basic engineering principles as it is to fail to come up with a design because resources are not exactly as stated in a learned procedure. We learn that it is important to have both. We need to have mental processing ability to be able to apply an apposite level of complexity resolution to solve a problem at the appropriate level. Equally we need knowledge, experience and skills, both technical and social, to be able to come up with a practical design and more importantly to implement the solution with other people. There is no golden key here. To succeed under these circumstances we need it all.

If we assume that the knowledge and technical skills are slightly easier to specify and evaluate (as in criteria for selection, for example, must have clean driving licence, degree in chemistry, keyboard skills or computer literacy), we are left with three dimensions: *mental processing ability*, *social process skills* and *application* that are more difficult to assess. We can see those in comparison using the example of three people A, B and C (see Figure 8.1).

This representation is not strictly accurate since *Mental Processing Ability* should be represented discontinuously i.e. divided into categories rather than a continuous line. However, we can see that person A may be very impressive in terms of drive and energy but may well fail to address or even understand the work really required. With luck they may not cause too much damage as poor social process skills may cause them to be isolated. However in a leadership role this person would be catastrophic. Person B is certainly bright enough and relates fairly well to people but does not have the energy to get much done. The saving grace may be that the person is bright enough to find the short cuts! Person C is heading for a heart attack or breakdown since they are highly committed (as evidenced by the high application score), and relate really well but just cannot do the work (solve problems) required. They will put in more and more hours and be at a loss to know why efforts are failing.

All three of the authors have actually observed situations where an individual died because of this type of mismatch between capability and job requirements. This tragedy can be avoided if one understands what is happening and the potential consequences.

The point here is that we must be wary of believing that a high ranking of one element will compensate for another; that a high degree of energy will make up for a lack of MPA or really good MPA will compensate for poor social process skills. Application and social process skills can be improved but not to the extent that they make another element irrelevant. In determining what is required in each of these five elements it must be borne in mind that each is a necessary but not sufficient condition.

Perhaps the most important caveat is not to confuse capability and the worth of a *person*. These elements refer to the capability to do work. It is a very significant problem for all of us that a hierarchy of capability to do work of certain types can become confused with a hierarchy of personal worth. That is to fall into the trap of assuming that 'if I have a higher MPA than you, I am a better person', that singularly unpleasant classification of the worth of people that assumes operators are less worthy as people than managers. This has echoes of feudalism

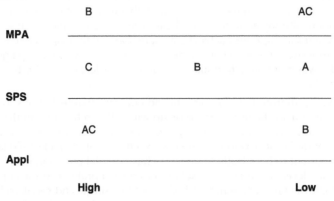

Figure 8.1   Comparison of Mental Processing Ability, Social Process Skills and Application in Persons A, B and C

and aristocracy and is still evident in many industrialised societies especially in Europe, although such ideas are of concern in the U.S. as well (see *The War on Stupid People*, Freedman, 2016). It also reflects a confusion between a meritocracy and other types of social organisation.

We have had the experience of some of these concepts of capability, work complexity and level of work, becoming substitutes for older status symbols such as title and pay grade in organisations. Leaders need to be aware of this possibility, monitor it and address it, as the practice can become destructive, particularly around the use of mental processing ability as the symbol because of its fixed nature in adulthood.

This model of capability, with its five elements, can be used not only to consider an individual's suitability for a role or task but also to review an entire organisation or part of it. The leadership can review the organisation's capability in more general terms: how do we score in matching mental processing ability to the work of each role? Do we have enough technical skills and/or knowledge? How good are we at our social process? Do we have people who are committed and have the drive and determination? Is it a high or low energy organisation?

The issue of capability is highly significant in organisations that are producing goods and services because the most effective way of delivering them is through a meritocracy based on work.

Conclusion

We have outlined a model of human capability to work in terms of five elements: knowledge, technical skills, social process skills, mental processing ability and application. We have described these elements and considered how far each can be influenced especially by external factors.

We have also drawn attention to the dangers of labelling and the misuse of these concepts. Despite claims over the years by many writers, we recognise these concepts are only *hypotheses* and not absolute truths. We have found, however, that they explain and bring order to our efforts to understand the processes of the organisations we have worked in and those we have studied. We recommend strongly that managers and leaders considering this material take the time to reflect upon how well the concepts bring order to their experiences as well. We offer this model as a way for people, especially managers, to consider the capability and suitability of people to carry out tasks and/or fill roles. We recognise fully that the decision is still a matter of managerial judgement.

We cannot emphasise too strongly the importance of being clear about *what the work is*. One of Jaques' favourite, and one of his best, questions when confronted with organisational puzzles was *what is the work to be done?* We regard this as one of the best organisational questions anyone can ask. This must be addressed before considering who might do it or where it should be done. Far too often we find, despite the fact that the first question has not been answered, selection or task allocation still occurs.

Finally, we have also found that most people have a very good sense of their own capability. They are neither passive nor waiting to be told by their superiors. We do, however, have a cautionary saying, bred of caustic experience: 'Beware anyone whose ego is bigger than their intellect – no matter how big the intellect.'

It has been our experience, however, if a person has a real understanding of what is required (the work to be done), they have a good sense of whether they can do it, even if it involves acknowledging it will be challenging, or will involve learning new skills. The majority of the problems we have seen have been generated by the absence of a thorough appreciation of the work to be done.

This assessment of capability should not be something that is done *to* someone but should entail mature, adult discussion. We hope the elements described above will help to make that discussion more realistic and constructive.

9 *Levels of Work Complexity*

Organising Work

Large organisations are characterised by layers or levels of structure. We refer in general terms to shop floor, operators, even workers. We talk about supervisors and first-line managers, then middle managers, executives, managing directors, vice presidents, presidents, chief operating officers and chief executive officers. In the civil and public service and the armed services there are ranks and grades forming a quite deliberate hierarchy. Even in smaller organisations there are managers and reporting structures. People over the years have criticised or attacked hierarchy but it is surprisingly robust and can be traced back through history (Jaques, 1976; 1990). Notable writers such as Weber, 1922; Blau and Scott, 1962; Burns and Stalker, 1961; Dawkins, 1976; Lane, 2006; Mintzberg, 1979; Morgan, 1986; Simon, 1962; Whyte, 1969 and many others have all described and analysed this organisational feature.

Like Jaques, we regard this form not as coincidental, but as indicating a deeper human requirement and a potentially effective and constructive way of organising work. Also, like Jaques, we see many current fads, criticisms and alternatives as misleading, sometimes vacuous attempts to cash in on the fact that many hierarchies are not nearly as efficient or effective as they could be, often because several different concepts are muddled together to form a tangle, which is not easily unravelled. To quote Jaques: 'The problem is not to find an alternative to a system that once worked well ... the problem is to make it work efficiently for the first time in 3000 years' (Jaques, 1990). We are sure that there have been examples of hierarchical structures working very efficiently and constructively over the last 3,000 years, or the concept would have died out centuries ago.

What is muddled?

When people design, operate or criticise organisations, they can confuse several quite different, albeit related, elements:

1. Level of management: The underlying structure of an organisation is actually a structure of management; as such it is an authority structure. It defines or clarifies who has the authority to:
   a. Require someone else to carry out some work (assign tasks).
   b. Review that work and apply consequences (positive or negative) in the form of recognition and/or reward.
   c. Depending upon work performance or upon a changed context, begin processes to remove a person from a role. (The corollary being the manager also authorises the person into the role.) This is what Jaques so clearly identified and with colleagues, including the authors, researched in many organisations. They found similarities across organisations in many fields of endeavour.

      Grades (or ranks): Many organisations (perhaps most obviously in the public sector) also have grading structures; these do not automatically confer authority over

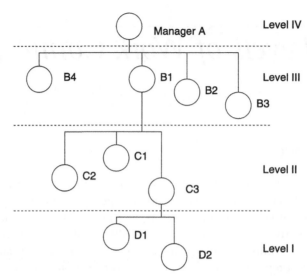

Figure 9.1   Grading Structures

others but are primarily concerned with career development and/or salary and purport to recognise differences in skills or qualification. These operate within management levels. For example, in Figure 9.1 there are actually three levels of management. Manager A manages B1, B2, B3 and B4, but note that B1, B2 and B3 are differently *graded*. There are invariably severe repercussions if B1 thinks and behaves as if he or she is actually the manager of B2 and/or B3 by assessing their performance, issuing instructions and so on. B1 is, however, the manager of C1, C2 and C3 (who are also graded differently). Note that C1 and C2 are not actually managers at all (perhaps stand-alone technical specialists) while C3 manages D1 and D2.

There is a dangerously implied hierarchy of authority in grading structures which causes significant distress, anger and resentment: *pulling rank, overbearing,* the exercise of power: these are multiplied when movement through grades is purely based on seniority or time served and has no relation to ability or achievement.

2. *Complexity of tasks*: All tasks have an inherent complexity. We all recognise this in terms of how difficult we find a task. The critical factor here is to separate out skill and knowledge from the underlying complexity of a pathway to, or method of, achieving a goal. If we imagine that there are thousands of tasks that need to be done in an organisation, it makes sense to order these in some coherent way. This is almost always done by gathering or bundling tasks of equivalent complexity together and calling that a *role*. We have found this concept adopted across organisations, regardless of whether they had any notion of work complexity.

3. *Mental processing ability*: As explained in the previous chapter this refers to the ability of an individual to complete tasks (or solve problems) of a specific complexity. This too varies. Some people will be much more comfortable with tasks of a particular complexity than others.

It is fundamental that we distinguish between these concepts of managerial level, grade, complexity of task and mental processing ability. While they are clearly distinct, there is also a fundamental and critical relationship between them.

How Are They Related?

To answer this question, we must ask why a hierarchy of work underpinning organisational structure, despite its many detractors, is, and has been, so prevalent. If the purpose of an organisation is to provide the goods and/or services then such a depth structure is or can be the most effective. Over time, many forms of organisation have been tested and the managerial structure based on a hierarchy of work complexity has been found to be extraordinarily resilient. Our experience and work supports Jaques' basic propositions that this is for two main reasons: first, that tasks can be categorised into qualitatively different types according to their complexity and second, that this reflects the way people construct their worlds, that is, the way they process information.

A careful consideration of Jaques' propositions shows them to be closely related. Work is a construct of the human mind; we see the world as each one of us constructs it. Some people are able to make sense of numerous variables interacting simultaneously, others are not able to do this and generate a much simpler representation of the chaos in which we are all embedded.

The distribution of work through all organisations is a recognition that different people are capable of different work, even though very few organisations have a clearly defined concept of differing work complexity. In no organisation do we find a random distribution of work to roles, but rather a very definite distribution of work to roles at different levels.

In Chapter 8 we outlined our definition of human capability and gave examples of how this was demonstrated by people doing work. We described how for one person a malfunctioning piston is technical hands-on repair; for another it is a reflection of how the vehicle is driven and for a third it is a design problem or transport issue. Each perception is relatively more abstract.

Thus we see that *mental processing ability*, an individual quality, gives rise to an analysis and solution of a particular *complexity*. Tasks of similar complexity can be bundled together to form a role that can be placed at an appropriate *level* in the organisation (level of work). This is what organisations do now, often in a muddled way because they do not have a clear means of differentiating between levels of management, salary grades, complexity of tasks and mental processing ability.

Being clear about these issues allows each level upwards to reflect a qualitatively more complex and abstract way of perceiving and acting in the world of work. More importantly we have a specific rationale for the generally vague term of *adding value*. Each level, potentially, adds value to the work of the level below by setting it in a broader, more complex context.

This is what employees intuitively refer to when they comment as to whether the person in their manager's role *adds value*. Most critically, in terms of power and authority, if the manager does add value, it is more likely that the team members will accept the manager's authority. This is in contrast to the power exercised by the more senior, higher-graded colleague who adds no value through his or her work and is resented.

We have referred to these *levels of work*: qualitatively different types of complexity of tasks and mental processing ability. How to describe and recognise them is, however, not easy. Jaques, with the authors and many others, especially Cason, has described these levels and mental process in slightly different ways (see for example *General Theory of Bureaucracy*, *Requisite Organisation*, *Human Capability Theory*). We have laboured also with the help and input of many others to generate our own descriptors, which have been articulated in published and unpublished work, often for specific organisations. There are two issues here. The first is what we mean by qualitative differences, or discontinuities in both the complexity required to complete tasks and the mental processing ability of people. The second issue is how to describe such discontinuities in a way that is useful. By discontinuity we mean that an approach or method is fundamentally different in kind from another. It is not simply faster or increased volume. Think of the difference between a bicycle and an internal combustion engine.

There is ample evidence of discontinuity in the way that people order their worlds and go about their work. In the book *Levels of Abstraction in Logic and Human Action* (Jaques, Gibson and Isaac, 1978), chapter 2 describes a range of theories of discontinuity and compares them; chapter 17 (by Stamp) compares a further range of theories including Bennett (1956–1966) on mathematics, Bloom (1956) on education and Kohlberg (1971) on moral development. Further theories even more well-known such as Piaget (1971) and associated researchers have hypothesised and experimentally demonstrated such discontinuities in the way people perceive and act in their worlds. Stamp (in subsequent work) clearly describes similarities between the discontinuities found in her own work and that of Jaques, Macdonald and others. The summary of the descriptions is shown in Table 9.1.

Whilst these are general descriptors, there is a need for those trying to design and run real organisations for more precise, behavioural descriptors.

After some thirty years of effort, including years of work with Jaques, Stamp, Rowbottom and Billis, the authors believe that the perfect set of descriptors is somewhat like the search for the Holy Grail. The difficulty in coming up with perfect descriptors stems from two causes. First, any description in words will be ambiguous because of the inherent ambiguity of words, and their changes in meaning over time. Second, we have found that useful descriptors are best written and most readily understood in the context of a particular organisation, describing work in terms of that organisation. Thus, we see a comprehensive set of descriptors for the work of social services in the UK by Rowbottom and Billis (1977).

Despite these reservations, the following is an attempt to provide a general set of descriptors. Again, like Jaques, we note the importance of time to completion, what Jaques called time-span.

The further we look out, try to predict or plan for the future, the more uncertainty we have to manage. Complexity increases as we project into the future.

However, we have also found instances where due to the rapid change in the immediate environment, for example in the chaos of combat in war, complexity is also very high in short time periods.

Stewart argues that what time-span is measuring is the length of time a person can make order in a chaotic universe. We now believe time-span measures the time to disorder, which appears to have a relatively stable pattern in what we would consider *normal* environments. As the environment becomes more chaotic, the time to disorder at all levels is compressed, as in war or in emergency situations.

Whilst we agree that a task which will take more than three months to complete will be more complex than a task of type one complexity, there may also be tasks of high complexity that have to be completed quickly if they are to be done successfully. For example, reacting to the Deepwater Horizon disaster.

Below are our general descriptors of each level of complexity.

LEVEL I – COMPLEXITY I (R1)

Box 9.1   Level I
Hands on – completing concrete procedural tasks.

Typical tasks might be completing forms, cleaning a room, servicing a vehicle, entering data. The completion of tasks at this level does not take longer than three months.

At Level I there is direct action on immediately available material, customers or clients (see Box 9.1). There is a clear understanding of the work to be done, the procedural steps to be followed and how they are linked. Direct physical feedback indicates whether the work is being performed correctly. The work is often immensely skilful, with significant use of practical judgement, discretion and adjustment by *touch and feel* or *trial and error* if previously known solutions or learnt troubleshooting methods do not work. A known pathway is followed until an obstacle is encountered and then practical judgement is used to overcome the problem or assistance is called for.

Useful input to improving working methods can be expected from the day-to-day experience built up, sometimes over many years, by using the procedures, the observation of repeated patterns of concrete events, and from trial and error. The patterns observed and described are all physical events.

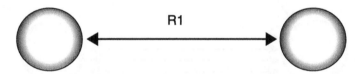

Relationship one is direct. The person and their work are rarely separated. This also gives rise to the reality that people doing this type of work do not take their work home. At the end of the day or shift the person goes home and leaves their work until their next shift.

LEVEL II – COMPLEXITY II (R2)

Box 9.2   Level II
Monitoring and diagnosis of operational processes.

At Level II, the key work is diagnosis whilst observing people or events, working in with established, known systems and processes (Box 9.2). Significant data collected in the form of suggestions from those operating the process and from the flow of concrete events observed in the process are compared with a known model or system. Improvements and modifying actions may be taken on the basis of this information. Diagnostic patterns may be learned through training and education, for example, in engineering, social work, financial analysis or nursing, or through years of experience. Indicators of learned patterns (algorithms and systems) are sought to recognise significant data and so identify the specific pattern or system that is operating in this instance in order to formulate alternative methods of performing tasks, to decide whether the diagnosis is correct or that the case is from another pattern.

This and the general work of task assignment demand the mental construction of how tasks might be envisaged and solved without direct physical, hands-on feedback. Trial and error solving of problems will not be sufficient. Problems are treated as a particular case fitting a known type rather than a new trend or pattern needing identification of a system. *Every case is unique.*

There is still direct access to the area of work and often-physical contact with the work. Leadership roles characterised by work at this level will include managing those who are operating the production process and applying the systems and so will have regular direct contact with them. They will be accountable for ensuring that the work of those they are managing is not constantly interrupted so that they may achieve their outputs reliably.

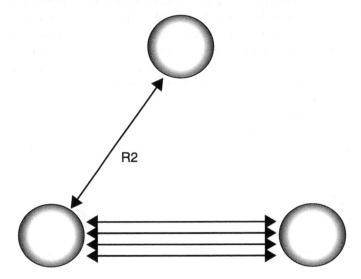

Here the person now can reflect (R2) on the work (R1). They can think about it away from the activity. They can mentally compare ways of approaching it. This is the first level of real planning and the first level of *professional work* associated with teachers, social workers, nurses, solicitors and others. Such work examples include designing individual care or teaching plans for individuals, comparing and identifying different ways of servicing vehicles.

LEVEL III – COMPLEXITY III (R3)

Box 9.3   Level III Focus

Discerns trends to refine existing systems and develop new systems within a single knowledge field.

Work of III complexity requires the ability to recognise the interconnections of significant data from a flow of real events within a single knowledge field, or discipline, and to discern the linkages between them. Trends are developed and systems are derived to mesh the interlinked activities in a way that will achieve the desired end result. The process is one of conceptualising alternative means to achieve a goal by forming, *if this, then that – if that, then the other*, chains of hypothetical activities that are tested through to completion. Alternatives are seen as either/or. This system which best addresses the current situation and links it to projected desired objectives is selected, taking into account local conditions, cost, risk, time to completion and the need to conserve human and material resources.

Because the work of hypothesis generation and test remains within one knowledge field, Level III capability will not recognise the often confounding effect on the proposed system caused by variation in another field generated simultaneously by the activity of that proposed system. Information that arises from what is not there (negative information) is not recognised as significant. The inability to comprehend the simultaneous effect of planned activity in other fields causes many system failures.

Work of III complexity can create high efficiency productive systems or optimise existing systems through the application, for example, of rigorous cost analysis, work method development and risk analysis. III complexity work is well suited for the leadership of a department of up to 300 people in a typical enterprise, recognising that geographic spread, technology variation and work type all have a bearing on the number of people and resources being managed. It is also well suited for highly specialised stand-alone roles requiring great depth of knowledge in a particular discipline.

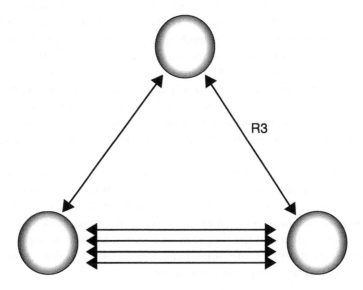

Here the triangle is completed. The person here is able to consider the difference between a *special cause* or *one-off* and a *systemic cause*. That is the system itself is at fault or needs improving. This level is suited to Lean Manufacturing, analysis and interpretation of actual data, benchmarking and comparison. However it does not go into the abstract world of imagining what is not there or does not currently exist. It is the world of best practice or rather, common practice and is the bread and butter of many large consultancies.

At Level III, work turns into the development of an understanding about the nature of the relationships between concepts and or physical phenomena that make up a specific domain or field of knowledge, held in the mind of the person doing the work. The knowledge is expanded through time as a result of work and the exposure to new knowledge. This expansion of knowledge can lead to the appreciation of potential new systemic relationships within a field which are then examined.

As new understandings of the interrelationship between entities in the knowledge field are developed and confirmed, they are then applicable as a predictive mechanism for future action.

Whereas work at Level II requires the determination, of which previously learned systemic relationship fits the data discernibly in a particular discipline or field of knowledge, work at Level III is the determination of the systemic relationships that exist between the data that is available and then the search for data from the field to confirm the relationship. Such data is often not readily distinguishable and may need to be searched out to prove or disprove the validity of the systemic relationship hypothesised.

Within the individual knowledge domain, work at Level III is that of system construction and while this ability is a powerful mechanism for producing order from chaos, it also leads directly to a significant trap as follows.

In most instances it is possible to see, after a more complex problem has been solved by someone else, how it could have been solved by the application of Level III problem-solving methodology: *If only those additional pieces of information had been available to me and I had more time; If I had known those elements were part of the knowledge field.* Sadly we do not live our lives in hindsight.

A distinctive element of work at Level III is the non-appreciation of the simultaneous effect of variation from several different knowledge fields upon the problem at hand.

A maintenance manager who can work effectively in a Level III role will be able to optimise the direct cost of repair by effectively systemising a repetitive major maintenance activity. However, this solution will not be one that will incorporate the effect on the capital cost to the enterprise and the other ramifications of holding a greater or fewer number of spare components available in stock for immediate use. Nor will it allow for the social impact of requiring a maintenance team used to diverse work being required to perform repetitive work.

It is the inability to appreciate the simultaneous effect of variation in other domains upon the apparent domain of the system that results in the *law of unexpected outcomes* and *gaming the system.*

The field of knowledge, or domain, that is most frequently missed when it comes to the carefully considered systematising of work, when it is done at Level III, is that of the people, the social domain. This results in systems of work that are designed to deliver a superior outcome but fail to do so due to no regard being given to the effect caused by the interaction between the designed system and the people upon whom it impacts in their work lives. This leads, invariably, to short and long-term financial and social detriment, examples of which abound in our regulatory and legislative environment.

LEVEL IV – COMPLEXITY IV (R4)

Box 9.4   Level IV Integration

Integrating and managing the interactions between a number of systems.

At Level IV there is a need to imagine and construct relationships between systems that are working in parallel and simultaneously, in order to develop a functioning set (Box 9.4). This demands a quality of thinking that crosses and integrates a number of fields or disciplines (if this *and* that, then the other) in order to see the risks, benefits, costs and potential delays. A key feature is that this integration may well involve a sacrifice in the effectiveness or efficiency, or both, of the functioning of one or more of the systems or processes so that the overall set works more productively. The language is often of *trade-offs* and *conflicts*. Thus, being able to identify and predict conflicts, some or all of the systems may need to be modified or adapted. Alternatives are seen as both/and rather than either/or.

This is often referred to as the first strategic level where an organisation's policies have to be understood, articulated, expressed and promoted in the design and operation of an integrated set of systems. Things, however, may not be as they appear. Production rates may be up but the facility may still be in trouble. Negative information is significant and made use of. Design and monitoring of a range of systems at this level has to be done without being able to observe the entire physical area of work.

Level IV is also the first level of *sacrifice* where resources must be sacrificed in order to achieve priority objectives. In business this is typically money or time. In the military it is far more difficult, as a commanding officer must send men and women he has trained and knows well into a situation where they are likely to be killed in order that the overall battle may be won. Officers who have been in this situation have described the incredible pain of doing so. (At Level III, leaders will try to conserve resources even when this leads to a bad outcome.)

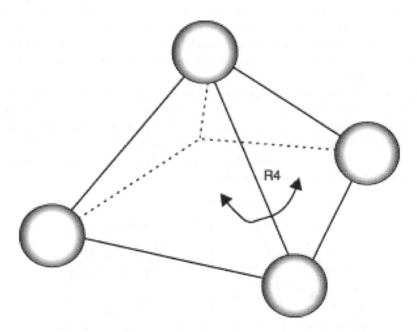

Imagine now a pyramid. The R4 complexity means that the person must imagine how one system impacts or might impact on another from a different field. A person may be imagining what the social implications are of a Technical Change (see Chapter 3). This is the first real level of systems design since most organisations have systems interacting with each other. We might think of this as system design that appreciates and allows for the effect of first order consequences.

LEVEL V – COMPLEXITY V (R5)

Box 9.5   Level V

Shaping and managing an organisation within its environment – maintaining the organisation's systems and processes so that it is self-sustaining within that environment.

At this level, entire theories and not just principles are used to link multiple knowledge fields or disciplines (Box 9.5). As a result of understanding and predicting the environment, the organisation is modified to address and minimise any potential negative impact (social, political or economic) from the environment, for example, by deciding what line(s) of business the organisation should occupy in five years' time, and managing the effects that a change of direction will have by changing the systems of the organisation and the capability it has to meet the new conditions, while ensuring the organisation is still achieving its purpose. Whilst not only being able to construct the relationships between systems, the second-order and third-order consequences of those relationships will also be foreseen. This includes understanding what impacts changes in another part of the organisation, of which this entity may be part, may have on its productivity and viability over time; understanding what impacts systems may have on people. Management by example and the use of symbols are crucial tools.

At this level, the entity, for example a whole business, constitutes an accepted whole with a complete boundary within the external environment. Consequently, work at this level is associated with boundary conditions and the interactions between the environment and the entity. The objective of leadership at this level is to have the organisation maintain a productive contact with its environment – economic, social, cultural, technical, legislative, natural – as this boundary changes.

The work will involve complex organisational projects such as major information management systems and new technological or people systems. The data on which the work is based is both abstract and concrete, observable and unobservable, with a need to recognise remote, second or third-order consequences and multiple linkages between cause and effect. Negative information, the absence or non-availability of specific data, i.e., what is not there, becomes much more important and is used extensively.

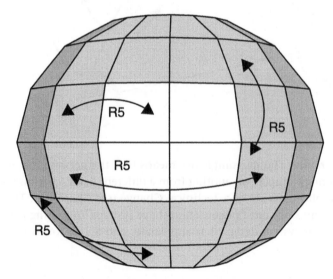

At Level V the pyramids have formed a sphere with all the apexes at the centre. We have a complete system. At this level the work involves understanding and predicting consequences and impacts of change in any one part of the system on ANY other. Thus R5 encompasses the system. We are now in the world of second-order consequences. It is interesting to hear how often politicians or leaders will refer to *unintended consequences*. They may claim 'we could never have predicted this'. They dismiss criticism by saying 'only with the benefit of hindsight'. In fact our view is that such unintended consequences are the result of poor analysis, over simplification of a complexity IV or V problem being reduced to complexity III or below. A classic example being George W Bush's comment 'Mission Accomplished' in Iraq in 2003.

LEVEL VI – COMPLEXITY VI (R6)

Box 9.6   Level VI

Shaping the organisation of the future – creating the ethic on a national and international basis that allows entities to function and manages the relationships between entities of a significantly different character.

The work at this level demands direct appreciation of and interaction with the external social, political, technical and economic environments in order to influence and mitigate any possible negative impacts on the organisation/businesses, or promote changes that will be to its advantage (Box 9.6). Essential to this is constructing an overall framework in which the relationships between fundamentally different types of organisations can be understood and managed. This may involve managing the relationships between two organisations built on very different organisational assumptions, principles and purposes, such as the relationships between a commercial company and government or a mining company and an indigenous community. It also involves the ability to form relationships by understanding sometimes very different perspectives and how they might be addressed productively. Managing this framework of relationships enables you to construct policies that influence and, if done well, enhance the organisation's reputation, often internationally. Level VI requires the ability to build mutually beneficial relationships between people from organisations with possible competing purposes. It requires the ability to construct mental models that are entirely new. It often is characterised by the ability not only to handle, but to live with, even enjoy, paradox.

Compliance with the legal framework is insufficient at this level; ethical frameworks for behaviour need to be created through the development and application of policies and systems, which will make the organisation acceptable within its environment over the long term. Such actions may well be seen as an unnecessary burden in the present. The organisation does not simply comply with local laws, such as those involving child labour or safety but sets its own (higher) standards.

Long-term goals are set and policies and corporate systems are shaped and audited to achieve them. If this work is not done well, organisations are constantly exposed to unexpected, major, destabilising problems, which distract attention and drain energy from the business. If done well, this work will add significant national and international value to a brand or reputation over time.

The work at this level is often seen as *political* and involves building constructive external relationships with relevant leaders and opinion formers. Within the organisation, leadership will be demonstrated primarily by symbolism and observable example.

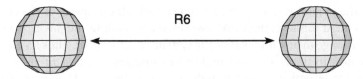

R6 looks very much like R1. However, instead of the poles being a person and their work, the poles at Level VI are made up of level five entities.

LEVEL VII – COMPLEXITY VII (R7)

Box 9.7 Level VII

Sustaining a successful long-term future by understanding, predicting and influencing world-wide trends that will affect the viability of the organisation.

The work at this level entails comprehending the fundamental forces driving changes in the environment (national and international). These are worldwide trends that affect economic, social, political, technological, environmental and intellectual forces as they come to bear far into the future. On the basis of that understanding, predictive hypotheses are developed to position the multinational or major organisation or corporation; working at Level VII involves taking account of these fundamental forces, constructing long-term plans and actions for the organisation's growth and viability. This will involve the creation of new Level V entities and the winding down of existing Level V entities pre-emptively as a result of the development of institutions, relationships and interactions within societies and technologies. The work at this level of complexity requires the ability to appreciate the unknowability of future worldwide contexts and to allow for this in generating the various possibilities, which can be realised, for your own organisation; providing goods and services for potential, entirely new, markets well into the future.

Leadership of an organisation at this level entails the creation of an ethical framework that will allow the organisation to thrive in its various social environments: *we have to do what is right*. There is a demonstrated concern for the whole of society and not just narrow self-interest in the behaviour of the organisation and its people. The setting of the ethical framework may be for a whole sector (non-governmental agencies, banks, manufacturing), and not just for their own corporation.

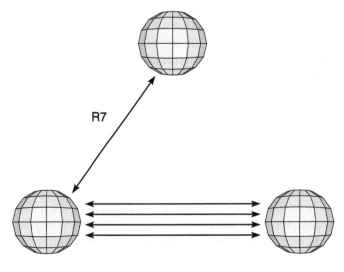

R7 looks very much like R2 except now the person is reflecting upon ways of building level VI complexity, mutually beneficial relationships. We are now generating theory.

LEVEL VIII AND ABOVE – COMPLEXITY VIII (R8 +)

Box 9.8   Level VIII

Creating worldwide institutions that enable fair governance on global issues: conflict or climate change.

We can continue to describe ever more complex work and relationships. Technically we can do this ad infinitum through the diagrams. We may be able to describe the work but it is ever more difficult to find examples of people who can actually work at such levels.

Level VIII complexity is such that it requires the building of level VII and level VI organisations (See Box 9.8). In effect it is creating the worldwide institutions (systems) that can deliver justice and good government. Attempts have been made, some much more successful than others. One example is the United Nations. It is of course flawed in its own title, as the nations are representative of their own views not integrated into a transcendent organisation that operates globally. Other examples are the World Bank (etc.). We might criticise them but they are trying to address quite the most complex problems on Earth: conflict, wars, poverty, climate change and population growth.

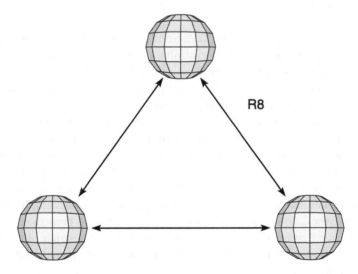

The poles at this level are represented by complex institutions and social theories of human organisation and existence.

All Levels of Work are Essential

While we can recognise the extraordinarily high Mental Processing Ability of certain individuals, and it may be interesting to speculate as to who they might be, the vast majority of us work at less exalted levels. This does not mean we have less worth as human beings; it simply means we pattern and construe the world differently and that we have differing abilities to carry out work.

The environment presents us with problems that require the application of all levels of work discussed and, perhaps, more. All these levels of work are essential if a society is to survive and thrive over time. If a problem requires Level IV capability for its solution but an MPA of II complexity capability is applied to solve it, the result is failure.

People and societies do learn from trial and error, but at a cost. With effort, time and the correct environment, a useful solution to a problem can be delivered, and providing the effect and cost of error is not too damaging to the person or the society, such a process of problem solving can be tolerated. If there is not time to learn from this process or if the results of the inadvertent experiment are too disastrous, there may be no person, business, or society left to take advantage of the result. If the environment presents a problem and there is no one who has the mental processing ability to deal with it, the society will be damaged or fail.

If businesses, government agencies and non-profit organisations are to meet their goals and survive, they must have people within their organisations who can work at the levels required to achieve their goals in their respective environments. The quality of work carried out at all levels of the organisation will determine the quality of results obtained. Thus, as human beings, we should delight in all levels of work. We all have something to contribute to the whole.

Role and Person

Under normal conditions, all work roles have minimum mental processing requirements, if the work of the role is to be performed successfully. Individuals who fill those roles, however, may or may not have an ability to match those minimum requirements. There are people in roles with requirements that exceed their mental processing abilities; others are in roles that require less than their full mental processing abilities.

The issues that surround the match, or lack of match, between the capability of the person and the complexity of the work of a role are of vital importance to the organisation, which must set up and operate systems to deal with them. For example, what does the future CEO look like in a Level II role a year or two after he or she has joined the organisation at age 24? How does this compare with another individual who will be happy and productive in a role at Level II throughout her career? These are issues for career and staff development.

These are not issues, however, which bear upon the concepts embedded in the levels of work complexity save that overriding concept of work being a construct of the human mind as it seeks to build order from the chaos of the environment in which the individual is performing the work.

The level of work of a role does not tell you much about the MPA of the role incumbent. If the person is successful in role, it is safe to assume they have the required knowledge, skills, application and MPA. Beyond this minimum, the role the person currently fills tells you little about the person's MPA. Should you have the opportunity to examine closely the work a person is doing in a role, how he or she does the work and why it is done that way, you can make a judgement about the MPA the person brings to the role. This is not, however, a simple exercise and it is *always a judgement*, not a certain determination. This is a very good thing because it makes it clear we cannot pigeonhole people based on their current job. Because the question is always open, the intrinsic humanity of the individual is easier for all to respect.

It is important that the terminology must always be 'a person in a Level II role' and never a 'Level II person' (see Box 9.9).

Another Perspective

Another way of looking at complexity and level of work is to think about what it is reasonable to expect from someone in that role. As we have discussed there will be occasions where the person in the role has a higher mental processing ability than is currently required. However, here we might look at what it is reasonable to expect from anyone in that role if they are doing the work appropriately.

One way to think about this is to consider what might happen in the case of a disaster or a serious safety incident. What questions would it be reasonable to put to somebody in a particular role?

If we consider a Level I role then it would be reasonable to ask the person if they followed procedures that they had been trained in. For example we might say ask: 'When the dial went into the red zone did you shut the valves four and five as in the operating procedure? Did you then inform the supervisor and other operators that this procedure has not reduced the temperature and the situation was becoming extremely dangerous?' If the person has been trained and followed all the procedures as taught then, even though a disaster may have resulted, it would be unfair to attribute blame to the person in the level I role; after all they did their work.

It is also an interesting characteristic that in level I roles we do not ask people to write reports or formally propose written recommendations. In such roles we ask people to complete forms or make verbal recommendations.

However, at Level II expectations change. We might reasonably ask somebody in a Level II role as to whether such incidences had occurred previously. We might ask what their views were with regard to the operating systems and procedures including whether they had reviewed them and what, if any, formal recommendations they had made with regard to improvement. We would expect such person in a Level II role to have collected data as well as implemented training procedures for operators.

In a Level III role we would ask the incumbent as to what analyses they have done with regard to all data with regard to operating procedures and practices and if they had identified from such data a systemic problem and reported formally with regard to the possible cause of that system problem.

In the Level IV role we would reasonably be asking questions about how this operating system was designed and modified in the light of other systems perhaps in the Social or Commercial Domains and what impact they thought the systems had on each other. We would ask what design work had they done to mitigate any negative interactive effects.

In a Level V role it would be reasonable to ask questions about second-order consequences; had they been identified, if not why not? What about the design of all of the systems throughout the organisation including how they all interact with each other? Is the techno-logy used inherently stable? Thus we can consider complexity in the context of what is it reasonable to ask a person to manage and address. Expectations differ in kind and the nature as we worked through levels indicating the discontinuous nature of work.

We are not alone in using a discontinuous model. We reproduce a table from Levels of Abstraction in Logic and Human Interaction (refer to Box 6.2) which comprises various items.

Table 9.1   Levels of Abstraction

	Gibson & Isaac Logical Analysis and Dualities	Jaques Levels of Organization and of Abstraction	Rowbottom & Billis Work Levels	Gillian Stamp Assessment of Managerial Capacity	Ian Macdonald Assessment of Mental Handicap	Summary Generalization
Level One	T and F refer to unambiguous behavioural entities, T being used concretely in that it is strictly behavioural, that is associated with an object actually discriminated by a subject: if P (a 'statement' in the sense of an actual response) is T (accepted) then $\sim P$ is F (rejected) and vice versa. This sample behavioural acceptance–rejection (go–no go) pattern, however, is seen as expressing the mutual exclusion and exhaustive alternation in the ambiguity of the and/or connectives.	Perceptual–concrete relation with prescribed task. Working relationship that of a person working in a concrete manner to transform a thing or to produce an effect on another person. No manager–subordinate relationship. May be collateral working together, but not with one person accountable for the work of another. (P → thing, person-thing)	Prescribed output: working towards objectives which can be completely specified (as far as is significant) beforehand, according to defined circumstances which may present themselves.	Concrete rule-obeying: rules are immediately obeyed. Prime focus of behaviour is to relate abstract shapes to concrete objects. No ambiguity is perceived and uncertainty is strictly limited by translating the abstract into the concrete. Frequent use of the exclusive 'either/or' when discussing solutions.	Externally fixed goal and plan: person very concretely tied to a particular goal and plan as completely prescribed by someone else. Dominated by uncertainty without external help.	Emphasis is upon concreteness, intuition, and uncertainty. The goals of activities are given in concretely prescribed form. Strict rules and procedures are either provided or assumed. The relationship with the object of activity is direct and concrete. Work is by the immediate process of operation upon the object, usually referred to as skill. This skill is based upon the 'touch and feel' of the situation, that is to say, it operates by intuition, by induction, within an externally given context. Based upon intuition, the situation is one of considerable uncertainty.
Level Two	The basic truth tables are introduced: the duality between the 'and' ($\wedge$) and 'or' ($\vee$) conjunctions is taken as having become explicit, and is joined by the at this level implicit duality between the 'if-then' ($\rightarrow$)' and the 'if-and-only-if ($\leftrightarrow$)' conjunctions. Level 2 thus introduces explicit ambiguity.	Imaginal–concrete, with specific tasks and solutions imaginally (ambiguously) dealt with. Manager gets work done through subordinates; or professional works with clients within a general objective. Relationship in which one person experiences uncertainty of being accountable for another person (a subordinate) achieving a transformation in a thing or client. (P → thing, person-thing)	Situational response: carrying out work where the precise objectives to be pursued are ambiguous and have to be judged according to the needs of each specific concrete situation which presents itself.	Judgement and action within rules: Rules seen as limiting the context within which judgment and action will be taken. Awareness of ambiguity emerges but the capacity to tolerate uncertainty is limited and ambiguity is handled by separating situations one from another.	Externally fixed goal and flexible plans: if a fixed goal is externally set, person can deal with ambiguities in flexibility of his own plan for reaching that goal.	Ambiguity enters into the situation in the form of incompletely specified goals or means. The ambiguity is handled by a flexible use of rules (deductive context) within which intuitive inductive process can be used to fill out the objectives and needs of each concrete situation. Each activity is handled in its own right. The flexible use of rules, and the elimination of complete dependence upon intuitive inductive process, gives greater certainty than at level 1.
Level Three	Truth tables are extended in the usual way, now making it possible to make a qualitative jump to the use of truth tables as such. The conjunctions or implicit duality arise out of relational statements between the items in the truth table columns. The ($\rightarrow$ and $\leftrightarrow$) duality is now shown to be explicit, but at a higher level of denotation and connotation in dealing with relations between truth table columns and not just with items from each column. The operations on the extended truth tables are shown to be irreversible, so that level 3 takes on the quality of a system of items occurring in uni-directional series from which extrapolations can now be made.	Conceptual-scanning operating through serial scanning. Manager in control of a unit in which he works through two rows of individuals; or professional working without externally set objectives; the situation is sufficiently concrete for them to know all the members or clients, and all that is going on, by serial scanning and extrapolation. (tree diagram: person or person-thing)	Systematic service provision: making systematic provision of services of some given kinds shaped to the needs of a continuous series or sequences of concrete situations which present themselves.	Extrapolation from a given rule as a starting point for the development of systems of solution for a serialist approach to the problem. Assumption that the solution will emerge in time. Uncertainty not seen as a potential resource for action but as defining the limits of the system for solution. 'If-then' statements often used as a basis for a serialist approach to solution.	Goal and plan self-established: person now able to set own goals and plans, but can cope only by establishing rigidly fixed system in which he proceeds serially through each successively fixed step towards that goal.	Emphasis in all the data is now upon activities occurring seriatim. The work remains concrete in the sense that each task is specifically given, or in the use of the logical analysis each specific truth table item can still be used. But system introduced, giving a feeling of maximum certainty and allowing for extrapolation from the trend of specific instances taken serially.

Level Four	The new implicit duality arises out of the use of truth table columns as sets, and the relations are now between the truth table columns themselves. Individual T and F items are absorbed into these columnar sets. With the disappearance of individual items, genuine innovation begins, and the implicit duality being that between the concept of relationship itself and the terms or poles of that relationship. Thus, at level 4, intuitive generalization emerges and behaviour becomes intuitively abstract in the innovative sense of detachment from specific items.	Abstract modelling, with genuine innovation. A manager can no longer know all his subordinate staff, nor a professional all his clients, nor can they serially scan all that is going on. Anonymity begins, and genuine innovation. Similar to the fact that in the columnar sets of level 4 not all the terms of the sets can be known: imaginative innovation from general principle becomes essential.	Comprehensive service provision: making comprehensive provision of services of some given kinds according to the total and continuing needs for them throughout some given territorial organizational society (rather than concrete extrapolation). Application of intuitive judgment to detect gaps in service.	Search for and maintenance of a pattern for a rule structure. Hypotheses explicitly stated in general form and tested. Negative information can be used after a hypothesis has been built. Phrases like 'as well as, not instead of are used as a means of acknowledging both sides of an issue or two possible strategies.	Own fixed goal but flexible plan: behaviour now sufficiently generalized to be able to set own goal but to keep it fixed, while adapting flexibility to unanticipated obstacles (i.e. the unknown).	A distinct and important change in the focus of activity. All the concrete items of activity can no longer be known. The individual is thrown back upon the use of inductive generalizations related only to particular examples of the concrete case. Recourse must be made to hypotheses about the unknown (identification of gaps), and the testing of hypotheses. The level of true abstraction and innovation has emerged, with increase in uncertainty as compared with level three.
Level Five	The analysis moves to the most general universe of discourse. The truth table analysis becomes that of relations between the columns combined into classes of columnar sets. The shift is now to a predicate calculus, the implicit universal introduced being that between the universal quantifier ($\forall$) and the existential quantifier ($\exists$), giving an underlying intuitive foundation of implicit theory—the relationship between the universal and the particular—in a 'specified domain. At level 5, the analysis thus returns to level 1 but in a general and encompassing form in that at level 1 T and F are implicitly or intuitively used, whereas level 5 starts and defines in principle how T and F are to be used.	Work by use of theory and theory construction, including concern for overall nature of enterprise. A manager has innovative subordinates, and is two levels removed from the level-3 manager who is still able to be in direct contact with the shop and office floor. The level-5 manager must be capable of working with universal principles, or theories, within which he can contain the general principles used by his subordinates in their work.	Comprehensive field coverage: making comprehensive provision of services within some general field of need throughout some given territorial or organizational society, i.e. the domain is now universalized.	Rule-making: Individuals will define the situation for themselves. Disorder may be deliberately induced and uncertainty welcomed as a possible source of further information. The importance of the not known as a possible source of information is often stressed and the necessity of being sensitive to things which do not happen. Negative information is readily formulated and used.	Own flexible goal and plan: person now able to function towards tasks as generalizable domains, i.e. to shift either or both the goal or the paths, depending on the particular circumstances which may obtain.	Emphasis changes to intuitive relationship with the universal—with theory construction or general rule-making—to be applied in relation to particular cases in a comprehensive domain. Uncertainty again dominates, as in level 1, because of the inductive intuitive relationship with the universal. This level completes the total system, for it exhausts the particular universe of discourse within which the five levels may be applied.

Box 9.9   Appropriate Terminology

The appropriate terminology is to refer to 'a person in a Level II (or III, or IV, and so on) role'. *Never* a 'Level II person' or a 'Level V person'. That form of description is both insulting and demonstrates ignorance of the theory.

Conclusion

Thus, in summary, what we are saying is that as people work, each pathway they develop to achieve a goal is unique. There are, however, patterns common to the differing pathways that allow them to be sorted into discrete groups, or levels of work. The levels of work are discrete because the problem-solving methodologies employed by individuals up to their own personal maximum ability are discrete. Because we need to make goods or services, we formulate tasks, and each task will have a complexity for its resolution based on the degree of variance in the chaos that needs to be resolved for the task to be successfully completed. The mental processing ability of the person who identifies and performs the work of the task will determine the complexity of the work. If this complexity is equal to or greater than the inherent complexity of the task, the resolution will be successful.

At higher levels of the hierarchy, the pathways needed to formulate and to accomplish a task will be constructed in less certain conditions relative to tasks at lower levels. In general, as one moves from one level of work to the next, complexity increases in that:

- there are more variables to take into account;
- more of the variables are intangible;
- there is an increasing interaction of variables;
- results are further into the future;
- the links between cause and effect are extended in time, space and logic;
- apparently negative information (what is absent or does not occur) assumes more importance;
- the achievement of the objective may require the *simultaneous* ordering of variables from more than one knowledge field.

We must recognise that the patterns we have described are incomplete. Although it is tempting to want precise descriptions that would allow us to place everyone in their specific box, such an ability would be disastrous for human freedom and the ability to control one's destiny. Of necessity, the descriptions of the patterns of complexity resolution apply to identified problems. They do not apply to the process of the thinking that identifies the problem and its potential solution while this is in progress. That would require describing what was going on inside somebody's head while it was happening, the thought process itself. We are left with the need to draw inferences after the event. The investigative studies conducted by Isaac and O'Connor (1978) and others have produced data that shows a set of definite discontinuities, but even here the descriptors are at best a result of viewing through a glass darkly.

Instead we describe what are, we believe, transient patterns in the chaos, rather like clouds. Although no two clouds are alike, we can recognise the patterns of cumulus, cirrus, stratus or cumulo-nimbus clouds. The same is true of levels of work. No two people are alike, but with practise we can learn to recognise the patterns of complexity resolution they demonstrate. We can never be certain of our judgement, but we can do this well enough to select people for organisational roles more effectively than we can without this knowledge.

Essentially what we are providing is a language to describe differences probably already familiar to managers and others who have had the experience of working with people and assigning work. It does not take long to appreciate that some are more capable than others, and, what is more, they stay that way. This description is made easier when there is a language to describe the differences in complexity. The levels of work described are only a summary. These levels of work have been identified in several different research studies, and they have been tested in practice in business, governmental and voluntary associations.

Box 9.10   The Importance of a Person's Worth

We cannot overemphasise the danger of equating MPA with the worth of a person. A person's worth, in our view, is not calculated just by how 'clever' they are, and we must not confuse an organisational hierarchy of work with hierarchy of worth. People contribute much, much more than intellectual ability to life and society. (For the dangers of misuse, see Freedman, 2016.)

We also stress that we have talked about a meritocratic, managerial hierarchy based upon a hierarchy of complexity of work. Not all work has to be done in a managerial hierarchy; not all organisations are appropriately managerial hierarchies. Churches, universities and law firms/partnerships, for example, are properly organised in different ways, but all will need to understand the complexity of work to be done and who is able to do it. For examples of descriptions of work at different levels, please refer to the website www.maconsultancy.com.

10 *Organisational Structure and Authorities*

Levels of Work and Organisational Levels

In much of the management literature, the structure of an organisation is treated as 'boxes on a chart' – only vaguely related to 'how things really work around here'. As a result, structure is often perceived as an impediment rather than an opportunity to clarify roles, relationships and authorities.

We argue that, when an organisation is established to achieve a purpose, that structure is the framework for the distribution of authority and work. Structure involves vertical, horizontal and diagonal relationships. The vertical, or managerial, structure forms the spine of the organisation, though it often gets muddled because most organisations of any size not only have managerial roles, but also have ranks or salary grades. These are often confused with managerial levels – thus the excess layering found in many large organisations. As a result of such muddles hierarchies have been and are, criticised as being messy, cumbersome, stultifying to their employees, slow, and inefficient.

Here we make an argument for a set of ground rules that have been tested in many organisations and found to improve their efficiency and effectiveness as well as improving the quality of working life for their employees.

The appreciation of the qualitative differences in levels of work as shown in Chapter 9, the differences in Mental Processing Abilities, explains, we believe, why the hierarchical structure has remained so prevalent over centuries even when the actual designs have deep and recognised flaws.

The logic is as follows:

Box 10.1   The Logic of Stratification

1. Work is the process of turning intention into reality.
2. To do this work individuals must use their mental processing ability in order to make choices as to what will achieve their purpose and then act upon those choices to bring the purpose (intention) into reality.
3. People have different ways of processing information and solving problems.
4. There is a pattern to the differences in the ways human beings process information.
5. If one wishes to get work accomplished (as required in any organisation), it makes sense to structure the organisation in a way that is in accord with the different ways that people go about their work.

When Designing the Organisation we need to be clear about

PURPOSE

To structure any organisation requires a clear understanding of its purpose and objectives.

CREATING THE VERTICAL STRUCTURE

Once the purpose is clear, the levels of work must be reflected in the vertical structure of the organisation. Each level of work corresponds to a different level of work complexity. In organisations employing a number of people doing a range of work, we have found the levels of work can form a vertical structure that allows the best use of human capability because they reflect the distribution of Mental Processing Ability (MPA).

The organisational levels reflect the qualitatively different mental processing abilities found in the population. Each organisational level requires the creation of pathways of complexity unique to that level. As one moves up the organisational hierarchy, the complexity of these pathways increases. The complexity of the work required of the chief executive of the organisation establishes the top level of the organisation.

We can then consider how many levels are required based on the complexity of the work to be done. For example, if the CEO must work with the fifth level of complexity (Level V) and the products are produced by workers in a traditional factory at Level I, the organisation requires five levels of work. As we will show further on, this means there will be four levels of managers, including the CEO. In another organisation, the CEO may work in Level V, but the output of the business is carried out at Level III. In this case there would be a need for three levels of work.

The work required by a specific organisation depends upon its purpose and the complexity of work to achieve that purpose. A shoeshine stand may require only one relatively simple level of work, while a large public agency or corporation might require seven or in the largest organisations, eight levels of work such as the Chairman of the Joint Chiefs of Staff of the U.S. Military. Partnerships, a form of association, usually have no more than three levels of professional work – for example a law firm with associates, partners, and senior partners.

PLACING A WORK ROLE AT THE CORRECT LEVEL

A role can be conceived of as a bundle of tasks. Placing a role in an organisational level is an executive decision that should be based on an understanding of the level of work required to effectively handle the bundle of tasks in that role. If the level of work of the core tasks is judged to be Complexity III, then it should be placed in Level III even though it will have an array of tasks including some of I and II complexity. It is the complexity of the core tasks which should determine placement in an organisational level.

MATCHING PERSON TO ROLE

To be effective in a role at any specific work level, individuals must be able to work at the required level of complexity. They must have the capability (knowledge, social and technical skills, application, mental processing ability) to carry out the work.

They must also have an understanding of the next level up, that is, they must be able to follow the processes involved in the next higher level of work, and critique and contribute to that work but not be able (as yet) to act effectively in the higher role or take accountability for it. This understanding is part of the basis for communication and teamwork.

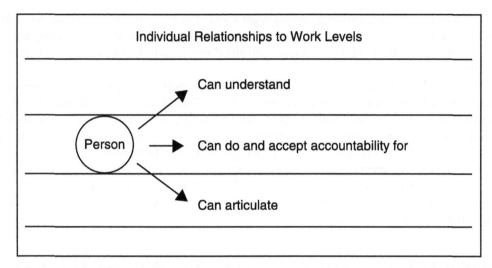

Figure 10.1 Individual Relationships to Work Levels

Similarly, to be effective, a person must also be able to fully articulate and encompass the next level down – have a complete understanding of the processes involved in creating pathways such that they can teach and/or delegate work. This does not mean a manager must have all the technical expertise of his or her direct reports. It does mean she or he must be able to articulate the tasks, their context and purpose, so that the direct reports can use their expertise effectively to achieve organisational purposes.

SIGNIFICANCE OF COMPLEXITY OF WORK LEVELS FOR ORGANISATION DESIGN

The work levels form a depth structure for employment hierarchies. They form the vertical skeleton for an effectively functioning organisation. The skeleton is based on two principles:

1. Managers are placed and are able to work at one work level above their direct reports.
2. In a single chain of command, there is never more than one manager within a given work level.

For an individual to add value as a manager of a direct report, he or she must be able to do work of different and higher complexity from the direct report. This broader horizon allows him/her to set the context for his/her direct reports and thereby provide a stabilised and understandable environment to allow the direct reports' work to proceed.

The manager's work must be significantly different from his or her direct reports, if he or she is to add significant value by articulating the work to be done by the direct report and by ordering the direct reports' work environment. There must also be enough difference in the ability to handle complexity to justify the manager's authorities consistent with a managerial relationship.

Research has shown that people in the hierarchy who are said to be the 'real boss' are people who are perceived to do qualitatively different work and to have a range of authorities in relationship to their direct reports. The common elements in this range of authorities are the VARI authorities described further on.

Too much difference between the manager's and direct report's work also causes difficulties because the direct report will not be able to understand the manager's perspective. The manager, in turn, becomes impatient with the direct report's lack of understanding and inability to 'keep up'.

Whether the distance between manager and direct report is too great or too small, the result is a work environment that is not well ordered. There is a waste of effort and energy because direct reports are frequently unsure about what they are to do and which factors are within or outside their authority. Management must reduce uncertainty and anxiety by taking accountability for the environment within which their direct reports work.

This can only be accomplished when there is neither more nor less than one work level difference between manager and direct report. This allows each individual to understand the work above, generate and accept accountability for the work at his or her own level, and articulate the work below.

Benefits Associated with Getting the Organisational Structure Correct

- Removing excess managerial layers clears the decks making possible other benefits as well, such as cost reduction.
- Priorities can be set because the manager has a larger perspective than his/her direct reports.
- Direct Reports gain a clearer understanding of what is expected of them.
- Direct Reports are given an opportunity to use their full capabilities in exercising discretion in roles which are the right size – neither too difficult nor too simple.
- Role relationships can be regularised with no need for bypassing to get adequate direction for work.
- Information systems can be targeted to the right level of work, avoiding excessive monitoring, reporting and other such time wasters.
- It also provides people within the organisation an opportunity to increase order in their social and working lives – to create conditions that meet human needs for predictability, meaning and purpose.

MANAGERIAL AND PROFESSIONAL WORK

When it is recognised that it is the complexity of work which determines the level of work, it becomes obvious that technical specialists or professionals may do work at the same levels of complexity as that done by managers. In each work level there may be a need for high level technical work as well as managerial work depending upon the goals of the organisation.

The unfortunate practice of requiring expert engineers, computer scientists, geologists, police officers and other technical specialists to enter managerial roles if they wish to be promoted creates a situation where important technical work does not get done (or is done badly) because there is no one available at the higher levels to do it. Organisations that place technical specialists in a level commensurate with the complexity of work they must perform (with pay and recognition comparable to managers in the same work level) have a significant competitive advantage.

Such professionals may at times work as stand-alone independent contributors (IC) doing the high level direct output work, or they may have a few (three to six maximum) direct reports to assist them with their direct output. When ICs have direct reports, they must manage those direct reports, but the managerial workload is lighter allowing them to carry on their professional work.

To reinforce understanding of this equality of work and to maintain the depth structure of the organisation, it is useful to assign titles to roles that indicate the level of work and whether or not the role is managerial or professional. Such titles should be picked with care since they become drivers of the principal function of the role. The examples shown below provide an example of how titles might be structured, though in different societal and organisational cultures different titles may be chosen. The principle is that titles should indicate whether they are managerial or professional contributor roles and at what level they are assigned.

MRU stands for Mutual Recognition Unit. Some organisations prefer to call any three level organisation under a single manager an MRU whatever the level of the work. Output Team may refer to any two level part of the organisation under a single manager. This reminds managers at all levels about the necessary social processes required.

Titles for Level V Business Unit – Examples			
Work Level	**Organization**	**Manager**	**Professional**
V	Business Unit	Vice President	**Corporate** [Corporate Human Res Cons] [Corporate IS Tech Cons]
IV	Division	General Manager	**Chief** [Chief Applied Technology] [Chief Organization Advisor] [Chief, PC Technology]
III	MRU or Unit	Unit Manager	**Principal** [Prinicipal Personnel Advisor] [Prinicipal Syst. Programmer]
II	Output Team or Service Team	Superintendent	**Specialist** [Operations Sched. Spec.] [Applications Devel. Spec.]
I	Crew		**Supervisor*** **Operator/Clerk** [Printer Operator] [Library Clerk]

* Not a managerial role.

Figure 10.2   Titles for Level V Business Unit – Examples

PROFESSIONS, TITLES AND MPA

No matter their education, most people begin their working lives in a role at Level I. Even people with a professional education in law, medicine, engineering, social work, financial analysis, architecture, etc., begin in roles with a short time-span even though the complexity of the work may fully use their capabilities. As they move up, their title may or may not reflect the level of work they are actually accomplishing.

Some technical specialists are not particularly interested or good at leading people, yet in order to get to the level of work commensurate with their abilities, they are required to become managers. It will be more productive to place people at the level of work appropriate to their capabilities, and not confuse technical skills with social process skills or MPA.

An important point here is to note that a title does not tell you what level of work an individual is actually carrying out. It tells you what the role requires, not the MPA of the role incumbent.

GETTING THE HORIZONTAL STRUCTURE RIGHT

Once one eliminates the excessive layering of the vertical structure caused by the muddling of managerial levels and salary grades, it is relatively simple to get it right. Relationships which define the horizontal structure must be clear and authorised if the organisation is to achieve its purposes and survive and thrive in the market place. This is also true of public agencies, which must perform certain essential functions, as must businesses, if they are to exist at all.

There are three mainstream functions that are customer-focused and 'do' the business. All must be present, though one or two may be purchased from the outside, and all three may vary in size and scope depending upon the nature of the organisation. There are also two sustaining functions, which are internally focused to support and improve the mainstream functions.

Box 10.2   Three Essential Business Functions:

OPERATIONS, SERVICE AND SUPPORT

Operations are the Mainstream Business Functions

- **Produce** a product/service to meet customer needs
- **Sell** product/service to customers
  - Inform customers about products and their qualities and capabilities
  - Discover customer needs for which business might provide products
  - Negotiate agreements to meet customer needs
- **Service** work underpins the productive capacity of business
  - Account for, and control corporate financial resources
  - Maintain corporate resources
  - Keep the business up and running
  - Assure continuity of business
- **Support** work improves the productive capacity of business
  - Identify, evaluate, implement better ways of operating or servicing the business, give advice as to improvement
  - Improve work flows and processes
  - Improve technical processes
  - Research and develop new products/services

Note: All employees have some operational, service and support components to their job. Every employee is expected to use her resources productively. Every employee is expected to use his resources properly and maintain them in good order. Every employee is expected to continually seek to find a better way of using or maintaining the resources.

ALL ROLES REQUIRE CLEAR AUTHORITIES

The structural principles presented here are all based on authority that is distributed throughout the organisation. As we explained in Part1 *every* role must have authority, for without it work can only be done on the basis of power. Also if people in roles have no discretion, they are in effect no more than machines. Apart from the ethical problem this poses (see Part 1), it is a waste of resources because people do not make good machines and their abilities transcend those of machines.

Authority is not, therefore, the prerogative of leaders alone but a necessary component of every role, if real work is to be done. There is authority in peer relationships. There is authority from team members towards team leaders. Our proposition is twofold:

1. Every role should have clear, explicit authority.
2. This authority should be allocated on the basis of the work to be done in each role.

Because organisations are established to achieve a purpose, we are confronted by a situation where:

- there is some clearly defined work to be done by someone;
- they need authority to do it – and this needs to be explicit; and
- there should be someone else whose work includes determining whether and how well the assigned work has been done and what consequences, good or bad, follow.

All too often we have found that the above conditions do not exist. People are unclear what they are really meant to be doing; they are unclear about what authority they have and are even unclear about who they report to. We have had this lack of clarity praised and lauded to us as 'flexible' or 'democratic' and allowing for 'creativity'. In our experience such organisations are riddled with power and have a hidden rigidity. Personal agendas and implicit rules cause damage to all but the brightest or strongest. It is interesting to hear some critics of hierarchy and authority implicitly supporting and encouraging the law of the jungle – survival of the fittest. We do not regard this as a just or effective way of achieving purpose and releasing potential.

We argue that to be effective not only should all roles have authority but as some roles appear in many organisations or many times in one organisation they can be categorised generally. We have found five vertical relationships in employment hierarchies, while there are many horizontal relationships. The basic vertical role is that of *manager*.

What is a Manager?

There are almost as many definitions of a manager as there are managers. Unfortunately, most of them do not clearly distinguish between those who have leadership work to do, and those who do not. Using the many common definitions manager, it is difficult to determine who in the organisation is a manager and who is not.

> **Box 10.3   Definition of Manager**
>
> *Manager:* A person held accountable for his or her own work and for the work performance over time of people reporting to him or her.

If one wants to build an organisation in which each employee may be fairly called to account for his or her work, it is essential to have a precise definition, as it is the manager's work to hold people accountable for the quality of their work performance. It is essential that everyone know who is accountable for what and to whom (see Box 10.3).

This definition excludes all persons in an organisation who do not have people reporting to them. A managerial role is pre-eminently a leadership role. As we have said, the distinctions made by some scholars between 'leaders', who are visionary and charismatic, and 'managers', who are rather dull drones, is both insulting to managers and seriously destructive of improved management practice and hence leadership.

If you are a manager, you are a leader of people. You have no choice in this matter. Your only choice is whether to become a good leader or a bad leader. To be fully effective a manager must work at one level above his or her direct reports and thus be able to articulate and fully encompass the work of the next level down.

For managers to accept that they will be called to account for the work performance of others, they must have certain minimum authorities that relate to the work of those others. These authorities must always be exercised within company policy and the laws of the land. By definition authority is never without limits. There are constraints on the authority an organisation can grant to its managers, and there are further, and often more subtle, constraints based upon the acceptance of a manager's authority by their team members.

Managers need to behave within, and act through, authority systems within limits that are subject to review if they are to be effective over time. Their ability to act derives from a clear grant of authority from the organisation that needs to hold role incumbents accountable for the proper exercise of that authority. It must be recognised, however, that authority is not only limited by organisation policies, but also has limits that are beyond the ability of the organisation to control easily. Failure to exercise this control leads to abuse by power and in time creates the need for unions and regulatory legislation.

The work of a manager is critically concerned with people. Accountability, when it applies effectively, is an integral element of the social relationship, that is, part of the social process that exists between a manager and the people who report to him or her. The manager's work involves reviewing, recognising and rewarding work performance of team members, which only makes sense if the manager can actually assign tasks. Further, it makes sense that, if managers are to be accountable for the team's work performance, they must have some say in who is a member of the team and who stays in or leaves the team. The proposition is simple, if a person does *not* have these authorities, they will not feel it is fair to be called to account for the work performance of their team members. The converse is also likely to be true, providing they have the appropriate capability. Jaques, Rowbottom and Billis and others at BIOSS (Brunel) have articulated this need and the authorities they arrived at were further developed and refined in work with CRA (now Rio Tinto) under Sir Roderick Carnegie in the 1980s.

The authorities represented in Figure 10.3 are the minimum required by managers if they are to accept accountability for the work performance of team members. The VAR[3]I authorities are the foundation underlying the definition of the term 'manager'.

Manager–Direct report relationships

V - Veto selection

A - Assign Tasks

R³ - Recognise, review and reward work
     performance differentially

I - Initiate removal from role

Figure 10.3   Authorities of a Manager

V: *Veto selection.* A manager may veto the selection of a new team member. In practice this means that the manager who is exercising the veto cannot be required to accept an employee whom the manager believes, with cause, would be unwilling or unable to contribute positively to the work of the team. [A manager who has direct reports placed on the team against his or her will cannot be fairly called to account for their work performance.]

It is important to note the difference between the authority to veto and the authority to select. Even when a manager is authorised to select a person for a role in an employment hierarchy, that selection is subject to veto by his or her manager, the manager-once-removed, manager-twice-removed, and so on. Veto means you do not have to have anyone you do not want. It does not mean you can always have your first choice.

It is also important to note that the veto is an authority and must be exercised within policy limits that include no unfair discrimination. A manager who seeks to abuse the authority to veto selection to role is rapidly exposed by his or her manager monitoring the sequence of vetoes and requiring an explanation for a skewed statistical distribution, e.g., a consistent veto of female or minority candidates for role.[1]

A: *Assign tasks.* This is the authority to assign tasks to direct reports. No one else in the organisation may assign tasks to a manager's reports unless they first gain the approval of the person's manager. (See Chapter 19 for tasks with an inset trigger where it may appear others are assigning tasks, but in fact the person is responding as his or her manager has authorised.)

R³: *Recognise, review and reward work performance differentially.* The manager reviews and recognises the overall work performance of direct reports in order to improve their work performance and the manager's own work performance. Managers evaluate individual work performance and, within limits set by organisation policy, recognise and reward people differentially based on the manager's judgement of their work performance. No one else in the organisation may differentially reward a manager's direct reports without his or her approval. We do not just rely on reward such as money but note how significant review, feedback and non-monetary recognition are in influencing behaviour.

In the application of differential recognition, it is important to acknowledge its significance – public recognition, special assignments, public representation of the company at events, etc. The focus should not be entirely on money, though obviously these are very important. It is essential that recognition of poor work performance is also the work of the manager and

---

1   The authority to select without a veto being available to someone else, and the authority to dismiss, does exist for the owner-manager of a small business. He or she, however, must still operate within the limits set by law or wind up in court.

must be timely done. All the other team members know if a person is delivering a poor work performance, and lack of recognition of this by the manager demonstrates either incompetence or a lack of courage. (As one angry employee wrote, 'Manager X either has no guts or no brains.') It also degrades the worth of any recognition they receive for good work performance.

I: *Initiate removal from role.* This authority means a manager is not required to keep a non-performing member of his or her team after the requirements of organisational policy have been met. The manager will be required to give valid and fair reasons for initiating removal from role, and the person to be removed must have been given proper warning and offered adequate help and opportunity to improve but has continued to deliver poor work performance.

The process is iterative as the manager's manager (M+1) may ask the manager (M) to take specific actions to coach and counsel a person whose performance is not satisfactory. This is done to ensure fairness and, where necessary, to determine a case for dismissal. When all company policies regarding warnings and help have been given, M+1 may not require M to keep a person who is not satisfactory.

Once the person is removed from a particular role, the M+1 must decide if the person is to be transferred to another role within his or her organisation (subject to the veto of the manager who is to take this person into their team), or is to be removed from the organisation (see Figure 10.4). In some organisations M+1 recommends dismissal to M+2 who decides whether or not to dismiss.

M+1 MANAGER-ONCE-REMOVED RELATIONSHIP TO MANAGER'S DIRECT REPORT

The same constraints determine the reality of the authority held by the manager-once-removed as those that determine the authority of the manager, namely: law of the land, corporate policy, social custom and work practices and acceptance by the team member(s).

The authorities of the manager-once-removed are:

Box 10.4 Managers' Additional Authorities

A manager may, in practice, have additional authorities – to spend money, allocate resources, sign contracts or select team members, subject to the veto of superiors – but the VAr^3I authorities are the base minimum.

If a manager lacks all the VAr^3I authorities, it must be recognised that she or he cannot be fairly held to account for the work performance of their reports over time. If the realities of corporate policy or industrial practice limit these authorities of the manager, M+1 must make adjustments to match accountability with the reality of authority limits.

Even though the organisation authorises a person to use the VAr^3I authorities, there are still limits on their right to veto appointment and initiate removal from role. There are limits on the tasks they may assign to their reports. There are limits on the rewards that may be earned.

The authorities also carry with them an accountability to exercise them well. A key element in the judgement of managerial performance is how well these authorities are exercised. Decisions made in the exercise of these authorities by a manager are subject to appeal to M+1.

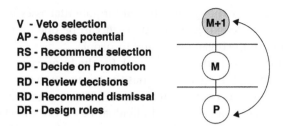

V - Veto selection
AP - Assess potential
RS - Recommend selection
DP - Decide on Promotion
RD - Review decisions
RD - Recommend dismissal
DR - Design roles

Figure 10.4   Authorities of the Manager-Once-Removed (M+1)

V: *Veto selection.* Authority to veto, in the same manner as the manager, above.

AP: *Assess potential.* This involves a judgement about an individual's capability to do higher levels of work and their potential for promotion. M will be expected to comment on potential or to recommend promotion, but the authority to decide lies with M+1. This must be the case since only M+1 is in a position to decide if P is ready to work at the level of M.

The individual whose potential is to be assessed must be informed that M+1 has this authority and is accountable for this process. M+1 needs to learn about the person's interests, knowledge fields, skills, ambitions, and the tasks on which the Manager believes P has shown his or her capability at its best. This allows the decision to be made soundly on the basis of data.

M+1 needs to discuss the assessment with the individual and learn more about the person's interests and ambitions in the light of this assessment. M+1 may indicate possible career paths, educational or training opportunities and other steps that might be taken, and their timing, to allow P to undertake self-improvement more effectively. This assessment should indicate when the organisation should be taking steps to provide developmental opportunities to P, taking into account M+1's assessment and P's career aspirations. The M+1 must also advise P if he or she is judged not to have any potential for promotion to a higher level. This is often, but by no means always, found to be a liberating judgement.

The process of potential assessment is difficult. It is often the case that an employee who is performing the work of the current role does not demonstrate the capability to perform tasks of a higher work complexity but nonetheless is performing very well in their current role and is keen for promotion.

It is not the purpose of the potential assessment to shatter the aspirations of good employees, but no one benefits from the appointment to a role of a person who cannot perform the work of that role. It is also unfair and dishonest to suggest that some form of development activity or course of study will overcome a shortfall in the ability to perform work of higher complexity.

A technique used in some organisations is to assign specific tasks of higher work complexity to such people. The outcome for this work serves to confirm, or disconfirm, the judgement of the M+1, and in the event of a failure serves as a vehicle for the individual to appreciate the basis of the judgement. The proviso with this approach is that the person to whom the tasks are assigned does the work without assistance from others. This includes tasks of higher complexity where the individual needs to bring others into the process and part of the task is leading others.

It is important to recognise the system applied for potential assessment needs to be carefully designed and well controlled. If poorly done, it can be one of an organisation's most damaging systems, for both the organisation and its people.

RS: *Recommend Selection.* As part of M+1's work for the improvement of overall performance and the development of P, he or she also has the authority to recommend selection to a manager to fill a role as one of his or her direct reports. The manager's authority to veto selection still applies. M+1 may recommend an individual based on knowledge of the person's capability, the belief that a particular role or project assignment will be good for the individual's development, or any other reason which is within M+1's authority and the limits of law and policy. Managers need to understand the reasons for this authority and accept its validity as part of the process of providing development opportunities for people who may be able to work successfully at the manager's level in due course.

DP: *Decide on Promotion or Upgrade.* As noted earlier, only M+1 is in a position to decide if an individual is ready to work at the level of his or her direct reports.

RD: *Review decisions.* This includes the authority to hear appeals from their manager's reports. It is necessary that everyone in the organisation know that the M+1 level has the authority of the organisation to review a manager's decisions. The manager must know this and factor it into the approach adopted when confronted with a problem. The person must know this, so neither the person nor the manager feels that the person is stabbing the manager in the back by going 'over his or her head'.

A practice adopted by several good managers we know, at the end of a discussion resulting in a decision that the direct report may not agree with, is to say, 'Now you have the authority to have my manager review this decision and possibly reverse it. You should feel free to ask for a review; that is the way we work here.'

RD: *Recommend dismissal.* The authority to initiate removal from role will, after appropriate processes, remove a person from the manager's team, but not from the organisation. The decision to dismiss from the organisation may rest at a higher level to ensure another review and fairness when someone's livelihood is to be removed.

Some organisations give M+1 the authority to dismiss; in others this lies with M+2. If it lies with M+2, then M+1 recommends dismissal. Where the authority to dismiss resides is a policy decision of the organisation.

DR: *Design roles.* The authority to design more roles (for more Ps) rests with M+1. (This includes the authority to re-design roles.) There are two main reasons for this. M+1 is in the best position to understand the context of the specific work involved and to judge whether a new role is required to undertake that work. He or she will have a better understanding of the wider business purpose and how the new role helps achieve that purpose. M+1 can ensure consistency of role design and fairness of the work volume for each role across the teams.

Notes on Sponsorship: The M+1 is sometimes called a sponsoring manager to emphasise his or her work of assessing potential and providing opportunities for an individual's development and demonstration of his or her capability.

While something like sponsorship goes on in many organisations, it is often done only for a favoured few, and it is often the vehicle for the use of power. A system of clear authority for the M+1 reduces this problem, and assists in ensuring that everyone in the organisation is able to get fair consideration from someone who should be able to discern potential capability given their role one level above the person's manager.

Authorities of the Supervisor

Although in some organisations the title 'Supervisor' refers to the first line Manager in a Level II role. In many industries the Supervisor occupies a lead role in Level I, which is how we are using the term here.

Box 10.5   Definition of a Supervisor

Supervisor. A leadership role in Level I. The leader of a crew within an output team.

Understanding the authorities of the Supervisor in relation to the Manager in Level II has been a source of contention both in theory and in practice. To clarify, we have represented the Supervisor role in Figure 10.5 including its essential authorities:

- RV: Recommend veto on selection
- A+/–: Assign tasks within limits set by M
- R3+/–: Review task work performance, recognise and reward differentially within limits set by M
- RI: Recommend initiation of removal from role.

This does not mean an intervening manager but someone in a leadership role with clear authorities as shown in Figure 10.5. What is most important, as always, is:

1. What is the work?
2. What is the authority?

In our experience, the term 'supervisor' is most often used to describe leadership work at the level of direct output of the organisation:

- the work cycle spreads across more than one shift per day;
- the desired output requires numerous identical roles;
- the manager at the level above has too many direct reports to give them day-to-day attention and the feedback they may require;
- the work can be ordered into demonstrable procedures in which people can be well trained and that do not require frequent intervention to resolve higher complexity problems and
- The nature of the work is such that a single team performing it will not generate the volume of higher complexity work required to keep a manager fully occupied in his or her role.

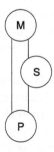

Figure 10.5   Authorities of the Supervisor

Box 10.6   Managers and Supervisors

The practice of good leadership on the part of managers requires that they make known to the crew where the limits of the supervisor's authority to assign work, and recognise differentially, are. Managers must also make clear that they will not breach these limits without letting the supervisor know, unless it is an emergency.

The same constraints on authorities that apply to managers also apply to supervisors. In addition, there are other limits on the authority of supervisor roles, which are determined by their managers in line with organisational policy – for example, a manager may not pass all of his or her authority to a supervisor.

Supervisors may have budgets for reward: a dinner, social occasion, gift voucher or presentation, but not cash. The supervisor does have the authority to recommend to the manager who should receive pay increases, or not. However, like Veto and Initiation of Removal, this is a recommendation. These authorities sometimes become confused because, if supervisors are good at their work, they may rarely, if ever, have their recommendations rejected. This does not change the authority.

It is important for managers at all levels to understand the sensitivity and subtlety of managerial and supervisory relationships. Where the organisation requires supervisory roles, the success of these relationships is crucial for the effective functioning of the organisation. It is also essential that the differences in authority and work of the roles be reflected in the systems of performance review, performance evaluation and differential reward.

A General Theory of Role Relationships

There are many other roles and role relationships with appropriate authorities, M+2, project leader (see website) also there are many other role relationships which are critical to an organisation.

In addition to the vertical work relationships that operate through a more or less clear authority regime, every organisation has many horizontal and diagonal relationships that are essential to the success of a hierarchical organisation. Diagonal relationships occur when a direct report to a manager has, for example, a working relationship with the manager's personal assistant or the manager's peer manager.

Often these authority relationships are left to chance, or are termed the 'informal' organisation. We believe this is the cause of much difficulty in organisations – the 'silo' effect; the miscommunications between individuals in different organisational units; or the unwillingness of some people at a higher level of work to work with, or in some organisations even to speak with, someone at a lower level of work.

Much is to be gained from clarification of these multiple role relationships. We have found that to be consistently productive it is useful to have a clear understanding of what a work role relationship is and the authorities that may productively exist between roles (see Box 10.7).

Work relationships are mutually interdependent. When trying to understand them, we always argue 'start with the work'. From there we can build the circumstances and systems of work relationships, and their associated authority regimes to promote the effective and

---

Box 10.7 Principles

Our major point here is that to determine working relationships the following principles need to be applied:

- Determine the work required of the people involved; be clear about expectations.
- Allocate the appropriate authorities to the people concerned clearly and openly, so all know what they are and why.
- Ensure that these authorities do not conflict with other authorities but rather take them into account. For example, ensure that the managerial relationship and project leader relationship do not conflict.
- The authority should match what is necessary to achieve the work the person is assigned and will be called to account for.

---

efficient performance of that work to the principles we outline above. We urge people to be as accurate and creative as possible within these. There is no need for the rigidity often wrongly associated with hierarchy. Authority and authoritarian are too easily and sometimes deliberately confused.

All role relationships are part of the fabric of the social processes of the organisation. The nature of authority can be fundamentally affected by the way it is exercised. The exercise of authority is subject to the same principles as described in the discussion of the work of leadership. It must take into account mythologies, current systems and capability. Whilst all managers have (or should have) the same minimum authorities, the way these authorities are exercised will be slightly, or even wildly, different, according to the person and context.

Finally, we emphasise that authority is not simply top down or even sideways or diagonal but can be upwards as well. In Chapter 15 we will look, for example, at the authority of the team member with regard to the team leader.

We have come across many situations where team members have taught their leaders technology and skills. People are not just given authority to direct or instruct. They should have the authority to negotiate, consider, teach, recommend, ask, give advice, inform. These are all significant authorities and can be distributed in many different ways according to the work to be done.

In our experience it is not authority that is the problem but rather the lack of clarity of authority, leading to the use of power. Lack of clarity is not resolved by 'being democratic' or 'flexible'; it is resolved by understanding what authority is needed either temporarily in project work or as part of a permanent role to allow the role incumbent to perform his or her work without needing to rely on the exercise of power. It is then part of the work of anyone to exercise the authority accorded to them with skilful social process.

Conclusion

We have argued that people think differently and approach problem solving in their own unique way. There are, however, patterns to these differences that can be categorised as described in the Levels of Work. Further, by following these patterns as the vertical structure of the organisation is created, your organisation will work with human nature and not struggle against it.

Three of the five vertical authority relationships are found in all organisations, and they create the stratified structure. They are, however, only part of the structural picture. The horizontal authority relationships between the essential business functions must also be understood and made clear with a much more diverse set of authorities given the diversity of the horizontal role relationships.

Whatever the eventual design, we argue that the work should be clear and known to all as should be the authority to do that work.

11 *Associations, Boards and Employment Hierarchies*

In Chapter 5 we discussed broad categories of social organisation. Here we examine many different types of organisations more specifically. A scout troop, the Anglican Church, General Motors, the City of Pasadena, the Red Cross, a Law Partnership and the Army can all be accurately described as organisations, yet their purposes, structures, financial sources, systems, leadership, members and employees (if any) all differ. It is important to distinguish them because their purpose and nature lead to appropriately different work relationships.

One common classification separates organisations into public, private and voluntary, but that is of little help in understanding in detail how they operate.

Although the tripartite classification serves some useful societal, political and tax purposes, it does not help to inform us regarding leadership, organisational structure, internal and external processes or the design of their systems. Here we separate out two concepts, those of association and employment hierarchy. These concepts have been identified by Brown (1971) and Jaques (1977). Here we describe the qualities of each, including critical issues that need to be considered if organisations are to be effective. We start with a summary.

Associations

Box 11.1 Wilfred Brown's Definition of Association

Associations are people coming together for a purpose. The purpose is either agreed tacitly or expressed in a written document. (Brown, 1971: 48)

Almost all of us are members of one or more associations. As a shareholder, you are a member of a business corporation. Many workers are members of a union. You may be a member of the Red Cross, which is a voluntary association.

The written document, providing guidance to the governance of the association, may be a constitution, a charter, and articles of incorporation or authorising legislation. Some associations such as neighbourhood groups may not have a written document or formal rules, but they will have, at a minimum, verbal agreement about who they are and *their purpose* for associating.

Box 11.2 Members are Equal

Whatever the relationships between members, each member of an association has the same authority. One share gives one vote, one citizen has one vote, or one union member has one vote. In a corporate association additional shares command additional votes.

Table 11.1 Characteristics of associations and employment hierarchies

Associations	Employment Hierarchies (Bureaucracies)
Primary	Secondary (to the Association/Board)
Independent	Dependent (on an Association)
Authority relationships based on the law, charter and social customs and practice	Authority relationships based on the law charter and the policies of the Board of Governors. Social customs and practice set some of the limits on authority
Members	Employees
Members are equals	Employees are in superior/subordinate relationships
Act through representatives who are held accountable by members	Act through employees who are held accountable by higher-level managers. Top manager held accountable by elected Board of the association
Leaders held accountable by members	Leaders hold direct reports/employees accountable
Operate through consensus, debate, persuasion, voting	Operate through executive decision processes
Set objectives and policies of the association within the authority of the charter and the law ... Where necessary seek vote of members	Receive initial objectives and policies from the association. Formulate plans and policies for Board decision/vote
Take instructions from members and advise	Listen to suggestions from subordinates, decide, assign work
Representatives, relationships collegial	Manager/subordinate relationships hierarchical
Representatives have term of office	Employees have open-ended employment contract
Members need not perform in order to remain a member; only obey rules of the association	Employees must perform or lose job

Membership in these associations has a different meaning for the members according to their commitment and the purpose of the association.

Associations operate through discussion, debate and persuasion and makes decisions on the basis of voting and/or consensus. Except in the case of very small associations, members usually elect a few of their number to be their representatives in a governing body that is authorised, usually through articles of incorporation, a charter, or authorising legislation, to act on behalf of the members. These representatives set overall association policy within the limits allowed by their charters, and when necessary, ask the membership to vote on changes that go beyond the charter or seek to amend the charter. When the workload of the association becomes too large to be handled by the Board and its members, the Board can be authorised to employ staff (employees) to carry out the association's purpose.

Figure 11.1 illustrates generic patterns of member, representative, 'governing board' and employee relationships.

In a business, the articles of incorporation set the authorities of the Board and indicate the requirements for election to the Board. Once the Board is created, shareholders must vote to accept the Board Members and annual elections are held where the shareholders must reaffirm

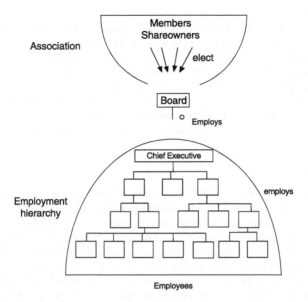

Figure 11.1   Corporate Business Structure

all or part of the Board. If an original entrepreneur controls a majority of shares, then he or she may also, in effect, control the Board.

As businesses grow, organisations have found it to be much more effective to have the entire Board made up of outside members except for the Chief Executive. Should employees subordinate to the Chief Executive be members of the Board, their work relationship with the Chief Executive can, and often does, come into conflict with their work as a Board member to represent the best interests of the owners – members of the association.

It is our position that it is preferable to have an outside chair of the Board rather than the CEO acting as chair. Again, there is a potential conflict of interest if the CEO holds both roles. In fact, these practices are now being put forward as proposed legal requirements in the US after recent abuses and scandals. In some jurisdictions it is now almost universal as it is considered to be current best practice.

Box 11.3   Essential Work of the Board: The failure of Boards to do their work effectively has had catastrophic results not least the Financial Crisis of 2008

The authority of the Board is a collective authority. Members of the Board are authorised to act as a body, not as individuals. As such, it is their work to articulate and review the purpose of the company and submit its proposal to the association for their approval that authorises the Board to organise the work required to achieve that purpose. It is the work of the Board to ensure there are policies and systems in place to maintain that purpose so that the company continues over time. This is highly significant work, even though the Board requires others to enact the policies by way of systems (this is the work of the CEO and other executives).

The Board is not there simply to ensure that the company complies with the law. It is a much wider brief and needs to be more active in assessing on-going performance to ensure the employment hierarchy is working as it is intended to work. All its activity, however, can be traced back to the fundamental work of defining the purpose and authorising on behalf of the owners, the business plan by which the purpose is to be achieved. In this way the work of the Board is consistent with our definition of work: 'turning intention into reality'. The Board's work is turning the intention of the members of the association into a functioning social reality in the world that achieves the purpose it approved. In doing so the Board must also assess risk to the purpose. Systems Leadership can provide the tools to do this through Systems and Symbols Audits, the Design of Systems and the analysis of Critical Issues. Boards that cannot see into their organisations and assess reputational risk are in danger of major disasters (see below).

Morality and Ethics

We have argued, and will argue, that higher-level work must go beyond the concrete and deal with the abstract in all its complexity. The intangible variables become more critical as the work becomes more complex. For a company to be successful, it is not just a question of having cash in the bank but also whether the company is trusted by the people it hopes and relies upon to support it. Only a company that sustains the trust of the society in which it is embedded will be allowed to exist over time. It is part of the work of the Board to ensure the company and the behaviour of its employees is acceptable to society at large. It is for the Board, working with the CEO and executive team, to establish a general ethical framework, which in turn will inform policy.

This ethical framework does not have to be articulated in detail, as it gains its expression through policy and its enactment through the systems of the organisation. It is the policy statements that provide the overall sense of 'what we stand for and how we do business'. The ethical framework is experienced by stakeholders whether they be employees, customers or members of the community. It is what the advertisers try to express in their campaigns, usually implicitly, and may vary according to the business or sector. While superficially it may be referred to as 'image' or 'brand', it is in fact much deeper. It is the reputation of the organisation based on the reality and experience of *how* it behaves as it goes about achieving its purpose.

Failure to set and enforce an ethical framework can be extremely costly. On 2 December 2001, Enron had to declare bankruptcy as a result of fraud; its share price went from a peak of $90.75 to $0.26, costing shareholders billions. Thousands of employees lost their jobs, a major accounting firm was also put out of business for obstruction of justice, and some top executives went to prison. More recently Wells Fargo Bank was fined $185 million, and had to dismiss 5,300 employees for cheating their customers. Volkswagen was fined $15 billion by consumers and the State of California for falsifying emissions in their diesel engine vehicles. In addition they had to pay $4.3 billion to the federal government, six top executives were criminally indicted and the damage to reputation may prove to be more costly than the fines.

Policies

As stated above, the formal expressions of the organisation's ethical framework lies in the policies of the organisation. Policies are statements of intent. They are often aspirational and must be formulated to act as clear directions for behaviour. While an overarching policy is clearly 'do not break the law', again this is not sufficient. Policies often reflect dilemmas. For example, what is the policy with regard to equal opportunity if you are a UK-based firm with a subsidiary in Saudi Arabia? What is your policy with regard to minimum wages? Is it purely determined by the country you operate in? Similarly, with age of employment, benefits and all terms and conditions of employment? What about environmental issues, land usage, relations with indigenous people and local communities? The formulation of policies in these areas will determine the nature of the organisation and how it is perceived. This is core work for the Board with advice and recommendations from the CEO and the executive team.

EMPLOYMENT HIERARCHIES

Employment hierarchies begin, in the simplest case, when a governing Board is authorised to employ an individual to work to achieve the association's objectives. This person is authorised, when the workload becomes too large for one person to handle, to hire additional employees within constraints of the association's objectives, budget, personnel and policies as set by the Board, a legislature or directly by the membership (see Box 11.3).

An employment hierarchy is a form of organisation that is subordinate to an association. In such an employment hierarchy, people are employed for a wage or salary to carry out the purposes articulated for the association by its governing body. Authority is distributed hierarchically, in that the Chief Executive is authorised by the governing body, while the roles subordinate to the Chief Executive have authority determined by the Chief Executive such that they form a coherent hierarchy of order and scope of authority. In such a hierarchy, the authority of any role is subordinate to the authority of the role of its manager. All are subordinate, however, to the policy and systems authorised by the Board.

The exceptions to this hierarchical order of authority apply to some specified roles in larger organisations in which audit, legal and financial roles are required to report directly to the Board on specific tasks.

The CEO agrees to be held accountable by the governing body for his or her own work and for the work performance of his or her direct reports. This form of work relationship where acceptance of accountability forms an essential element is required between each manager and his or her individual reports throughout the organisation. It is the work of the CEO to distribute the authority to each role that is necessary for it to function correctly.

If the organisation is based on a meritocracy (see Chapter 7) this enables the organisation to cope with a changing environment and to have people in roles performing the work required for the organisation to achieve its purpose. An employment hierarchy is not, and by its very nature cannot be, a democracy; it is an authority hierarchy.

Individuals can have dual roles, being both members (perhaps through owning shares), and employees of the corporation. There has been considerable discussion of how the ownership of shares may change the behaviour of the employee. Often higher-level managers are encouraged to be shareholders, as well as employees, based on the belief that they are more likely to increase shareholder value if they themselves are shareowners. In some businesses share ownership is required of Board members.

Unionised workers are members of one organisation, the union, and employees of another organisation, the business or public agency. Union members' commitments to their unions may vary depending upon the felt need for protection from perceived management abuses and the competence of the leadership of the union.

Members of voluntary associations may have greater or lesser degrees of attachment to their association. Some members may simply write a cheque to a cause they support. Others may take a more active role as a paid or volunteer worker. One of the interesting dilemmas in voluntary associations is to manage the work of both employees and volunteers, often a highly

---

Box 11.4 Wilfred Brown's Definition of Employment Hierarchy

Employment hierarchy: 'that network of employment roles set up by an association of people to carry out work required to achieve the objectives of the association'. (Brown, 1971: 49)

sensitive issue (see the case study on the website 'Parish Life in the Anglican Diocese of Perth, Western Australia – the Bellevue–Darlington Story').

Employees' ideas and contributions to the setting of policies and direction are essential for success over time. What employment does mean, however, is that the authority to act comes from the association and that employees can use those authorities as a resource to perform work on tasks assigned to them by their manager. This allows them to accept the basis for review of their work, and accept that they will be called to account for their work performance by their manager. The Chief Executive is called to account for his or her work performance by the Board.

Employment hierarchies are both secondary and dependent institutions. They are secondary in that they cannot be formed in their own right; there must first be an employing body that decides to establish an organisation and provide the authorities within which employees carry out their work. They are dependent in that their continuity depends upon the continued existence of the employing body.

A variation on this theme is the entrepreneur who sets up a business and initially embodies both the association and the employment hierarchy. The entrepreneur decides the purpose of the business, the business plan, whom to hire, whom to fire, how to structure the organisation and what systems will be used – albeit within the law of the land. Once the business moves beyond the sole proprietor stage and must seek articles of incorporation, then the association of shareholders is brought into being. The entrepreneur may still control the association through majority share holdings, but there is now both an association and an employment hierarchy though the entrepreneur may control both if he or she chooses to remain as Chief Executive officer.

The differences in the roles and relationships within associations and within employment hierarchies are illustrated in Table 11.1. The failure to make such distinctions leads to significant difficulties and confusion, both theoretical and practical. These two institutional forms differ and the roles of individuals within them differ fundamentally. To be an elected representative of an association is profoundly different from being an employee of that association. Even where terms like 'leader' or 'accountability' are, correctly, or incorrectly, applied to both roles, the ideas and the lived reality behind these terms are significantly different.

The elected union leader is in a very different relationship to the workers who elect him or her than is the CEO of the corporation who employs those same workers. In the case of the union leader, the workers are members who can, through the election process, throw the union leader out of office. The CEO is in a position to hire the workers and to fire them within the limits of law, organisation policies and the union contract if such exists. They, in turn, are not in a position to remove the CEO (though very bad CEOs may find their subordinates undermining them, which can result in dismissal by the Board).

Unions also hire staff who are employees of the union and therefore part of an employment hierarchy. They too may have their own union. The executive director of a union and the employed staff are in the same relation to the union leadership as is the CEO and staff of a corporation to the corporate Board. Much to the embarrassment of employing unions, their staff union may, and some have, called strikes and have walked out over pay or working conditions.

Voluntary associations may become even more confusing since they too may hire an executive director and staff who are employees, while at the same time using volunteers who are members of the association to carry out some of the work. Employees and volunteers of such organisations can testify to the difficulties that occur in this situation. As members, the volunteers are the ultimate 'bosses' who elect the governing Board. As workers, they may be subordinate to a full-time employee – a tricky relationship unless authorities and work of each role are fully articulated and understood.

Wilfred Brown (1971: 48–59) has discussed some of these relationships extensively, particularly for those working in government and voluntary associations where the association/ employment hierarchy relationship is more complex. The theories and models presented in this book apply to all types of employment hierarchies, though the primary model we are using is the simplest model, that of a corporation. This, we believe, will allow us to make the general principles clear, and in turn, they can be applied in other organisational settings.

While many of the theories and models we present apply in a variety of human interactions, the theory of a stratified structure initially developed by Jaques and Brown, applies primarily to the employment hierarchy. The structural concepts have relevance in other settings such as partnerships, but that requires some alternative ways of applying them in practice. The theories of human capability apply to all humans, but their significance is different in the association and the employment hierarchy. Just because the association governs the employment hierarchy, it does not imply the members or their representatives are, or should be, of higher Mental Processing Ability. The knowledge and skills required to be a representative are significantly different from the knowledge and skills required of an employee. Although it is very helpful to have at least one member of a governing Board who is equal to, or preferably one step above, the Chief Executive of the employment hierarchy in Mental Processing Ability, it is not a necessary condition. We can therefore see that employment hierarchies as bureaucracies operate very effectively as meritocracies (See Chapter 7).

Conclusion

It is important to understand the difference between associations and employment hierarchies because they have appropriately very different structures and decision-making processes. When they have become muddled, as we have seen more generally in Chapter 5, they become inefficient and counter-productive. It is especially important to distinguish the work of the Board and the Executives. The poor understanding of the role and work of Board members has led to catastrophic results, perhaps the most spectacular being the global financial crisis.

4 *The Work of Leadership*

Introduction to Part 4

So far we have discussed what Systems Leadership is; its core concepts and how we build organisations. This part concentrates on the work of leadership: how a leader creates a culture, how a leader works with policies and systems and how work is properly assigned. We also look at teamwork. While there are many books written on leadership there are far fewer written about being a good team member. This is strange because organisations are social structures and as such everyone in them is a team member but not everyone is a team leader. We provide practical guidance as to what makes a good team member and how she or he can contribute to their team and the purpose of the organisation.

In the West particularly there is huge emphasis on the role of the leader. There is an idealisation of individuals who can "save the day", be inspiring and take an organisation forward. Along with these unrealistic expectations go huge salaries that in themselves drive discontent. Our argument is that too much emphasis has been placed on the individual and that such lofty expectations are indeed unfair. Leaders can only get their work done my working with others. Leaders also always work within constraints that may be enabling, hindering or even crippling. We need to understand the nature of the context and how the leader can use social processes in order to release the potential of the team and all of those working in the organisation.

Again we find that in this field there is a lack of shared definition of terms including leadership, team, culture and even work. We aim to clarify not only the meaning of these terms but also how to go about creating a culture of working effectively with others and reducing frustration and wasted effort through clarity of mutual expectations.

12 *The Work of Leadership: Creating a Culture*

The Work of Leadership

This is probably the most written-about topic of all. It ranges from the more descriptive biographies and autobiographies of people who have been in significant leadership roles, for example, Mandela and Churchill, to theories of leadership such as Hargreave and Fink's *Sustainable Leadership* (2006). Arguments abound as to whether leaders are 'born, not made' and to what extent leadership can be taught or learned.

In order even to discuss these ideas, it is first of all important to determine what leadership is and how it might be recognised. It is interesting to think about what current definitions of leadership come to mind, if any. Could you write down an attributed definition? Leadership, like so many other concepts in this field, has wide social meaning but no scientific, shared meaning. We hear that leadership and management are different, but how and why? We have argued that this differentiation is not very helpful. In Part 2 we distinguished between two types of relationship: between one person and another person or persons, and between a person and an object or objects. The distinction between leadership and management sometimes implies this difference: that, somehow, leaders are concerned with people whilst managers look after resources such as plant, equipment, stores, budgets and so on. In contrast, we associate both leaders' and managers' relationships with specific sets of authorities. Thus all managers are leaders but not all leaders are managers.

So what do we mean by leadership? Most people will associate leadership not only with people but with influencing these people to act in a particular way (see Box 12.1).

The work of a leader is clearly a social process. A very important element for us is the term *over time*. We are not referring to a short-term process, which, whilst it may be effective, does not necessarily last. To take an extreme example, a person may go into a bank with the objective of getting the staff to give him the bank's money. He points a gun at them and they do so. Hardly good leadership? A CEO visits a site. Employees rush around for a few days beforehand, clearing clutter, painting or removing obvious eyesores so the place looks good. Is this good leadership?

Leadership is certainly about having people act in a way that results in productive social cohesion. But how is it made possible? We argue that many of the traditional tools: fear,

---

Box 12.1   The Work of a Leader

The work of a leader is to create, maintain and improve the culture of a group of people so that they achieve objectives and continue to do so over time.

Box 12.2   What Makes a Good Leader?

In our view, good leadership involves effectively directing the behaviour of others without the primary use of force, manipulation or power … Good leadership engenders willing participation.

---

coercion and intimidation are inappropriate. Yet we still want the leader to influence others to behave constructively, productively and creatively, and all of this for the most part willingly. This is not an easy task in any social setting whether at home, in the office, in a religious organisation, a political party or a voluntary organisation (see Box 12.2).

If leaders are to be effective, they must be skilled in the management of *social processes*. The ability to comprehend a social process and intervene to produce a productive outcome is at the heart of leadership. It is a huge advantage if the leader genuinely likes people and is committed to using good social process. One of the worst leaders we came across explained his *process* of leadership as follows: 'First, I give them the chance to agree with me. If they don't, I sack them.' There are still many leaders who use this approach and are even admired for their strength.

As we have said leadership is a social process. We have already discussed this in Chapters 3 and 4 … But how is this used effectively? We have identified some work for the leader to do. The leader must be able to answer the following questions to test his or her understanding of social process:

1. How do team members (that is, those whom the leader is leading) perceive each other?
2. How do they perceive the organisation?
3. How do they perceive the leader?
4. Can the leader predict how they will perceive particular changes, for example, of working practices, organisation, benefits, and so on?
   Note: In attempting to answer questions 1, 2 and 3, the leader needs to be able to relate the perceptions to the values continua and position them on these continua.

This is not a superficial process that can be solved by simply saying, 'Well, if the change is positive, they will view it positively.' People often perceive situations in quite different ways. The key to understanding this perception is to understand their mythologies and to be able to see the proposed changes through their mythological lenses. This is not a question of right or wrong. Their mythologies may be based on stories and experiences from years ago.

One of the authors asked a group of people if they trusted the leadership of their organisation. One of the group answered, 'No, not after what they have done in the past.' On exploration, the examples he came up with were more than 15 years old and from a time when none of the current management were even at the organisation! Such stories echo down the years and may still influence people today. We have found that some organisations are better than others at telling and relating to stories, and building and sustaining mythologies. Union leaders are often good at this, and excel at reminding people of the past, relying particularly on tales of untrustworthy or dishonest management. Some organisational leaders may find this frustrating. Frustrating or not, it is part of the reality of organisations, unionised or not, and must be addressed.

This is where the values continua: trust, love, honesty, courage, respect for human dignity and fairness, when expressed positively, are applied. The leader can use the universal values to help answer the questions above. Do people trust each other and the leader? Do they think the organisation is fair? Is the leadership courageous? If the answer to some or all of these questions is no, the leader must ask why and try to explore the underlying mythologies. This is often best done by listening; a very simple technique, but one which is frequently underused by leaders. Leadership is often assumed to be all about the inspiring speaker, the person who leads from the front; someone with apparently boundless energy and determination. Yet good leadership is almost always the result of good, careful observation and listening followed by considered action.

This is not to imply that good leadership is doing what is most popular. It may be the case that what needs to be done will initially be seen negatively, for example cost reductions, changes in organisation or location or new work methods. The understanding of mythologies (Box 12.3) provides the basis for more effective leadership behaviour, improvement of systems, better setting of context and the considered use of symbols to provide believable answers to the questions that are concerning people.

One organisation we worked with eventually faced closure. The economic argument was compelling. Employees were, not surprisingly, unhappy at the prospect. However, the leadership used their understanding of mythologies to design information systems, relocation options and retraining to make this process as positive as possible. This was well received and employees left with mythologies that placed their own experience and the leadership as positive on the values continua. They felt they had been treated with respect for their dignity, told the truth and that the leadership had openly confronted the difficult issues (see Box 12.4).

If the purpose is unclear, ambiguous or in any way covert, the social process will place it at the negative side of the values continua. Others will articulate alternative purposes, and

---

Box 12.3   Understanding Mythologies in a Tough Situation

The world market and price for bauxite was falling as a result of a recession. Employees at an Australian mine had had the potential impact of falling sales explained to them by their Managers. Expenditures would need to be cut, rostered overtime would be removed, and if the sales predictions fell further, employees would be laid off. The mood of employees was, understandably, described as glum, at best.

Managers were quite aware of underlying Australian mythologies including, 'All managers are bastards who tell lies and don't give a bugger about their workers.' Thus the problem was to have the sales predictions believed. The figures were based on long-term contracts and were accurate, but this was not the issue; it was the believability of the local managers.

The answer was to have the actual information that was sent weekly giving the latest sales figures pinned to the main notice board with no comment. It was a business sensitive document, but confidentiality was never breached, even as the sales numbers fell and the process of reducing the number of employees began.

In a meeting to announce this to one group, the Manager was asked what selection process would be used for those to go. His answer was, 'The worst go first.' There were no further questions about the selection process.

The symbolism of using the information to keep people informed, even though all the news was bad, and the bluntness of the answer about selection helped considerably in making the messages believable, in spite of the mythologies about managers.

Box 12.4   Countering Negative Mythologies: PURPOSE

A leader must have, and be able to articulate, a clear purpose ... Just having a clear purpose, however, will not overcome negative mythologies; it is only the beginning.

---

energy will be dissipated. The exercise of power will result and an alternative, subversive, purpose is likely to be promoted. Clarity of purpose is an essential part of the social process. Articulating a clear purpose does not guarantee agreement, however. The leader must also understand why people disagree. Using the values continua, concerns or objections must be examined, which requires an understanding of the mythologies that apply. We once worked with an organisation whose workforce went on strike because the company increased sick leave benefits! The leadership had overlooked the negative placement of the action. Seen through the lens of suspicious and negative mythologies about the purpose of the change, the workforce feared that increased sick leave benefits would be linked to a loss of benefits elsewhere (which had happened in the past). It is tempting in these, often tense, circumstances to dismiss these sorts of objections as irrational. Do not dismiss them. The mythology which explains their rationale must be found (see Box 12.5).

As we have said people often resort to three simple explanations for behaviour they do not understand and often turn to one or more of three simple answers: they must be *bad, mad* or *stupid*.

Why did they damage that vehicle by running it without checking the oil? Why was he not wearing the proper safety harness, causing him to fall from the scaffold? Why does she keep complaining about lack of information when she has access to our new intranet?

Frustration can offer quick explanations: they are bad, he is mad and she is stupid. We ask leaders to explain a range of behaviours that they see as negative in the workforce without resorting to any one of these simple explanations or excuses. It can be a tough task. It is even more poignant to see politicians and world leaders resort to such simplicity to explain others' behaviour. It always seems easier and more rational to see *other* people whose behaviour as falling negatively on the values continua than it is to reflect on our own behaviour and what drives it.

In the example above of the employees who took strike action over an increase in sick leave benefits, it is easy to classify this behaviour as stupid and bad. If you are a member of the group who took this action and you knew that in the past such actions of appearing to be

---

Box 12.5   Avoiding Purely Emotional Arguments

When seeking to understand other people who are behaving, to our eyes, in an irrational way, it is often easy to enter into an emotional argument. When two Macdonald Associates consultants presented a report to a managing director that revealed some strong negative mythologies about some changes he had made, he became upset. He had worked hard at these changes, which he genuinely believed would, over time, benefit employees and the organisation. He eventually became exasperated and just kept saying, 'Well they are wrong, just plain wrong.' It took considerable time and discussion to move away from an absolute position to consider the questions 'Why, if you have made these changes in good faith, would someone also genuinely, not trust they are beneficial?'

Box 12.6 The Purpose of Leadership

The purpose of leadership is to change behaviour.

---

loving by the managers (as they would classify it), always led to an overall reduction in benefits in total, then strike action is completely rational and courageous.

Leadership is obviously not merely a matter of responding. While the development of an understanding of the current situation is critical, creating a new, different situation is essential (see Box 12.6).

All leaders must change behaviour, their own and their team members'. Even if the current situation is quite satisfactory, the context will always be challenging and so demands will change (see Box 12.7).

We have defined culture as a group of people who share common mythologies. The leader's work is to create a single, productive, culture; often from a starting position wherein the leader is in one culture and his or her subordinates are in a completely different culture – one that has no shortage of mythologies to interpret the leader's behaviour as falling on the negative side of the values continua. Leaders must have a clear idea of the desired behaviour they need for constructive and productive results. This is no abstract matter. The universal values of trust, love, honesty, fairness, dignity and courage only have meaning in relation to actual behaviour.

Exactly what behaviour is fair?

A client of ours came across one of his crew fishing in a nearby river. 'I thought you were on shift today?' said the client. 'Yes, I am', said the crew member, pleasantly. 'Then why are you here fishing?' said the client. The reply came, 'Oh, I'm on a sickie'. He then sensed that he might be in serious trouble and quickly said, 'Oh, it's OK. I phoned in before the shift so they could arrange cover.'

To this crew member, *taking a sickie* was not unfair or dishonest. Letting his leader down by not giving notice was. His calmness in the face of the manager suggested this was common practice (which it was). The leader had to change this behaviour. He needed to create a culture where taking a day off sick when you are well was not perceived as fair or honest.

What was he to do next? What do you think would have been the reaction, in a highly unionised mining operation, if he had disciplined the crew member there and then? Instead he said he would see him back at work and then thought carefully through the mythologies and what influenced them. Through understanding the mythologies, changing the behaviour of leaders and changing critical systems he created new mythologies and, by the time he left that mine, the behaviours had changed. This was done over time by a series of system changes which included redesigning the sick leave system and the holiday/leave systems. They were applied equally to all the workforce. This system change was preceded by discussions with employees and especially line leaders. Leaders were trained both in the new systems and social process skills concerning briefing their teams and dealing with difficult issues.

Box 12.7 The Leaders Work

The leader must create a single productive culture.

So far we have highlighted the need for:

- clarity of purpose;
- understanding mythologies as part of social process and
- the need to create the desired culture.

One measure of a desired culture in an employment organisation is that all employees willingly work toward the achievement of the purpose of the organisation. In such an organisation, improvement and innovation directed toward the achievement of this purpose occur as a matter of course.

The Three Tools of Leadership

Creating a culture builds on clarity of purpose and is achieved through three main leadership tools (see Box 12.8). Since we first articulated this set of leadership tools in the mid-1980s, they have been used to great effect in a wide range of circumstances ... We see it as an integral part of the system leadership framework. We referred to these tools earlier in Part 2.

BEHAVIOUR

The leader's own behaviour is highly significant. Phrases like 'walk the talk' or 'practice what you preach' are typical. A saying used in child development also underlines its importance: 'Do not worry if your children don't listen to you. They're watching you all the time'.

The consistency of a leader's own behaviour will be scrutinised by team members. It is not helpful if, in trying to improve timekeeping or housekeeping, the leader is a poor timekeeper or walks past litter at work. Role modelling is essential in challenging behaviour. People really do notice and either take heart or are discouraged according to what the leader actually does.

Use and misuse of the term *attitude* is almost universal. My attitude is what I think; my behaviour is what I do. You can observe and record my behaviour; at best you can only infer my attitude, you can never know it. Over the millennia, many noble men and women have given their lives so you and I may think as we please. This freedom and their memory are surely sacred. We do not use the term attitude, as behaviour is so much more important. We can see behaviour; we can only infer an attitude. What a leader must seek to do is to change behaviour that will produce results.

SYSTEMS

Karl Stewart coined the phrase, 'systems drive behaviour' when he was working to develop a theoretical understanding of systems. When he took over the leadership of the Comalco

---

Box 12.8   The Three Tools of Leadership

The three tools of leadership are:

- behaviour
- systems and
- symbols.

Smelting business, there had already been a considerable process of helpful structural change, but the business as a whole was not delivering the performance it should have been or was capable of. By concentrating on changing the systems, he was able to accelerate that change and obtain the results he saw as possible.

Systems are so important because they operate all the time, all day every day. Unlike the behaviour of a leader, the systems are ever-present; they do not get tired or dispirited. The alignment of systems and behaviour is very influential. It is difficult for a leader to counter bad systems and behaviour by others by his or her behaviour alone. Leadership dependent upon role modelling alone will not last in an organisation of any size beyond that of the owner-manager. Behaviour will revert unless reinforced by systems. Bree Macdonald found many instances in health service institutions, mental hospitals and hostels, where excellent staff who were struggling against countervailing systems of depersonalisation, ended up suffering significantly because of burn-out (see Macdonald, B., 2001).

SYMBOLS

Symbols can be used by all leaders but become more significant as the organisational distance increases between the leader and the employees or team members. Behaviour itself is highly symbolic, but there are other examples of symbols: uniforms, staff facilities, flags, logos, office size and placement, car parking, housekeeping. How people perceive symbols offers very clear examples of mythologies (see Box 12.9).

If the systems and behaviour are aligned, symbols can be very positive and helpful. If they are not, they can be counter-productive and very rapidly and strongly reinforce the negative mythologies that place the behaviour of leaders and the systems of the organisation at the negative ends of the values continua, for example, lack of trust prevalent in the organisation. The workforce can appear to become even more cynical.

Some organisations are much more aware of symbols than others. The Church, religions and armies are usually steeped in symbols whether that be a plethora of gold, colour and ritual or a simple plain, unadorned chapel. The clothes of leaders – priests, officers, soldiers – are highly significant to those in the organisation. One of the most significant symbols in any organisation is title. What are you called? What titles apply and are they similar (or not) to other organisations? Changing titles can be one of the most contentious and difficult tasks to undertake in any organisation and go way beyond rational argument, as to the words being used. So-called *re-branding* initiatives are often viewed with scepticism by people within and outside an organisation. How much does it cost to come up with the new logo? Company values as symbols can be looked at with similar scepticism when disconnected from behaviour and systems.

Box 12.9   An Example of How Symbols May Be Perceived

A coal mine in Australia was taken over by new owners. It had a history of poor industrial relations. The new owners wanted to make a fresh start and appointed a new general manager for the mine. He issued good-quality baseball caps on the first day printed with the new company colours and logo. Every employee was given one free. At the end of the shift, each side of the road leading to and from the mine was littered with discarded caps. This behaviour demonstrated the depth of negative mythologies. As one miner commented, 'They are not going to buy us with a bloody cap!'

Symbols become more important as we move up through the organisation: presentations, awards, letters of recognition, visits, commemorative plaques, office space, furniture, decoration and cars/vehicles can all have very significant meaning.

Process of Building a Culture

A recent cover of *Harvard Business Review* carried the headline, 'You Can't Fix Culture'. (Lorsch and McTague, 2016) Of course we disagree, and in this chapter we have shown how it can and should be done. In the article which followed, however, the examples shown as exemplars were in fact changing systems (the authors used the term processes) and the authors reported, 'Rather, in their experience, cultural change is what you get after you've put new processes or structures in place to tackle tough business challenges like reworking an out-dated strategy or business model. The culture evolves as you do that important work.'

Lacking our language and theory, the linkage between cause and effect was not explicitly stated in terms that could provide guidance to other managers. Nor did they have any understanding of the shared mythologies as the definition of a culture. Yet despite the article's title, 'Culture is not the Culprit', their actual findings directly support what we have discussed in this chapter.

This chapter has described the work of leaders in creating the desired culture. The following diagram (Figure 12.1) summarises not only that work but also a central message of Systems Leadership and this entire book.

The diagram itself is a simple gap analysis, in that it describes where you want to be, that is the Desired Culture, where you are now, that is the Existing Culture and how to get there. What is less common is that this diagram provides leaders with specific tools as to how to articulate and then create that Desired Culture.

STEP ONE: THE DESIRED CULTURE

When using this model with organisations we ask people to describe the culture that they want to create in terms of actual behaviours. That is we ask people to describe, in concrete

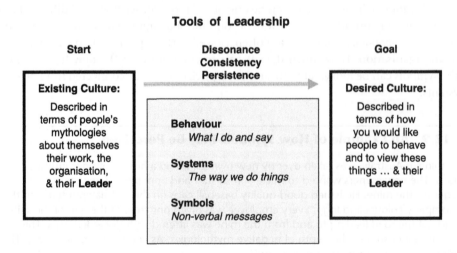

Figure 12.1　The Tools of Leadership

terms, how they would like people to behave, how they would like people, including customers and other stakeholders to describe the organisation and what sort of productivity or result they would be expecting. A simple way of doing this is to ask the question: 'If I was to visit your organisation when it was operating exactly as you would like it to operate what would I actually see? How would I be treated and what would people say about the organisation and its leadership?' We ask people not to use general terms such as: 'people would be working well together', but to go to the next level of detail such as; 'when somebody makes a suggestion the leader will acknowledge and listen to that suggestion'. 'People actually make eye contact with each other and greet each other when walking through the organisation.' 'There is no litter, offices are tidy, people ask other people if they need help or if they want any help' and so on. These behaviours are observable. Similarly we ask what would employees say about the organisation and why. For example in the desired culture we might want people to say that they look forward to coming to work because they feel they are listened to and given recognition and feel part of the team. They may say; 'you're never asked to do anything unsafe or unethical here and you are consulted about changes'. That is, you are treated fairly, with respect and love.

STEP TWO: THE ARTICULATION OF THE EXISTING CULTURE

As for the desired culture we ask people to describe what the current behaviours are and what people actually say about the organisation and why. Some of these comments and behaviours may be very close to the desired culture others may be very distant. As with the desired culture again we are asking people to be very concrete and explicit and not to over generalise by using terms such as 'it's not too bad', 'some aspects are fine'.

STEP THREE: TO LOOK AT THE TOOLS OF LEADERSHIP: SYSTEMS SYMBOLS AND BEHAVIOUR

We ask the question: 'What is helping and what is hindering the creation of the desired culture?' For example what current systems are encouraging people to behave as you would like and what are actually making work life more difficult? Similarly, are there behaviours making the desired culture difficult to achieve especially the behaviour of leaders, and thirdly what are the symbols the people are proud of and represent the culture you are trying to build and what symbols are sending messages that are counter-productive? For example, when visiting an organisation are safety exits and equipment clear and accessible? Are people at reception actually welcoming and helpful? One telling comment about such observations being symbolic is when someone says, 'Well, that's typical' (either positively or negatively).

From this analysis we can construct a plan of work to redesign systems and symbols that encourage the desired behaviours in order to create the culture. As we mentioned before this also requires an understanding of the mythological lenses of various stakeholders.

When implementing the plan of work to create the desired culture we also see in the diagram the need for Dissonance, Consistency and Persistence. When implementing the plan there should be some experience of dissonance; that is people are experiencing something they do not expect. For example; people getting feedback and recognition for their work where previously there had been very little. Perhaps the systems are now more reliable and equipment does not break down as it has always done in the past. In order for the plan to be effective there needs also to be consistency. Changes may be made in organisations but they may be experienced as a one-off and not expected to last or to be significant.

Box 12.10   Three Data Points

Interestingly we have discovered that for people to change their behaviour and/or build new mythologies they need a minimum of three data points to show that things have changed. One experience may be an exception, when something happens twice it may be a coincidence but when something happens three times in a row a people we tend to infer that there has been a systems change.

Here is a simple test: if you take your children swimming for three Saturdays mornings in a row we would predict that if anyone asks your children: 'What do you do on Saturday mornings?' they will say: 'We always go swimming.' Or conversely if you do not go swimming for three Saturdays in a row they will say: 'We never go swimming any more.' As people we like to see patterns that make our lives predictable. In organisational change, a new mythology, and consequential new behaviour is even more effectively reinforced if those data points come from three separate sources, For example (i) my own experience, (ii) a colleague's observation and (iii) a third-party comment or observation.

We also need persistence. Many so-called culture change programmes are embarked upon with great enthusiasm, fanfare and exuberance but everyone has seen this before. After about six months if not earlier the so-called initiative runs out of steam and people slowly revert to their usual or habitual pattern. This is partly because such initiatives do not usually combine the tools of behaviour systems and symbols but concentrate on only one or sometimes two of those. We predict that in such circumstances that change will not be sustained. What we are putting forward here is that the combination of systems, symbols and behaviour along with dissonance, persistence and consistency will create the desired culture. Relying on only one or two of these elements will not produce sustainable change.

CULTURE: CONNECTIONS

All of the above discussion can be connected by Figure 12.2.

The diagram connects all of the elements we have been discussing: Systems, Symbols, Behaviours, Statements (these are the actual words that people use in describing their experience of the organisation). Each of these elements influences each other element. It also means that we can start anywhere on this diagram and ask the question as to how one element connects to the others. Let's take an example and start with a Statement. Supposing somebody says: 'I am very anxious about going to work'. We can take that as a starting point and then consider what might be the underlying Mythologies that underpin the statement. It might be that the person experiences the workplace and leadership as unloving and perhaps disrespectful or worse, be subject to bullying. So what systems might underpin that mythology? Well, there might be a payment or bonus system that is entirely based upon output numbers which are all that matters. How might that be represented Symbolically? Perhaps there are production figures and targets posted everywhere but no information about well-being or safety. The Symbolic message is: 'We don't really care what happens to you as long as you reach your targets.' So what Behaviour might that drive? Perhaps senior managers only ever ask about output or use aggressive questions about why targets hadn't been achieved with threats of dire consequences.

Let's take another example and start with a leader giving honest and accurate recognition to a team member. This in turn might symbolise positive and respectful relationships in the

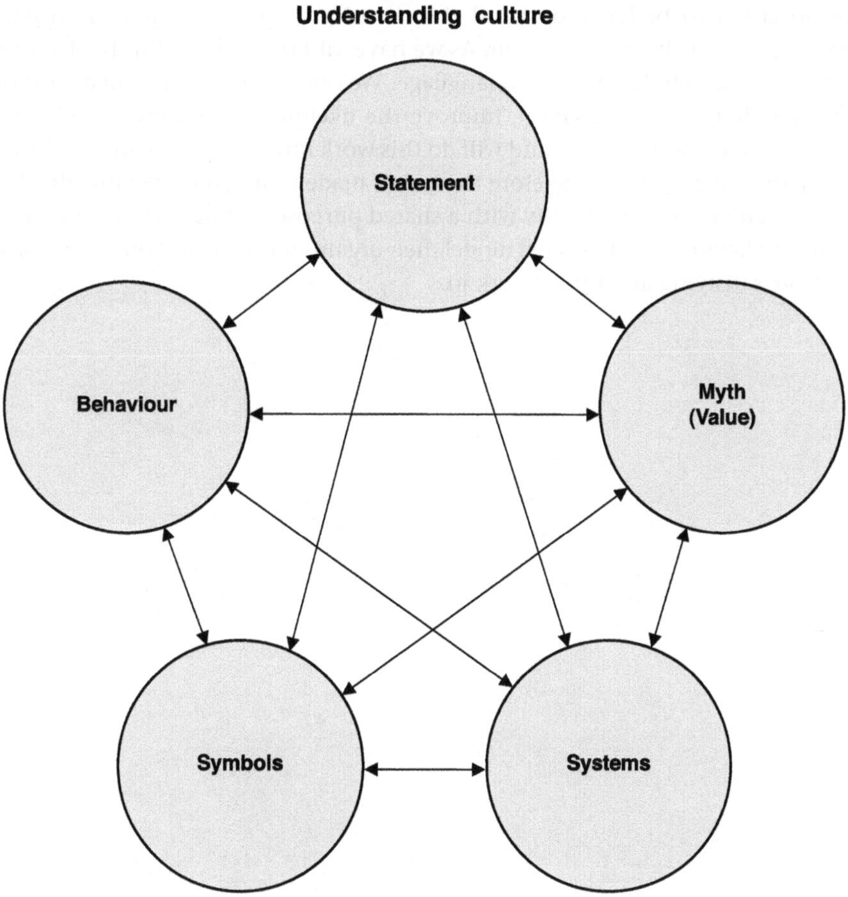

Understanding culture

Figure 12.2   Understanding Culture

organisation and be underpinned by a system of task assignment and performance review that is well designed and implemented. This might create the mythologies that people are treated not only with respect but fairly with regard to work performance leading again in turn to a statement made by an employee that people are really interested in what you're doing and want you to do well.

You can use this diagram to explore in some depth and detail what is going well and what is not going so well. Whether the desired culture is being realised and whether the leadership has created a positive organisation with productive social cohesion.

Conclusion

THE WORK OF LEADERSHIP IS TO CREATE CULTURE

In this chapter we have emphatically argued that the work of leadership is to create a culture. Indeed we believe that all leaders create a culture. It is just a question as to whether it is the culture that they had intended. We have offered a range of tools that should help the leader in any organisation to better understand the situation they are in and to create a more productive culture and change behaviour. As we have said throughout this book a key part of this is that people need to have a shared language. We offer terminology and definitions that, if applied throughout an organisation, improve the likelihood of creating productive social cohesion. While many leaders have and will do this work intuitively, they may be hindered by the lack of shared language and therefore the task is made so much more difficult. Our experience is that when people can identify with a shared purpose and have clarity about the work through a shared language and a shared model their organisations are not only more productive but much more satisfying and fun to work in.

13 *Leadership, Policy and Systems*

The Role of Policy and Systems

We have discussed the importance of creating a culture using the tools of Behaviour, Systems and Symbols. This chapter explores the role of policy and systems in more depth.

The purpose of the organisation can only be achieved through work. Purpose reveals intent; the policy and systems provide the boundaries for the enactment of the how of turning intention into reality. For our definitions of policy and system, see Boxes 13.1 and 13.2.

Box 13.1   Definition of Policy

Our definition of policy is 'a statement that expresses the standards of practice and behaviour that are required of people who work for the organisation.'

Box 13.2   Definition of System

Our definition of a system is 'a specific framework for organising activities to achieve a purpose within which variation is acceptable to the system owner'. The framework orders the flows of work, data, information, money, people, materials and equipment required to achieve the system's purpose.

LEADERSHIP AND POLICY

In the previous discussions of work, we saw that all work is necessarily carried out in the context of constraints. For example, we never have unlimited resources or time. We also saw that some constraints were imposed by an external authority, for example, by law. Others were chosen such as the make or type of equipment to be used.

If an association employs people to help achieve its purpose (in the form of an employment hierarchy), it cannot act as if it has no constraints. There are legal constraints and resource constraints – the capital available, the nature and size of the market, the availability of people and materials, social customs and practices. In addition, we argue that the board and the executive leadership must go beyond simple legal compliance. *The purpose of any activity implies ethical principles being observed in its achievement.* If the organisation acts amorally, the result will be fragmentation not only of the association, but of the employed group.

What we mean by this is simply that in all human endeavours, the end does *not* justify the means; if this implies that any means will be acceptable providing the end is achieved. We have discussed how human beings are social creatures and thus also moral creatures, as evidenced by the values continua. The demonstration of behaviour that is ethically and morally acceptable is essential for the maintenance of group cohesion. There will always be opinions and differences of opinion as to the nature of the process to achieve the purpose. Our view is that while it is necessary to discuss the technical aspect of this (that is, will the process actually work?), it is also essential to consider the ethical principles of the social process.

The association and leadership must determine the constraints around how the purpose is to be achieved. These constraints are articulated in the form of policies as we have defined them, *standards of practice*. Policies are critical, especially if the organisation works in different states or countries with different laws. For example, if the law in one country with regard to employment conditions, health and safety, or the environment (pollution) is different from the law in another, does the organisation merely comply with such laws, or does it have a policy on safety that requires a particular standard even if the law does not? Answering these questions is part of the work of the board and the CEO's team.

The policies of an organisation have a strong bearing on its identity and reputation.

The policies of a company will have a significant bearing on who associates with it and who supplies it or buys from it. Some investment companies have policies not to invest in armaments or military supplies companies, or companies with poor environmental or human rights records irrespective of the return to shareholders of such companies.

Rio Tinto (a London-based mining corporation) has a community policy that requires all its global operations to develop a positive programme of engagement with the local communities whether local laws require, encourage or ignore such issues. Rio Tinto also has a policy that explicitly requires the settlement of land rights and access to lands without relying on the pure technical, legal rights tested to the full in courts where laws are often ambiguous and the legal process lengthy.

Collins and Porras (1994) provide numerous examples of ethical behaviour in the companies that are *built to last*. For example, Merck states, 'We are in the business of preserving and improving human life. All of our actions must be measured by our success in achieving that goal' (Collins and Porras, 1994: 89). Johnson & Johnson says, 'The company exists to alleviate pain and disease' (Collins and Porras, 1994: 89).

Merck chose to provide streptomycin to Japan immediately after World War II to help eliminate the tuberculosis that was rampant and severely eroding that society. They did not make any money, but the CEO Roy Vagelos said, 'the long-term consequences of such actions are not always clear, but somehow I think they always pay off'. It's no accident that Merck was the largest American pharmaceutical company in Japan in 1994 (Collins and Porras, 1994: 47). In more recent years, the leadership of Merck appears to have forgotten that statement of purpose when they did not immediately reveal an arthritis drug, Vioxx, could also cause increased risk of heart attack, ischemic stroke or sudden cardiac death. Merck's stellar reputation suffered and they paid $4.5 billion to settle lawsuits. In 2008 Merck agreed to pay $650 million to settle federal charges it had overbilled Medicaid. Merck's share price has still not returned to its peak in 2000. Merck did not change its policy but it did not behave in accordance with it.

Policy sets the standards intended for the organisation and indicates the behaviour required of its people. The chief executive is most directly involved with policy, and the CEO and his or her team have the work of developing a long-term business plan that will achieve the purpose of the organisation while operating within the policy standards. This is one of the reasons why work at this level is both abstract and complex. It also has the potential to develop and improve the organisation or, when done badly, to endanger the very existence of the organisation. Problems in this area are well documented as the collapse of Enron, Worldcom, Global Crossing and other corporations has demonstrated. Indeed the most significant economic crisis in recent times (2008 Global Financial Crisis) can be linked to the unethical and deliberately deceitful systems and practices that generated and hid bad debt. The purpose of the organisations (banks) as societal engines was hijacked by a drive for short-term individual gain and reinforced by the design of systems (especially bonuses) that rather than curb such excess actually encouraged it.

LEADERSHIP AND SYSTEMS

The leadership of any organisation must work to ensure that employees act in such a way that they contribute to the purpose of the organisation while at the same time working within the law and the organisation's policies. Leadership is, as we have said, about behaviour and changing behaviour.

If we consider ordinary human interaction, it is well accepted that non-verbal behaviour can be more important in conveying meaning than verbal behaviour. If we are talking to someone whose eyes are half-closed and who is yawning, we are not going to be convinced that they are paying attention to what is being said.

Systems become embedded. Like habits, they require a specific repertoire of behaviour and eventually people just get used to them and act according to their dictates. *It's the way we do things round here; Oh, you can't do that!; We don't do it like that round here!; We've always done it like that.* The major problem is that systems, like all habits, can be good or bad. Even good systems over time can become outdated and counter-productive (see Box 13.3).

Systems need to be designed so that all activities help in achieving the organisation's purpose. This is a very difficult task. Many systems actually run counter to the organisation's purpose both actively and symbolically. Take a very simple example. If you run a service business that is intended to be *customer focused*, you may have a system that receives customer phone calls for inquiries, orders and so on. Now, such a system may be technically very advanced. The system may be automated and start with a variety of options: 'To place an order press 1, for overseas sales press 2, for technical support press 3 ...' and so on. Having negotiated the system thus far, the customer may eventually work out an option that seems relevant and then get a message stating that 'All representatives are currently busy. Your call is important to us. Please stay on the line. A representative will be with you shortly.' Then (the crowning glory), the customer listens to some form of music or sales spiel for fifteen minutes while intermittently being told, 'Your call is very important to us. Please hold.'

After this experience, will the customer feel that their call is really important to the organisation and that they are receiving good service? Is the company customer focused? Here we return to the values continua. All systems can be, and are, rated on the values continua in a similar way that behaviour is rated. Do the systems, in the way they treat people, demonstrate fairness, honesty, courage, respect for human dignity, love or trust? Clearly, in many cases, they do not. Reflect for a moment on your experience either as part of an organisation or relating to an organisation as a customer or supplier. Clearly some systems are actually frustrating the purpose of the organisation, undermining its strategy and even contradicting stated policy.

Box 13.3 The Importance of Systems and Behaviour

In organisations, systems are the equivalent of non-verbal behaviour in human interaction.

Policy is enacted through systems. They are the means by which policy becomes reality. They might not, however, accomplish this in practice. Intentions to have good relations with the local community are undermined if no one in authority in the organisation is familiar with the local culture, or speaks the language or is properly trained in the field of local community relations.

Equal employment opportunities can be frustrated by unfair recruitment systems, poor communication or advertising, or opportunity requirements that effectively exclude certain groups. However well-intentioned the leader, however hard he or she works at leading by example, the systems may be frustrating the leader's purpose.

An organisation may claim to be performance based – a meritocracy – but the reward systems may not allow any significant differentiation in pay. Poor performers may be protected by highly convoluted procedures that effectively mean it is impossible (or at least extremely difficult) to remove poor performers from their roles. Proper exercise of authority may be hindered by too many levels of organisation that slow decision-making and cause inefficiency.

Overtime systems may become so complex that the supervisor spends an inordinate amount of time calculating time and rates. There may be bureaucratic rules about who can be asked to work overtime so that, even if the supervisor finds someone to do it, because of the existence of a seniority system, it may not be the appropriate person.

Such inefficient systems are extremely costly, not only in immediate time and money; they often have a much higher long-term cost in terms of affecting people's willingness to use their capabilities to the full in their work.

Tools for Analysing Systems: Systems Drive Behaviour

TWO TYPES OF SYSTEM: 'WE ARE' AND 'I AM'

As mentioned above, Stewart coined the phrase 'systems drive behaviour'. This has become a very popular phrase, taken up by Jaques (2002) and others. It recognises the significant influence that systems have on behaviour, but it can be too simplistic unless followed up by a clear analysis.

We have found it useful to distinguish between types of systems and so understand their influence. The first distinction that we make is between *systems of equalisation* and *systems of differentiation*.

All organisations are social entities. They are in existence to achieve a purpose. To maintain social cohesion and shared purpose there must be a sense of belonging, a sense that *we are*. However, people in organisations are chosen and appointed because of their particular, perhaps unique, skills and abilities. This too needs recognition: *I am*.

Systems of equalisation treat people the same way. A system of equalisation does not distinguish between an operator or a manager, a supervisor or a CEO. The most obvious example of this is safety. It does not matter who you are; if you enter a certain area you must wear a hardhat and boots, ear protection and eye protection so on.

Systems of differentiation treat people differently. That is, they distinguish people in roles. The most widely used system of differentiation is remuneration or compensation. Some roles are explicitly paid more than others. Within a group of people in similar roles there may be further differentiation on the basis of individual performance or grading.

It is important here to be careful not to be confused by a system that applies to everyone and then assume it is one of equalisation. Remuneration applies to all paid employees. A disciplinary system may be available to all. In fact, all systems that flow from policy should apply across the whole organisation. The way to understand if a system is one of equalisation or differentiation is to consider its intent. Is the intent to differentiate or to equalise? We may all be subject to disciplinary systems but they should only be applied on the rare occasion when someone breaches the code or rules; in such cases not everyone in the organisation is to be disciplined.

GOOD OR BAD?

Sometimes, particularly in organisations based in democratic countries, it is easy to slip into the general view that equalisation is good and differentiation bad. This is certainly not the case. Whilst it is very important to reinforce a sense of belonging, this involves the proper use of both types of systems (see Box 13.4).

We might think of a range of systems that could fall into either category, for example, car parking, clothing/uniforms, health care, cafeterias, facilities, transport, leisure facilities, company supplied vehicles or office size.

Our argument is that, if you are going to differentiate, there should be a clear work-related reason. Why should some roles in an organisation have a set number of days for sick leave and others in the same organisation have no set maximum? Why should a certain group park

---

Box 13.4 Basic Principle of Systems of Differentiation

All systems of differentiation should be based on the work (to be) done.

---

within the site boundary and others not? The answer to these questions depends upon whether there is a good work-related reason. For example, most sites have disabled parking bays near entrances or lifts/elevators. We understand the reason for this, but why should a manager have a reserved parking space when he or she can walk as well as anyone else except the disabled? In one company we know, sales representatives had reserved parking because their work required them to go in and out several times a day to meet with customers, and this was deemed entirely fair by the work force. Differentiation can be justified, for example, if the company has a health insurance scheme, which may be enhanced for some roles where the people in those roles travel to countries where health care is less available or more expensive.

Conversely it is demoralising if systems that are supposed to equalise really differentiate. One of the authors, Ian Macdonald, was running a workshop in a remote Australian mine site. He asked a group of tradespeople what they saw as the most unfair system in the company. They were all members of a union and from a generally very egalitarian culture. The answer came back: 'hourly rates are the same'. What they meant was that pay for electricians was the same rate no matter how well, hard, poorly or carefully a person worked. Further, they all knew who the good performers were and who were the poor performers but there was little anyone could do about it, especially with regard to pay. This, in turn, did not encourage good performers or allow the organisation to provide monetary recognition of their particular individual contributions.

In our own work in the United States, Australia and Great Britain, we have found that in employment roles, differentiation based on the work of the role is acceptable, even necessary, as different pay based on different work and differing levels of performance is seen as fair.

Equalisation is more likely to be perceived as fair in instances that are not directly related to individual work behaviour, for example, if everyone in the plant wears the same uniforms. Other examples where equalisation is perceived as fair and differentiation unfair are in health benefits, safety systems, cafeterias and company services.

Another example comes from General Roderick Macdonald based on his experience as the leader of a British Royal Engineer Commando Regiment. He took over the regiment at a time it was experiencing severe leadership problems. There were a number of elements he had to change, but one in particular illustrates the importance of systems and symbols.

At the time he took over the regiment, officers were allowed to wear any boot they preferred as long as it was black. The soldiers were required to wear the military issue boots only. This was a source of dissatisfaction among the troops. Macdonald was aware of this, so one of his first acts was to allow soldiers the same freedom as the officers. While this may appear trivial, it was widely appreciated by the soldiers who recognised that this commanding officer was different. Commandos operate on a basis of greater equality between officers and soldiers, so the change was not disturbing to the officers. The mythologies supported equality as fairness. This was, of course, one of many changes, but its symbolic importance began the change process. Interestingly, he was asked if he would do that in other Army regiments. He said, 'No. In a Guards Regiment, many of the officers were from aristocratic families, and the soldiers took pride in having a commander who was an Earl or a Duke.' The mythologies of the Guards Regiment held that differentiation in boots, uniforms and other elements was appropriate and fair.

A company in New Zealand was considering a major change in employment systems as the finale to a period of significant leadership change by offering staff contracts to all employees. This had the effect of equalising all benefits except pay. Prior to this offer, the general manager and his team met with one of the authors, Ian Macdonald, to perform a task set by the Managing Director (another author – Karl Stewart). The team examined every system in the company in detail over several days. If there was no work reason for the system to differentiate, the system was equalised. This included not only the obvious systems: transport to work, uniforms, car parking, canteen facilities and benefits such as holiday and sick leave, but also the highly symbolic systems such as biscuits provided with coffee and tea (previously only a *staff perk*) and the staff Christmas party, now open to all. It was interesting that for most employees, previously employed under a collective arrangement, these smaller, symbolic changes were seen as the *real* demonstration that the company was serious. Within a matter of weeks well over 95% of the employees who had previously worked under a collective agreement had chosen the new arrangement. The results were dramatic rises in productivity at the plant. (For a fuller and detailed account of this significant process and its elements, see the case study New Zealand Aluminium Smelters Limited, see Chapter 20 and website.)

All systems should be designed deliberately according to their respective purpose taking into account the mythologies of the people who must work within them. To be a good leader you must understand your own mythologies and the mythologies of the workforce. When you implement a system, you must know whether it will be perceived as fair or unfair, honest or dishonest, as demonstrating respect for human dignity or lack of respect. Understanding how people perceive systems is as important as understanding how people perceive behaviour.

Systems should be designed to be productive, to achieve a purpose and in doing so encourage positive behaviour. If people see the system as unfair to them or showing the company does not trust them, they are unlikely to behave in a constructive or enthusiastic way.

AUTHORISED AND PRODUCTIVE?

Another tool that we have developed to analyse systems and their impact on behaviour is one that asks how authorised and productive systems are. This model has been of significant practical value to many organisations we have worked with over the years.

You will note that we use the terms *authorised* and *unauthorised*. That is, they are either approved or ratified by the organisation, or not. This distinction reinforces the distinction we made earlier between authority and power. We do not use the terms formal or informal because some so-called *informal* systems are enforced by intimidation and significant pressure and are not informal at all.

An officer giving a command in combat is not in the business of influencing his or her troops to do what he or she requires. The troops have each signed an agreement that they will follow a lawful command – authority because it does not breach a boundary. Employees of an enterprise sign a contract of employment to perform any task assigned to them that they are competent to perform safely; the requirement of the leader in both cases is that they exercise authority, the authority of their role. The outcome of not adhering to the contract of employment is removal from the organisation or more severe in the armed forces. A citizen of a country is subject to the authority of the law in its various manifestations. Failure to do so results in removal from the role of citizen for a period in jail unless the country has the death penalty in which case the removal is permanent for some offences.

Obviously we are trying to design and implement systems so that they fit into box A: authorised by the organisation, and productive because they contribute to achieving the purpose of the organisation. We are all familiar, however, with systems that, while authorised, are actually a hindrance to working effectively (box B). We often describe such systems as bureaucratic, red tape or irritating. They are obstructive and often people will 'get around the system' in order to do their job. They cut corners to be more efficient or effective. Thus we get box C.

Box C behaviours and systems can be very creative and productive, but they can also be dangerous, especially if any safety rules and behaviours are compromised. In some organisations, box C may be the only way to get the job done, but there is a danger of denial of due process, inequities, as well as safety issues. Box C may provide ideas for positive change and innovation, but the ideas must be examined carefully to ensure other problems are not being created through the box C behaviours.

	Productive	Counter-Productive
Authorised	A – Well designed and implemented	B – Restrictive practices that have been adopted by the organisation
Unauthorised	C – People 'cutting corners' or breaking rules in order to get their work done	D – Alternative leadership based on power, e.g. intimidation, racism, sexism, stealing, work quotas, etc.

A Good
B Area for change
C Positive opportunities for change or education
D Must be addressed immediately, and done away with

Figure 13.1 Matrix for the Analysis of Systems

Box D behaviours and systems are not acceptable. Very simply, box D behaviour results in personal gain at the expense of the organisation. It may involve theft, racism, sexism and may be maintained by covert methods of intimidation. Behaviours and systems in box D must be crushed. Their existence is evidence of poor and weak leadership. As one worker put it, '[the boss] either has no guts or no brains'.

Thus, while box C and D both involve the use of power they are predicated upon very different motives and intent. It is essential to differentiate between them. A leader who disciplines someone who is well intentioned but who bent the rules, yet takes no action to crush racism, sexism, intimidation or theft has very effectively destroyed his or her own credibility with the workforce (see Figure 13.2).

We will examine the model and how to use it in more depth in Part 6. We have found its application to be a very useful model in practice. It is important to see it as a dynamic model.

It is common over a period of time for systems that were well designed and operated in box A to move into box B because of a change in work context, technology or regulation. The understandable response, and it is often led by very capable employees, is to develop a box C system. However, any employee using a box C system is open to disciplinary action because they are breaking the rules. In fact, a clear demonstration of the existence and inefficiency of box B systems is the effect on an organisation if its employees decide to work to rule. Productivity invariably collapses.

We have argued that organisations, as social entities, not only have purpose but also have standards which need to be adhered to if purpose is to be acceptably achieved. These standards are effectively the ethics of the organisation in practice and help inform and create its culture. These ethical standards are most clearly expressed by the leadership in policy. Policy is not merely compliance with the host society's laws; it must go beyond this to express the nature and culture of the organisation itself.

The leadership of the organisation, the Board, CEO and senior executives may be able to articulate policy but to employees, customers, suppliers, the local community and other shareholders it is the systems and behaviour that demonstrate the reality of the policy. In this way

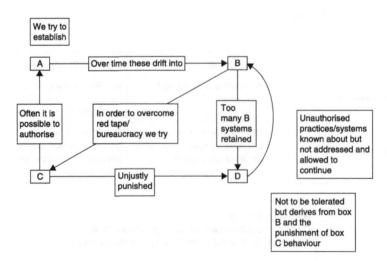

Figure 13.2   Possible Processes Driven by Different Categories of Systems

systems frame the work (turning intention into reality) and are critical to the actual achievement of purpose.

We have looked at ways of understanding systems: equalisation/differentiation, authorised/unauthorised, productive/counter-productive and will use these and other models later to look in more depth at the design and implementation of systems. This chapter has highlighted their significance in the enactment of policy and the identity of the organisation.

Key People Systems

It is crucial that the leader has available good systems to help build a productive work culture. The next part of this chapter outlines some key systems that should be operating well if the culture is to be effective. Those systems are described in more depth on the website.

PEOPLE SYSTEMS

We, like Jaques, always start with considering the work to be done. Some organisations place too much emphasis on building structures and grades and salary for career development and career opportunity. This can result in confused or over-complicated structures which do not help to get the work done. The circle of people systems are represented in Figure 13.3.

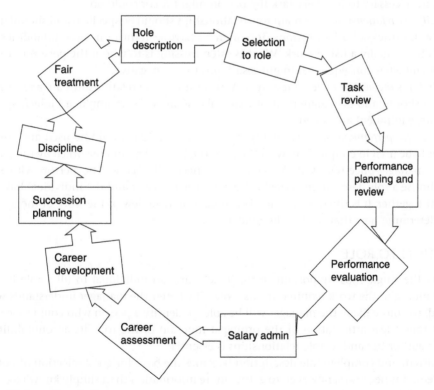

Figure 13.3   People Systems

ROLE DESCRIPTION

We start with the need to do work and the bundling of that work into roles. As we said earlier, a role contains a group of tasks and it is usually productive to have the core work of the role focused around a level of complexity. There will always be work of differing complexity in a role but it is important to be clear what is at the heart of the work of the role. Therefore, role descriptions should describe the work specifically.

Role descriptions should:

- Have a clear and simple purpose statement, that is, a positive description in one sentence, without using the word 'and'.
- Have a simple title. Role titles are one of the most significant symbols in an organisation.

We have seen 'deputy, assistant coordinator' and 'assistant, vice principal, head of support services'. We recommend titles common to level and to role type, for example, the title manager, principal at level 3, specialist at 2, general manager at 4, and so on. The role title should tell you the nature of the work and what level it is.

- *Describe in simple terms the key work of the role in terms of type of work.* For example, is this primarily a leadership role, a support role or a service role? It should also include the *outputs* expected. These outputs are not the same as individual task outputs, but are more general. For example, there may be a general output: 'to make sure you and your team work safely'. It might include a task, which could be: 'to design and implement a new safety system in your department to reduce lost time injury frequency to zero'. It should not be necessary to list every task the person might do or could do.
- *Specify role relationships.* The main role relationships should be specified and should include the authorities in both directions. Too often we have seen the term 'accountabilities' used, which is actually a list of work. What is often missing is to whom the person is accountable and what consequences might result: positive or negative.
- *Include a statement of material resources.* Authorities in role relationships are a resource but there should also be a statement of material resources, for example, a budget, spending limits, equipment and so on.
- *Provide for performance review.* Finally, the role description should be used and useful. It should be used in conjunction with the performance review and reworked by the manager and manager-once-removed (M+1) when it needs changing. The person who should authorise a role description is the M+1 even if the manager and the individual have put a draft together. It is the work of the M+1 to have an overview of the work of the team and to determine how that work is distributed.

SELECTION TO ROLE

Probably the single most important factor in selecting an individual to fill a role is a clear understanding of the work required in that role. The better the manager understands what is required, the more likely the manager will be able to identify a person who could successfully fill that role. Clear articulation of the principal function of the role, its accountability and tasks, its authorities and its role relationships is essential.

A current and complete role description becomes the basis for good selection of potential employees. It is necessary, however, to gather more information than simply knowledge about the role and the person being interviewed.

From the role description it is important to use the capability model to create a specification for the role in terms of the capability model:

- mental processing ability
- knowledge
- technical skills
- social skills
- application.

The qualities with regard to social process skills may be determined by the required role-relationships. For example, what are the characteristics of the current team? What sort of customers might the person have to deal with? Are people in other areas, specialists and services easy or difficult to relate to? List other requirements that may be important. For example, is significant travel required?

THE SELECTION PROCESS

Do not just rely on interviews. Consider what other methods may be relevant. We have found that giving the person an actual problem to solve; an in-basket exercise, for example, is very helpful. A team problem-solving exercise or case study can also reveal useful information with regard to social process. We are not very impressed with psychometric tests, especially if they are done separately and standard reports not specific to the role. It is too easy to use psychometric tests as substitutes for judgement. If they are used, then be clear about their validity and reliability, exactly what quality or skill is being tested, and how this fits with the role.

It is very important to clarify the authorities of anyone who is part of the selection process. For example, we have seen people appropriately involved in the process but confused as to whether they have a veto or recommendation or advisory authority.

Mistakes

We have all made mistakes in selection and no judgement process is foolproof. It is important to reflect on past errors and successes. We are all susceptible to certain distractions. Some typical distractions include:

- *Energy and drive* (application) – it is easy to be over-impressed and mistakenly see it as a compensation for other areas.
- *Appearance* – looking good or not is a classic example. Remember appearances can be deceptive.
- *Assumed similarity* – the fact that a person has been to a particular college, has a certain qualification or worked for a particular company can invoke assumptions that are actually not warranted. One of the authors remembers a particular comment 'He must be good. He was in the first eight [rowing]'. Think of how many distractions have fooled or are likely to fool you.
- *References* – it is really worth checking these directly by talking to referees where possible. We have also learned a great deal from people who have worked for a candidate. Many people are good at managing upwards but treat their team members poorly.

MONITORING YOURSELF (CONTROLS AND AUDIT)

When you select an individual, note in writing what you observed that led you to believe the person would be good in this role. Specifically record your interpretations of your observations and your thoughts as to why you picked this individual. Six months or a year later you can compare what was observed and how you interpreted those observations with the reality of the person selected.

If you do this every time you select an individual for a particular role, you will quickly learn your own strengths and weaknesses in the selection process. As we noted earlier, every human being has blind spots when it comes to selection. Some are fooled by a person who is very articulate; others rely too heavily on experience. Some prefer a person who appears very energetic or politically astute. All of these characteristics may be useful in some circumstances and may be just what is needed by the manager. On the other hand, they may also fool a manager into believing the person is capable of something they are not. You must be aware of the need for the mental processing ability of the person to match or exceed the complexity of the work of the role.

Task Feedback and Review

We have already discussed tasks and task assignment. The task doer also needs to know how their work performance is judged by the manager. This is necessary if the manager's judgement of performance of the task is to be accepted as fair. The key elements of task feedback and review are:

- context
- purpose
- quantity
- quality
- resources
- time.

TASK REVIEW

The purpose of task review is to learn lessons from both success and failure in order to improve work performance in the future. A task review is one form of task feedback, and is recognised in many organisations as the number-one system needed for improvement.

Task review is an informal process carried out on a regular but random basis by a manager as they comment (in a few words or at length) on task performance. Here the manager's role as trainer/coach is predominant. The emphasis is on a two-way, not a one-way process.

The employee may also initiate a task review when the employee thinks it is needed to improve their own work performance or the manager's work performance. It is valid and necessary to tell a manager from time to time, 'I could do my job better if ...'

Task review is intended to be an analytic process anchored in the concrete reality of specific tasks – where both the manager and employee look back at the task assignment, what was expected, and why – how well this was understood. Then they look at the execution of the task – what was done, whether the task doer in fact met the expectations.

Task review is the time to look at whether the task achieved its intended purposes. It is the time to analyse the chosen pathway and perhaps discuss other pathways which might have been more effective or efficient. There should be discussion as to whether changes in the environment required changing the task assignment and how a similar task might be assigned and done better in the future.

Where things have not gone as well as they should, this is a chance to inquire as to what went wrong and what might correct the problem in the future. This is where, on a regular basis, the manager and the person talk about their work and where the manager can provide coaching to help the person improve their work. The person may also provide information as to what the manager could do which would help the subordinate to achieve task goals.

Coaching and counselling are the everyday processes of leadership and management and should be anchored in the concrete: what the person did; how they did it; how the task was assigned (clearly or not); and whether the performance was good, poor or failed entirely.

Performance Planning and Performance Review

PERFORMANCE PLANNING

The purpose of performance planning is to make clear what is to be accomplished this year (or in a time-frame appropriate to the role – one year, two years, three to five years, ten years, and so on). This process:

- links the work of each individual to the corporate business plan;
- clarifies what the manager is expected to do and where the person fits into the manager's plan; and
- provides clear articulation of what constitutes excellent performance:
  - outputs can be measured and
  - work performance of the employee can be judged by the manager.

It is a good idea to discuss the manager's plan with the entire team to get their input and ideas. After the manager's plan is set, then individual plans can be made. It is also a good idea to have another team discussion, so that each knows what the other is doing and why.

Performance planning is the beginning of the performance management cycle, which includes task assignment, task review, performance review and performance evaluation. Task assignment and task review are ongoing throughout the year. Performance planning, performance review and performance evaluation form an annual cycle with performance review required at mid-point of the cycle. (More frequent performance reviews may be productive if managers or their reports wish to do them, but only one is required.) Performance evaluation is the end of the cycle and is immediately followed by performance planning for the next cycle.

In addition to the essential tasks, which the person must complete in order to meet the manager's requirements, the plan should indicate the resources allocated and the freedom of action available to the person at this time (areas where the person is encouraged to exercise initiative to improve the quality of work). This is also the time to discuss context, purpose, quantity and quality of output, resources, and planned time to completion for the significant activity planned.

PERFORMANCE REVIEW

The purpose of a performance review is to improve future work performance by examining how well both the manager and person are doing in carrying out their respective elements of the plan and their specific tasks. Performance review is a formal two-way analytic learning process for both manager and team member in order to:

- review what they planned to do – their purpose and plans – and what they actually have accomplished to date;
- review their work performance as individuals and as a team and
- make specific plans to improve their work effectiveness for the rest of the year (or next year).

Performance review must be carried out at least once a year, typically about six months into the performance plan. For persons new to a role, a performance review should be given after six months, or even quarterly, in addition to the annual performance review. We also recommend that it be done again, at the end of the year to inform the next year's performance plan.

A manager has the authority to decide that a formal performance review is needed at any time during the year due to particular issues or perceived problems. This is particularly important if someone is performing poorly. Such a discussion may uncover the source of the difficulties and provide a solution that will allow the manager and person to devise clear steps which need to be taken to improve performance.

In addition, a person may ask for a performance review whenever they feel this is needed. The requested performance review needs to be done within the time specified within the system given overall work commitments.

Note: As with all task and performance reviews in a work environment, the focus must be on the work, not on the person.

The performance review process involves an analysis of the work and tasks of both manager and team member to assess what has been accomplished over the six months or year, to evaluate the quality of what has been accomplished and to discover better ways of working together to achieve better results.

This is, in effect, a summing up of the task reviews that have taken place on a random basis during the year and provides a longer overview of performance – a look at the forest as opposed to the trees. It is a joint effort designed to reduce defensiveness by involving both manager and team member in an appraisal of what was accomplished and an analysis of what happened.

At the end of this review both manager and person should agree as to what work will be done to improve performance in the future. For example, they may agree on steps to be taken by each of them to clarify task assignments. Any other steps agreed to for either party should be noted. This should be written down and signed by the manager and the team member.

Performance Evaluation

UNDERSTANDING PERFORMANCE

We have found that the term 'performance' is used to mean two different things when organisations come to evaluate individual or team performance and when they wish to 'pay- for performance'.

OUTPUT AND PERFORMANCE

1. *Output or results*: Hard measures of same, which may include:
    *   relationship between targeted output and achieved output;
    *   outputs such as tonnes produced, number of cheques processed;
    *   results such as market share, industry rank, operating costs.

2. *Work performance*: How well or poorly a person has achieved the results, or output taking into consideration the quality of leadership, team membership behaviour and all relevant circumstances.
    *   How has the person exercised discretion?

OUTPUT OR RESULTS

Output or results can, and must, be measured. Valid measures are usually different at each level of work. Each employee's measures of performance must be relevant to his or her role, purpose and task assignments. Measures are essential:

*   to compare achieved outputs with target objectives;
*   to allow a manager to make adjustments in quantity, quality, resources or time in task assignment to ensure objectives are reached;
*   to provide employees with feedback about how they are doing and
*   to provide a clear statement of what is important, what should be monitored.

The caveat with all measures is that systems drive behaviour. It is important that the measures are valid and that the manager knows both what behaviour the measure drives and what systems surround the measure. The measure must be explicitly linked to the individual's work, and the linkage to behaviour must be understood. Choosing a measure or measurement system that drives counter-productive behaviour is a serious error. For example, a manufacturing company provides certain financial or psychological rewards for safety performance, which leads to non- or under-reporting of safety incidents; a social work agency decides to assess performance based on numbers of cases closed and, as a result, the most difficult cases are set aside and fester while the easiest cases are dealt with and closed.

Box 13.5   Output

Output, correctly measured, is very important. It must be taken into account as an indicator of work performance, but it is not, by itself, the measure of an individual's work performance.

Work performance

Work performance is how well or poorly a person has worked to achieve the results detailed above, and cannot be measured. It must be *judged* by a manager.

The question the manager is paid to answer is, 'How effectively has the person worked to achieve the assigned output or result in the situation in which the work was performed?'

WORK PERFORMANCE VERSUS OUTPUT MEASURES AND RESULTS

Work performance is a judgement made by the manager of the use of all the elements of capability – knowledge, social process skills, technical skills, application and mental processing ability – by a subordinate, based on the tasks that make up the role. The manager must take into account:

- the output or results achieved as measured by various indicators;
- the complexity of the situation in which the work was performed;
- the person's effectiveness (or lack thereof) in the light of that situation;
- how the person balanced competing long-term and short-term demands and
- how well the person responded to changing conditions (see Box 13.6).

While there may be many objective measures of output and results, when it comes to the work performance of the individual employee, there are always mitigating circumstances that can demonstrate the objective measures are incomplete.

Work performance evaluation is often the task most dreaded by managers. Many attempt to avoid problems by rewarding people with the average salary increase. This not only leads to salary distortion but also undermines the concept of meritocracy by creating a seniority system wherein a person's pay increases with length of service and is not related to work performance.

Properly done, a face-to-face evaluation of work performance is a healthy element in an honest work relationship.

The purpose of performance evaluation is to assess the work performance of employees in order to recognise and reward differentially.

If done properly it:

- confirms to an employee the worth of his or her work;
- makes visible what the organisation and the manager desires by what they recognise and reward;
- recognises differences in the work performance of different employees;
- allows the demonstration of managerial capability, fairness, honesty and courage and
- provides an evaluation methodology that can apply to a variety of salary administration systems, for example, straight salary adjustment, at risk salary adjustment, bonuses and profit-sharing.

Summary of Performance Evaluation Systems

1. Why are many performance evaluation systems not effective?
   - Poor design causes the forms to be too time-consuming to fill out.
   - Reliance on allegedly objective measures rather than the combination of objective measures and the subjective judgement that is required.
   - Subjectivity disguised with so-called objective standards. As one manager put it, 'The system asks the manager to create an objective-looking document to explain what is really a subjective judgment.'
   - The system asks the manager to perform two psychologically contradictory processes simultaneously: the manager is expected to help the person improve his or her work performance – to act as a trainer/coach, while at the same time evaluating a

person's work performance and making decisions that will have impact on salary – to act as a judge. These activities need to be in separate systems, operating at different times.

- The evaluation process may even require a recommendation regarding the future potential of the subordinate, all of which must be done at the same time using the same system. This creates confusion between work performance evaluation, the work of the manager; and potential review, the work of the M+1. This creates deep psychological and practical problems. It also encourages defensiveness on the part of both participants.
- These factors cause managers to fudge their thinking and their statements (in effect to tell lies), which is known to both manager and team member. This dishonesty puts the relationship at much greater risk than any honest evaluation of work performance.
- If the system will have an impact on an individual's future career, there is a tendency to soften a negative evaluation for fear of doing long-term damage to the person's career or to escalate a positive evaluation to ensure future potential for advancement.

2. Some possible inadequacies which the manager may need to confront:
    - Were task assignments really clear?
    - Did I give recognition, task feedback and conduct task reviews?
    - Did I let the person know I was dissatisfied with certain aspects of their performance at the time it occurred?

    If the answer to these questions is 'no', evaluating work performance will most probably be perceived as unfair by the subordinate: 'If that was what you wanted, why didn't you say so?'

3. Some managers have told us of concerns that their ratings will be different from other managers.
    - Some managers have said they are concerned they are being too hard on their people as compared to other managers.
    - Some managers say they are concerned about being too easy on their people as compared to other managers.
    - The real issue is equity – similar treatment across units, divisions, and business units.

4. Fear of legal challenge: the words written by managers on performance evaluation forms may come back to haunt them. There are enough cases of legal challenges regarding discrimination and unlawful dismissal that managers often are concerned about the legal consequences of what they say or write.

    This concern has been argued as a case for bland, innocuous statements, which are less likely to be used in court, but which, in turn, have little or no positive impact on individual performance. They are seen for what they are, an exercise that demonstrates a lack of courage: everyone knows performance evaluation is an exercise we must go through, a lot of sound and fury signifying nothing.

    The threat of court action has been put forwards as a reason for managers to give everyone a good or adequate rating and an average salary increase. Later when it can no longer be denied that someone needs to be dismissed from role for poor performance, these 'good' ratings over the years make legal challenge of the dismissal easy for the plaintiff and often costly to the organisation and the individual manager.

The courts openly recognise the requirement for managers to make judgements. They are concerned that the judgements be legal, consistent, fair and supported by clearly articulated and understood systems that do not differentiate on non-work-related grounds.

Salary Administration

One of the reasons that performance evaluation creates so much anxiety is that it is linked to pay. Task review and performance review leaves open the possibility for improvement prior to a judgement that affects what a person can earn.

PAY FOR PERFORMANCE

The basic salary should reflect fair pay. However, there is also a need for a component that reflects the nature of individual contributions. The relative amount of performance pay in terms of percentage of salary may vary but we argue that:

* *It should be clearly understood.* The rules and triggers in some systems are almost impossible to understand.
* *It should be clearly linked to personal performance and contributions.* Whilst this is still a matter of judgement the evaluation should be fairly based on what a person has done. Deming has been very clear about poor systems that offer reward but where the control of the reward is out of the person's control or even the organisation's control. For example, neither a person nor an organisation can control international prices of commodities. An operator cannot operate if machinery and equipment is unavailable. Some so-called performance components are almost impossible to avoid. We have seen systems where simply turning up is almost enough to trigger the full performance component.
* *Do not confuse this system with bonus or profit share systems.* Many organisations pay a bonus for reaching targets that, as mentioned above, may be the result of many people and departments achieving objectives. Whilst these systems have the advantage of appearing to share wealth, they can also cause confusion or a sense of unfairness when 'I have done my best but because of X I have lost my bonus'.

Finally, with all payment systems the questions in the systems design chapter remain highly relevant. It is particularly relevant to ask:

* What is the purpose?
* Is it really a system of differentiation?
* What behaviour do you expect this to drive? Why?
* Does the person understand it?

We have seen many other components of salary given in other forms: cars, allowances, stock options and so on. We are very wary of such systems as they can create negative mythologies.

Our approach, consistent within this book, is to keep systems clear and simple with an unambiguous purpose. One operator at a plant in Australia commented 'I like working here, I have exactly the same contract as the General Manager except for the salary'; he paused and then said 'and I wouldn't want his job for love nor money'.

Identifying and Developing Potential

CAREER ASSESSMENT

While some people are content to stay in one role for almost all their employment career, most people do like change and do want a career. Even staying with 'one role' it is inevitable that that role will change and the person will need to learn new skills and knowledge.

Identifying potential and providing opportunities for people to develop and use their capability is essential. It is very important to distinguish between the work of the immediate manager and the manager's manager in this process (see Box 13.6).

In order to be effective, the M+1 should have a clear understanding of the various roles, career patterns and career opportunities in the organisation. It is helpful to know something about future corporate or departmental directions in order to guide people into new roles that are likely to be needed by the organisation. We use the term *mentoring* to describe the work of M+1 in preparing people for future roles. *Coaching* is the term to describe helping someone improve in his or her current role.

THE MANAGER-ONCE-REMOVED

The manager-once-removed:

1. Identifies people who are ready for promotion to the level of their immediate team and takes steps to see they are offered such a promotion either within their team or elsewhere. This ensures the business gets the best use of its most talented people by placing them in a role that matches their capabilities.
2. Makes a judgement of the likely career paths based on their abilities and interests.
3. Discusses career options on a regular but varying basis depending upon the stage of a person's career. For bright young people who are judged to have high-level potential and who, therefore, should move rapidly through the organisation, an annual or biennial review might be appropriate. A longer review period of three or even five years is appropriate for people who are comfortable at their current level. Toward the end of a person's career, one assessment of potential may be enough for the person who will not advance further in the organisation and knows it.

Box 13.6   Management's Role in Developing Potential

In essence it is the work of the immediate manager to provide for the development of people who report to them directly in their current roles. That is, the manager should be working to develop their knowledge, technical and social process skills and encourage them to be more effective in doing their current work. It is the work of the M+1 to assess who, if anyone, has the potential to work at a higher level and who needs to change role in order to improve their contribution at the same level.

This is not to say this is exclusively the domain of the managers and M+1s. The immediate manager may well identify people whom they think have potential and recommend them. Peers, colleagues and others may have an influence. The individual concerned has critical work to do. The person's own ambition, view of their own capability and valuing of the work is critical in this process. Understanding the difference between current performance and potential and who to discuss this with allows this process to succeed or fail.

Conducting assessments of potential too frequently is unnecessary and may cause difficulty especially if they imply promises of promotion.

Keep in mind that each person is responsible for his or her own career. The M+1 is in a position to advise people regarding many important aspects of their careers:

- the kind of organisation this is – its culture, what is valued in its employees;
- career patterns, how people advance in this organisation;
- M+1's assessment of the person's career potential;
- what types of roles and tasks the individual might undertake to gain needed knowledge or skills;
- education and training programmes the person might find useful;
- opportunities for special assignments;
- estimated timing of various elements of the person's career progression.

With the views of the M+1, the individual can put together a career development plan indicating interests and setting some target timetables to move into particular roles. Discussions with the M+1 should also make clear if certain positions are essential if a person is to advance to higher levels of work. For example, in the US Army, few become a major general who have not had experience as a company commander and a battalion commander.

The M+1 is in no position to promise that the person will attain a particular role or a particular level of work in the future. This will depend upon the person's performance, when openings at a particular level or in a particular field come open, and who is available to fill those roles. The best person available at the time a role is open should get that position.

Career development as part of the M+1's work

In many organisations the manager of an individual is assumed to be accountable both for the person's work performance and for their career advancement. There are major problems with this assumption in regard to career advancement.

1. The manager is in the wrong position to make a decision about promotion of a direct report. They have neither the authority nor the perspective to make a decision regarding promotion.

   Promotion moves the team member to the level of the manager. This requires a decision by the manager's manager (the M+1) to determine if the person is ready to fill a role at this level.

   Only the M+1 is in a position to know and encompass the work of the manager and the manager's peers. Thus it is only the M+1 who can make an effective judgement if an individual is ready to work at a level immediately reporting to M+1. This does not mean that the manager cannot, or should not, make recommendations with regard to promotion. It is an important managerial task to bring capable people to the attention of their M+1, but the decision regarding promotion is made by M+1.

2. The M+1 will also have a better perspective on organisational needs and opportunities across the organisation, far beyond that available to the immediate manager.

3. Without an organised process of potential assessment, an organisation will draw from a small pool of talent (those who are noticed or are good at self-promotion). The people promoted may not be the best people, and the organisation accepts what happens rather than working to get the best use of talent to cope with the competitive challenges it will

face over the years. Having able people to fill key roles is far too important to be left to chance and individual initiative.

Despite appearances to the contrary, business organisations do try to promote the best people, as the managers making the decision define 'best'. Yet without an ordered and known system based upon a correct understanding of managerial and M+1 authorities in the organisation, the process of promotion will be flawed to a greater or lesser extent.

4. Any given manager may have a team member who is more capable than them, one who carries much of the load for their manager. (In some cases incompetent managers may hide their shortcomings for a considerable period of time by having others do their work.)

Even with a competent manager, it is always tempting to keep an able team member beyond the time they should be promoted. Such talented people feel buried beneath a manager who has a vested interest in keeping them down, and they rightly feel resentment over this fact. Such people may leave the organisation, or if they stay, they may become resentful and work less effectively than they might if they had the opportunity to be noticed and promoted at the right time.

Finding and fostering the organisation's human talent

It is the work of the M+1 to identify the most able employees early in their careers and take steps to foster their development.

M+1s need to be held accountable for assessing the potential of *all* their people one level removed. This has the effect of opening up the talent pool by including people who usually go unnoticed in more informal systems.

Special training and job opportunities can be assigned to people who are judged to be most able – testing the M+1's judgement. This allows possible errors of judgement on the part of the M+1 to be corrected early in a person's career to avoid either too rapid or too slow advancement. It also increases the likelihood that the most able people will have challenges commensurate with capability talents, making them more productive for the organisation over their entire careers. The best people are more likely to stay in the organisation rather than seeking opportunities elsewhere. In this way the work of the M+1 helps to reduce (and eventually eliminate) the power games of informal mentoring systems.

The authorities of the M+1 to assess potential as well as the manager's authority to veto selection provide a system to inhibit such power games. Each is held accountable for exercising their authorities.

By giving all employees assessments as appropriate, the maximum benefit may be derived from the talent pool of the organisation. In doing this the M+1 can learn about the quality of managerial work exercised by their immediate reports. The insights gained from the M+1 relationships makes it possible to give their immediate reports better feedback and coaching to improve their managerial practices.

The M+1 authority leads to communications with people one level removed and these in turn may make it easier for these people to initiate discussions on other topics, including potential problems and opportunities which might otherwise remain hidden from higher level view (see Box 13.6).

In summary the M+1 is the appropriate person to assess potential, albeit with input and information from a variety of sources. The person being assessed will usually have a realistic view of their own ability if they really understand and have confirmed the nature of the work required. Once the assessment is made, career development can occur: finding opportunities inside and outside the workplace for the person to fulfil their potential.

Succession Planning

The work on assessment and development with the associated information then should become part of succession planning. Succession planning is the proper ordering of all the information in career assessment and development to create an overall view of the organisation. The identification and development of a talent pool is necessary if the organisation is to survive and grow. If the systems of performance management, career assessment and development are in place these can form the basis of the succession planning system.

This system requires the M+2, with M+1s and input from HR specialists to review the organisational structure. The present structure and the proposed structure (based on the business plan) must be articulated. For every current and proposed role three names need to be identified as possible successors (unless the role is to go).

The identification should be made according to three categories:

1. *Ready now*: This is someone who could take the role today and perform well immediately.
2. *Ready within three months*: This is someone who could, within a short time, be ready for the role and only needs some knowledge or the addition of some technical skills that can be quickly learned.
3. *Ready within one year*: This is someone who may need some significant development in knowledge, technical skills or social process skills. They may need to experience a leadership role or sales or financial/business work.

Names can then be discussed and the M+2 can decide on the final list and the category each is in. One rule is that no name can appear more than twice on the shadow chart. We now have a measure of how well prepared the organisation is for succession. Clearly fewer names or significant gaps give cause for concern. The context must be considered, however, and having three names in category 1 for every role might indicate an organisation where people are ready to leave. As one leader (M+2) explained to us, 'We only have one role at level 5. We recruit highly capable people. The trouble is the best leave if they see their chances diminish.'

Discipline and Appeal

Throughout this book we have emphasised the importance of human judgement and human relationships. We are all subjects, and hence subjective. We have our own lenses through which we view the world and make those judgements. We do not want to be 'objects'. We are not simply at the mercy of scientific materialistic laws. The fact that judgement is subjective does not make it necessarily biased and idiosyncratic.

Human judgement can and should be informed by data and information. We can and must use evidence. Courts are a good example of the need for evidence, not merely speculation, but there is still a judge and a jury. Human judgement is informed but not replaced by facts and information.

At the heart of leadership is an attachment between people. People are not inspired solely by a sheet of objective facts or cash reward.

However, it is clear that judgement can be flawed, can be prejudiced, can be plain wrong.

If someone has a manager and, in our model, accepts that the manager has the authority to judge performance, what can be done if the person believes the judgement to be wrong?

In this section we will look at different situations and how they can be addressed before recourse to third parties or the law. We will examine the importance of disciplinary processes.

We have noted that many managers find performance feedback, review and especially evaluation difficult. Very few people enjoy giving bad news whether that is concerned with performance or potential. Most people have been in this situation either as giver or receiver.

It is often characterised by a knotted stomach. Nonetheless, avoiding the issue of poor performance and disciplinary consequences is perhaps the most costly activity in a business. Avoiding difficult issues causes good workers to be demoralised. It gives rise to negative mythologies and a resort to power.

In this area, perhaps more than any other, the most important principle is that the systems and processes must be clear and accessible. Leaders, especially managers, must ask 'Do people know about and understand the limits?'. These limits include:

- policies
- systems
- code of conduct
- operating procedures
- safety regulations
- limits of a task
- limits of authority.

How easy is it to find out about the limits? If people are not aware of the limits, how can they be disciplined fairly for breaking them?

Do people know and understand the consequences? Again we would argue that all disciplinary systems should be clearly communicated and widely understood.

Do people know and understand disciplinary procedures? These procedures should include:

- verbal and written warnings
- authorised actions, for example suspension, stand down, dismissal
- legal rights.

We must start from the proposition that disciplinary systems should be known and/or easily knowable. These topics should be part of induction process and training. If that is the case, then we must start from a clear statement of the problem.

FAIR TREATMENT SYSTEMS (FTSs)

The person involved in procedures outlined above may not want or feel able to raise the matter with the manager or even M+1. The matter may be too personal, serious or demonstrate a fundamental breakdown in trust. This is such a critical area that we recommend all organisations have an internal fair treatment system (FTS). We have helped design many such systems and depending on the size and nature of the organisation they may vary in detail. However all FTSs have core principles in common.

The system is enabled by the presence of advisers, called fair treatment advisers (FTAs). These are people who are chosen for their maturity (not necessarily age related), social process skills and reputation for keeping matters confidential. They are trained in the system details and their purpose is to advise on the process. Does the person (complainant) know how the system works? Is it serious? Is it another matter? They do not act as advocates.

FTSs are not a substitute for legal complaints. The system should not attempt to replace legal complaints. The FTS is designed to investigate unfair treatment, not illegal treatment. Thus the FTA may advise only on the existence of a case of sexual harassment, assault, fraud, negligence, and so on. This immediately suggests a limit may have been broken and therefore puts it in the first category (see above). If it is not (at least initially) a legal issue then the person can initiate the FTS process with the advice but not advocacy of the FTA.

The system requires the appointment of a fair treatment investigator (FTI) to carry out an inquiry. The FTI must be at least the peer, or, more usually, a level above the person against whom the complaint is directed. Thus, if I am complaining about my manager, then a person of at least his or her equivalent will investigate. We recommend one level above, but it depends upon the size of organisation. It must be remembered that this system now operates like an audit: it is a corporate policy and system owned and authorised by the board and CEO. The FTI has the delegated authority of the CEO. The FTI, who must be trained and also advised by the FTA, then has full authority to question, look at papers, emails, and so on, in order to investigate the complaint and make a recommendation.

The recommendation is then made to the manager of the person who has been accused of unfairness. In larger organisations it is the M+1 of the person unless these people have been a subject of the investigation (and perhaps involved in the complaint). The line manager then decides whether to implement the recommendation. Whatever the decision is, it must be communicated to all involved including the FTA.

APPEAL

If the complainant is not satisfied, they can then appeal to the CEO (if the complaint is not already at that level). The CEO then reconsiders the evidence, the recommendation and the decision and makes a final judgement.

We have also considered the involvement, during the FTI stage, of an outside party. While not ruling this out absolutely we recommend against this unless such a person is very knowledgeable about the organisation and is well respected in it, for example, a recently retired executive. The FTS is an internal process and should be appreciated for this.

Using the FTS does not prejudice the person from using other avenues, such as an agreed process involving a union or industrial tribunal. However, if the complainant uses this first then they forfeit their right to use the FTS for the same complaint at a later date or if the outcome is unfavourable.

It should be emphasised that the FTS is not an HR system. Although FTAs may be from the HR stream, it is an executive system.

SUMMARY OF FAIR TREATMENT SYSTEMS

The FTS is not an alternative to other means of complaint. It is available as a control on managerial judgement, particularly with regard to task assignment and performance review. It is there to demonstrate that a person does not have to rely on third parties to achieve a fair treatment. Some may say it will only support 'the bosses'. If that is the perception, it already demonstrates low trust and poor leadership. Healthy relationships do still have problems, whether at work, in families or outside relationships. We regard it as important to first try and resolve these matters in house. The FTS is a system which is necessary if that is to be possible. For us it is one of the critical systems for a high-trust organisation.

Conclusion

All of these systems work together. They should be integrated and owned in the line not by HR. Failure to pay attention to careers and succession means the best people will leave and capability is wasted. While the processes need to be well designed, they still require and rest upon managerial judgement. There are no quick and easy short cuts. Although advice from a range of sources can be helpful, it can also be confusing unless authority is clear and the concepts compatible.

Most importantly, the one trap it is important to avoid is that of promising a future that cannot be delivered. It is easy at the time to either explicitly or implicitly give a person an impression that either their performance or their prospects are much brighter than they are in reality. This is often unintended, but dishonesty will cause disillusionment if not anger and plays back into power games.

Our experience is that people are quite realistic about themselves when given accurate information and feedback. They also do not need to have their entire careers mapped out, false ceilings or limitless sky.

Not everyone performs well; some break limits and this must be dealt with. As with all systems, controls and audits are essential. The fair treatment system is itself a control on managerial judgement. Without it mythologies will grow that poor judgement rather than poor performance is the real problem and trust will diminish or evaporate. These systems are discussed and described in more depth elsewhere (see website).

14 *Task Formulation and Assignment*

What Are Tasks?

We have put forward concepts and a framework for understanding work, leadership, authority and systems. An essential part of leadership work and achieving success in general is the proper assignment of tasks.

Like many other concepts, assigning tasks may appear deceptively simple, but we have seen and experienced a significant amount of wasted time and effort because of poor task assignment. When one person is not clear and another has misunderstood, the result is waste, inappropriate blame, poor performance review and the creation of mythologies that place the behaviour of leaders at the negative ends of the values continua – dishonest, untrustworthy, no respect for dignity, unfair.

Again, these various social meanings are useful, but for the purpose of improving our understanding of management and organisations a sharper definition is needed.

If work is *turning intention into reality*, a *task* is a statement of intention with *context, purpose, quality/quantity, resources* and *time* (CPQ/QRT), stated explicitly to provide boundaries within which the work is to be done (see Box 14.1).

Box 14.1   Definition of Task

Task: An assignment to carry out work within limits that include the Context, Purpose, Quantity and Quality of output expected, the Resources available and the Time by which the objective is to be reached (CPQ/QRT).

Human Work, Tasks and the Exercise of Discretion

Given the large body of literature on delegation, and our experiences in a variety of organisations, it appears that many managers have considerable difficulty in the task assignment process. Some behave in a way that shows clearly they do not trust those to whom they have assigned work, to do a good job. They spend considerable time and effort checking and re-checking their progress and interfering (micro-managing) the employee's work. Others give little or no direction or advice and apparently assume their direct reports know what to do. Many managers never explain why a task is to be done – its purpose – or the expected circumstances in which it is to be done – its context – which remain a mystery to those who are supposed to carry it out.

For the purpose of this section we will assume that the manager is assigning a task, although there will be circumstances where people assign tasks to others outside a managerial relationship. The manager must provide certain information to the person and also leave room for the person to create a pathway (exercise discretion) to achieve the objective. There is considerable research to suggest that when people speak about work, and when they assign worth to their own work, what they really appreciate is their use of judgement and choice as they turn intention into reality.

As we have noted, the ability to use judgement and make decisions to achieve a goal is a distinctly human characteristic. By allowing and encouraging the application of the full capacity of employees in using this judgement, managers demonstrate their recognition that employees are people with minds and ideas as well as their trust in them.

Inhibiting or preventing the use of judgement treats people as if they were machines (objects). It is not unusual in these circumstances for employees to breach a limit just to prove they exist. The result is inefficiency, work-to-rule, non-adherence to standard operating practices or even industrial action (slow-downs or strikes).

PEOPLE AND TASK ASSIGNMENT

People are able to understand overall objectives and purpose, ask questions for clarification, take note of changes in their environment and adjust their work accordingly by exercising judgement and coping with uncertainty. It is absolutely essential that for people the pathway be left open for the exercise of judgement, so that variations in the environment which might be expected but which cannot be predicted can be managed.

This is where people have an advantage over machines: they take into account purpose and they can adapt and change in furtherance of that purpose as conditions change.

If people are to use judgement effectively and efficiently for their organisation, they must understand the purpose of what they are doing.

TASK ASSIGNMENT PROCESSES

The purpose of these processes described below is to ensure the persons assigned the tasks:

- have a clear understanding of the task they are to do;
- believe they are able to commit themselves to doing it; and
- are in a position to accept their manager's judgement of their work performance as fair.

Clear understanding requires that the task be Formulated and Assigned correctly. To gain commitment it is usually helpful to provide people (task doers) with the opportunity to be involved in the task formulation process, though there will be occasions when time pressure does not permit this. To place employees in a position where they are able to accept their manager's authority to judge their performance as fair, task doers must know what the manager wants them to do, and they must know the basis on which the manager will judge their performance. They must have an opportunity to have their task performance reviewed and recognised in the context of the actual conditions under which the task was performed.

Task assignment, properly understood, is a subtle and complex process – one which requires considerable practice to master.

The guidelines are not a statement of absolute requirements to be articulated and recorded at every step. As the relationship between a manager and team members develops, clarity in task assignment may be achieved without a complete articulation as provided for in the guidelines. Attempting to articulate everything at all times and under all circumstances is likely to become mechanistic as well as time-consuming for the task assignor, annoying for the task doer and thus, unproductive.

IMPORTANCE OF CLEAR TASK ASSIGNMENT AND ACCOUNTABILITY

There have been endless discussions of delegation and how advantageous it is to do it, but there is little consistency regarding exactly what is to be delegated, why or how to do it. Delegation can mean passing on a notion from someone higher in the organisation. It can mean abdication of work and authority on the part of the person who is delegating. It can mean giving orders or suggesting something might be a good idea.

We use the term *task assignment* to make very clear what is to be done and then to provide advice on better ways to accomplish the work. Businesses and public agencies are created to produce goods and services through people who are employed to do work. Therefore it makes sense to assign that work in such a way that people are prepared to accept accountability for ensuring it gets done properly.

It is important to realise that accountability only exists in reality if the person being called to account accepts it. No matter what managers may believe, accountability cannot be imposed on people. To gain the acceptance of accountability requires an understanding, and the achievement of, the conditions that are necessary for such acceptance. Accountability is a function of the relationship between a manager and a direct report. The manager calls a person to account by requiring an answer to the following questions:

What did you do?
How did you do it?
Why did you do it that way?

In this way we can see the judgement is *not* just about *output* but also should take into account the *input* and the *process* chosen to turn the input into the desired output. Work performance covers *all three* aspects (see Box 14.2 Problems with Accountability).

The purpose of accountability is to inform the manager about the performance of work, so he or she may make a judgement about the efficacy of its performance as well as the judgement of the capability of the person who did it given the context in which the task was performed.

A good manager will always allow discussion of the judgement.

If work is to be done effectively and efficiently, it is essential that people be recognised and rewarded based on the merit of their work.

To build a system of merit, just as with accountability, we must understand and deliver the necessary conditions for the acceptance of differential reward as a measure of merit for work performance before we can create acceptance of a system of merit.

If, however, those carrying out the tasks are to accept accountability for their work and accept differential recognition and reward as one measure of the merit of their work, they must know the criteria against which their manager will make his or her judgement on accountability and assess their work performance. Therefore the manager must assign tasks correctly. There is enough uncertainty involved in working out how to do something without confusion and uncertainty as to what needs to be done or what dimension of a task needs to be optimised.

Box 14.2   Problems with Accountability

The word accountability evokes different responses some quite emotional even visceral. Many equate the word with blame or punishment or at least being told off for doing something wrong. Again this is a problem that arises from a lack of a universal shared definition of accountability and people believing that their understanding of that word is the correct one. Our view is that accountability is an essential and potentially very positive part of good working relationships. We have found that people in most organisations are very happy, indeed enjoy, talking about their work. We have found that people are very open about the factors that enable or hinder them in achieving their purpose and completing tasks. So why does the term accountability receive such a bad press?

We believe that a negative view of accountability is based on several factors. First people intuitively understand that being held accountable for the outputs of work but not being given the authority and/or resources to do that work is inherently unfair which is why we argue so strongly for clarity around the nature of authority. It is not unusual for people to have to 'account for' results when they do not control or even influence parts of the process that affect that result.

Secondly, accountability gets a bad name because of poor task assignment. This entire chapter stresses the need for clarity around expectations and offers a model to help in the clarification process: CPQ/QRT. Again people find it unfair and/or disrespectful and/or unloving when they are told something is not what was expected when those expectations have not been made clear in the first place!

The third source of negativity around accountability stems from a lack of clarity around what part of the work process is being focused upon and discussed. We use a simple diagram, familiar to many, especially anyone involved in system design, lean manufacturing or simple scientific process. We can see that work involves inputs, outputs and the process(es) chosen to turn those inputs into outputs. See Figure 14.1.

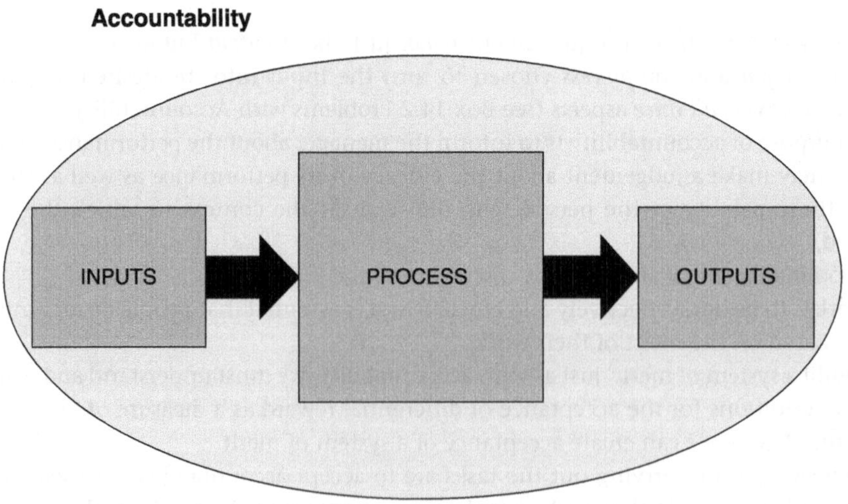

Figure 14.1   Accountability

Many performance management systems, and hence accountability discussions focus on one of these elements rather than how they fit together. Thus, if target setting and output measures are the only real concern then this distorts and undermines the opportunity for a full and proper discussion. This focus on outputs or targets is unsatisfactory because it pays no attention to the two other critical parts of the process: the inputs and the process. It disregards how difficult or easy it has been to achieve that output. It effectively says I don't care about the pathway or process that you have chosen I don't care about the inputs, all that matters to me is the outputs. This is the sort of distortion that leads to highly counter-productive and destructive work processes such as those that led to the global financial crisis.

Similarly, however, a focus purely on process causes distortions. This is similar to our discussion of Box B behaviours and systems. All that appears to matter is that a particular process was followed whether or not it was appropriate with regard to the inputs and whether or not it actually achieves the outputs. Focusing on any one of these elements or even two of these elements does not result in creative and productive accountability discussions. The real heart of accountability is to understand how and why inputs become outputs and why certain processes successfully transform those inputs into desired outputs and other processes do not. An accountability discussion should have at its heart learning and the production of new knowledge, improvement and consequently more efficient and effective work.

Accountability should be concerned with all the three elements and how they interact. For example if we compare a private school with a state school a critical difference between these two similar organisations (they are both about educating young people) is that one; the state school does not have the authority to manage inputs. They usually have to take a range of children due to geographical location rather than other criteria that can be used to select out more challenging and demanding pupils. Therefore to compare the outputs directly between such schools is simplistic and misleading secondly the processes that are used in both institutions may be properly quite different because the inputs, that is the students, are different with different qualities.

We have found that where discussions include the consideration of all three elements there is a much higher likelihood of creativity and innovation. Finally most of us actually enjoy discussing our work if it involves the consideration of how and why we chose to do certain things in that context. As such we see that accountability discussions can be a very productive part of the social processes of an organisation which in turn can lead to improvement and the sense of real appreciation and worth for the people working in that organisation.

TASK FORMULATION

All tasks that are to be assigned to another person begin in the mind.

Task formulation is a process whereby the manager assesses the situation, including input from others, determines what is to be done, why it is to be done, the deadline for its completion, the resources available to perform the task and the limits within which it must be accomplished. As will be shown later, it is usually good practice for managers to seek ideas from the task doers as to some, or all, of these elements during task formulation. Indeed the discussion between the manager and his or her team members will often be very helpful in determining what the task actually is (see Chapter 15 work and authority of team leaders and members).

Such a formulation always contains assumptions about the environment in which the task will be carried out. It is like the water in which the fish swims: present, but not consciously considered unless subject to drastic change. We must bear in mind that tasks are always assigned in the present for performance in the future, and no one is able to predict the future with complete accuracy. Therefore it is good practice for managers to give consideration to the expected environment and provide the context for the task's performance.

STATING PURPOSE/SETTING CONTEXT

The most vital element in the task assignment process is the statement of the *purpose* to be achieved by the accomplishment of the task as shown in Box 14.3 Too often the purpose is assumed or ignored when telling someone to 'do this'. This is particularly true at the lower levels of organisations where there is a far greater demonstrated tendency for employees to be treated more as objects (machines) than as people.

Setting the *context* involves answering questions about the circumstances in which the task is to be performed, the background as to why the task needs to be done and how it fits in with other work as shown in Box 14.4 Is there a specific problem or an emergency? Other key points:

- Why the task is important?
- How does it relate to other tasks?
- Who is doing related tasks?

You may have had the experience of being assigned a task and had your manager say, 'You will need to be a bit careful with Fred for a few days. His daughter is ill, and he is not his normal self.' This is a manager assigning a task to be performed in an environment that is different from what the task doer has been accustomed to.

Knowing the purpose of the task and its context will enable the task doer to use judgement more effectively. It will allow the task doer to recognise that if the context changes and make it more likely that the unforeseen change will be overcome. Most importantly, knowledge of context and purpose will allow the task doer to come back to the manager quickly to advise him or her of the unforeseen change in context or if the task does not appear to be achieving its intended purpose. In this way errors, injury, damage or waste may be avoided. This point is of critical importance for safety at work.

Too often we see examples of good people continuing to complete the assigned task in the face of a markedly changed context, and being caught up in an unfolding disaster that takes lives or damages people severely. One of the very substantial changes for the better in

---

Box 14.3   Definition of Purpose

Purpose: What is to be achieved by accomplishing this task? A purpose statement should be able to be expressed in a single sentence without an 'and' (as conjunction). If we have 'ands' there will inevitably at some point be lack of clarity, competition and conflict between 'purposes'. There can, however, be subordinate outcomes, e.g. 'The purpose of this training is to learn how to drive a car. We hope you enjoy it and have fun doing so.' Here it is clear that the purpose is to learn to drive a car. If we enjoy the process and have fun but fail to learn the purpose has not been achieved. If we learn to drive but do not have fun the purpose is achieved but not in the way that was ideally intended.

Box 14.4   Definition of Context

Context: The situation in which it is most likely the task will be performed, including the background conditions, the relationship of this task to other tasks and any unusual factors to be taken into account.

Box 14.5 Context and Purpose

There is an old story about two medieval stone masons, one bent and drained from a day's work, one singing. When asked what they had been doing, the first said, 'I have been lifting heavy stones all day.' The second, 'I have been building a cathedral.'

---

industrial safe work practice over recent decades has been the spread of the dictum and the practice of: 'If you are unsure, STOP and seek advice.'

Knowledge of context and purpose has other benefits as well (see Box 14.5).

We have stated our definition of a task as an assignment to carry out work within limits described by the context, purpose, quantity and quality of output expected, the resources available and the time by which the objective is to be reached. We have also noted that all work is carried out within boundary conditions that include all the prescribed limits of law, social custom and practice, corporate and department policies. These boundary conditions are the *givens* that the person assigning the task cannot change in the task assignment process.

Many of these limits should be known to the task doer, but we highlight them here as a reminder that people who are new to role, or people who may not be able to keep up with all the changes in laws and regulatory policies, may have to be reminded of the boundary conditions if they are to be clear regarding the area for discretion in the task assignment. When things begin to go wrong, it is always a good idea to review whether or not the boundary conditions were known and not applied or if the boundary conditions were not clear. There will be some tasks in which a boundary condition is particularly important; this needs to be articulated in the context discussion.

TASK DIMENSIONS

These must be set by the manager and include output, time and resources:

Output: Stated in terms of quality and quantity.
Time: The targeted completion time – a deadline indicating when the task is to be completed.
Resources: Defined in terms of cost or resource use. Resource use is required in circumstances where the task doer has no control over the item cost but may influence the number of items used. Other resources include people, authorities, access to information, facilities and assets assigned to facilitate completion of the task.

Issues in Task Assignment

Before a task can be assigned, managers must not only formulate the task, often with help from others, but he or she must also consider the task doer's capability (mental processing ability, knowledge, skills and application). Is this the right person for this task? If the person does lack the capability to complete the task satisfactorily, resources will be wasted, the manager will not meet his or her own targets, and the person's sense of self-worth may well be adversely affected.

The manager must also consider how much of their own input will be required if the task is to be carried out effectively. Some complex tasks may be done by someone less capable if the manager is willing and able to break them into smaller tasks and provide considerable feed-back and coaching as they are being carried out. This may be acceptable with an inexperienced person who needs to learn the elements of the role.

The manager must also consider the person's workload. In the case of overload, the manager may choose to extend the deadlines on other tasks, provide more resources, or modify the output required, that is, change the tasks. In properly functioning managerial relation-ships it is a part of everyone's work to advise the manager at any time they believe a task will not be completed within its limits. Judging a person's workload cannot always be done with precision, so the establishment of this information flow is crucial to both the task doer and the manager.

INVOLVING THE TASK DOER IN TASK FORMULATION AND ASSIGNMENT

In most cases it is helpful to involve the task doer in the process unless the tasks are already familiar (as is the case in many roles at Level 1). Doing this allows the manager to gain inform-ation from the person to help the formulation of the assignment. It may also produce a better understanding during the task assignment and help to gain the commitment of the person to achieve the desired task result.

Managers must use fine judgement in deciding when, or when not, to involve people in task formulation and to what extent. Involving a person in the task formulation process may also expose any preconceived ideas which are held by either manager or the task doer and which often inhibit clear communication, leading to errors and waste.

We have found that, as tasks become more complex, so does discussion as to the clarifica-tion of the dimensions. We have found that discussions with regard to what quality is required is often most helpful as that dimension can be more ambiguous than say time to completion or quantity. All dimensions clearly impact on each other. For example, if you want higher quality it may take more resources or time.

The person may be a technical expert on the task in question. The manager may be clear on what is needed (the purpose or the output) but does not know exactly how long the task is likely to take or what resources will be required. In these circumstances, discussion of the task is essential. Input is required from the direct report and the manager to arrive at the desired outcome. Such involvement does not mean the expert determines what is to be done. The final decision on the output required, the targeted completion time and the resources to be used must be made by the manager. The manager may decide to do exactly what the expert proposes but it is still the manager's decision, and one for which the manager is accountable.

In practice, the person to whom the task is to be assigned may understand clearly some or many aspects of the task, in which case there is no need to discuss them. The point remains, however, that the manager must be sure that this is the case, not just assume that it is.

THE USE OF INITIATIVE

Does clear task assignment as we have described here mean people never do anything on their own initiative? Of course not. The intelligent exercise of initiative is essential if any organisa-tion is to survive and thrive over time. It is precisely when a person has a clear understanding of the purpose and objectives that the task doer is free to use initiative, and where necessary, to deal with conditions which change unexpectedly in order to achieve the purpose.

It is good practice for the task doer to check with the manager when he or she has ideas on other tasks to be done, in order to ensure his/her actions are productive. Should the task doer develop a task pathway, using his or her initiative and discretion, that is a radical departure from the normal methodology, it is advisable for this to be discussed with the manager before it is applied.

In our experience over many years we have found clear task assignment to be liberating, not constraining. Clear limits and boundaries provide external reference points that allow the task doer to assess and control the exercise of discretion based on objective outside standards. When properly formulated and stated, the reference points provide a clear space for the use of judgement. Unclear task assignment or the lack of assignments are the real constraints that leave people confused, sap energy and make it less likely initiative can be exercised effectively.

SCOPING AND SPECIFYING

In assigning a task it is possible to prescribe exactly what output is required in terms of the quality and quantity, precisely what resources should be used and on what day and at what hour the task is to be completed. However, this is rarely the case in reality. There are nearly always tolerances within which there is no preferred position and scope within which any outcome is acceptable but one is preferred. Therefore the dimensions can be explained in terms of an acceptable ranges. This also allows for better judgement of work performance; depending upon where within the scope the task is completed.

When a leader gives a team member an exact definition of a dimension of a task, they are allowing no variation from that target. This we call *specifying* the dimension. It is, however, as mentioned, possible to allow the task doer a range in the quantity/quality of output, resources or time dimensions. This we call *scoping*. This allows the task doer to express their capability in finding ways to get, for example, the fastest, the cheapest or the best output they can within the given range. Quality and quantity are both elements of output and one cannot exist without the other, hence output is a single dimension of a task. We find that in task assignment, if output is the scoped dimension, the range of variable worth is placed either on quantity or quality and the other is specified.

A leader will need to take a range of factors into account when deciding on the scoping and specifying of the dimensions of a task. Some of these will arise from the context and purpose – what is it that is more crucial and less crucial about the task, for example. The capability of the team member will play a part in this decision; it is advisable to specify more and give tighter scoping for someone who is new in the role or who has never done the task before.

TYPES OF TASKS

Although the examples given assume the manager will make a specific task assignment to a specific employee, not all tasks are so assigned. There are many variations in the process, and direct assignment may not be the one most frequently used.

DIRECT ASSIGNMENT

The manager assigns the task directly to the task doer. For example, 'The Board has changed the timing for the preparation of the monthly accounts to give them more time to analyse them before each Board meeting. So I am able to compile our report to them, I now need your cost report by the end of the fifth working day after month end. Will you please develop for me the plan for how you are going to achieve this? The Board have given us six months to make the change, so I will need your plan no later than two weeks from now. You have the resources available in your team for advice, and if you need mine, come and see me. As you would expect, the quality of the plan is what is really important.' C, P, QQ, R and T are all given. Output is the scoped dimension (quality), and it is assumed the task doer knows what the cost report is.

TASK WITH INSET TRIGGER

The manager assigns the task to a person with the statement that when a trigger event occurs, the person will carry out the task. These are the most common type of tasks: Sam, Zak and John are authorised to request equipment for their work. For example, a manager may say: 'When an order comes in to you from one of them, make sure it is processed within 24 hours. If this cannot be done due to other commitments, let them know and inform me. The processing of such orders should average no more than one error per month and you should not have to use any staff overtime. If the order is for an item not coded for their use, refer it to me'. It may appear as if Zak is assigning a task when issuing an order but Zak is triggering a task authorised by the manager.

Most of the work done in organisations that supply a service or goods involving interaction with customers falls into the classification of tasks with inset triggers.

Organisations that appreciate the need for excellent customer satisfaction ratings and the maintenance of them over time, put a lot of time, money and effort into training their staff in the performance of tasks with inset triggers.

Staff are taught the specific triggers for a particular work response and the behaviours required to be demonstrated to the customer during the performance of the task. They are also taught the limits of their own authority and the means of referring a customer with a request or questions they cannot satisfy to someone in the organisation who can do so.

It may appear to the customer that he or she assigns a task to an employee in these organisations, but this is not so. The task is very clearly assigned by the manager who specifies the criteria for good work performance and often monitors it through customer feedback.

The customer does not assign a task to the service person in a bank. He or she sets the trigger for the performance of work in a task for which the service person has been well trained.

There are of course other types of tasks with inset triggers. An industrial assembly task is triggered by the arrival of the next assembly at the workstation. An invoice will trigger a response in accounting to pay the bill. A hazardous condition in a plant will trigger action to correct it or report it to someone who can correct it.

TIME-BOUNDARY CONDITION AND RESOURCE

Often there is confusion and difficulty with the idea of time in the task assignment process since it is both boundary condition – one of the key dimensions of a task assignment – and also quite clearly a resource. Both are measured in the same units – minutes, hours, days, years, but there is a crucial difference when thinking about good management practice. The boundary condition is a deadline (target completion time); the amount of time available prior to the deadline is a resource. Often this resource is expressed in staff hours available or overtime hours available, but it is clearly different from a deadline.

THE 'HOW' – SPECIFYING THE PATHWAY

One of the things we have learned both as managers and as employees, no one likes to be told *how* to carry out a task unless the person is new to role and has no idea how to tackle a new assignment. People who know their job say, 'Tell me what to do, but don't tell me how to do it.' Think about how you have reacted to the 'helpful' advice offered to you about your driving, cooking or how you should raise your children (see Chapter 2 What is Work?).

The 'how' is the creation of a methodology (pathway) to achieve the goal and that must remain within the task doer's area of discretion. There may be some limits on the methodology or pathway that needs to be created. For example, hiring consultants to do the work may not be allowed, or developing a new computer program may not be allowed. These are effectively additional limits applying for the task; they do constrain the 'how,' but within these limits the 'how' of the task is open to the discretion of the task doer. They are, in effect, resource constraints.

When employees claim they are being micro-managed, more often than not, the manager is telling them not only what to do, but how to do it. That is why we said earlier that the pathway must not be specified for people in task assignment. Work for people is turning intention into reality by exercising their discretion. Correct task assignment for humans must concentrate upon our abilities to learn, to create and to innovate.

The clear exception to this is training where the purpose of the relationship is to learn *how* to do something – to build skills, knowledge or both.

The decision to write or not to write a task assignment is a managerial judgement. It should not be made a requirement in all cases because it will then become a mechanistic and non-productive process. As a managerial relationship progresses, each will develop a clearer understanding of what is expected, and a few words 'on the fly' may be all that is necessary to make clear what is to be done and how performance will be judged. In other cases, a manager may decide a written task assignment would be a more productive means to communicate his or her intentions, and therefore decide to put it down in that form. Several managers have noted that this process helps to clarify their own thinking as they become accustomed to this task assignment process.

In some societies where we have worked, for example in Russia, we have found that most tasks are written down. However, they are called orders and rarely contain context and purpose. While being clear, they do not encourage discussion.

NOTES ON 'EMPOWERMENT' AND 'SELF-ORGANISATION'

When boundaries and the area for discretion are clear, people are able to feel and be truly 'empowered' to get on with their work. They are able to organise their work processes and carry on to achieve their goals for the organisation. Too often the terms 'empowerment' or 'self-organisation' are used as if employees can do anything they want; that there are no longer any boundaries or controls. This is nonsense as virtually all employees subject to these programmes of empowerment and self-organisation recognise. Thus imprecise and confusing language and the ensuing misunderstandings, lead to cynicism and the view that 'empowerment' is just another fad, and a fraudulent one at that. It appeared to mean one thing, while the reality was quite different.

In some cases where organisations claimed to be empowering their workers, nothing changed: excessive controls were maintained even though management denied they were there. In other cases, managers were taught these concepts in a way which led them to believe they should not tell their employees what to do – just let them 'get on with the work'. The managers, in effect, abdicated their work to develop and provide a clear statement of context and purpose and to provide clarity.

True personal empowerment comes from a clear task assignment that states context and purpose and sets clear boundaries, but leaves appropriate space for the exercise of discretion.

More recently, software development firms have promoted Scrum and Agile approaches to work by emphasizing self-organising teams which management 'doesn't interrupt during a work cycle' (Denning, 2011). While some using these practices claim productivity increases of 400%, 'the overall picture of implementation has been quite mixed. More than 70% of Scrum implementations have failed to achieve their goals'.

The ideas underlying Scrum and Agile have similarity to what we propose in Chapter 15 on Teams and Teamwork. What is missing, at least in the literature, is an understanding of the need for leadership in a Team and the need for a clear articulation of tasks. Task assignments appear not to be clearly articulated as the team decides how much work it can do, decides how to do the work and measures its own performance. This approach to teams is likely to lead to the use of power rather than authority with all the damage that can do to individuals and team productivity. Failure of Scrum has been ascribed to not implementing all the practices of Scrum as well as interference by traditional management where 'the prevailing culture of hierarchical bureaucracy is triumphant' (Denning, 2011).

This may well be true, but we would argue that greater understanding of structure, team leadership and team management as well as use of well understood methods of task assignment and other essential people systems would allow Scrum to have more consistent successes. We say this not to denigrate the new ideas, but in the hope that the ideas in this book will make their ideas work more effectively.

Conclusion

The task assignment methodology described in this chapter provides a clear statement of what is required for true empowerment of employees; it also answers the questions that were raised above. The examples in this chapter used simple tasks with short times to completion in order to make the principles clear. We recognise that at higher levels of the organisation the tasks will need to be significantly more complex, and the term task (which often implies something small) may not even appear to be the correct term. However the need for good task assignment applies at all levels of the organisation.

Obviously tasks will be assigned very differently at different levels of the organisation. As one moves up the organisation, the area for discretion grows, and often the limits have much broader tolerances. Many of the prescribed limits are assumed to be understood though we still recommend a conversation to make sure there is full agreement even at the highest levels of the organisation.

15 *Teams and Teamwork*

In Chapter 12 we looked at how a leader creates a culture and uses the tools of Behaviour, Systems and Symbols to do so. We have emphasised the need for clarity in working relationships, especially with regard to authority and tasks. Here we look in more depth at another popular topic, teamwork. *Teamwork* is another term that has broad social usage, with a general agreement as to its meaning but lacking precision. It is simply not sufficient for leaders to exhort people to remember they are a team or to just work as a team unless there is a deeper and shared understanding as to what this means: what is the behaviour required from the leader and the team member?

In order to answer this question we need to return to the proposition that people are essentially social; that we form social groups in order to achieve together what we cannot achieve as individuals. There is, and always will be, the potential for a tension between what is advantageous for a particular individual and what is advantageous for the group. The key to a good organisation is managing the social process so that individuals are encouraged and allowed to use their capability to achieve the overall purpose of the group. The individual gains personal satisfaction and reward for their work whilst achieving the common goal.

There has been, and continues to be, great emphasis placed on teams and teamwork in writing about organisations. It is clearly recognised that effective teams can be highly productive and satisfying to the members. The obvious example of the well-functioning sports team demonstrates the need to blend individual talents into a complementary process.

Recently there has been concern about the excessive use of teams and what is referred to as collaborative overload. Data collected over two decades shows 'the time spent by managers and employees in collaborative activities has ballooned by 50% or more' (Cross et. al., 2016). They warn of the imbalance in contributions to teams and the excess demands this places on certain individuals. Their recommendations to improve the situation are similar, though less specific than ours – more clarity of roles, authorities and task assignments as well as appropriate recognition for both individual and team accomplishments.

Other research indicates the importance of social process skills. Woolley (2010:686–688) led a team from MIT and Carnegie Mellon that found one of the key factors in team success was 'high average social sensitivity.' 'They were skilled at intuiting how others felt based on their tone of voice, their expressions and other nonverbal cues' (Duhigg, 2016b).

Beginning in 2012, Google began Project Aristotle, conducting extensive research to learn why some teams perform very well and others less so. Initially they studied 180 teams, looking at numerous variables and could find no patterns that explained their performance. After looking at the research of Woolley and others, Project Aristotle finally identified 'psychological safety' as key to team performance – the existence of a social environment in which people listen to each other and show sensitivity to each other's feelings and needs (Duhigg, 2016b).

Research also indicates the importance of clear understanding of the purpose of the team and the impact of their work. This chapter suggests ways of achieving effective teams and teamwork.

The False Duality

Underlying much of this discussion about the form and processes of the organisation is an implication, and at times, the statement that there is some sort of basic choice between two types of organisation. One is the traditional hierarchy, and as we discussed in previous chapters, hierarchy, authority and bureaucracy have acquired negative connotations. The arguments put forward assert that these forms of organisation equate to command and control, top-down instruction, rigid structure and highly directive manager–subordinate relationships.

On the other hand we are invited to believe in the *organic, empowered*, non-hierarchical, creative organisation. People in these forms of organisation, it is asserted, work willingly and unencumbered; teams form and reform, often without leaders. This was the vision (or mirage) of the dot com companies of the 1990s and 2000s. In truth, neither of these options is viable in the medium or long term. It is misleading to present them as a choice. Social organisations need both structure and authority, clearly understood by all of their members, to be effective. At the same time people need to work together in teams if organisational goals are to be achieved. So let us put aside this false duality and look at effective teamwork, what works and what doesn't.

We all need to balance our need for individual identity with the need to belong to a social group or team. It is both productive and comforting to belong. Just as with systems of differentiation and equalisation, an over-emphasis on one or the other can be detrimental. For example, *equalisation* does give a sense of belonging but if over-emphasised can blur identity into a homogeneous collective, against which the members react negatively. An example would be a structure where in all people in a particular role are paid the same no matter what their efforts or achievements. *Differentiation* gives a sense of individual identity reinforcing the self, but on its own can lead to feelings of isolation or extreme competitiveness at the expense of other team members. An example would be basing all pay on apparent individual output, piece rates or bonuses, with no regard to input from other members of the team.

For us teamwork is not just about the collective. We reject the slogan 'There is no i in team'. Teamwork is about people collaborating for mutual benefit, clear about their mutual authority, their work and their relationship with their leader. The word *team* is used very generally, as are many terms in management. We have chosen a more specific meaning:

Box 15.1   Definition of Team

Team: A team is a group of people, including a leader, with a common purpose who must interact with each other in order to perform their individual tasks and thus achieve their common purpose.

There is nothing greatly contentious in this definition. However, the phrase 'who must interact' is crucial. It demonstrates the mutual interdependency of the team members. This distinguishes the work of a team from a *network* where some members of a network have no real relationship with some others, and there is no requirement for mutuality even if all the network members do have a common purpose. It also distinguishes the team from a group of people, say, passengers on a plane; all have a common purpose but do not need to interact to achieve it. We emphasise the need to interact and the mutuality. This is the difference between, for example, the members of a shift or project team and the group comprising all the employees of an organisation as a whole.

This does not mean, however, that there is a blurring of accountability. The leader of the team needs to hold team members accountable for their work as individuals – including that part of their work that requires establishing constructive and co-operative work relationships with other team members. If an organisation is serious about good teamwork this co-operation must be a part of the work of each role and reflected in review, reward and recognition system results. The leader must do the work of setting the context for such co-operation by creating the appropriate social processes. We outline such a process in this chapter.

In an employment organisation, people are employed as individuals and paid as individuals. A significant part of this employment role is to work constructively with others and the extent to which this is achieved should be recognised. Good teamwork is more likely where there is no role demarcation, that is, where team members are not artificially prohibited from helping each other provided each is properly trained and can work safely. This lack of demarcation does not mean everyone is the same or that there is no leadership.

If people are employed and paid as individuals, then they need to be accountable for their work performance to someone. It only makes sense if they are accountable to the person who assigns and reviews their task performance: the team leader.

Team Tasks, Goals and Rewards

Confusion may be generated by the use of language, socially defined. Can a team have a task? Should a team be rewarded? Can a team be set goals?

In employment roles a *team* cannot be given a task. A task is given to an individual. If that individual is in a team leadership role, he or she may then say to the team members 'we' have to 'change all the beds on the ward by the end of this shift'; 'complete all our team's performance reviews by June 30'; 'lay all the tables in the restaurant properly before opening time at 6.00pm'; 'produce X tonnes this shift' and so on. This is an appropriate way for the leader to define the *purpose* but he or she may not simply walk away at this point, or even say 'right, get on with it'. Even sports coaches who end their pre-match exhortations by extolling the whole team to 'go out there and win' are only able to summarise in this way if each person knows what they are expected to do in their role and the plan, i.e., the team tactics. If the coach has previously ensured that each individual team member knows what is to be done and has the ability to do it, then 'right, get on with it' is in fact the trigger to a set of previously assigned tasks.

The fact that there are team leaders does not mean that the organisation has to be authoritarian (see Chapter 4). Authoritarian behaviour by a supposed leader is an excellent way to destroy constructive team work and may well generate destructive teamwork. An observer may at times find it difficult to spot the leader once an activity is underway, especially if everything is going well. The empowerment of team members is another way of expressing that the team leader is using all the capabilities of the team members. This can be more precisely described as encouraging the use of appropriate discretion, encouraging suggestions for improvement and only intervening to add value by improving the outcome or preventing a problem. If the organisation is working properly, people will be in roles that not only encourage but also require good teamwork and sharing ideas.

Teams are not an alternative to a hierarchy; they are *part* of an accountability hierarchy. An organisation that reduces discretion, inhibits creativity and does not encourage people to work together is *not* operating as a typical, authority hierarchy. It is simply an organisation working badly because of poor leadership.

There is quite some debate about team rewards. First, it is important to distinguish these from business bonuses, profit-sharing or gain-sharing. These are systems that apply to everyone and are, in more and more organisations, a variable component of normal income. However, should the team (a shift or project team for example) be rewarded collectively for their work? There is nothing in our principles that prevents a leader from recognising the efforts of all team members equally, for example, giving everyone a dinner, a day off or public statement of achievement and effort. This is not to be confused, however, with salary. The credibility of the leader rests upon his or her ability to recognise relative contributions. For example, the team may have achieved the output *despite* the poor contribution of one of two members. Giving *only* equal recognition will merely say that the leader is unaware of relative contributions. It is important that individual feedback is always given. It may be more appropriately reinforced at the time of a performance review and later recognised in salary differentiation.

It is *not* divisive to recognise individual performance unless it does not reflect actual contribution. The team members know better than anyone else who contributed what and whose contribution was lacking. As such, poor leadership is extremely divisive especially if the leader insists on treating everyone the same whatever the circumstances or, attempts to abdicate, from the leadership role.

It is quite consistent with our principles, especially with regard to improved quality and measurement, to have run charts and output figures that reflect the combined output of the team. However, it must be clear what these are measuring. They may not necessarily be a measure of team performance. They could refer to one of several processes, including some indicator of the social processes of the team. As such, figures and charts may serve to enhance that process but only if there is complementary evidence that the leader knows in more detail what or who contributed to the result.

Team Decisions

A rich area of confusion concerns the approach to decision making reflected in phrases like the 'team decided', or 'the team was against it'. These are examples of poor or muddled leadership. Individuals are paid to make decisions: it is at the core of our understanding of work. In Chapter 5 we distinguished between an executive structure and a democracy. Of course, good leaders are concerned and listen to ideas and suggestions. A good leader will know whether members are comfortable with or even understand a proposed course of action and will not ride roughshod over team members. If the leader does lead poorly an alternative leader will emerge over time or members will simply find ways to subvert the original leader. Good leadership and teamwork in a meritocracy is not, however, based on a formal system of consensus or majority voting. A leadership role is far more than simply reflecting or representing members' views. Members must be free to voice concerns without feeling that this is a vote against a course of action. It is important to know what authority is operating, and not to muddle democracy, consensus or seniority with effective team leadership and teamwork.

Team Processes

So far we have discussed team leadership and team membership in general terms. The team leader must also create and maintain the appropriate social processes for its members and its purpose. Team members need to establish constructive and co-operative work relationships with other team members. In our work with a diverse range of organisations around the world, we have developed some specific and practical steps to guide how this can be done. In particular we have developed a training course, *Working Together*, which helps people learn how to improve their understanding and practice of effective team processes. This experiential course uses exercises, which are filmed to help people see their behaviour so they may to better recognise their own strengths and weaknesses, and to observe and learn what behaviour makes a good team and what behaviour detracts from this. In 1992 Ian Macdonald articulated this into a complementary process outlining the steps and traps that team leaders and members can use (and avoid) to improve their contribution and effectiveness. The following is an account of this process, which has been used and referenced by many organisations worldwide. It had its origins in work with CRA (the corporation that owned all the companies like Comalco where the modelling was largely developed) and is used in slightly different forms by organisations not only in the private sector but also in the public sector, including schools, indigenous organisations and even religious organisations.

LEADING A TEAM

There is a wealth of material on leadership and teamwork; theories and examples emphasise a range of qualities. There are debates about *born leaders* versus learning to lead. While there are many concepts, we have found it useful simply to describe what good leaders do, and consequently what is expected of someone in a leadership role. In our experience it is at best pointless, and at worst dangerous to ask people to change their personalities, but you can ask someone to explain tasks clearly. The latter can be observed, recognised and improved.

   We have observed good leaders in practice in a range of organisations over many years and analysed good practice in the experiential courses (*Working Together*). Leaders in employment roles do work in the context of an organisation; if the structure, role, authorities and work requirements are unclear, good leadership is virtually impossible. Power replaces authority. Leaders' apparent effectiveness will be more determined by strength of personality, physical strength and the ability to influence personally or even coerce. The context required for effective leadership can be improved in terms of structure, systems, capability, authority and clear tasks, using the models in this book. The following set of steps and frequently observed traps are set out in order but are not a rigid, linear process. It may be necessary to return to earlier steps to review and reassess a plan or a particular step.

Box 15.2   Authority and Teams

The Team Leader and Member Steps described below should be seen as authorities. Many organisations that have adopted this model require these steps from both leaders and members. They are part of work reviews and performance assessments. This demonstrates that, even in an executive hierarchy, authority does not simply flow downwards. Team members have the authority to require the leader to be clear about context, purpose, tasks, etc., and can demand a review. This is a clear and proper flow of authority upwards. Also team members have authority with regard to each other requiring collaboration, information and feedback. This approach confounds the simplistic assertion that hierarchy is, by its nature, 'authoritarian'.

TEAM LEADER AND TEAM MEMBER STEPS

The following is a practical guide to good leadership and perhaps even more importantly good team membership.

Explain the context and purpose

In setting the context for a task the leader needs to explain the situation: an order may be overdue, production may be behind. There may be environmental issues; there may be a concern with the market or even the weather. Safety may be a particular concern.

It is surprising how many team members are unsure why they have been brought into a team and what they are meant to achieve. It is not sufficient for the leader to assume they know. The leader must spell out a clear and overall purpose in a single statement without an 'and'. If leaders can't do this, they probably don't understand that purpose clearly themselves.

A significant part of the context will be the constraints within which the team is working. These are known limits and may include safety, reputation, budget, time limits, fixed resources, geographical boundaries, company policy or the law. It is important at this stage to understand and communicate clearly what these explicit boundaries are.

Identify and address the critical issues/problems

It is important to identify, prior to action, the significant problems that will need to be overcome for the task to be completed successfully. This is not a case of listing everything that might go wrong (an infinite task) but selecting, in your judgement, what the key threats are likely to be and seeking proposals to overcome them if they do arise. As such this is similar to a risk analysis, often done for safety reasons, but we apply it generally.

A *critical issue is something that threatens the purpose*. People have described them as *showstoppers*. We describe them as *what-ifs* and we address them with *'how-tos'*. For example, what if a key team member phones in sick? How do we clean the trucks well enough to service them if they have been in mud and the weather looks bad? How to cover all the classes in the school while we train some teachers in the new exam marking system? The point here is not only to identify the critical issues, but also to work out a proposal of what to do if they occur. This is often called contingency planning.

In our experience there are usually only three or four critical issues, no matter what the task. They are the sorts of events that are revealed in enquiries after disasters, as issues that have, prior to the event, been mentioned or recognised but not acted upon. A classic, and tragic, example is the case of failed *O rings* on the Challenger space shuttle where the fault had been identified but not acted upon.

The social process of critical issue identification and solution planning must be managed by the leader. Team members are thinking through their plan for completing the task within the limits and context they have been given, identifying critical issues and thinking of ways to overcome them. They are asked to articulate critical issues as they think of them as well as their thoughts on a solution if they have one.

Critical issues can be usefully categorised in terms of the Social, Technical and Commercial domains (see Chapter 3). It is recommended that each domain be considered as to whether there are critical issues associated with it.

Not all team members will identify the same critical issues, nor will they think of the same solutions, even if they did. Some solutions will result in more critical issues. Out of this intellectual cacophony the leader has to do the work of comparing and contrasting concepts, integrating proposals, answering and asking questions, correcting misunderstandings, providing due recognition, sequencing input, and finally, producing a plan of action to achieve the purpose. Clearly this is more readily achievable if the social process of doing so is ordered and disciplined.

For the process to operate well, it is also important to distinguish between Critical Issues and Constraints. Constraints are known limitations. They would include the resources, laws, policies, time to completion, quality requirements. One participant on a course in California explained it well by saying: 'So constraints are what you know, critical issues are what you have to work out.'

Also, as mentioned, critical issues may be related to the three domains referred to in Chapter 3 (Social, Technical and Commercial). We need to identify critical issues associated with each domain.

Encourage contributions

Most leaders need help in order to identify critical issues and contributions to their solution. Even if you, as the leader, don't think you need help, there is always a risk in going it alone. Not listening to others and therefore implying they have no contribution to make is almost always a mistake. The solution to the entire problem may come from another team member, but most often it is the solution to specific critical issues that come from different team members, and these need to be integrated into the solution for the whole problem. This is the work of the leader. Not being able to generate the complete solution personally is not a failure – the leader is being paid for his or her judgement.

Some ways of encouraging contributions:

a. After explaining the purpose, give the team members time to think.
b. Ensure that each person really has an opportunity to offer the result of the think time. A member must feel comfortable even if they do not have earth-shattering ideas. In this phase the leader must be *accessible*. The positioning of people is important. If the group is standing the leader must see and be seen by everyone, as shown in Figure 15.1.
c. Be careful not to talk only to those next to you or to the most vocal. If you are sitting, the same principles apply. Long tables are a disadvantage. Do not be afraid to sit at the head: you are the leader. Non-verbal clues are critical at this time. People will give clues if they are bored; obvious ones are yawning, wandering off or sitting/standing back. They give clues if they wish to contribute (leaning forward, increased body movement, hand gestures, raised eyebrows). The leader must be sensitive to these actions. Ignoring them leads to a feeling of not being listened to, even if words were actually spoken.
d. People may also work remotely and therefore not be in physical contact. It is even more important to be aware of the steps and traps described here when working electronically. It is so easy to ignore others or over communicate or simply see the issue through your own eyes.

Make a decision about the planned action

As we have said, in an executive structure leadership is not a matter of democracy or consensus. If you are in a leadership role, it is likely that you are getting paid more than the team members. Your position in the role is based upon your perceived capability to make decisions and your role is accorded the authority to do so. It is important to end the discussion stage in a timely fashion to avoid paralysis by analysis. The leader has work to do to make sure all the critical issues and contributions have been considered carefully and integrated into the construction of the plan. When he or she has decided on the plan, the leader needs to articulate the plan to the team. If some team members' suggestions have not been used, they will need to know why. The leader should clearly indicate to the group what the intended actions are and what the critical issues are, including how they will be dealt with.

The leader should consider where he or she is in relation to the team members (see Figure 15.1).

Assign tasks

The decision or plan should be broken up into a number of tasks. These will be assigned to team members based on the leader's judgement of capability. Team members must know what they are required to do. Using the task assignment model (CPQ/QRT) that is Context, Purpose, Quantity, Quality, Resources and Time, team members must know:

a.   what their tasks are – and what to do next;
b.   if and how their tasks complement other people's tasks and
c.   how their tasks will help to achieve the purpose and overcome problems – *why* they are doing these tasks.

If team members cannot answer the questions above, the leader has failed and the team members will not know how and when to use their initiative when the situation changes (as it inevitably will!).

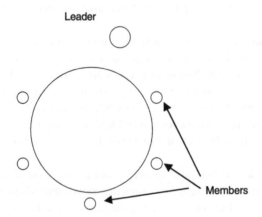

Figure 15.1   Accessibility of the Leader

Monitor progress

The leader needs to do the work of monitoring progress of the team. If the leader does this, then team members are free to get on with their work. Progress is monitored along several dimensions (at once):

a. *Technical* (the most obvious): Are the solutions working? Do they need to be modified? Will the methodology/plan actually solve the problem?
b. *Social*: Is the team cohesive? Are people involved, using initiative, interacting or are they forming sub-groups, fragmenting, only doing 'what is necessary'? Do they look interested? Engaged?
c. *Temporal*: Is there a programme, a timetable/schedule? Is it being achieved?
d. *Environmental*: The *leader* does the work of monitoring the environment, allowing team members to concentrate on the task at hand. What is happening around the team and what intervention is required to help overcome problems?

Finally if any or all of the above are going wrong, what contingency plan does the leader have? Can he or she answer this *before* a problem arises, even if only in outline? Here the leader may have to revisit critical issues, stop the process and re-evaluate.

Coaching

As team members work they may need help to complete their tasks or improve their methods. Leaders are helpers. This is a very sensitive area because the *way* in which a leader coaches will affect whether people will accept help. First, a leader must make it clear to the team member whether he or she is:

a. *Giving an instruction* – telling someone to do something differently and expecting him or her to do it.
b. *Giving advice* – suggesting a person think about using your ideas but leaving it up to them.
c. *Teaching* – showing/telling someone how to do something because they recognise that they don't know how. This area is critical to a leader as few people like being told how to do something while they are in the middle of work unless they think they are having problems. Consequently do not be afraid to ask.
d. *Asking* – gain information from members: for example Why do you do that? Do you want any help?

Although an important part of the leader's work is coaching, do not forget the leader may well learn from the team.

Review

At the end of the activity, whether the purpose has been achieved or not, the leader needs to review the process. This is the opportunity, when everything associated with the task is still fresh in people's minds, to give recognition to team members and to comment on the leader's perception of his or her leadership behaviour, in particular, those things that were not done as well as they might have been. There is an adage, 'teams win; leaders lose,' that carries a considerable truth.

Box 15.3   Individual Perspectives

The leader must be able to see the world from each team member's viewpoint.

It is very important for a leader to draw out the views of team members, a process that will usually be easier if the team has been successful than it will be if the outcome was poor. It needs to be done, however, if all of the team is to learn from the experience. The leader has work to do to prevent the development of mythologies that will be disruptive of team cohesion. The objective of this work is to deny a team member who has performed poorly the refuge of believing such poor performance was really caused by the behaviour of other team members. The social process of these reviews will determine, to a large extent, how successful they are at engendering improved work performance. It is vitally important to recognise people's work and to encourage individuals and the team to learn from what they have done – what they can build on and what they need to change. We all benefit from knowing if we have achieved our purpose (see Box 15.3).

TRAPS

There are some common traps that we have seen leaders fall into. In our experience these are the most common:

Not seeing the problem from the member's viewpoint

This involves the leader making assumptions that team members know and see what he or she knows and sees. Given that in most instances the leader will be better informed and better able to generate order from complexity (a higher MPA), such assumptions are open to question. It does take a conscious effort at times, but a leader should be able, mentally, to step into someone else's shoes. What does the problem look like from their point of view? How anxious or confident are they?

Getting over-involved in the action

There is a temptation, especially if there are problems, for the leader to dive in and take over. This not only interferes with team members' work and may well show that the leader has assigned tasks badly, but becoming over-involved in the action also prevents the monitoring work and good coaching. At times of great personal risk, it may be correct for a leader to demonstrate leading from the front. In most instances, however, it shows a lack of capability or confidence or both, and can result in dependency and/or resentment.

Feeling you have to have the answer

It is the leader's work to make sure the best solution is implemented. The solution to the entire problem may come from another team member, but most often it is the solution to specific critical issues that come from different team members, and these need to be integrated into the solution for the whole problem. This is the work of the leader. Not being able to generate the complete solution personally is not a failure – the leader is being paid for his or her judgement.

Often a leader fails to take note of an excellent suggestion because he or she is anxious because an answer has not come to mind or is too busy trying to make the present solution work.

Being the technical expert

Like the trap above, this one arises because the leader behaves as though he or she has to know more than anyone else in the team. This is a particular risk if the problem or a critical issue has to do with a technical issue about which the leader does have some knowledge. Superior technical knowledge and expertise is often mistaken for leadership by those who seek to demonstrate it, and by many observers, when in fact it masks poor social process and, at times, questionable capability. We argue that the leader does not have to be the best at any or all subtasks. The leader must, however, be able to understand and question the logic of technical proposals. 'Explain to me, in simple language, how that is going to resolve the critical issue'. The ability to give such an explanation is a real test of the depth of technical knowledge.

Ignoring social and programming issues

Part of the culture that emphasises technical knowledge also downgrades the importance of or difficulty in the other areas of social process and programming. In most cases the technical solutions can be found within the team. It is critical, however, that people have the opportunity to put forward their ideas and that there are time lines, controlled strictly by the leader, applied to the planning process and then to the performance of the task. Programming is not simply recording or telling the time but checking progress against plan. At the same time, the team leader should be monitoring how the team members are relating to each other.

Issue fixation

Often one problem area will gain enormous attention. It may be a critical issue but it gets blown up, out of proportion. This may occur during the planning phase or during implementation. All resources are then directed toward the resolution of this issue, resulting in a failure to see how this affects other areas and what impact a new solution has on the rest of the problem. This also leads to a blindness to outside issues; there's not much point if, while changing a tyre, you get run over by a truck.

Not willing to stand out in a crowd

This is one of the most common and damaging traps – when a leader is reluctant to appear to be a leader. It is often perceived as against the grain to stand out, especially in a superior position. Consequently there is an over-dependence on consensus, an attempt to achieve a *collective accountability*, leadership behaviour directed toward a merging with the group. The result is a rudderless slow approach, conservative because it lacks direction and clear programming. Be reassured that groups/teams *do* like the leader to be *decisive*. Consult, certainly, but team members may become very frustrated with a leader who will not be decisive when a decision is required.

TEAM MEMBERSHIP

Everyone is a team member but not everyone is a leader. However very few people have a clear or shared idea about what behaviours make for good team membership. The emphasis on team leadership overshadows the critical work of the team member. We hope to provide some clarity about what this means.

If there is a library of material on leadership, there is scarcely a small bookshelf on team membership. This section describes some of the constructive behaviours that all team members can demonstrate in order to achieve their common purpose.

The point about teams described here is that, from the viewpoint of each team member, in order to contribute effectively as a team member he or she is dependent upon others with whom the establishment and maintenance of direct working contact is essential, perhaps not all at once but in the process of achieving the purpose.

Like the leadership section, this section draws on general observation of people in organisations and of specific behaviours by team members in activities in their normal work and on training courses. One preliminary point before discussing behaviour: team members in employment roles clearly do not work in isolation. They operate within the organisation. If the structure, roles, authorities and the tasks and the accountability relationship are unclear, then team members will have difficulty working with each other and the leader. Teams may then be run on power, the power of personality or vocal, even physical strength. This is not the context that will create an organisation that will continue to be productive over time. We have described in earlier sections the need for clear authority and for accountability so that teams can work more effectively. However, even in this context there are ways of helping the process.

So how should team members behave and what are the traps? This section describes practical behaviour for all team members. It is described, as for team leadership, as a series of steps:

CONTEXT AND PURPOSE

If you are a team member (and the great majority of people in employment are), are you clear why you are here? If you are not, then ask. If you are not clear what the purpose is, the chances are that others will also be unclear. How many times have you failed to ask a stupid question and found afterwards that other people were equally in the dark? If you don't ask, the leader will probably assume that you do understand.

CONTRIBUTE TO THE 'HOW'

If you think of problems and ways of solving them, then you have work to do to put these ideas forward. You may identify a trivial point that is crucial. It is for the leader to decide in the end what is relevant. It is not only the leader who pays attention to the social process. Timing is critical if you want to be heard. Be available and accessible within the leader's sight. Don't give up if not heard initially. However, do not continue to press a point if it has been recognised.

LISTEN TO OTHERS

It is important to make a contribution, but equally important to listen to other points of view. It is difficult for the leader if all members are switched to send and none to receive. You may find this difficult especially if you think others are making apparently silly or trivial suggestions or ideas you had already thought of and dismissed. Listening is really hard work. It is not a passive process.

ACCEPT DECISIONS

In many types of organisations there are rarely appropriate times for voting. If you have had a *fair go*, you must commit to the chosen path even if your worst enemy has had his/her suggestions accepted. You are there to achieve the common purpose not simply to prove that you are right. The ready and constructive acceptance of the ideas of others is much more likely if the team's social process prior to any decision has been handled well.

CLARIFY YOUR TASKS

Are you sure:

a. What you are meant to be doing (CPQQRT)?
b. What you are meant to do next?
c. How your effort contributes to the purpose (why)?
d. How it fits with what others are doing?

If not, *ask*. Being a team member is an active process not a matter of blind faith. People working in parallel are not a team. You must be in a position to use your initiative especially if (or when!) something goes wrong (that is not to plan). In short, can you think into your leader's head? If in doubt, *ask*.

CONCENTRATE ON YOUR TASKS AND CO-OPERATE

Try to complete your tasks while ensuring that you help and co-operate with others. Be prepared to give information and feedback on your progress and give encouragement to fellow team members. Do not hide information or use it to exercise power.

ACCEPT SOME COACHING

No one is perfect and you can learn from others. It may be uncomfortable at times but try to listen to other people's ideas as to how you might improve your work.

DEMAND REVIEW

At the end of, and at times during, the process it is important to check and review your performance. You must ask the leader what he or she thought and give your own view. It is also your work to suggest how it might be done better (next time). This does not mean proving your idea was right all along (see Box 15.4).

Box 15.4   Teamwork

You are part of the whole. It is only by active co-operation, however, that the whole will be greater than the sum of the parts.

TRAPS

These are some of the most common traps for team members based upon what we have observed over time.

Keeping quiet

This is where the team member does not ask questions or put forward ideas, behaving in a way that suggests that passive acceptance and blind obedience is what is required. It is not sufficient for a team member to assume that he or she will find things out from other team members after the briefing.

Not listening

Allowing other people to speak does not equal listening. There is a difference between waiting for some idiot to finish and actively listening. It is remarkable how often we have seen people in meetings and on training courses repeat almost exactly the same point someone else has just made thereby showing clearly they had not been listening. Women often note that when they put forward an idea, it is ignored; it is then repeated by a man in the team and everyone reacts by saying it is a great idea. Women do not appreciate this, nor do minorities who often confront the same issue.

Getting on with my job

This involves ignoring the situation and the needs of others, with blinkers on, and continuing to do your own work whatever the circumstances. This is a situation where a person isolates him- or herself and has nothing to do with the rest of the team: 'it's not my problem'. This behaviour may not be habitual practice but may stem from such close attention to the issue at hand that external issues that should be noted are not.

Getting on with other people's jobs

Some team members interfere with other people's tasks because they think they know better. This is sometimes because they do not know what they are supposed to be doing or because they are not capable of doing the work they were assigned. Such behaviour can also be an attempt to exercise power, disguised as co-operation, but is very different from co-operating.

Wandering off

We have seen team members wander off either mentally or physically and often both, exploring possibilities without reporting back and in doing so missing vital information. Often it is with good intention, or due to boredom. However, it causes distraction.

Fragmenting the team

This is a variation of wandering off, and involves setting up ad hoc sub-groups to re-work the problems, changing the tasks and redefining the purpose, again without feedback. This is an exercise of power – setting up internal factions that polarise the team and undermine the leader.

'I knew I was right'

Going along with a bad plan, while actually undermining it in order to prove it was bad and having the dubious satisfaction of seeing it fall apart. This behaviour is especially common when the team member is convinced he or she had had a better solution that was not adopted. This behaviour is also an exercise of power directed at destabilising the existing leadership and may be driven by an inflated ego.

Ignoring coaching

Being overly sensitive to questions from others (especially the leader) as to why you are doing something in a certain way. This may mean that you miss ways to improve. The statement, 'we have always done it like that' is usually an indicator that coaching will be ignored unless the leader or another team member forces the issue through the exercise of authority. It is also, unfortunately, an issue when safe work practice is being discussed, 'no one's been hurt before'.

Fear of taking over

Holding back because you worry you might take over the leadership inhibits your potential and the team's resources. There are mechanisms some subtle, some not so subtle, that fellow team members will use, apart from any intervention from the leader, that will tell you if you step out of line too much. While it is good not to dominate discussion, it is unlikely that the leader will be undermined if you are constructive in your behaviour.

PROCESS

It is important to emphasise that although we describe these as 'steps' they are not necessarily a linear process. Depending upon the result of consideration, we may go and revisit one or more steps. The critical issues may require a re-evaluation of purpose, coaching may result in changing tasks and performance monitoring. The important aspect is that all of the steps are covered. They are linear in that one cannot logically start anywhere. It is not helpful to assign tasks before clarifying the purpose!

Conclusion

In this chapter we have taken a very practical approach to understanding team processes. We have stressed that *hierarchy* and *teamwork* are *not* alternatives. We do not believe there is such an entity as a *leaderless team*. In all teams, leaders emerge. It is a question of whether they do so by authority or power. One of our most successful clients commented on his competitors, 'I do hope they adopt leaderless teams. It will give us a great competitive advantage.'

Teamwork is an overworked and often vague term. We have been specific in terms of both definition and process. Good teamwork is an essential component of an effective organisation. It is at the heart of an organisation's social process. Without good teamwork and co-operative

Table 15.1   Complementary Roles of Leaders and Team Members

Leader	Member
Explain context and purpose	Clarify context and purpose
Identify critical issues	Contribute to the 'how'
Encourage contributions	Listen
Make a decision about the plan	Accept decisions concerning which plan
Assign tasks	Clarify tasks
Monitor progress	Co-operate
Coach	Accept coaching
Review	Demand review
Avoid traps	Avoid traps

membership an organisation will fail even if it has excellent technical and commercial processes.

Our unique approach has been and is used to explain how the leadership role and membership role complement each other. This is a major reason why our model has been used so widely. The complementarity of the team leader and member steps can be seen clearly in Table 15.1.

AUTHORITY

We have argued that these steps in the process do not merely form some helpful practical advice. We recommend that they be actually confirmed as authorities of roles throughout the organisation. That is, team leaders should be held accountable for working through this process and team members held accountable for their part. Thus, it is not a luxury to review a task but a requirement. It is not just important or helpful for team members to ask questions and clarify but an essential part of their work. In organisations that have used this model as a set of authorised tasks assigned with an inset trigger, the improvement in the team process after the training has been significant. As such it is an extension of the understanding of authority. It demonstrates that authorities are not just 'top-down'. The team member should be authorised to call the leader to account for following this process and to call other team members to account for their work in implementing this process. As with all behaviour, the way this is done, the social process, will determine the effectiveness of the teamwork.

5 *Making Change Happen*

Introduction to Part 5

Much of this book has described not only what to do but has also given practical material and guidance as to how to do it. In our experience this is a fairly unusual in books of this kind. Most are much stronger as to the What rather than the How.

This section concentrates even more specifically on how to make change happen and how to embed that change. It deals with the realities of organisational life and under what conditions real positive change and social cohesion can occur. There is a lot written about managing change and the change process as if there is a stable state that is from time to time interrupted by change. Our view, although not unique, is that change is occurring all the time and indeed the work of the leader is to change behaviour. We have worked with very many organisations around the world and have found that whatever the organisation: public, private or not for profit very similar conditions apply if the organisation is to achieve its purpose and build socially cohesive culture. We outline how successful change is achieved, how we carry out organisational health checks and how to create high-performance teams.

We then examine actual case studies from very different organisations in different parts of the world where these ideas have been put into practice. We do not have space in this book to include all of the examples and so we refer to the related website which contains many more examples. Finally we acknowledge that there are other approaches that are in use and we look at some of those. Many people in organisations complain about the jargon, fads and trends in this area. Some approaches are lightweight, have no theory base and are thus short lived but in the meantime can cause significant distress and wasted effort which detract from the real work and purpose of the organisation. Systems Leadership is designed to be the opposite of that, so we examine some of these approaches in terms of basic criteria that we apply equally to our own work.

Then we consider overall what is required to create an organisation that encourages Productive Social Cohesion. We propose a Charter of Employment that if implemented provides checks and balances to arbitrary decisions, the exercise of power and exploitation. This can then create the environment where people willingly give of their best and are able to use their capabilities productively and creatively.

16 *The Process of Successful Change: How is it Achieved?*

The authors and Macdonald Associates have been involved in many change programmes with many different organisations around the world. Associates have worked with schools, churches, international mining companies, hospitals, financial organisations, voluntary organisations, indigenous communities, local authorities, manufacturing, public utilities – in fact, a wide range across the private, public and voluntary sectors.

In all of this work we have provided advice and support to the leadership and members of such organisations. Such advice has been intended to encourage creativity by helping to create a set of conditions whereby people are able to express their potential through work.

Amongst the many projects and programmes in which we have been involved, not surprisingly some have been more successful than others. This chapter concentrates not so much on content but process. It draws on our experience to summarise the main elements in a successful change or transformation process. It is not a rigid prescription and depends upon specific circumstances, and we accept that it cannot always be followed exactly. However, it does provide a framework that, if followed is likely to lead to success. Where the process has been followed carefully and with attention to detail, it has resulted in significant, positive change; in some cases exceeding expectations. Where the process has not been followed in this form, changes have been slower and have yielded less significant gains. The main argument we are making is that there needs to be considerable attention paid to the process. A good idea can be ruined by poor implementation. Throughout this book we have emphasised the importance of understanding social process. This understanding applies no less to the social process of implementing change.

A change process or transformation can occur without specific outside consultancy. There is, however, always a need for specialist advice and considered reflection, from either an external or internal source. The nature of the work and the demands it places on the organisation's leadership makes such an arrangement desirable. The process must be led by the leadership of the organisation or it will fail to achieve the purpose of the change programme. This will always require some degree of behaviour change by the leaders as individuals, so they demonstrate what is required and generate dissonance. Personal behaviour change is not easy; it takes time. The leader will have to provide his or her input into the redesign of the significant systems of the organisation. Although this seems an obvious point, it is interesting to see that many change management processes are led by Human Resources and are not clearly owned by the executive leadership.

While all of this is going on, the leader must continue in his or her day job running the organisation. Much of our experience in such processes involves external consultancy. There are advantages to external advice, largely its independence and specific technical expertise. Also external advisers are not competitors for a potential career in the organisation. The advice can be considered and the relationship ended more easily, and the consultant never enters into a managerial authority relationship. In our work as consultants we endeavour to work in partnership with the leadership.

Two phrases we do not allow a consultant to utter are 'if I were you' or 'you should'. We recognise executive authority; who has the authority to make the final decision over structure, systems or removal from role. Our advice tends to be analytical and predictive rather than coming in and doing the work. If the partnership is not characterised by high trust between adviser (internal or external) and client, the process will fail or have at best a short-term impact. Applying a set of externally predetermined ideas will rarely, if ever, work unless the leadership has gained ownership of these ideas and helped to shape them in terms of the particular organisational application (see Box 16.1).

Because an external adviser may not be continuously available to members of the organisation, including the leader, Catie Burke has found that working with both an internal and external consultant is often useful. The internal adviser is present on a daily basis, and is required to learn the theories and processes we recommend, such that they can assist in the analytical process and help the leader and other members of the staff when questions arise.

The length and nature of this working relationship varies depending upon the circumstances. We do not favour two-, three- or six-month programmes with grand project titles. Such programmes or projects give the impression that there is a definitive start and finish

---

Box 16.1   Two Types of Consultancy

In our experience there are two fundamental types of consultancy relationship:

SUPPORT AND ADVICE: The way that we have all worked is to offer advice and help the leadership create the Desired Culture. We seek to transfer knowledge and skills into the organisation and eventually create the situation where we are no longer needed, certainly not full time. This is a common clinical or therapeutic model that enables the client to do their work. This works best when the client(s) have the current potential to do the work but may be helped by technical expertise.

DEPENDENCY: Here the consultant wants to do the work. It works best when the client is incapable of the work and is not able to succeed without the 'consultant'. Work is characterised not so much by advice but by large teams of consultants working together to tell the client what to do but also to look for more work. The purpose is to create dependence and secure a revenue stream. This model relies on fads, constantly re-badging and reselling content.

Box 16.2   Examples of Consultancy Relationships

There are many examples of these relationships. One example was the relationship between Wilfred Brown (chairman of Glacier Metals) and Dr Elliott Jaques at Glacier Metals (1947–1977). In the 1980s a major restructuring of CRA (now Rio Tinto) in Australia was led by Sir Roderick Carnegie supported by Jaques and internal consultants including Leigh Clifford (who became CEO of Rio Tinto), Jack Brady, Terry Palmer and Karl Stewart. When Palmer and Stewart moved to managing director roles, they built similar relationships externally with Macdonald and others to bring about very significant change, as has David Murray at the Commonwealth bank of Australia with Les Cupper as an internal adviser. There are many similar relationships involving both internal and external advisers to CEOs such as Burke who worked with John Fielder who became President of Southern California Edison along with his internal adviser Dr Dan Smith. These relationships are critical since it is helpful for a CEO to have someone with whom to test ideas, where that person is not a competitor. The function of the adviser is to give honest, direct feedback and evaluate these ideas against a set of principles and concepts.

time. We remember one surprised general manager who, when asked to work on some new systems, said; 'Isn't this what we pay you for?' Our relationships tend to be longer-term but may vary significantly in intensity and level of involvement at any particular time. The fact that the relationship is one of active collaboration between consultant and manager does not mean it is purely pragmatic. The consultant must bring a depth of knowledge that can predict which adaptations to principles will actually enhance the process and which will inhibit it.

The conceptual material in this book, as well as Jaques' theories, need to be seen as a discipline; that we must attempt to be rigorous in definition and analysis, not merely pragmatic or political. An impediment to such discipline is the adoption of the transformation process as a belief system. This is partly because all social processes have an emotional content and partly because of the ease with which belief becomes a substitute for understanding. The concepts and models or principles then move from a set of predictive tools to be tested and become a dogmatic belief system with evangelists and sceptics. Failures are perceived from both sides as proving their case. If a change fails to produce the desired result for the sceptic, it proves the belief system is flawed; for the evangelist it has been deliberately undermined by the sceptic.

When the debate becomes suffused with intransigence and emotion the distinction between content and process becomes blurred. As with systems, it is important to be clear whether the outcome (or lack of it) suggests inherent problems with content (the ideas and concepts) or problems with how it has been implemented: if the sound coming from my violin playing is alarming and tuneless, is it because the instrument is faulty or simply that I have never learnt to play the violin with sufficient skill?

Box 16.3 Failure Predicted and Change Implemented

Catie Burke had the experience of working with a Departmental Vice President where he and his staff designed a Performance Assessment system based on her analysis using the concepts in this book. It worked so well, he recommended it for use corporate wide. The task of designing the corporate system was given to the HR department, which assigned the task at too low a level. The result resembled what had been done in the Department, but with significant (and negative) changes.

Burke wrote a memo to the VP listing several things she thought would go wrong with the new system. The VP recognised the systems were different but thought the corporate system could still work for his Department. Burke left the country and was out of communication for a month. When she returned, her voice mail was full – the VP wants to see you as soon as you get back. She went into the office where the VP was visibly upset and angry. His first words were, 'Don't tell me I told you so'. All but one of the predictions had come true, and the people in the Department who had experienced a system that worked were furious as was the VP. Because the workforce could send e-mails anonymously, the VP showed her his favourite, 'This system proves (the VP) either has no guts or no brains.' He kept it as a reminder of his mistake.

'I want this fixed, NOW.'

'But it won't conform to the corporate system.'

'I don't care. I want this done right.'

A team from the Department was created, led by a very able General Manager in a IV role. Burke helped the team in their analysis, and they designed a highly workable system that was deemed fair and effective, even by those whose assessments were not a good as they expected.

The Moral Is: The ability to predict failure based on the concepts in this book can lead to positive change over time.

Successful Change Process

The following section outlines the process, not as dogma but as a set of steps or criteria that can be used to examine where and why there might be problems. The process outlined below has, in our experience, been successful in terms of results over time. It is written assuming the positive relationship described above is in place between a person (or persons) in executive roles (the leadership) and those in support roles (that is, consultants providing specialist advice).

STEP 1: ESTABLISH A GOOD WORKING RELATIONSHIP BETWEEN THE CEO AND ADVISER(S)

These relationships can occur and develop in many ways and over different periods of time. Our experience is, however, that a direct, working relationship between adviser and the line executive is essential. This may not always be with the overall CEO. If not, then the scope of change will be limited to the area of discretion of that line manager. For example, it may occur in a division, a site or sector. If this is the case then at least those in the line roles above must be supportive if not driving the process.

Whilst the requirement for the change process to be led by the line manager may seem to be a very obvious point, it is surprising how many so called change programmes do start and continue under a specialist banner, for example, HR or IT. They are doomed to failure or at best slow progress until the CEO (or equivalent) in a level IV role or above not only owns it, but also is seen to own it. It is virtually impossible for someone in a level III role to drive significant change because the role does not carry the necessary integrative authority. This is not a negative representation for the person in a level III role and does not refer to that person's capability. If a highly capable person in a level III role does drive change without executive support, again by definition, they will have to use power, not authority. If we assume, however, that the relationship with the CEO has been established, then several critical issues need to be addressed.

WHAT IF OTHER EXECUTIVES ARE NOT ALIGNED?

Teamwork is critical and the CEO must lead a functional, productive team. Time and effort must be put into this alignment and, if particular team members cannot support the process, it is important that they leave. This need not be done punitively. In one particular instance we experienced, an honest difference of opinion led to a very dignified exit with each party demonstrating mutual respect.

If external consultants are employed, their work must be complementary to internal consultants. A change programme must rest on common principles and language. Different models and conflicting advice will hinder the process. Essentially the problem is the same as that of alignment in the CEO's team and must be addressed.

WHAT IF OTHER PARTIES ARE NOT ALIGNED?

Depending on the organisation there may be other parties to consider, for example trade unions. What is their view? How are their concerns addressed? This is a critical issue and must be addressed in the context specific to the organisation. We have worked in organisations where third-party response has been as diverse as literal, violent opposition or highly constructive engagement. How the third-party issue is addressed is, of course, a decision of the leadership of the organisation. It is, however, a decision that must be made to avoid confusion and uncertainty through the change process.

HOW BEST TO ENGAGE THE BOARD?

If the change process is significant it is crucial that the board knows about it, knows what is trying to be achieved and at least in general terms how it is to be achieved. If this is not the case, then early costs are difficult to accept. For example, during initial stages there may be a reduction in productivity, training costs may be high and there may even be some industrial unrest. This is critical work for the board, as explained in Chapter 11.

It is inevitable that any significant change process will generate comment. For an organisation that regularly appears in the financial press, there is no guarantee the commentary will be positive. It is essential that the Board be fully informed about, and in support of, a significant change program within the organisation. It is the work of the CEO to keep the Board informed.

The process of addressing these critical issues is helped considerably by the next step.

STEP 2: ARTICULATE WHAT THE CEO IS TRYING TO ACHIEVE

Often this articulation is called a 'vision' or 'mission,' sometimes both are present. A vision is, by definition, an hallucination, and while it may seem to be a good thing to display publicly what the CEO believes the organisation should be aspiring to, it is our experience that in most instances, such public declarations serve little constructive purpose. Statements of vision or mission that begin with 'We are ...' or 'We do ...' pose the potential problem of the CEO having to explain from the witness stand why the organisation about which he or she made the claim, is, in fact, not doing what it claimed it was.

These declarations are often vague, even vapid, watered down truisms or platitudes. They are often hard either to agree or disagree with or to know specifically what needs to be done and who is to achieve them. Our experience has been that sometimes the CEO will have a clear picture in his or her mind but will be frustrated that it is not obvious to everyone else. We do not use terms as grandiose as 'mission' or 'vision' (except in the Church), but prefer 'purpose', 'goals' or 'objectives' because such terms are clearer and less abstract. Often it is useful to express this in very simple behavioural terms, for example, 'a place where people want to come to work', 'where people are listened to and their contributions recognised'. It is important in this process to take into account the following critical issues. (See also Creating a Culture in Chapter 12).

HOW TO MAKE AN INTEGRATED STATEMENT?

Any process of change should integrate the technical, commercial and social processes. As has been discussed, they are intrinsically related within an organisation, and any significant change process must recognise this relationship. It is not helpful to drive a technical and commercial change process such as six-sigma 1 unless the potential social process change and its impact is clear to everyone. A structural reorganisation (social process) is not helpful unless it is linked to a business case and how the new organisation structure will better achieve the application of the technical speciality of the business.

HOW MUCH VARIATION IS THERE THROUGHOUT THE ORGANISATION?

Are some areas good/bad examples? Are some divisions or departments currently near or a long way from achieving these goals?

WHAT IS THE OVERALL BUSINESS CONTEXT?

Is it obvious that change is needed or can it be argued that 'if we aren't broke why fix us?' The answers to this will clearly have significant impact on the timing and speed of the process (see step 5).

STEP 3: HOW DO THE CONCEPTS OF SYSTEMS LEADERSHIP THEORY HELP?

It is critical that there is real and in-depth understanding by the executive leadership of how and why these concepts and tools can form a pathway to achieving the goals. This statement may seem to be a self-evident truth, but it contains a deeper issue. The possession and application of a real and in-depth understanding of the concepts and the tools leads to an appreciation by the CEO of the work he or she must do if the change process is to be a success. It has been our experience that the removal from role of people who do not have the capability to perform the work of the role has been the prime determinant of success in significant change programmes. This is the work that confronts the CEO with his or her team members. An understanding of the process makes clear the absolute necessity of these personally difficult decisions and actions.

The construct that mental processing ability is a component of human capability that does not change in adulthood is difficult for many to accept. A common belief, which contradicts this idea, states everyone is able to achieve whatever he or she wants, provided he or she is prepared to work at it hard enough. This idea has had people sent to training courses to overcome a fundamental inability to perform the work of a role. If it becomes obvious in the change process that a person is not and will not be capable of the work, no amount of 'development' or 'coaching' will help.

If a member of the leadership team introducing the material upon which this book is based as part of a change process is unable, for his or her own good reasons, to support the use of the material, he or she should leave and be given the opportunity to do so with dignity.

HOW BEST TO CREATE A PRODUCTIVE RELATIONSHIP BETWEEN EXTERNAL AND INTERNAL CONSULTANTS?

Until this understanding exists, the change process cannot be owned by the executive and what we have found is that the change programme is put forward as a technical exercise in which questions are passed to the 'specialist', usually Human Resources, with or without the advice of the consultant. This process almost always leads to the 'belief system/dogma' approach discussed above. The critical issues are outlined below.

HOW TO AVOID THE PROCESS BEING A 'BLACK BOX'?

We have seen executives reluctant to devote the time to understand the concepts and saying 'Oh well, that's HR' or 'That's why we pay consultants. Just fix it'.

There must be education and engagement at the highest levels. This is not just teaching but dialogue and discussion which may result in changes in both content and presentation which relates to the critical issues associated with the specific organisation:

Box 16.4 Teaching the CEO and his Direct Reports

After some examination of the ideas herein, plus a test of the consultant's analysis in one small division, the CEO of a large department decided to implement these ideas. He did not feel he or his staff fully understood the concepts and relationships. One of the authors suggested they meet with two of his most trusted direct reports – one young, and recognised as someone who would move up the hierarchy. The other was fully capable in role, experienced and highly knowledgeable regarding the Department and its history. Both were able and willing to challenge the CEO and the ideas.

Given the workload each carried, the CEO decided they would meet with the consultant one afternoon a week to explore, test and consider the concepts and theory. They did this for 12 weeks without fail. At that time, the CEO decided he would teach all his direct reports the concepts, such that they could understand and support the changes. He decided to teach the ideas himself, though the consultant was present to help out. The team studied, discussed, argued and learned how the ideas might work in their organisation during two three-day off-site workshops. The two direct reports who had learned the ideas in the earlier sessions were invaluable in explaining to their peers why they thought the ideas would be useful and improve their operations.

Later, the CEO's direct reports taught the ideas to their direct reports, again with the assistance of the consultant. This cascading on the ideas made possible major change and improvements in the Department.

HOW TO INTEGRATE SYSTEMS LEADERSHIP THEORY WITH OTHER MODELS AND CONCEPTS?

It is highly unlikely that a CEO or equivalent will have reached their position without having their own ideas based on their own experience. Others in the organisation will have their own concepts ... It is important not to be overly precious, pedantic or dogmatic. It is the rigour and discipline itself that is important and some terms may be changed. These may be highly symbolic. One organisation did not like terms such as *level* or *stratum*. The concern was allayed by using general role titles and describing the type of work. Another leader insisted on no name for the process of change, which was highly successful because the organisation did not use technical or general terms. This ability to integrate without losing the integrity of the concepts is at the heart of the relationship and makes the difference between successful transition and imposed compliance.

Once there is an understanding and articulation of the change process, at least amongst the CEO's team and support staff/consultants, then it is important to take the next step.

STEP 4: CARRY OUT A DESKTOP STRUCTURAL REVIEW

This is a paper exercise in that it requires the CEO team, with advice, to consider whether the current structural arrangements are appropriate and what needs to change to achieve the new purpose and goals. Using stratified systems theory and systems leadership theory an analysis can be made with regard to the critical issues:

- What is the work?
- How to structure the required work?
- How to address the gap between what is required and what exists?
- What if there is not sufficient clarity of role relationships and appropriate authority?
- How to understand the use of power and assess where it is being applied?

There should be shared understanding with the team of the change required and what the structure might look like in terms of levels of work, operations, services and support roles and other structural concepts discussed earlier (see also Chapter 11).

At the same time or just after, it is useful to carry out the next step.

STEP 5: CARRY OUT A SYSTEMS AND SYMBOLS AUDIT

This process is described in detail in the next chapter but is essentially an organisational health check. A review and interviews are carried out by an external consultant to determine, for example, how people view the leadership and systems. This is done by the careful collection of mythologies, linking them to how they position the systems and symbols of the organisation and the behaviour of leaders on the values continua (honesty, trust, love, respect for human dignity, fairness and courage). The audit identifies different cultures and their uniting mythologies (stories about the organisation that underpin value judgements). Observations are made about internal consistency, for example, safety slogans visible around the site whilst extinguishers are missing and exits are blocked, or there is poor housekeeping, litter and waste during an apparent cost-cutting process.

Critical issues are:

- How to ensure that this process is explained and authorised by the leadership so that consultants are not seen as spies or the police. It may be better not to call it an audit but a review.
- How to avoid this being seen as if it is a survey based on statistical results. It is a process of interpretation where one person may have highly significant and insightful views and observations.

The desktop structural review and systems and symbols audit thus provide the data to check:

1. Is organisational practice currently internally consistent? Is it doing what it is intended to do?
2. To what extent is organisational practice working for or against the purpose and goals of the organisation?

As a consequence of this, the next step is for the CEO.

STEP 6: THE CEO FORMULATES A PROGRAMME FOR CHANGE

Bearing in mind other business/organisational issues and the current context, what is the order of change and who will do what?

Critical issues here are:

- How far down the organisation is the diagnosis and the process shared? This may be influenced by the extent of information shared from the structural review and systems and symbols audit.
- How to ensure the proper choice of people who will engage in this process? This will be highly symbolic and indicate the seriousness of the process.

- What qualitative and quantitative measures are to be used to measure the progress and judge success against cost?
- The process for review of progress and change pace or direction if needed?

The next part(s) of the process depends, of course, on the nature and extent of the programme including what are judged by the CEO to be priority areas. Certainly steps 7, 8 and 9 could well proceed in parallel, and the order in which they are presented here is not any preferred order.

STEP 7: TRAIN

It is important that people understand what is expected and why. The Working Together course described in Chapter 19 is helpful as it combines context setting with knowledge and experiential learning. It is essential that courses are run top-down and are co-led, that is with internal course leaders and an external consultant/trainer. It provides an opportunity to discuss the business plan and important information about how the change program forms a part of that plan. As a result, people may choose not to be a part of this process and so will change roles or organisations.

It is critical to train internal co-presenters (*train the trainer*). Although the roles of the two co-presenters are different, the internal co-presenter must be able to demonstrate knowledge of the concepts and be able to present the business case.

STEP 8: RESTRUCTURE

The extent of this process will obviously depend upon the gap between what is needed and what exists. A restructuring can be a very extensive exercise, and the time it takes will depend upon the resources devoted to it. The new structure must be based on the work required to achieve the purpose of the organisation and the distribution of the complexity of that work, the levels of work. Authority necessary to do the work of the role, and the work of each role, needs to be articulated using a simple effective role description format. The process's success is dependent upon the obvious leadership of the relevant executive head with support from internal and external experts.

1. It is critical that the process is not dogmatic or overly bureaucratic, though it must be disciplined.
2. It is also critical that a differentiation is made between the work required in a new role and the capability of the current role incumbent. All the roles in the new structured are reformulated, even though some may look similar to roles in the pre-existing structure. There will be significant differences, so it is counter-productive to refer to roles by people's names, for example, 'what about Jim's role?' or to have people to 'apply for their old job'. When it comes to selecting people for the new role, it is most important that there be no assumption a person, in what seems to be a similar role, is able to perform the work of the new role to the required standard. We have seen a number of otherwise excellent restructuring programs fail because the assumption above was made and people appointed on this basis.

STEP 9: SYSTEMS DESIGN

In Chapters 12, 13 and 17 the significance of this work is explained. In Chapter 17, we articulate a very practical process for designing systems. Our experience and a consideration of the descriptors of complexity in levels of work (Chapter 9) suggest this work is both complex and demanding of resources, primarily time. It is so highly significant because of the influence that systems have on behaviour and their potentially symbolic role.

Therefore, the critical issues in the process are:

- How to have small teams work on systems (four or five team members as a maximum), whilst taking input from others.
- How to ensure that there is sufficient capability in the design team so that the systems are effective, efficient and that they are designed quickly. The key systems to examine are:
  - safety
  - performance management
  - fair treatment.

These systems affect all employees and the latter two are fundamentally about managerial judgement, which is at the heart of a meritocracy.

The key to the analysis is to look at the purpose of systems and to review all current systems in terms of differentiation or equalisation. Significant gains can quickly be made by changing systems that currently differentiate for no good reason to equalising systems, for example, car parking, uniforms, canteens or benefits. Similar gains can be made the other way (equalisation to differentiation), for example, performance pay from fixed hourly rates.

It is often helpful quickly to initiate some symbolic (but not cosmetic) system changes to demonstrate intent. Some systems may have irritated people for years and yet are relatively easy to change, for example, authorisation for stores, car parking, and good safety equipment – even, in one case, decent work boots.

STEP 10: REMOVAL FROM ROLE

This step is absolutely critical. We have seen many change programmes slowed, halted or fall into disrepute because, despite good structure and systems proposals, people are left in roles when they cannot effectively carry out the work and everyone knows it. This is especially true for those in leadership roles. This is perhaps the most difficult element of all. In successful change programmes we have often seen between a 30% and 40% change in leadership roles within a year. Some of the role changes may be by choice; others by requirement. It is rare that positive behaviour change will occur amongst those in level I or II roles if they see poor leaders left in the roles higher up. The symbolism of and dissonance produced by the removal from the organisation of a manager who has regularly and consistently used box D systems (that is, unauthorised and counter-productive systems as explained in Chapter 13) and behaviour can be highly advantageous to the overall change process.

Any person who attempts to perform his or her work to achieve the purpose of the organisation and does so to a high standard while being subjected to poor leadership behaviour, the exercise of power and poor decision-making must resolve the internal psychological conflict these contradictions generate the entire time he or she is in the employment environment. It is little wonder that poor leadership is so destructive as well as wasteful of resources and human capability.

The critical issue is, of course, how to manage this process of removal from role in a fair and courageous way. It is important to differentiate between those who change roles (or leave) because they do not have the capability but are genuinely well regarded and those who leave because they are bullies or are operating in unauthorised or unproductive ways. The former should leave with dignity; the latter should be dismissed. Of course this distinction may not be so clear, but a sound understanding of mythologies about the work the person has (or has not) been doing will inform such decisions. There should be an opportunity for good employees to change role with dignity, which may require a period of training and the opportunity to build the knowledge and skills needed in the new role. The choice of taking this path must lie with the individual concerned. The critical issue here is not to use training as an excuse to avoid facing the hard truth or in the hope that it will improve mental processing ability.

There may well be a subculture of people who oppose the changes and are not aligned with it. The rest of the organisation will be watching this group carefully to see how they are treated. This is a key leadership issue and relates directly to performance management. Many initial *opponents* have in time not only been won over but have also become enthusiasts. The critical issue is whether they are doing the work of the role. Removal from role of a poor performer who also opposes change can be very positively significant and symbolic. Retaining a critic who is very productive may also be positive.

Despite the criticality of this step we have seen this avoided because it is too difficult, especially at higher levels. It is surprising how simple it seems to cut numbers, that is, objectify the loss of jobs lower down, whilst leaving a person in a level IV, V or VI role who is clearly *not* capable of the work of the role, or who uses power to obstruct the process.

We have found it advantageous to provide the members of an organisation with the option of leaving with the payment of full benefits during a significant change programme. People have their own deep-seated mythologies and established personal relationships that they need to retain to be who they are. These may conflict with the fundamental constructs of the change programme we discuss here. Under these circumstances the preferable outcome may be for them to leave with dignity and fairness.

STEP 11: CONTINUE TRAINING THROUGH THE ORGANISATION

In our experience it is important to take the training programmes about the change process, the reason for it, the concepts underlying it and the opportunities it presents through the organisation, not to stop at the top. Courses may differ in length or content but it must be clear these differences have a work or business reason. The obvious similarity between courses for all employees helps in several ways:

- It reinforces common language.
- It helps build a culture (people at all levels can discuss their experiences).
- It is a positive symbol of equalisation.

There are, however, two critical issues:

A. How to determine change? What is the purpose of the training?

There needs to be demonstrated attempts at change in behaviour by people who have been through training. The worst comment made on a course is 'I wish my boss had gone on this' – when the boss already has.

On the other hand, behavioural change does not result simply from training. As we discussed; behavioural change is driven by the exposure a person has to the example of leadership behaviour. 'Don't worry if your children do not do what you tell them; they are watching you all the time.' It is even more powerfully driven by systems, the organisational analogue of human behaviour, and symbols, the visual manifestation of organisation behaviour.

It is completely unrealistic to expect behavioural change to result from a training course where the content is directed toward an increase in knowledge. It makes sense to set an examination after such a course to test the knowledge gained. A training course, or courses, designed to result in behavioural change needs to incorporate demonstrations of the behaviour required (and not required) along with the opportunity to practice the desired behaviours.

The form of training courses we recommend, such as Working Together, are experiential with opportunities to try new behaviours and learn from the results. No matter how well such a course is designed and run, however, it is unrealistic to expect changed behaviour to be maintained and built upon if the leadership does not demonstrate that its behaviour, systems and symbols support those changes.

Forming communities of practice within the organisation after training can also be very helpful as individuals confront situations and issues where it is not clear how the theory applies, or should be applied. Having a group of peers to turn to with questions can be very helpful as long as they also have access to others in the organisation who are more expert in the application of the theory.

B. What if the course becomes ritualistic?

The course must not become a substitute for change. That is, we must avoid; 'we have nearly finished our change programme as 90% have been through the course'. Such training is at best ritualistic, and at worst destructive because the organisation is demonstrating, through the training course, that its leadership does know the way it is leading its people, but is wilfully choosing not to do so.

Keep in mind that training must be on-going as people change roles and new people are brought into the organisation. Refresher training may also be useful.

STEP 12: SYSTEM TRAINING, DESIGN AND IMPLEMENTATION

System design and implementation takes time, and it is critical to select and train people to do the work of systems design and implementation. This is high-level work requiring high-level capability. The leadership of the organisation must then select those systems whose redesign will most support the change programme and have them done first. There needs to be processes put in place that give measures of the effect of the change programme so that it can be readily monitored. Some of these, such as the change in the number of reporting levels or the number of people who have attended training will be simple. Others such as the reduction in processing time for a set of transactions will be more difficult.

However good the system design is, it must involve training in the knowledge and skills needed in the new system and its implementation. This is an essential, but often overlooked part of the process. The critical issues here are:

HOW TO ENSURE THAT SYSTEMS ARE SEEN AND EXPERIENCED TO BE OWNED IN THE LINE?

If people systems are, or are seen to be, owned by 'HR' or information systems by 'IT', it is unlikely that the purpose of the system is directed toward the achievement of the objectives of line management. If the purpose is correctly directed, ownership of the system by a service function will lead to it being subverted to that function to the detriment of the users. We have seen this result in long, protracted wars breaking out between users and apparent owners.

HOW TO BUILD CONTROLS INTO SYSTEMS THAT PROVIDE INFORMATION FOR AUDITS AND REVIEWS?

Too many systems are implemented with no or poor controls. In our experience, system control is poorly understood. (For a more complete discussion of system control see Chapter 17.) A new system may be well designed and implemented, but without control will drift over time and may become counter-productive without the leadership's recognition of the problem.

Further, it is important to identify priorities. Some systems are in urgent need of redesign; others can be left for later in the program of change and others can be abolished. It is important to link the systems work with the training and structural work so that they are seen to be interdependent.

STEP 13: REGULAR REVIEW

This is a critical step. The CEO, his or her team and relevant others must regularly review progress against expectation. This highlights the need:

1. to integrate the whole process;
2. to have good control and audit information;
3. to have good measures.

The review then will inform any decisions that may be required to rebalance the various components of the change programme, or for targeted intervention by the CEO to deal with a critical issue, for example, restructuring, systems work, training, implementation.

It is essential that this work continues through the programme and is visible to the people of the organisation. It is vital work of the executive leadership. If this leadership by the executive is not visible and undeniable, the way is left open for those within the organisation who perceive themselves as being under threat from the change programme to exercise power and subvert it.

The whole process can be summarised in terms of Figures 16.1 and 16.2. This process is not one that can always be followed exactly, nor can it be applied mechanistically. However, our experience is that leaving out steps or failing to address the critical issues hinders the change process and can be counter-productive.

Conclusion

If productive transformation is to occur, then the social process must be managed as carefully as the technical content and the business case. Benefits to the organisation must be explicit and demonstrable. In summary the main lessons we have learned are:

• To ensure that the CEO or equivalent leads the process. Establishing a relationship between advisers and CEO is critical. It must also be clear that the relationship is advisory, and the quality of the relationship must be such that the adviser is free to deliver bad news to the CEO. Note that the CEO's job can be a lonely one; a good relationship with a capable consultant allows the CEO to use the consultant as a sounding board – not to give advice but to provide analysis and an external perspective.

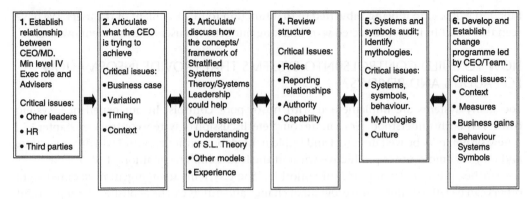

Figure 16.1   Successful Change Process (Part 1)

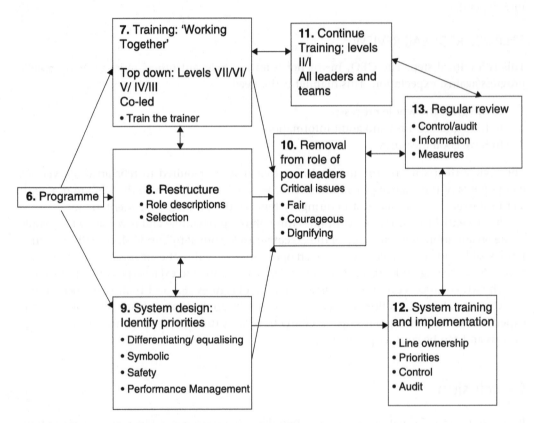

Figure 16.2   Successful Change Process (Part 2)

• During a change process a CEO (or the executive leading the change) may leave and be replaced. We do *not* assume that the process will simply continue. A new CEO may have different priorities. If the Board understands and is supportive of the goals and process, it may well continue albeit with a different timescale, priority and certainly style. We have experience where the use of concepts and models has continued through a succession of CEOs (in one case four succeeding CEOs), and others where the new appointment has resulted in a different direction and the advice declined or put on the back burner. It is important to accept that an advisory relationship, which is based on mutual trust and respect, cannot be built overnight.

- The external consultants (and their team) must develop productive relationships with the CEO team. This is not likely if the consultants are perceived as 'zealots'.
- Although people in HR roles may seem to be the obvious allies of this process, this is not always the case. Indeed, people in the HR roles may see external consultants as rivals or threats. Building a positive relationship and engaging with current concepts used by HR is important. At the other extreme the HR department may be seen as owners of the process and that the head of HR is the client. This must change over time or the whole process will likely be curtailed.
- It is important to understand the role of other external third parties, for example, union leadership. There may be vested interests in maintaining a distance between the organisation's leadership and its employees. It is important to discuss a clear strategy of if and how such organisations relate to or are involved in the change process.
- It is often a good idea not to name the process or the teams involved. Although this paper describes it as a particular transformation process, if it gets named, it is easy for the work to be seen as separate from the business. It is also easy for it to be seen as a 'project' (which will end or go away or fizzle out).
- All through the process it is important to keep in touch with mythologies within the organisation. These may be positive or negative to the changes and will affect both training and pace of change. Most successful transformations have been supported by the advice from 'wise counsel', that is, a few people in the organisation who do have good reliable networks and who have sound judgement and are prepared to give honest feedback.
- In relation to this point, both internal and external members of the change process team must have a heightened awareness of their own behaviour. People will be actively testing for consistency and inconsistency and waiting for dissonant behaviour that might undermine confidence in the process.
- The pace of change will vary; timing is very important and clearly relates to resourcing. There is no fixed time for this process. However, it is likely to take more than a year even when conditions are favourable. Pacing will depend on many factors, resources as mentioned but also the current state of the organisation, capability of those involved and the perceived need for and benefit of change.
- Finally, it is important to build internal resources to sustain and improve on the change process. Although some consultancies might regard this as bad for business, it is not helpful or productive if the maintenance of the new way of working is seen to be dependent upon outsiders.
- There are several pitfalls the consultant, the leader and the process can drop into, and some key overall lessons. From a consultant's perspective:
- It is essential to be disciplined but not dogmatic.
- Advise in such a way that avoids a class or even worse a caste system developing over levels of work: 'she's just a level I', 'he can't do that; he's a level III' and so on. The concepts of capability and complexity must be distinguished. *Never* allow people to be labelled based on their level of work. This advice may seem trivial and self-evident, but it has been a problem of a greater or lesser extent in every organisation in which we have worked. The propensity for humans to classify other humans is astounding. In written history it goes as far back as Plato who had gold, silver, bronze people and slaves who were not people at all.

- Spend a significant amount of time and effort on systems analysis and what behaviour results from it. Especially use the differentiation/equalisation and system matrix models.

From the perspective of the executive/leadership:

- It is essential to demonstrate the process is owned by the line management.
- Establish the business case and link the change program to clear results, both qualitative and quantitative.
- Embed the work into the organisation with systems.
- Remove poor performers from roles.

All involved must keep in touch with mythologies as they develop and work to build new ones that place the behaviour, systems and symbols of the organisation at the positive end of the values continua. Be aware that the advisers and leaders will be constantly judged as to whether they are examples and role models of what they are saying is desired practice.

17 *How to Design Systems*

We have emphasised the importance of systems. Our view that 'systems drive behaviour' underlines how important they are. How systems are designed and implemented has a significant effect on people's behaviour and consequently the productivity of any organisation. We have explained that leaders have three main tools: systems, symbols and behaviour. A leader may individually set a great example but, if the systems are counter-productive, it will be like swimming upstream. If the systems are counter-productive, then it is likely that the organisational symbols will be perceived negatively. If you do not perceive that your work or you as a person are valued positively, then it is unlikely that you will take great care of the organisation's property, pick up litter, keep an area tidy, wear company clothing with any pride. It is not a very big step to see how this might affect the quality and commitment to work.

We argue that systems are the non-verbal behaviour of the organisation. In ordinary life if there is a contradiction between words and behaviour, people believe the behaviour. This experience applies to systems. Words in vision and mission statements are no match for the experience of actual systems. If leaders make statements that are contrary to the experience of people in the organisation or its customers, they become a confirmation, from the mouths of the leaders, that they do not tell the truth.

Putting 'safety first' is only tested in practice by the way systems operate or are tolerated. Missing fire extinguishers, blocked exits and out-of-date safety information tells the real truth. In this way slogans, visions and other vapid exhortations can be replaced by a single statement: 'This organisation tells lies' – unless the systems are authorised and productive.

We have introduced a simple definition of work: 'turning intention into reality'. Systems provide a framework within which flows of activity, including the work activity of people, take place. They help turn the intention of the organisation, as expressed in its purpose and policy, into the reality of day-to-day experience. The effectiveness of the organisation depends upon how well those systems are designed and implemented. Given the importance of systems it is surprising, in our experience, how many organisations do not properly resource their design and implementation. We believe this is largely for three reasons:

1. Their significance is underestimated or misunderstood.
2. The difficulty or complexity of the work of design is underestimated and/or assigned poorly.
3. There is not a simple set of criteria to guide the work of system design and implementation.

Significance

We have already offered tools to understand systems; the systems of differentiation and equalisation and the systems matrix looking at authorised/unauthorised and productive/

counter-productive activity. However, some organisations seem to spend time and money on the articulation of policy statements, grand vision and mission statements, but are relatively careless as to how these are enacted in practice. It is our experience that some organisations rely almost exclusively on behaviour. That is, the leadership assumes that people will make it happen despite the lack of systems. Actually the systems are there but are developed through trial and error, undocumented, and handed on by word of mouth. Their real efficiency and effectiveness are unknown. Paradoxically we have found the most exploitative organisations are the most *worthy*. Organisations with a true mission (religious, voluntary, health or educational) are more likely to exploit the goodwill of the staff than commercial organisations.

For example, there is not a great deal of intrinsic enjoyment or satisfaction in standing over a furnace changing anodes in an aluminium smelter. Few see this as vocational work, though many do it with great skill. Consequently if you want people to do this, they will rightly require good systems: pay, protective clothing, facilities and ideally, good leadership. If, however, people are saving lives, souls or feeding the starving, it seems tempting, given the number of examples we have seen, for the leadership of such organisations to not treat the people they lead very well; the behaviour these leaders demonstrate seems to be, 'I don't have to bother myself, after all, they will do it anyway'. It is surprising how many such organisations, including charities, are not run well nor are they anywhere near achieving what they could. This is often not a deliberate intent but a failure to understand the principles and influences that, when well applied, generate productive behaviour.

Complexity

The work of designing a system most often appears easier than it is in practice. Using the analysis of complexity, it can be seen that this is work of *minimum* level III complexity for systems that apply in only one field of knowledge. Most systems in organisations have effects on, and are affected by, the three principal fields of organisational activity – technical commercial and social. Such systems are of minimum IV complexity in that they require a mental processing ability capable of generating order from the simultaneous interaction of variable inputs from the technical, commercial and social fields within the organisation to achieve the purpose of the system efficiently and effectively.

If the system is organisation wide, its complexity will be higher, depending upon the size of the organisation. Corporate-wide systems of international companies can easily require level VI complexity work. This does not always mean that only people in level VI roles should work on them, but that level VI-type mental processing ability needs to be applied. It does, however, require that someone in a role at the required level (IV, V, VI) should be accountable for this work, its review and authorisation.

A very common mistake, seen in many organisations, is to underestimate the complexity of the work of systems design and to delegate it to a role too low in the organisation where the incumbent does not have the authority, the mental processing ability or knowledge to be able to build a *Box A* system. The output generated as a result of this error is a *Box B* system (if the system is completed at all), inefficient, frustrating to try to use, and which fails to take into account the full degree of variation in its operating environment. Instead of an enabling process we end up with a rigid set of rules that encourage people to find creative ways round the system (Box C) or worse promote the development of covert Box D systems.

A further and compounding error is to see system design as belonging to the technical experts. Thus, *people* systems get designed by HR teams, just as commercial, technical or information technology systems are designed by teams strong in those disciplines. The result is often a system which, although it *may* be technically elegant, is seen by most users as difficult to understand, overly complicated, time consuming to use, with no recognition of the needs of users and, not surprisingly, requiring constant help from the technicians who designed it. We have noted also that systems designed by technical experts function to the benefit of those experts and not the organisation as a whole. For example, People Systems are too often designed by HR experts to provide the data and information needs of HR, not those of line managers.

We argue that all systems need to be owned and authorised by line management. They are and should be executive driven. If not, the systems can be avoided, criticised or changed. Telltale comments that this is happening include 'HR requires us to do this', 'HR gave us little choice', 'The IT department doesn't realise we don't need this capacity' – and less polite critiques.

Criteria: The 20 Questions

It is easy to criticise, especially with hindsight. In response to leaders who were concerned to design systems properly we wrote a paper outlining the criteria for good design. These were developed from our experience and understanding of systems in organisations and our work of designing and helping to design systems that led to manifest and positive behavioural change. These have proved extremely helpful. These criteria have been articulated into a series of questions the designer(s) should address.

These questions can be used to both critique and design systems. This is similar to our model concerning Critical Issues. That is, while it is very important to identify what the issues are, it is also necessary to address them. People can use these questions simply to understand why systems are not working well but the real work and gains come when those issues are addressed and a new design produced. This latter work is where the real complexity lies. For example we might realise that the system has no clear or shared purpose but the work of articulating one, in a single sentence without an 'and' is tough. This work of addressing the issues takes time and effort but it is worth it. It saves an enormous amount of time and effort in the long run.

Before we even start with the questions it is essential to consider the context. If we are considering a particular system for examination why has this been done?

While we place a great deal of emphasis on systems, we are also aware of the amount of time and resources required to design and implement good systems. So it is important to ask that if there is a problem, is the system needed in the first place?' It is often too easy to respond to a problem in an organisation by saying 'It's the system', and then modify an existing system or bolt on additions. An effective organisation is not one with a plethora of systems. The purpose of system design is to simplify work and eliminate waste. That is why it is high-level work. As Mark Twain commented, 'if I had more time, I would have written less'. So we need to ask: how this system (or potential system) fits with the organisation's purpose. Does it relate to a current policy? How will the improved system integrate with what else is happening in the organisation? For example, it might be very useful to redesign performance review and assessment systems if the organisation is attempting to build a meritocratic, performance-based culture. However, we have found that sometimes systems are designed to avoid difficult issues. For example, rather than require managers to confront poor work performance, a new system for discipline or training is designed but not really needed as it does not address the underlying issue.

1. WHAT IS THE PURPOSE OF THE SYSTEM?

This is the most important question of all the twenty. Clarity of purpose is essential. We argue that the purpose of a system should be expressible in a single sentence without the conjunction 'and'. This is usually a difficult task involving significant debate, but without this clear purpose statement the rest of the design will not be coherent. The reason for excluding an 'and' in the statement is that it is almost inevitable that at some point in the design process these two halves of the purpose statement, one either side of the 'and' suddenly emerge in their true colours as two distinctly different purposes that are in conflict – a conflict that cannot be resolved consistently within one system.

For example, the system may be called 'review and development'. Should the design emphasise one or the other? What if the review is highly critical? We have seen this issue avoided by simply moving quickly onto the 'positive' development aspects. Review and development should be two related but separate systems. In system design it is not unusual to return to the purpose statement several times in the design process. This may seem tiresome but it is, in most cases, time well spent.

The purpose statement is the reference against which the various activities proposed for inclusion in the system are tested. *Is this activity going to help in achieving the purpose? Is there a better way of doing it?* It sometimes becomes clear that an activity is essential, yet does not meet the purpose. This requires a re-examination of the purpose statement. Beware of hidden purposes. For example, is the design really intended to catch abusers (for example, of petty cash) or to promote good practice? Ask what behaviour you want the purpose to encourage and reinforce. It is usually helpful to have a positive purpose. For example, 'to provide security for company property', rather than 'to stop stealing'. The latter implies lack of trust, and may result in a design that treats everyone as a potential thief.

One thing that is certain is that, as you work on the other questions, the purpose should be revisited many times. Don't worry; do not hang onto the purpose statement just because it has taken a long time to work out, when further work demonstrates it is inaccurate. The purpose must be clear for the design to be effective; frustrating though it may be these iterations are worthwhile.

When the purpose has been decided, it is essential to generate a flow chart of activities that will achieve the purpose. The first step may be to chart the existing system to learn precisely what is actually being done. This flow chart will be modified as the system design proceeds, but it provides a necessary reference document for subsequent work. The flow chart needs to incorporate all the activities required, the inputs and outputs, information requirements, decisions, reports, data storage along with a time line. (See also Q. 16.)

2. WHO IS/SHOULD BE THE OWNER?

The owner of the system is someone with the authorised discretion to implement or significantly change a system (not merely propose changes). Too often the system owner either is, or is perceived to be, a specialist. For example, the head of HR *owns* the people systems. Our experience is that many organisations dilute leadership to their detriment by handing over authority for a core part of this work of leadership – the design and implementation of systems

– to such specialists. They confuse expertise with leadership. Our experiences suggest that system owners should usually be line managers (rarely, if ever, below level III and usually appropriately at level IV or above).

This does not mean that the owner has to do all the design work, which leads to the next question.

3. WHO IS/SHOULD BE THE CUSTODIAN/DESIGNER?

The designer is the person whose work is to manage the work of system design to the point at which a proposal for the complete system can be presented to the owner for authorisation or for more work. This can be complex, time consuming and involve specialist knowledge. We have found that a small team (three of four members) with a range of knowledge and experience headed up by a highly capable person in at least a level IV role is an effective way to approach this issue. The team can call on people from all levels, especially users, for comment and advice. It should be clear to the organisation that, while the design team may work extensively on a system, it should be commissioned and authorised by the owner, that is, a line manager.

The custodian of the system is the person nominated by the system owner, to do the work of monitoring the application of the system and advising the owner of the outcome of the monitoring. The owner, designer and custodian could be the same person (same role), but for company-wide systems this is usually not ideal due to the time needed for both design and monitoring of the system, and the technical knowledge required, once implemented.

4. WHAT IS THE UNDERLYING THEORY?

All systems and processes are essentially methods of changing an input (or inputs) into an output (or outputs). Do you know why these (should) work? Too often systems are designed and implemented in an apparently pragmatic way or simply because 'other organisations do it'. Interestingly this is more often the case in HR systems than technical processes, although IT comes pretty close to HR. For example, suppose a company that smelts aluminium decides to try a new technology with regard to reduction cells. It is unlikely that the new technical process will be introduced without examining the underlying metallurgical, chemical and electro-magnetic theories. Further, the company is likely to conduct trials and try to gain information from other sources as to the efficiency and cost of the new technology.

Incentive pay systems, however, are rarely examined with such rigour. What exact change of behaviour is expected as a result of such a scheme? Why should it produce a change? Will people work harder or more effectively? On what evidence? Or is the purpose really one of retention of staff? It is not that such questions will all be answered negatively. The point is that often such questions are not even asked. Most people have experience of expensive computer systems being introduced on the basis of claimed technical improvements in the hardware or software that are either not relevant to the needs of the users, or not actually realised in practice, leading to a need for further upgrades. The articulation of the underlying theory or assumptions also helps with the consideration of relevant measures of success, which brings us to the next question.

5. HOW IS IT TO BE MEASURED?

Many systems do not have clear measures of success. Measurement, and all measures should be directly related to the Purpose. We need to know how or whether the purpose is being achieved? This should not be complicated by drawing up a very long list of measures. Which are the most important? How will they be displayed and communicated? Work in the quality field is very helpful here, such as statistical process control and run charts (see Deming, 1982).

Has the cost/value been fairly estimated? This may not always be easy but should be attempted and is part of the measurement of success. This costing includes the estimate of costs of design and implementation. In one business a good costing exercise resulted in the decision not to go ahead with a system redesign because the cost of redesign, new equipment and training was greater than the reasonable expectation of gain.

6. IS IT A SYSTEM OF EQUALISATION OR DIFFERENTIATION?

It is important to decide whether this is a system which is intended to apply to all employees or only to some, and if so, why? Should there be different benefits for health care, holiday or sick leave arrangements? The organising principle is that systems of differentiation should be justifiable in terms of the work to be done. If the reason for being treated differently is not explainable in this way, it may well be perceived by others as unfair or dishonest. If a person has improved insurance and health care benefits, it needs to be understood that it is because that person has to travel to countries that have poor public health services and not because they have become a vice president. Many systems of differentiation are about status not work.

A system of equalisation is not simply one that applies to all. Remuneration and disciplinary systems may apply to everyone but the *intention* is to differentiate in both, that is, to pay different amounts according to the work (roles) or to distinguish between those who have performed poorly or broken policy requirements and those who have not. Hence they are systems of differentiation where the differentiation is based upon work done, or not done.

7. WHAT ARE THE CURRENT 'BENEFITS' OF THE POOR SYSTEM? THAT IS, WHO GAINS FROM INEFFICIENCY?

It is important to know what you are up against. A new system may bring about cost savings and improvements, but some people may be gaining from the current inefficiency. For example, an overtime system may allow an employee to earn double time for four hours when he or she only has to be called out for half an hour. Some employees may be able to use company vehicles for their own use and have come to assume this perk as a right. A manager may enjoy his or her large office, but has no work related use for the space. Employees may gain extra payment for going to training courses, even though they do not need or use the skills taught. As with systems of differentiation the underlying benefit may be status and prestige rather than efficiency.

The question is whether there is an understanding that some people may feel they are losing out, as they should be expected to try to influence the way the system change is to be explained and communicated.

8. WHAT ARE THE BOUNDARIES OF THE SYSTEM?

There are no absolute rules for deciding where a system should begin or end. For example, we may have one system that is designed to fill roles in the organisation with the most appropriate people, or we could break this up into recruitment, appointment, induction, and promotion. Where the boundaries are depends upon the needs of the business at any time and is an executive decision (see also the discussion of system owner, Question 2 above). All we are saying here is that the boundaries must be clear and logical. They must be known to people so that overlap and confusion do not occur. Smaller is usually better than bigger when it comes to system design, particularly in the early stages when design teams and managers are coming to grips with the work and discipline necessary to do it well.

9. WHAT ARE THE LINKAGES WITH OTHER SYSTEMS?

When designing a system, attention needs to be paid to existing and new systems that interact with the system under design. This affects decisions about the boundaries and structural issues. This part of system design involves work of at least level IV complexity. It is a common fault that systems are designed in isolation and the conflict with other systems is not appreciated until the system is implemented. A classic example is compatibility with technical equipment, especially in IT where it is discovered, usually late in the process, that the hardware does not have the ability to run the new system as it has been designed. (This is a far less frequent occurrence now with the cloud, but the stories of IT system implementation disasters have not abated.) Another is where technological change is not considered in terms of its impact on social processes or current arrangements, for example the labour agreement, or even the availability of skilled labour. An incentive scheme may be introduced without proper reference to current appraisal systems or the general compensation system or grading system.

10. WHAT STRUCTURAL BOUNDARIES DOES IT CROSS?

Where a system flows across structural boundaries, for example, from one department to another, even from one organisation to another, there is potential for conflict and loss of efficiency. This is because the resolution of problems or misunderstandings may have to be at a relatively high level, where a crossover manager can be found. If crossing boundaries is needed, then it is even more important to have a detailed articulation of the system, including a detailed articulation of the work, tasks and authority on both sides of the boundary at the crossover. If management systems are crossing boundaries, it may be an indication of a need for a structural review. (This is often the outcome of business process re-engineering projects.) In general, it is useful to minimise these boundary issues, which may mean that a large system is better managed as several smaller ones that have a readily verifiable measure of the flow at the boundary.

11. IS THE SYSTEM ONE OF TRANSFER OR TRANSFORMATION?

A system is simply represented in Figure 17.1.

What occurs in the box is either a transfer or transformation. If it is a *transfer*, then the system is intended to deliver C in the same state as A. Obvious transfers are transportation systems like freight or postal deliveries. The system includes processes, which are intended to protect the object from unintended change, for example, packaging or refrigeration. Some business systems, however, are intentional transformations, that is, where C is significantly different from A. Typical examples here would be chemical processes, steel making, accounts or education (See Box 17.1).

Whatever the core activity, transfer or transformation, it is critical in system design to minimise the other. The customer is usually reluctant to pay for the alternative. For example, I am unhappy if the products I ordered are delivered in a damaged (transformed) state, or if the main cost of steel includes the costs involved in warehousing and storage (hence the

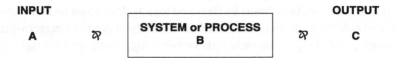

Figure 17.1 System of Transfer or Transformation

Box 17.1 Are Systems Magic?

Note: It is interesting to note that magic is essentially a clear transformation of something recognisable (as A) into a totally different entity (now it's C!) where the observer has no idea of the nature of the transformation (B). Too often systems appear more like magic than understandable processes.

---

reluctance to maintain extensive inventory). Thus, complex systems that involve moving and storing transformed goods are wasteful and are likely to damage the goods in the process. Of course, I am also reluctant to pay for failed transformation; for example, when I send my team members to a training course and they return exactly as they were, having learned nothing.

Therefore part of clarification of the purpose of the system is to determine whether it is transfer or transformation and to minimise the other, first of all in the purpose, and then in the design.

12. ARE AUTHORITIES AND TASKS CONSISTENT WITH ROLES?

In the design of the system it is important that a person's work in the system is not at odds with the work of his or her role and the authority of the role. For example, imagine the situation where a manager may have the discretion to spend up to $100,000 but has to send a form to his manager's manager countersigned by someone in accounts to justify an overnight stay in a hotel on business. Conversely, think of what would happen if a specialist in HR (level II role) were required to check on the CEO's quality of interviewing and give feedback.

There may be times when exceptions are required. For example, it is common that all overseas travel has to be approved by the CEO for a period of time because of tight business conditions. We must be very careful in the design that systems do not constrain the opportunity to use discretion, that is, reduce the level of work in a role or increase it by taking tasks out or putting them in, respectively. It is important not to limit the use of creativity and common sense with mindless procedural activity of no worth. This latter is a common pitfall and is most often the result of the designer's inability to identify sensible controls of the system.

13. ARE THERE PROPER CONTROLS BUILT INTO THE SYSTEM?

A control in a system acts to provide information as to whether or not the system is being operated correctly, that it is working as intended. This is done by taking statistically valid samples of data about work quantity and quality that informs the operator, custodian and system owner about the system in use. Controls are often useful around decision points. For example, if the 'assessment of potential' policy and system requires that only people who have been assessed as having potential to work at a higher level should be promoted, is this the case? What information is there concerning recent promotions? It is our experience that while controls are required inclusions in financial systems, and common in technical systems, they are often poor or non-existent in HR and some IT systems. In HR systems a common problem is to apply controls only to quantitative elements and not qualitative. Thus 'I have done all my performance appraisals', does not say how well I have done them. Whilst it is important to build in controls, as a part of the system design process, not as an afterthought, it is also important not to draw control data from every system activity. Too many control data streams are counter-productive. They become background noise that is understandably ignored. They are seen as demonstrating a lack of trust in the discretion of the people working in the system.

In addition to controls it is important to ask:

14. IS THERE AN EFFECTIVE AUDIT PROCESS?

Audit is different from control in that it first checks from time to time that the controls are in place, whether or not they are being used and acted on, and whether they are still valid indicators of system functioning. The audit then reviews whether the system is achieving its purpose and is the best way to achieve that purpose. It is typical that auditors are independent of system operators but report findings to the system owner. In the event of exceptional circumstances such as financial impropriety or breaking of the law, the auditor has the authority to have direct access to the board.

The process of audit being discussed here is most often internal audit, work that is done by members of the organisation. This is different from external audit which is a legal requirement, usually done annually and which concentrates on financial issues. The audit processes themselves are very similar.

Auditors, in most instances, are not the most loved people in organisations but do essential work. They can appear less like police or spies if it is understood that they are reviewing whether the system is operating correctly and whether or not it is achieving its purpose. A system may be operating according to its intent, and have effective controls in place but not achieving what it should effectively. An example would be a system for training people in skills that are no longer in use.

We find that one area of system design, which is often overlooked, is the people aspect, or attention to social process. So it is important to ask:

15. HAS THE SOCIAL PROCESS ANALYSIS BEEN DONE?

This is partly covered by the prior question, but involves a much more specific use of the values model by requiring an assessment of where an activity which forms part of the system will be placed on the values continua when it is viewed through the mythological lens of the people who will be subject to, or part of, the activity. This work requires an assessment of how the new system as a whole will be placed on the values continua. The designers and the system owner need to have a sound understanding of the current mythologies to do this.

They need to know the behaviours that are required to achieve the purpose of the system, and from that the mythologies that need to be created to deliver success. This analysis informs the implementation plan. It may be that substantial dissonance needs to be generated to prepare the ground for the seeding and growth of the mythologies needed to have the new system drive the desired behaviour. All of this is not simple work, it requires discussion to gather information and share ideas, and the capability to develop them. It requires us to look through the lens of others and ask how would people view and respond to this change. It is not sufficient to extrapolate from one's personal views as in, 'Well, I think that is perfectly fair, so it is okay.'

To help with this exercise, we use the following set of sub-questions. It is strongly recommended that time is spent on this aspect as some very useful and sometimes surprising information is discovered. This can have a significant impact on the way the system is both designed and implemented.

a. How is the system currently viewed?
   - What are the mythologies about it? (Or lack of it)
     ◦ How is it rated on the values continua?
     ◦ Is it a system of differentiation or of equalisation?
     ◦ Where is it on the systems matrix? (A, B, C or D)
     ◦ What behaviour is it driving? (Note that this may vary between groups)
     ◦ What symbols are associated with the system (or lack of)?
b. Desired outcomes
   - What behaviours should it drive?
   - What mythologies do we want about the system?
   - What are the assumptions and theory on which the new design rests?
c. What are the recommended changes/design? How will these/it be viewed?
   - On the values continua?
   - Differentiation or equalisation?
   - Systems matrix?
   - Will any of these changes be symbolic? How?
   - What behaviour do we predict it will drive?

As these questions are being addressed, the activities in the flowchart are worked through and confirmed, both for their inherent work behaviour and for their interaction with other activities, systems or people, as supportive of the achievement of the purpose of the system. Depending upon the system, this can be time consuming and iterative work of IV or higher complexity. At the conclusion of this work, the flow chart is a visual model of the system and how it has been designed to work.

16. IS THERE A FULLY OUTLINED FLOWCHART OR FLOWCHARTS?

There are many methods of flowcharting that are useful, and some excellent software packages exist to assist with it. Detailed flowcharting articulates the detail, whether it is a flow of materials, money, information, people, work or equipment. There need not only be one flow-chart. We can literally chart the flows of the any of the items mentioned in the previous sentence and from different perspectives. Our experience suggests that any flowcharts should be understandable to an outsider and practical like a good set of instructions. For example, it is not sufficient to say 'at this point customer requirements go from sales to production'. What customer requirements? Who in sales must do the work of sending them? Who in production must do the work of receiving them? Then we can ask what is the work that is required. The flowchart must indicate decisions points, all the discrete activities within the system boundary and the control.

If there is not a flowcharting system already being used, the design team will need to generate flow charts that it believes will result in the system's purpose being achieved. About the only thing that is certain about this first iteration of the flow chart(s) is that it will be changed as the design process moves forward and back through its many iterations. The flow chart is the working document upon which notes are made about why a certain choice has been made or what detail is required in a link to another system, for example.

While there are excellent software packages available today that help enormously with drawing and recording flow charts and notes, but they do not do the thinking work required to design the system. That is a uniquely human activity. This phase of system design is usually the most time consuming. The design team may choose to bring in people who now perform the activity that will be required within the new system boundaries and have them explain in detail what is done now and provide suggestions on how it might be done better or not at all.

The design team should field their ideas with these doers to test their proposals either for different work from that being done now, or for different work sequences. It is advisable to ask about the best source for necessary information and the channel through which it is delivered.

The work of building the flow chart(s) is the creative phase of system design. The inherent effectiveness and efficiency of the system is largely determined here. It is advisable to note the points in the flow chart(s) at which it may be desirable to extract control data. These are revisited when the control of the complete system is being considered. Any point that may require specific training for implementation and operation are also noted. During this phase of work it is common for the purpose originally chosen to be revisited.

Another way of thinking about the flowchart is to think of the way that the system treats someone, in particular the person who the system is meant to be serving for example a customer, a client, a visitor, the patient in hospital, children in school and so on. It is sometimes helpful to think of the flowchart as the script of a play all film with both dialogue and directions. It should describe accurately who does what when and what happens next.

The flowcharts are an essential part of documentation and so the next question is:

17. IS THERE A DESIGN PLAN THAT ADDRESSES THE CRITICAL ISSUES?

Answering all of the questions above should identify a number of critical issues and the work to be done to address them. Too often this work on how to address the critical issues is not properly addressed. A problem may have been identified but it is not articulated into a task; specifying what is to be done by whom and when. For example it may be that a particular system, say role design, is not compatible with the IT software in an HR system. What work needs to be done to make them compatible and whose work is it? It may be that the owner of a system should be in the line while currently the owner is a specialist. Who will make this change and how? Every issue should have a task associated with it in order to address that issue. Therefore there should be a design plan that identifies the work and which along with the flow chart and system documentation (see below, next question) articulates the entire system.

18. IS THERE FULL SYSTEM DOCUMENTATION?

System documentation is the unloved child of systems design. When the time comes for documentation, the system is ready to go. The designers want to see how their creation will work in practice, and it is often too easy to put documentation off until tomorrow. Too often system designs remain in the heads of the designers. This knowledge and experience may leave with the person, and even if it does not leave, it is not readily available for reference and will fade with time.

From the perspective of the users of the system, good documentation provides an insight into why the system has been designed as it has, providing context for their work. It gives a short description of the tasks that make up the activity of people, any specific authority that may be different from the authority of their roles, the flows of information, materials, money and the rationale for the controls.

While good system documentation is of worth to users, it is vital for system owners, custodians and auditors. It is the work of the owner to verify the system design meets his or her criteria, to authorise implementation and to monitor its use. The documentation is his or her reference point, and it serves the same purpose for the system custodian.

For the system auditor, the documentation provides the knowledge about the system that allows an audit to be done. The system documentation must not only describe the system, it must also provide the rationale for why it is structured as it is, and why the controls were chosen as they are. As mentioned the flowchart(s) are part of this documentation.

The process of system documentation in itself may reveal anomalies and deficiencies in the system that requires rectification. A note of caution here is that system documentation is a descriptive process. Be careful it does not become a bureaucratic rulebook limiting discretion. It should contain the flowchart and methods of recording the information flow of the system including control and audit information. It also needs to include all of the input and output documentation in the form in which it has been designed in Step 16. These need to be facsimiles of the actual forms or screens.

The importance of the design of these interfaces and their accurate reproduction needs to be appreciated. In many systems the interface generates a user's experience of the system and therefore its positioning on the values continua.

19. WHAT IS THE IMPLEMENTATION PLAN?

Sometimes systems fail because, although well designed, they are rolled out without proper education and training. Training in a new system can be a major undertaking, especially if it is a corporate-wide system. However, it is pointless to introduce a new system half-heartedly. Training and implementation programmes are not just about the technical details but should be informed by all these questions, especially the purpose, gains, and social process and behaviour required for the new system to be a success.

The work done to produce good system documentation informs the work of developing an implementation and training plan. It is advantageous to build these in parallel.

20. WHAT IS THE FINAL COST OF DESIGN AND IMPLEMENTATION?

Finally, it is important to revisit the cost.

In designing the systems, its processes and implementation, critical issues will arise which need to be addressed. It is very rare to come up with an initial cost estimate that is accurate. This last step should estimate more realistically the overall cost and calculate it against the gains. It is not a failure if at this point the system is regarded as too expensive and rejected. Making that decision may save a commercial and social disaster but requires great courage.

Box 17.2   The 20 Systems Design Questions

1.   What is the purpose of the system?
2.   Who is/should be the owner?
3.   Who is/should be the custodian/designer?
4.   What is the underlying theory?
5.   How is it to be measured?
6.   Is it a system of differentiation or equalisation?
7.   What are the current 'benefits' of the poor system?
8.   What are the boundaries of the system?
9.   What are the linkages with other systems?
10. What structural boundaries does it cross?
11. Is the system one of transfer or transformation?
12. Are authorities and accountabilities consistent with role?
13. Are there proper controls built into the system?
14. Is there an effective audit process?
15. Has the social process analysis been done?
16. Is there a fully outlined flowchart?
17. Is there a design plan that addresses the critical issues?
18. Is there full system documentation?
19. What is the implementation plan?
20. What is the final cost of design and implementation?

Practical Examples

The website for this book (www.maconsultancy.com) contains a number of case studies; they are actual examples of where these concepts have been applied in a wide range of settings.

There is a range of examples there; however, we include one example here as it was one of the first examples using concepts and design criteria.

The first full demonstration of the effectiveness of this work took place in CRA, a large Australian mining and metal smelting organisation, in the late 1980s and early 1990s. After the restructuring work was done, the managing directors of the new business units turned their attention to systems using the systems leadership model. Most notably Karl Stewart at Comalco Smelting and Terry Palmer at Hamersley Iron (later as CEO of Comalco) applied the full suite of modelling and concentrated on systems design.

Box 17.3   'NOT TO GO' – Lessons In Systems Design

CONTEXT

Hamersley Iron transports the iron ore it mines in the ranges of the Pilbara region of northwest Australia, by way of a rail system it built and operates, to its port at Dampier. The distance varies, depending on the mine, and is between 300 and 400 kilometres. The rail system operates around the clock – at the time of this case study it was transporting between 3 and 4 million tons per month. A train was made up of a rake of 210 100-ton capacity wagons, called a consist, and three locomotives. The wagons, steel boxes on wheels, are united in pairs by a solid draw bar so an individual unit is made up of a control car and a slave car. These units can be uncoupled from each other. They have two boxes, four cast steel suspension frames, two sets of brake mechanisms, eight axles, sixteen bearings and sixteen wheels. Each unit has an

---

identification number. The fleet was made up of 2,500 wagons and 47 locomotives plus 300 other items of rolling stock. The operating schedule called for seven trains per day with one additional on Fridays.

The entire rail system was and is one of the biggest in the world in terms of tonne/ kilometres per day and is technologically very advanced.

The rail operations and maintenance group totalling 560 people had, immediately prior to this case study, been the first part of the Hamersley Iron Business Unit to go through the restructuring exercise based on the ideas of Elliot Jaques and the knowledge gained from previous exercises elsewhere in the CRA (now Rio Tinto) group.

DISCUSSION

One of the tasks assigned to the restructuring team leader by the CEO of CRA (Sir Roderick Carnegie) was to develop an understanding of systems in business which would inform their design and implementation across the corporation. Some work on this task had been done by the team leader and a few of the team members during the restructuring exercise over the previous six months. This small group chose the NOT TO GO system for its first trial of its ideas. It was a system vital to rail, it was a system believed to be not working well, and it depended upon the transfer of data and equipment across department boundaries.

The system was organised around the work of 30 traffic operations people, called car and wagon examiners (C&WEs), and 30 tradesmen from rolling stock maintenance, called wagon maintainers. The cycle of work was begun when one examiner walked up either side of the consist visually examining each wagon for structural faults and then standing, one on either side, while the consist was slowly pulled past them so they could listen for noise which would indicate a bearing or a wheel fault. The examiners each carried a gauge that they used to test the shape of any wagon wheel they thought might have worn undersize on the wheel flange or tread. The purpose of this work, which continued around the clock, was the identification of faults that had the potential to cause a derailment. As the general manager of rail said, 'You start counting the cost of a derailment at a million dollars and it goes up by the hour from there.'

A wagon identified as having a fault had a card 250mm × 200mm marked up and placed in a pocket in one corner. The card had on it in large black print:

NOT TO GO

hence the name of the system. The supervisor of the C&WEs also walked the consist noting marked cards, checking to verify faults and recording the cars to be cut out. This data was provided to the shunting locomotive crew who cut the NOT TO GO wagons from the consist and delivered them to a holding track outside the rail maintenance workshop. Codes on the NOT TO GO card indicated the fault identified by the examiner.

The relationship between the examiners and maintainers was not good. Recently, in response to criticism from the maintainers about the inspection quality, the examiners had placed NOT TO GO on 200 wagons over a weekend, all of which were waiting for the maintainers when they arrived for work on Monday morning. The maintainers worked three shifts per day, five days per week.

The myths each group held about each other may be gauged from the following quotes (from which expletives, indicating the emotional state of the speaker, have been deleted):

'The wagon maintainers do nothing to fix the wagons – they hit them a few times with a hammer, tear up the NOT TO GO card and put them back into service.' 'The wagon maintainers are too lazy to do any work, they sit around all day in the shade and read Playboy.' 'The maintainers are useless, they don't know one end of a wagon from the other and their bosses are worse.'

'Car and wagon examiners are all apes – they find them in the gutter outside the pub in Roebourne [a small, old, local town] and give them a job as C & W examiners.' 'The C & W examiners are so stupid they keep losing wheel gauges. How do you expect them to inspect wagons?' 'We have got people doing nothing each day but make up wheel gauges.'

In fact, the work of the C & W examiners was difficult and unpleasant. It required intense concentration and at night, in spite of many powerful lights, shadows made examination more difficult. During the long summers the daytime temperature between the rows of wagons where the examiners worked was above 50 degrees C – every steel surface was too hot to touch with a bare hand.

The examiners and maintainers were members of different unions.

The systems team discussed the proposal to work on NOT TO GO with the GM of rail and were given approval. They then ran an information session with the managers (Level III), superintendents (Level II) and supervisors (Level I) who had a direct association with the system. These sessions produced some favourable commentary and a 'best of luck'.

The information session with the maintainers was not so forthcoming. The union delegate for the maintainers informed the team that, 'The union leadership has informed us that it will give no support for the work and we will not talk to you,' to which the systems team leader replied, 'I grew up in the union. It is the members of a union who make the decisions in a union, not the leaders. We will talk to all those whom we please. You can tell us what you choose.'

This response was confrontational, and well removed from normal practice, but the meeting continued. The team members then went on to explain the process intended for data gathering and feedback on progress. The reception received from the examiners was almost as frosty.

The individual response the systems team got from these people over the subsequent weeks as they gathered data and discussed ideas for a new system was very straightforward and helpful. They spoke to people on all shifts. The union delegate for the maintainers was one of the most forthcoming on his work and his experience of the current system.

FINDINGS

The examiners were copying data seven times between the notebook they carried and placement of the NOT TO GO card on the wagon.

There was no information provided to examiners on what maintainers had found or done. The maintainers expressed concern about standards of inspection. Sometimes they could not find a fault and sometimes they found a fault different from that marked on a card. The examiners had no idea what had been done to the wagons they marked. They were sure that on occasions a wagon they had marked was back in the consist a few days later with the same fault but they had no record unless they wrote the wagon number and fault down separately – which a few tried to do.

The leadership of both areas was satisfied with the system design and put the difficulties they were having with it down to poor quality employees and the fact they belonged to the union.

Both examiners and maintainers said their own leadership added no value to their work, and the other group's leadership was condoning poor work practice. The examiners were not losing the gauges; they were throwing them into ore wagons in rage because they were so awkward to use and heavy in their shirt pocket where they needed to be carried.

The maintainers were making the gauges bigger from material much thicker than necessary so the examiners could not lose them so easily.

Data on wagon faults was collected for analysis by the operations department. Data on wagon maintenance was collected for analysis by the maintenance department. The systems team could find no evidence of any analysis in the previous twelve months and no consideration had been given to the analysis of both sets of data together.

The last derailment had occurred some eighteen months previously and there was general concern that 'We are due for another one.'

NEW SYSTEM

The NOT TO GO card was redesigned. It now had a line drawing of the wagon on which the examiner could mark the position of the fault. The codes on the front of the old card were replaced by short descriptions of the fault with an 'other' category and columns for the examiner and the maintainer to mark. The card had sizeable boxes for comments from the examiner, who placed the card, and the maintainer, who worked on the wagon, both of whom were required to sign below their respective comment box.

Pocket-sized booklets with two-copy NCR paper were printed so the pages were a small replica of the NOT TO GO card. The examiners were to carry these and mark them up as the primary record of inspection. They kept one copy and the other was used as the data input for management and record keeping. The examiner transferred the data from his pocket book to the NOT TO GO card in the trackside work hut and then went out and inserted the card into the holder on the relevant wagon as in the old system.

The supervisor had a copy page from the examiner's book for each card placed.

As the design of the new system developed, proposals were taken out to the users for their comment. The management group advised that there would be trouble asking examiners and maintainers to sign the cards and that they would refuse. Very few examiners signed the present cards. The recognised 'leader' of the examiners was pungently critical of the system team's members and their work until he was shown the prototype of the pocket notebook, which he refused to give back to the team declaring it was 'A bloody good idea.' When it was explained that it had taken days to draw up each page by hand he laughed and told them it was about time they did some real work. From then on the team's work with the examiners was much more collaborative.

The new system required the NOT TO GO card to be completed and signed by the maintainer at the completion of maintenance work, checked by his supervisor, copied for maintenance records, sent to the examiner's supervisor for his reference and then given to the examiner who had initiated it.

IMPLEMENTATION

The systems team made a series of presentations explaining the new system to all users, answering questions fully and providing access to the new notebooks and cards. Immediately following the last training session the system was put into practice.

There was no objection raised to signing the cards.

OUTCOME

Two weeks after the implementation, a group of maintainers approached their superintendent with a proposal that they run a training course for the car and wagon examiners to teach them in detail about the parts of the wagons, the information which would most assist the maintainers, and special aspects of inspection which would improve and standardise inspection. Approval was given, the course developed and training began four weeks later. Training course attendance was 100% and at the course each examiner was presented with a thin polished gauge on which his name was stamped. Three weeks after the courses had been run, one examiner identified an unusual fracture in a steel casting. It was in a location that made it visible only through a triangular opening about 50mm wide and, had it not been found, the fault would have caused a derailment. The maintenance comment written on the NOT TO GO card was 'A spectacular save.' The examiner carried his copy of the card in his crib tin (lunch box) for weeks to show it to people.

At a presentation to the upper-level management of the corporation which sought to explain the system, its design methodology and its outcome, the crew superintendents of both the maintainers and the examiners said, 'It (the new system) has succeeded beyond our wildest expectations.'

POST SCRIPTS

The original NOT TO GO cards were printed on dull red paper, which made them difficult to see against the brown of the wagon, particularly at night.

The new NOT TO GO cards were printed on fluorescent red paper so they could be seen easily by the locomotive crews who cut the wagons from the consist and took them to the workshop. The colour faded in the intense sunlight and the cards became difficult to identify. New paper was sourced by the systems team and replacement cards printed.

The systems team reviewed the operation of the system twelve weeks after it had been introduced and found it had been changed. The NOT TO GO cards were not being returned to examiners on a regular basis and maintainers and examiners were being required to transcribe data from the cards onto newly introduced forms. The examiners and maintainers were highly critical of the changes and said they had no idea of why they had been introduced by their respective managers. The working relationship between the examiners and maintainers remained excellent.

The systems team intervened, with the general manager of rail, and the system was taken back to its original design. Eight months later the new system had collapsed completely. It had been changed back to its original form except for the design of the NOT TO GO card.

The working relationship between the examiners and maintainers was still good but showing signs of strain, particularly with new members of the examiner team (which had always had a high turnover, in part because of the difficult working conditions). The working relationship between both crews and their supervisors and superintendents had deteriorated significantly.

WHY?

1. The new system was owned by the systems team and not by the general manager of rail. He was very supportive but it was not his.
2. There was no clear articulation of the process of system change, nor of who had the authority to institute change. Changes were introduced by people in level II and level III roles who simply believed they had the authority to do so.
3. The design process itself did not incorporate the person who should have been the system owner, or the users. They were presented with the output of design work done by the system team for their review and comment. Relevant managers in Level II, III and IV roles were invited to join in the design team's work but they chose not to. Design work was slow and boring and they were busy.
4. Control and audit were not identified specifically as elements of the system; this activity was done by the systems team on an ad hoc basis. Only later was it fully appreciated that control and audit, carefully designed and formally authorised, are critical elements of all systems.
5. The system's purpose was confused: was it –
    a. To demonstrate the methodology of systems design?
    b. To improve the wagon inspection process?

c.   To reduce the likelihood of train derailments?
d.   To improve the relationship between the examiners and maintainers?
e.   To improve the data collection processes associated with wagon repair?
f.   To improve information flow across the boundary between two separate departments?

From the viewpoint of the system design team, the purpose was probably (a), but different groups or individuals associated with the system would have perceived it as one of the others.

The immediate impact of the new system was due primarily to the recognition of the work of the examiners and the maintainers. Neither group was receiving any recognition from their respective leaders; a common circumstance in a strongly unionised work environment.

This was, paradoxically, the primary reason for the new system collapsing. The old myths about the examiners or the maintainers being the 'enemy', depending upon the group to which you belonged, were not tenable with the behaviour generated by the new system, and the management of both groups depended upon this set of myths to maintain what they perceived to be leadership authority.

The new behaviours openly challenged this authority, often on the basis of the information provided by the new system.

For the system design team, it was both an outstanding proof of concept and a salutary lesson showing them they had more work to do if they were to develop a full understanding of the complexity of system design.

It was, however, a spectacular demonstration that 'systems drive behaviour'.

Conclusion

This chapter has emphasised the importance of systems within an organisation.

We have seen that in many organisations systems work is done poorly because of one or more of the following: the significance of systems is underestimated, the complexity of the task is underestimated and there is no shared process for doing the work. This is why we have articulated the '20 questions' (see Box 17.2).

We have worked with organisations which have used this model (and its earlier version) and those who have applied it thoroughly have benefited significantly. Systems are not well designed by a large committee but rather a small team led at the appropriate level (not below level IV) who then consults with others, especially users to collect accurate information about how things really do work in practice. As one of the fundamental tools of leadership, we argue that systems drive behaviour; it is a question of whether that behaviour is productive and ethical and whether the leadership understands the relationship between the system design and the behaviour it drives.

18 Systems and Symbols Audit: Organisational Health Check

Analysis of Systems, Symbols and Behaviour

This chapter[1] provides a method that we have developed for reviewing the current state of an organisation in order to test the nature of the gap between the aspirations of the leadership and the reality of the situation as it exists in practice.

The audit draws on the system leadership theory and in particular the analysis of existing systems, symbols and behaviour. We have used this approach in many organisations, the first of which was Hamersley Iron (now Rio Tinto Iron Ore) in Australia, in 1992 (see Box 18.1).

The requirement to develop an understanding about the interpretation of leadership behaviour at all levels, along with systems and symbols, underpins the audit process and serves as a guide for the specific process described below. The three tools of leadership provide the core of a structure for reporting the audit results. Further, the interpretation across all three elements reinforces how important it is to design and implement good systems, a topic examined in more detail in the next chapter.

The findings from this process can then contribute not only to decisions on what might be done but also, more particularly, on *how* this might be done. Prior to the audit it is important that there is some understanding of the theory by, at least, the upper level leaders in the organisation. This should be discussed as part of the context setting for the work, and may result in some prior explanatory sessions, pre-reading and/or organising the feedback to take this into account.

It is important to state that no two audits are the same. The current state of the organisation, the purpose of the proposed change process, and the current industrial relations/ employee relations' context will all influence the actual design of each specific audit. The underlying process and principles remain consistent, however, and are outlined in this chapter.

Purpose of an Audit

The purpose of the audit is to provide feedback to the leadership of the organisation on the effectiveness of systems, symbols, leadership behaviour and the interaction between these three as reflected in the workforce's interpretation of them. From these findings, the consultant provides analysis and recommendations for further action by the leadership team/general manager based on the insights gained during the process.

---

1   This chapter is based on a paper written for Macdonald Associates by I. Macdonald and J. Grimmond, March 2000.

Box 18.1 The Three Questions

Underlying a successful organisation in our experience is a shared understanding of the nature and purpose of the organisation. We have found that the organisational health of an organisation can be gauged by whether people in, or associated with, the organisation can answer some basic, simple questions:

- What am I meant to be doing?
- How am I doing?
- What is my future?

If people have clear answers to these questions they are probably able to concentrate on their work. It is clear that these questions in turn are linked to the structure, systems and plans of the business, short- and long-term. Each question is directly related to elements in the business. If these elements are not in place, or are poorly in place, the person will not be able to answer and our prediction is that people will spend time and energy trying to find the answers.

WHAT AM I MEANT TO BE DOING?

If a person can answer this question, then the organisation will have good systems of:

- Role descriptions: outlining the *purpose* of the role and types of task a person can be asked to do.
- Clear task assignment, including good *context setting* and again clarity of *purpose*, output, resources and time to completion.
- Clarity about role relationships, including authority.
- Clarity about the business plan and its goals: an understanding of how their work fits with others' and the wider business objectives.

HOW AM I DOING?

If a person can answer this question, then the organisation will have good systems of:

- Task review: giving a person feedback on individual tasks.
- Recognition: acknowledging the quality of performance (positively or negatively).
- Reward: salary and pay linked to a person's performance over a period of time (annually).

WHAT IS MY FUTURE?

If a person can answer this question, then the organisation will have good systems of:

- Career review/assessment of potential: by the manager's manager (M+1) regarding career progression, including promotion.
- Development plans: opportunities to develop skills and knowledge and enhance abilities, for example, that of leadership.
- Business information: information systems detailing how well the organisation is progressing, its place in the market and comparison with competitors.
- Long-term business plan: information linked to the above but specifically about where the organisation intends to go, how it will get there and what part the person might play in this depending on their role.

Audit Steps

STEP 1: INTRODUCE THE PROCESS

Careful consideration needs to be given as to how the process is introduced, explained and communicated. It is not always necessary or desirable to call it a systems and symbols audit.

These words may have negative connotations for some people, depending upon the mythologies they hold about audit, and many people may just regard such a title as jargon. Other terms can be used, so long as they honestly reflect the actual process, for example, employee relations review or employment systems review. It also depends upon what aspect the leadership would like to concentrate on.

This means, of course, that the specific purpose of the process for the organisation must be articulated beforehand. This work needs to be done by the consultant and the operations manager with his or her team. (The operations manager might be a site general manager, managing director or CEO, depending on the breadth of the review.) Then a communication needs to be made to the workforce from this manager. It may take the form of an email and hard copy as well as briefings from managers and supervisors.

The written communication should also contain more specific information about feedback from the audit. The nature and type may vary but should be clear so that the consultant can discuss this with people at the interview.

STEP 2: SAMPLE

Talk to about 10% of the workforce. This should give sufficient insight into the critical areas for attention, especially when coupled with other parts of the process (symbols audit, system documentation).

The employees may be interviewed individually or in small groups (maximum five). This should be determined beforehand. Some people may wish to be interviewed even if not chosen. This should be accommodated if practicable or, if not, a clear answer given as to why this is not possible. It should be noted that those who volunteer may have strong views and this needs to be taken into account.

STEP 3: WORK TOP DOWN

Initial interviews should be with the highest line manager (MD/CEO) and his or her team. If possible everyone in that team should be interviewed. Also, if possible, these should be one-on-one interviews. Then a sample of about 20% to 30% of the next level of management should be interviewed, again if possible one-on-one, but if needs be in groups no larger than three. Then about 20% of supervisors (or equivalent), probably in groups of three or four. Then about 10% of the workforce, again in small groups of three to five, but allowing for some one-to-one interviews especially if requested by the employee. Supervisor and workforce interviews can be interspersed but not integrated so that operators are not required to discuss issues with a person in any leadership role present.

Each interview session should take no more than one hour but with a gap of between 15 and 30 minutes to allow for key issues to be distilled and captured. If notes are taken, then this should be done in an open manner. Our experience is that people in manager/superintendent roles in some low-trust organisations can occasionally be disturbed by a lot of note-taking, but operators and tradespeople are often pleased that notes are taken because it demonstrates listening and indicates the process is serious.

STEP 4: THERE SHOULD NOT BE A RIGID INTERVIEW SCHEDULE

The interviews should be semi-structured and not programmed to a strict set of questions. A significant number of questions should be open-ended with the opportunity to follow up leads to more in depth information. However, the interviewer does need a framework and prompts to ensure coverage and a similar experience for interviewees. Consultants should prepare a basic question list prior to the assignment commencing and continue to refine that list as organisational input is obtained.

The interview process at first line manager / supervisor / operator / maintainer level should start with:

- A personal introduction from the consultant.
- A check that people understand the purpose and ground rules. In many cases people will claim to have no idea what it is all about despite having been sent emails and other advice. The consultant should ensure that a copy of the advice or email is available to refresh people's memories.
- It is a good idea, after the consultant has introduced himself or herself, to ask interviewees their first names and to ask people how long they have been in the organisation. People recently employed may have very different views from those held by 'long termers', and this can be used by the interviewer to good effect in discussing systems, mythologies and so on.
- The consultant should always clarify what the interviewees do. Sometimes a supervisor or a superintendent may have been inadvertently included in a group of operator/ maintainers (that is, someone who missed an interview somewhere else and has been sent along to catch up). This can be difficult and can affect responses from others.
- After the formalities have been completed, the consultant will generally start with questions regarding the safety system, for example, 'I am really looking at systems. Can you tell me what safety is like around here?' 'Can you give me some examples where safety always comes first?' 'Are there examples of production coming first?' 'Why you think this is the safest place you've ever worked?'
- For every general answer a specific follow-up question should be asked both negative and positive, for example 'Could you give me an example of poor leadership?' 'Why do you like working nights?'
- Topics covered should be from a list of prompts, including the systems listed in the letter relating to employee systems. Not all topics need to be covered in depth at each level in the organisation but should be mentioned for consistency.
- The GM or equivalent may have circulated the general headings for questions, which will indicate the range of questions that will need to be covered.
- General questions need to be asked, especially with managers: 'What are the big issues at the moment?' 'What has been going on here the last three months, last six months, last twelve months?' These interviews will also be critical in determining what are the current critical issues on the site, and can assist in developing follow-up questions during the interview process.

- These sessions can also assist in determining managers' levels of understanding of the current mythologies like, 'If I ask people what they think about safety, what will they say? If I ask whether they would use the fair treatment system, what will people say? Why would they say this?'
- Whenever mythologies are being collected, the value, or values, to which they apply need to be confirmed. When they are being discussed subsequently, they are best expressed as they were first articulated and the related values articulated. This practice aids in reinforcing the reality of the situation that exists and makes it harder to deny.

Care should be taken as to where interviews take place. They should be carried out in a setting where people cannot be interrupted and where they are comfortable. Operators are more likely to be at home in the lunch/crib-room rather than the boardroom. However, all interviews should take place on site.

STEP 5: THIS IS NOT AN EMPLOYEE SURVEY

It is important to distinguish this process from the usual employee survey where people tick boxes on a prepared interview schedule. The purpose of such surveys is to gain data for an overall statistical analysis. A systems and symbols audit is more of a qualitative, judgemental process where the comments of one person or a very small number of people may be judged to be both highly significant and important evidence of a critical insight (obviously maintaining confidentiality). These interviews give much richer information but depend on the skill of the interviewer. The systems and symbols audit does not preclude the possibility of a survey. Survey data may be a good input or for comparison, but should only be used if it is normal practice and then at the normal time. Any one-off employee survey at the same time as the systems and symbols audit will generate suspicion about both.

STEP 6: USE SOCIAL PROCESS SKILLS

The consultant (as interviewer) must have considerable social process skills. This is not a process that can be carried out by just anyone. The consultant needs to be able to establish rapport and build trust with the interviewees in a very short period of time. He or she must have some knowledge of the organisation, the sort of work done and ideally the general field of work (for example, refining, voluntary or social work, teaching, financial services, local government and so on).

The consultant must value contributions and seek to clarify them. They should never argue or correct unless it is to clarify purpose and ground rules. They must be at ease in virtually any setting, as mentioned above, the boardroom or the crib-room; a council chamber or a residential nursing home. The consultant must be able to modify style and language to fit the context without ever appearing false, insincere or patronising. The consultant should not try to 'fit in', for example, by swearing, colluding, overly dressing up or down, or through any other artifice. In essence the consultant must be able to identify honestly with the purpose of the process and be confident that results will be used constructively and for the improvement of the organisation. The consultant is neither the shareholders' representative nor the shop steward. The consultant is not there to 'take sides'.

The consultant must also value the work to a high degree to be able to demonstrate interest in the process and maintain this independent stance from the first question until the last during the interviews (see Box 18.2).

> **Box 18.2**
>
> We have been asked whether it is possible to carry out a Systems and Symbols Audit (SSA) with internal interviewees. Our view is that it is not. The issues of confidentiality, judgement and authority are quite different. This is not to say that leaders or people in support roles do not listen to views and pick up information similar to this process. SSA is, however, a particular process and its quality is based on the consultant's skills and independence.

STEP 7: USE SYSTEMS LEADERSHIP THEORY

The consultant must have considerable technical skill and knowledge in terms of systems leadership theory. The consultant must be fully knowledgeable about all aspects of the theory. This includes the values continua and system design criteria including the importance of symbols, steps and traps of team leadership and membership, as well as an understanding of levels of work, authority and accountability. The consultant must be able to interpret answers against these concepts, for example, the systems matrix, differentiation and equalisation, authority versus power and so on.

The consultant is essentially trying to articulate the mythologies of the workplace and link them to the systems. As such, in real time, they must be able to take a verbal statement ('management have no idea') and link it to one or more of the values ('they treat us unfairly and in an unloving way') through a reported behaviour ('the superintendent stays in his office most of the day, rarely enforces safety regulations and only makes negative comments about our work'). It can then be tested to see how general the myth is: is this view shared by others in the organisation? How widespread is this view? Is it only about one superintendent?

Further, the consultant must then be able to link this with the relevant systems. From the above example, there are questions about the safety systems, work assignment review and recognition, as well as personal leadership behaviour. This would also raise questions about controls and audits especially with regard to the safety system. It may also reveal some unhelpful authorities and role work content, for example, that the safety system is the work of safety experts (officers) rather than the work of the line management.

The consultant must discern warning signals and emerging mythologies which, while only currently held by a small number, may be indicative of things to come. For example, 'Several comments about the new bonus system and its links to safety results suggest it is encouraging people to cover up injuries.'

STEP 8: INTERVIEWS ARE NOT THE ONLY SOURCE OF INFORMATION

It is important that the consultant is not merely the conduit of opinion and comment. They must not only sift the information but also be alert to other data from the two other main sources of information reported below (steps 9 and 10).

STEP 9: IDENTIFY SYMBOLS IN THE WORKPLACE

The consultant needs to take time walking about the workplace observing. He or she must look out for examples of good or bad practice. Some direct observations include housekeeping.

Is the workplace tidy? Is there any rubbish or scrap material on the floor? Are the buildings in poor repair? What does the equipment look like? In particular, safety compliance can be observed and is a rich source of symbols. Are people wearing safety equipment? Are there locked fire doors? Are extinguishers in place? Another source is notice boards. What is on them? Are notices up to date? Are they in the language of the workforce? In one organisation the employees were largely non-English speaking but all the signs were in English. Who has put up notices? Are there union notice boards and what is on them? Are social events publicised? Is there a newsletter and what does it convey?

Behaviour can also be symbolic. While walking around, do people make eye contact? Do they talk to you or each other? What do they say? What is the leadership behaviour? Do leaders talk to their teams? Are they in offices? How do they communicate? Less direct observations include – What is the social process behaviour in the crib-room, staff-room, common areas, canteen and other places where employees gather? Do people personalise their workstations? Are there pictures? Of what kind?

Clearly this is not an exhaustive list but essentially the aim is to gain an impression of what it is like to work in the organisation, noting variances between areas if they exist.

STEP 10: REVIEW SYSTEM DOCUMENTATION

The other main data source is documentation. This includes actual system descriptions (if they exist), which can then be compared with reported practice. For example, if people have reported that they only get feedback once a year, is that consistent with the intent of the system? What are the policies of the organisation? Again, they can be compared with what people say.

It may well be difficult to find direct evidence of intimidation, racism or sexism – unauthorised, counter-productive (box D) systems (see Chapter 12) – because of their covert nature. However, indirect evidence may be available, such as a reluctance to speak or 'throwaway' comments such as 'I'd get the sack if I told you about that'. This needs to be considered carefully and additional data sought, with care.

It may occur, however, that either through direct observation or in discussion, examples of illegal or intimidatory behaviour become apparent. These incidents are probably the most difficult aspect of this work. The consultant must use his or her discretion in these cases. It is not simply a question of reporting or not reporting these incidents. While the person who raises the issue may be encouraged to use other channels to follow this up, the consultant must not become a conduit. This will be strongly influenced by the nature of the relationship between consultant and client. Hopefully it is such that it can be raised without specific reference but may well have a bearing on the continuation of the relationship. It is important never to betray a personal comment made in confidence.

STEP 11: THE REPORT

The report is not a scientific or statistical paper. The report does not stand on its own as a written paper but should be presented to the management team as the basis for discussion leading to a plan of action. The report should contain an analysis of the numbers of people seen by level and general role title. It should identify cultures that may not be simply categorised by organisational level and role type. Essentially the report should reflect the sources of data, that is:

*   the interview/discussions
*   observations from the consultant (symbols)
*   systems commentary.

The extent of recommendation will depend on the original purpose and the nature of the relationship between client organisation and consultant. At the debrief it is useful to explain to the leadership 'that some of this will most certainly be factually incorrect. What I am talking about are mythologies and mythologies may be wrong in fact, but they are what people believe to be true.'

It can lead to considerable and unnecessary debate if people do not understand this basic concept.

When we reported to one managing director that several of his key systems were perceived to be unfair and disrespectful he first said, 'Well, they are wrong; that system is quite fair – I designed it. Are you saying I am unfair?' It took a little while to revisit the concept of mythologies.

The report may be in the form of a presentation and/or a written document, depending upon need.

Conclusion

It is important to recognise that a systems and symbols audit is a general process that is highly interpretative and dependent upon the skills and experience of the consultant and the nature of the relationship with the client. It is not a rigid process or an employee survey but follows the principles as outlined above with emphasis directed by the original purpose. It is part of an approach (consistent with Macdonald Associates Consultancy work) that seeks to minimise the need to use power in organisations in order to get work done. It should lead to a programme of action, often centred on system design and redesign, directed to improve the quality of leadership and hence a more productive, effective and enjoyable workplace.

19 *Creating High-Performance Teams*

Working Together

There is a mountain of literature about the importance of teamwork. The most obvious examples come from the world of sport where individuals interviewed in the media seem compelled to stress the importance of the team above individual achievement or success (except, perhaps, when negotiating their contracts). Similarly motivational posters inform us that 'There is no i in Team' or the best performances come from a 'star team rather than a team of stars'.

While the statements expressed are admirable, they are simplistic; exhortation does not replace explanation. We regard the apparent conflict between team and individual as a false dichotomy. Of course individuals have needs but, as we have argued throughout this book, life and achievement is a social process. We cannot succeed without others. It is not enough to emphasise the need for good teamwork: we must also ask what it is and how to achieve it.

We have discussed in some depth the work of leadership and the steps and traps of team leadership and membership (Chapter 15). Putting this into practice is not easy, and so we developed a specific training course, called Working Together, which has been designed to help people to develop their skills in both leadership and team membership.

The original course was designed as a result of an observation by Dr John Cliffe, who was head of HR at the engineering company Tube Investment in the early 1980s. Macdonald and Stamp, whilst working at BIOSS, Brunel University, had been involved in some consultancy work for him when one evening he explained to Macdonald that he had run organisational theory courses for the organisation. He thought they were good in content but people found them boring. On the other hand, he had sent people on what were called outward bound courses, involving challenging exercises in the wilderness, which they had found exciting but, he noted, he could see no change in people's behaviour or clear learning. He consequently asked Macdonald if he could design a training course that combined the excitement with the learning. Macdonald took this idea to his brother Roderick Macdonald, who at the time was a serving British army officer teaching at the Army Staff College. Together they designed what was to become the Working Together course.

The key components of the course remain the same (see Box 19.1) although content and process have changed and developed considerably. Today there are a variety of forms of the course, of different lengths and with different emphases.

The original course, run by I. Macdonald and his brother R. Macdonald, brought in management theory, stratified systems theory and systems leadership theory, as well as exercises, presentations and case-study work. As far as we know this was the first course not only to use video, but also to use it reflectively to compare actual behaviour with concepts taught on the course. The focus was, and is, the analysis of social process in leadership and teamwork.

> **Box 19.1   Essential Components of Working Together**
>
> - The courses described are a collaboration between the company and Macdonald Associates, each providing a co-presenter.
> - Each co-presenter has a clear role, and has been trained in that role.
> - The course is a combination of presentation, experiential learning through practice and review of behaviour, indoor and outdoor tasks, role plays, case studies and discussion.
> - Exercises are videotaped and debriefed using the recorded material.
> - Exercises are analysed in terms of safety and a course report written which includes a safety report.
> - Each participant has an opportunity to experience a leadership role and team membership roles.

On a visit to the UK in 1986 another of the authors, Stewart, attended the course and after redesign, implemented it in his business unit in Australia, Comalco Smelting, then part of CRA. Terry Palmer attended in Australia and introduced the course into his business unit (Comalco Rolled Products) and later at Hamersley Iron. Both Stewart and Palmer used the courses as part of a much broader cultural change programme with highly significant results (see Chapter 20, What Difference Has This Made?).

There are now many types of organisations that have used the course around the world, each modifying the programme slightly and adapting the content but maintaining the essential components.

The Course

Although the course varies, the background, context and purpose usually remain the same. An example is shown below in Box 19.2.

> **Box 19.2   Working Together Course**
>
> *BACKGROUND*
>
> The organisational environment is never still: changes occur in demand, technology and opportunity that require changes in the way work is organised and carried out. Work, however, will always involve people who determine the success or failure of an organisation. This success or failure is in turn strongly influenced by how people are led and whether they behave as part of a team. Business is not simply a matter of understanding technology or finances; it is also critically about understanding people: the mythologies they hold about their leaders, their fellow employees, the work they are required to do and what they want to do.
>
> This course assumes that people want to be constructive and creative, and it is their environment and working relationships that influence how well their energies are directed toward this end. An organisation that treats its people like machines, constrained by petty rules and regulations that contradict common sense and a sense of fairness, will fail. Building trust is not a simple matter; what one person regards as fair or honest may not correspond with another person's view. Understanding how people see the world and acting on this understanding is a key element of leadership work and is central to this course.

PURPOSE

The purpose of this course is to help participants improve their understanding of leadership and teamwork so that they can apply this understanding at work to become better managers, team leaders and members.

OUTCOMES

Participants should come away with an understanding of the core ideas and principles on which the company bases its organisation, culture and practice in the behaviour required for good leadership and team membership. In particular participants should be more aware of:

- their own behaviour and how this influences leadership and team membership;
- the central importance of systems and how work systems may be improved;
- the expectations of their role and their work;
- the rationale behind what the leadership of the company is trying to achieve;
- the importance of clarity in assigning, reviewing and recognising work and task performance;
- the effects of leadership on organisation, structure and business culture.

METHODS

Most people become bored sitting in classrooms listening to presentations/lectures hour after hour. This course is intended to be participative. While there are some presentations on the core material, interaction is encouraged and the programme is adjusted, as necessary, to meet the needs of the course participants. In addition there are syndicate tasks and practical exercises both in the teaching room and elsewhere.

Participants are advised they should wear casual/work clothing that they do not mind getting wet or dirty. Any person with a physical disability should make this known to the course leaders (this will not preclude involvement in the course). As you would expect, everything we'll do, can and will, be done safely.

Courses are probably residential and for 12 participants, organised into two teams of six.

THEORY CONTENT

The 'theory' sessions cover Systems Leadership concepts. Depending upon the organisational needs and roles of participants, certain parts will be covered in more depth than others. What are always covered are the concepts of culture, values and mythologies and the team leadership and membership model.

EXERCISES

There is a range of outdoor and indoor team exercises. Two teams of six each rotate the leadership role and carry out the same exercises in parallel. We have developed a range of activities to be able to accommodate different abilities amongst participants and different physical settings and climates. No exercise requires above ordinary physical ability and no one is forced to participate particularly if they have any reservations (for example, if they do not want to do any lifting). Safety is always paramount and all exercises have safety rules (with articulated penalties for their breach).

CASE STUDIES

We also use a wide range of short case studies, which teams work on, analyse and present their answer(s), often in role-play format. We write them for a particular organisation or industry to address topics relevant to the organisation at that time.

ROLE PLAYS

Either as part of the case studies or in addition to them, participants are asked to role-play situations like interviews or managing difficult issues, often of a disciplinary nature. This is to give an opportunity to put answers into practice and highlight the difference between answers in theory and answers in practice (see also core social process skills for leaders, see Box 19.4).

FEEDBACK TO PARTICIPANTS ON EXERCISES

Participants discuss the way they have approached activities and the exercise. Following an exercise, they are asked their views as to how well they have achieved the output *and* worked as team leader and team members. This view is then tested against the video record. Often the experience of dissonance is profound. People are regularly surprised at how quickly they have rewritten history either more positively or negatively. The critical point about the feedback is that it is made against the criteria of the models, especially the team leadership and membership steps and traps.

This feedback can be highly sensitive. Often it is enough for people to see on the video that they have not clearly assigned tasks, or asked for contributions or co-operated by helping each other. It is common for people, visibly under pressure because of all the tasks have a fixed time for completion, to skip the thinking involved in identifying critical issues, preferring to relieve their anxiety by leaping straight into the action.

ROLES

The roles of the co-presenters are critical. We regard it as a principle that one be from the organisation (ideally in a leadership role) and one a consultant (accredited by Macdonald Associates Consultancy). The external presenter's work is:

- to manage the overall social process;
- to give primary feedback on exercises; to ensure technical accuracy of the concepts.

The internal presenter's work is:

- to behave as a role model and symbol that the organisation is serious about this work;
- to provide examples from the workplace of good and poor practice;
- to produce technical knowledge of the organisation, for example, policies, systems, processes;
- to reinforce the business case for the training.

Box 19.3 Social Processes and Behaviour

We always concentrate absolutely on behaviour, and then consider the consequences of that behaviour ... There is no consideration of 'attitude' or intent ... These are invisible and could be anything anyone chooses to say they are.

Box 19.4   Different Learning Experiences

On one course we had two teams, one that was made up primarily of people involved in research and development work, the other made up primarily of operators ... In one exercise the R&D team spent almost the entire time planning and constructing a prototype. They left almost no time to actually carry out the real task ... In contrast the other team started building before the leader had even finished briefing the team ... An exasperated leader asked what they were doing, as he was only halfway through explaining the task; 'don't worry' came the reply, 'tell us as we go along!' Neither team had a successful outcome on that task. With both teams present in one room for the debrief, it was an interesting learning experience ... The video records of the activity of each team ensured denial was impossible.

This is not a course that a managing director opens with a short introduction of how important the course is and then leaves it to external or internal consultants. The managing director must make very clear that this is the way business is going to be done and why he or she has made that decision.

We score each team's exercises in terms of output, social process and safety. The teams are left to themselves to determine how far they see the exercises as competitive. This also gives an insight into current culture.

The feedback at a personal level is mediated by the external presenter. If these courses were run entirely in house, even by trained co-presenters, there is a large risk of organisation appointed authority becoming dominant and it would be very difficult, if not impossible, for people not to experience the course as formally part of a performance appraisal (see Box 19.6).

Box 19.5   Terry Palmer and the Working Together Course

In one instance the top executive team made up the course. The two teams were fiercely competitive and at times actively sought to sabotage the other team's activities. In the debrief, which pointed this out quite graphically, the defence was: 'Well, these are just games. Of course we are not like this in the workplace.' The managing director, who was co-presenting, quietly responded: 'You are exactly like this in the workplace and that is why you are on this course; to learn some teamwork.' This demonstrated the importance of the role of the internal co-presenter. Behaviour changed very quickly.

In another instance a course participant wrote of Terry Palmer's involvement in the Working Together courses:

'Terry attended each of these courses in full. I believe that there were at least ten sessions that year, meaning that Terry made a personal investment of ten weeks of his business and personal time. Looking back now I still find this level of personal investment astounding. There was no sense of rush and Terry's focus was on the job in hand and as a participant you felt you had his individual attention.'

The courses were now being rolled out across the whole business to the entire workforce.

Thus attendees included many people who had never been on a course, and certainly not a residential one paid for by 'the company'. Sadly for Terry he couldn't co-run them all, or even personally attend them all so he had a videotape made of him giving an introduction to explain why he wanted people to go through this training. Courses were starting at all sites and Terry was dropping in to demonstrate his commitment to the programme. He went into the training room and sat at the back while introductions went on.

At a suitable break he got up to introduce himself which meant walking round the horseshoe of participants shaking hands. As Terry did so, in his usual relaxed yet confident way, one of the participants was heard to whisper to another,

'Who's that?'

'I think it's Terry Palmer.'

'What, the MD?'

'Yeah, I think so.'

Terry approached, held out his hand and said,

'How are you, I'm Terry Palmer.'

With a slightly cynical grin on his face the response came:

'Yeah, but who are you really mate?'

Quick as a flash, and with a smile as broad as the Nullarbor, Terry replied,

'I'm Terry Palmer all right and I've got a video to prove it!'

Terry had caused his usual dissonance and with his usual humour and good grace.

PURPOSE

This last point raises the question as to the clarity of purpose. The course can be run as an assessment centre or an educational process. It should be clear to participants, which is the case. We have run both types. Even when the purpose is educational it would be dishonest not to acknowledge that people will be making judgements. That is part of any endeavour where people work together. As Palmer put it:

> *'I am going to spend the next 3 days watching you solve problems and using leadership and team membership models. Do you think I can do that without forming some views?'*

It is advisable to recognise the reality that each course participant will make judgements about his or her fellow course participants.

It is, however, important to emphasise that it is a learning process, where mistakes made do not have the same consequences as in the workplace. Failing to build a cardboard tower is not the same as failing to install equipment. The external consultant must mediate and point out, for example, that implementing models should improve with practice, so that early leaders of activities have a tougher task than later.

CRITICAL ISSUES

Clarity of purpose, as with any activity is very important but there are also other critical issues that must be addressed if the Working Together process is to be really effective.

HOW TO LINK THE TRAINING WITH THE WORK OF THE ORGANISATION?

This not only helps to set an organisational context, but must show how this activity is to help the organisation and is part of an overall plan for change. We have seen many instances where an organisation decides that 'we need some leadership and teamwork training' and embarks on a series of courses. These may be of some benefit, but if they are not linked to an overall plan and a consistent demonstration of leadership support in behaviour, in the use of theory and language, they can become a 'sheep-dip' process with little long-term impact.

In the CRA manual 'Working Together', the members of a team that was assigned the work of advising on leadership training wrote:

> *Whilst an important aspect of implementing Systems Leadership is conducting the training course, which is now being done in a number of Business Units, this will not, in itself, achieve any beneficial, lasting change. Only when the Business Unit's systems have been reviewed and the changes necessary to align them with the vision and strategy have been implemented will the potential benefits be realised ... The work done in the Group (especially in Hamersley and Comalco Smelting) to provide training in Systems Leadership as part of an integrated process to change the culture of a Business Unit has provided considerable learnings. Most important is the requirement to undertake an integrated set of work for implementing Systems Leadership throughout the Business. This will contribute to all employees perceiving that their management has 'constancy of purpose'. It would be simplistic and incorrect to focus solely on conducting the training course.*

It also states:

> *Leadership training is a topical issue in the corporate world. The current fad is to use outdoor, experiential learning, which is loosely underpinned by behavioural theory. The linkage created* for the participants by the trainers and the leaders of the organisation's strategy is often tenuous. In contrast, the outdoor activities included in the Systems Leadership training course are used to reinforce the theory; the theory which CRA has played a significant role in developing and on which CRA's organisation is predicated.

HOW TO LINK THE TRAINING WITH INDIVIDUAL CHANGE?

Even if the organisational context is clear and this is seen as an integral part of the overall plan of improvement, individual participants need preparation and follow-up. Ideally participants should have a prior discussion with their manager to discuss the purpose of the course and what the individual needs to work on and improve. This might be social process in general or specific steps such as team member co-operation, better contributions, better task assignments or review.

After the course there should be a debrief. What has been learned? How can this be put into practice and monitored? Ideally tasks should be assigned and reported on. For example, people might be asked to apply that learning on the day-to-day social process of leading their own team, a system (re)design task, identifying mythologies or a cross-functional team project.

HOW TO HAVE CONSISTENCY IN PRESENTATION?

It is crucial that the course co-presenters be trained and competent in the skills and knowledge required and competent at delivering these in real time. As was mentioned, Macdonald Associates trains and accredits associates in the process. This competency is reviewed annually and new ideas and changes incorporated. There is a 'train the trainer' course designed for internal co-presenters. This intensive experiential course is not easy and the leadership of the organisation must ensure the quality of delivery. There are many courses on leadership and teamwork, but in our experience none is integrated as part of an overall coherent theory of organisation; none is a collaborative intervention requiring teaching partnership with the organisation's leaders.

We are not claiming that in all our practice these critical issues have always been completely addressed. What is evident, as our model of critical issues would predict, is that if they are not, the positive impact is significantly less than it could otherwise be, and indeed the process may be detrimental.

Cultural Relevance

Many courses and training are culturally biased and culturally limited. Because we have an underlying general model of culture these courses can be adapted to the type of organisation, industry and country. Courses have been run in the UK, Canada, Southern and Western Africa, Australia, New Zealand, China, USA, Indonesia, Russia, Ukraine and Thailand. Organisations have included, amongst others, schools, mining companies, banks and financial institutions, indigenous community organisations, non-governmental organisations, local government, health services, religious organisations and social services. Participants have included truck drivers, CEOs, miners, children as young as 14, aborigines in remote communities, priests and bishops, nurses, bank managers, traders, police, students and community leaders.

The courses have been adapted according to the context in which they are being carried out, for example, in the following two case studies (Box 19.7 and Box 19.8). However, the underlying process remains the same. In our experience the values continua have provided a valid, and valuable, cross-cultural link (as they would need to do to support the concepts upon which they are based), as have the concepts linking them to the mythologies and behaviour. We find the same values but different behaviours that are seen to demonstrate those values positively or negatively.

There are differences that we have noted especially with regard to leadership and teamwork. These differences could themselves be the subject of a separate book and there is always a danger of stereotyping. In general terms, however, we have found that, for example, in Australia there is still a strong mythology that standing out in a group is behaviour that falls on the negative side of the values continua. Amongst the jailed in a convict society, anyone who stood out was trying to show themselves in a favourable light to the jailers and was therefore not to be trusted. It is referred to universally across the culture as the 'tall poppy' syndrome where those poppies that dare to grow taller than their peers get their heads chopped off. In the USA, the opposite seems to be true and individuals are generally keen and encouraged to stand out from the group. We find that in Russia people are initially much more formal, more likely to make assertive statements, but reluctant to reveal emotion or inner thoughts until the formal parts of the course are over, that is, over dinner, in the bar or in the sauna.

The Working Together courses we have run have, too regularly, given us an opportunity to expose and endeavour to remove gender bias. It was suggested that the extent of such bias, almost universally unconscious, was engendered by the outdoor, physical activities, so we have included a wider range of activities. It is interesting to note that the early courses run in Comalco acquired the symbolic name 'Rambo courses'. This was partly due to the outdoor activities and partly because Brigadier R. Macdonald, commando trained, was a co-presenter. We tried to address this but failed. Eventually and paradoxically it became a help since the activities did not require great physical skills – but did require the application of appropriate mental processing ability and social process skills. The 'macho' approach, when taken, was

---

Box 19.6   Constant Constance

Constance has been an active member of the parish of St George's for the past seven years. Prior to the death of her mother, Constance attended church on special occasions but did not get involved in any church activities.

Her mother, Mary, spent a couple of years in a nursing home and was visited regularly by the rector James Swallow. In fact James was 'called out' a couple of times and in the final weeks of Mary's life called by every day. He conducted the funeral, which was much appreciated by Constance.

Since that day Constance has been to church every day. She participates in virtually everything, remembering to apologise for the things she cannot attend. She has also been parish treasurer and now remains on parish council as well as chairs the social committee, helps at the Op Shop, with the banking and with morning teas on a Sunday.

Shortly after her mother's death, Constance was operated on for the removal of cancer of the breast. Since that time she has been in good health and remains so.

Recently James was told by Constance that the church was to benefit from her will. It is clear that Constance has dedicated almost her whole life to the church.

Constance has a rather 'snappy' approach to people and from time to time she has been very bossy and people have come to James to complain.

Last week two people came to see him:

Pamela, the manager of the Op Shop (which raises £12,000 a year for parish funds), has had enough of her sharpness and bossy nature and has threatened to resign from her position if Constance does not remove herself from the volunteer helper list.

Annabel, a young parish council member and staunch helper each Sunday morning called James to complain about Constance and her abruptness and her off-putting approach to newcomers. 'I can't put up with it much longer!' she said. 'Something has got to be done, she is upsetting so many people.'

You are the rector: what will you do?

Role play (10 minutes) your meetings to resolve this problem, with Pamela, Annabel and Constance.

---

exposed, inevitably failed, and then provided valuable material for discussing sexism. There were women on all courses.

There have been over 30,000 participants on various versions of the Working Together course worldwide. It is difficult to measure the impact in overall terms since the purpose is not always the same. It is our experience that the positive impact depends upon addressing the critical issues outlined above. When this is done, and particularly when the Working Together programme is part of an overall strategy for change, the impact is significant at both an organisational and individual level. The case studies in this book (or on the website) examine this in more depth and refer to specific outcomes according to the type of organisation. It would not be valid to assess the Working Together courses on their own, since they are part of a process and part of an integrated theory and approach. Indeed this theory would predict that implementing the Working Together programme on its own would not have a major, positive effect and may indeed be negative. One recent analysis produced advice that made us wary of a proposed course implementation because the organisation was not assessed to have the quality in leadership and systems to sustain what is taught. The Working Together courses are only one step in the process of change.

WHAT IT IS NOT

This Working Together process does not seek to change personality. It seeks to change behaviour. We do not confront people at a personal level, nor search for their inner thoughts and feelings. The video record of each team's performance on the exercises is confidential to the team. They are only provided with a personal copy if all team members agree in a secret ballot. The Working Together course is not a T. Group[1] process or pseudo-psychotherapy course. We believe a person's thoughts are their own business. Many people of noble and courageous spirit have fought wars and died so that we may be free to think as we please. Their memory warrants great honour. While such personality-based courses often produce deep feelings, these do not last and do not result in behaviour change. The Working Together course clarifies what behaviour is required to help the organisation to be successful. It tries to help people improve their skills and practice in that behaviour.

It does require skilled and trained co-presenters. It requires people with a knowledge of stratified systems theory and systems leadership theory. It also requires people who enjoy the creativity of others. The course helps to embed a shared language to underpin the culture and provides a common experience that a CEO can enjoy sharing with an operator, an archbishop with a vicar or a teacher with a student.

We leave the last words on Working Together to Terry Palmer who, as MD, could not physically co-present on every course at Hamersley Iron and so he made an introductory video. This was the script:

Welcome to this four-day course on team leadership and team membership.

Please excuse this video introduction, but I am unable to be with you today. Nevertheless, I do want to welcome you and make some comments on why you are here.

Every Hamersley employee participates in these courses. This takes a lot of time and consumes a lot of resources but I am sure it is worth it. Once you have finished the four days I think you will agree it's an investment in our future.

Just a few words about the PURPOSE of this course and what we want each of you to get from it. Firstly, we want each of you to learn a lot more about what TEAM LEADERSHIP is all about.

Secondly, for you to learn a lot more about what TEAMWORK and TEAM MEMBERSHIP is all about.

However, that is not where it ends!

We want you to go away from this course and change the way you behave as leaders and change the way you behave as members of a team.

All of us, including everyone in leadership roles, are in teams as members of those teams. So we must learn about both aspects ... and then we must make a concerted effort to change our behaviour.

For almost every one of us, the effort in changing behaviour will be great, the change required is large.

---

1   Facilitated experiential learning, focused on the here and now, in an unstructured small group setting.

It is not easy to change your behaviour. But change we must. The task for each of you is this:

To learn as much as you can about leadership and team membership and then, immediately after this course, to apply that learning to the way you go about your day-to-day job. The resources you have to do this are quite considerable.

There are the course materials and leaders while you are here, plus your fellow course members.

Back on the job you will have your manager and the other people around you who will also be working to change their behaviour. They should also be a resource. What about timing? When are you required to make this change in behaviour?

I want you to change your behaviour as soon as you start back in your regular work roles. Immediately!

Why so quickly?

Because the evidence is very clear. If you do not make a really big effort to change in the first few days after you return to your job then there will be no change in behaviour at all.

So that is a task that team working demands from each one of you. It is the most important task that will be assigned to you for a long time. It is not the only task that will come out of this course but the presenters will tell you about these other tasks.

We are doing all this work on teams because we need to continue building a better Hamersley. That is possible only if each of you is heavily involved.

Over the last couple of years Hamersley has changed a lot. It must change a lot more. This will only be possible if we have your help and commitment.

Let me describe the sort of Hamersley we are looking to build. It is best described by how the average shop floor employee would feel about their leaders, their managers and their employer. The average employee would feel like this:

'My manager really cares for my safety and well being.'

'My manager trusts me because:

- *confidential information is shared with me.*
- *I am allowed to get on with my job.'*

Remember, you cannot expect the people who work for you to trust you if you show that you don't trust them. Continuing with how the average shop floor employee would feel:

'My manager involves me in planning the work that has to be done. My suggestions are valued. All in all I am involved in the decision making.'

'Tasks are assigned to me clearly and the priorities made clear – I am trained well and given interesting work to do.'

'Although my manager is not forever checking on me s/he keeps an eye on how I am going. If I get into real difficulties I am not left to flounder because my manager steps in with help and advice.'

I am sure almost all of you would agree that if the average shop floor employee were really going to feel like this then Hamersley would have to change a lot more yet.

Core Social Process Skills for Leaders

We have seen that just knowing what to do is not usually enough. People need examples, role models and practice. We have attempted to address this with the Working Together courses but it was evident that a short course, even if intense and residential, was often not enough to allow people to change their behaviour consistently. It was clear that many people would benefit from more skills training. One of the principals of Macdonald Associates, Tony Dunlop, a clinical psychologist, developed the next step: core social process skills training (Dunlop, 2000).

This grew out of the need for skills, not only in teamwork, but those required if systems are to be implemented effectively. The details of what was needed became clear from performance reviews and Working Together courses. These core social skills can be taught in a whole course, as a smaller set or directly in relation to systems implementation (see Box 19.7).

Box 19.7 Core Process Skills Training

Like the Working Together course, core process skills training courses require a fully trained, social process consultant who is able not only to teach but also to demonstrate the skills in role play and in real time. Like the Working Together course, variations of this programme have been run in many different countries, cultures and climates. And like the Working Together courses, the material can be dangerous if not delivered properly and professionally and with a clear purpose. There is no single template but again certain elements are necessary:

- collaboration between client and consultant especially as to context, purpose and delivery;
- fully trained leaders with a clear role;
- the 'course' in at least two parts, with learning followed by a period for practice with follow-up reflection and practice and use of video and observation to reflect and learn from a structured model.

Conclusion

As we argue throughout this book, it is easy to write about what needs to be done: 'create effective teams', 'build trust', 'collaborate'. It is much more difficult to explain what is meant by that in terms of actual behaviour and then give people the opportunity to practice. Exhortation and the written word are not sufficient. We have outlined how this can be defined and put into practice. Of course none of this is of value if people are not then required to practice this in the workplace. That is why such courses should not simply be 'H.R. training' but should be led by line managers and refer to behaviours and systems that are required back at work.

CHAPTER

20 *So What? What Difference Has This Made?*

There are many books about principles and modes of leadership, change management and organisational design. Very few attempt to link the ideas with actual, specific outcomes. Some may make general claims of significant increases in productivity or efficiency but do not provide data. Perhaps the exceptions here are in specialist areas: the internationally recognised Dupont Workplace Safety Training programmes and modular training materials for the support and further development of safety professionals, line and operations managers and line supervisors, or in technical processes such as six sigma and in general the Continuous Improvement movement.

This is understandable at two levels. First, and most important, causality is actually difficult to attribute accurately. For example, a system change or behavioural change in one area may affect another area positively or negatively. An improvement in productive behaviour or better teamwork may coincide with improvements in technical processes or an upturn in the market. How do we separate these strands fairly? Second, change is made by people putting ideas into practice. That practice may vary – even unintentionally – or the ideas may be misunderstood, or both.

Organisations are not easily made into laboratories with experimental and control groups. People will vary in their opinions as to what caused what. In the words of an old saying, 'success has many fathers, but failure is an orphan'. Despite these difficulties it is worth trying to ascertain what effect has occurred and whether it is attributable to the implementation of particular ideas. We look at implementation in a wide range of organisations. We examine work in the Anglican Church, schools, the public sector and diverse industries. They demonstrate that the concepts are not limited culturally nor to a sector or type of organisation, since the proposition is that they are based on fundamental principles of purposeful, human behaviour. We have applied them across the Public, Private and Not-for-Profit sectors. They all relate to creating Productive Social Cohesion.

We also have to bear in mind that not all change is measured in output alone. Qualitative measures such as personal job satisfaction, a sense of achievement and pride in work are also relevant and meaningful to members of an organisation and other stakeholders.

We have included several case studies here. Some are from the first edition as they provided the first really significant evidence of the potential of Systems Leadership and actually stood up to judicial scrutiny and were formally stated (Australian Industrial Relations Commission) to have delivered high productivity improvement. However, we have continued to see the ideas implemented in the last ten years and so have selected new case studies (more to be found on the website):

1. The implementation of Systems Leadership in the Australian Victoria State Judicial System.
2. The implementation in Mexico with regard to cross-cultural understanding and relationships that enabled a mining business to grow with mutual benefit.
3. The implementation in a state school in Far North Queensland, Australia.

4. The analysis of mental health services in Trieste in Italy.
5. The use of concepts to analyse combat in Afghanistan.

There are also other case studies; some from the previous edition and some since which can be found on the associated website www.maconsultancy.com. Also the websites Macdonald Associates, Bioss and SLDA provide other examples of the use of SLT.

The original cases were examples where the introduction of systems leadership concepts was careful and deliberate and did not coincide with technological change, where the impact was recognised not only in the organisation but also in the wider society.

Box 20.1

We encourage discussion of evidence. We look at any approach and ask three questions of *all* approaches including our own:

1. Does the approach go beyond the WHAT to the HOW i.e. does it describe how to create the desired culture?
2. Is it theory based: is there a set of principles and propositions that are internally consistent and predictive?
3. Is there evidence: are there examples of where this approach has worked and resulted in measurable positive change

---

Before examining these cases we would like to reinforce the argument that consultants do not bring about change. The leadership of the organisation brings about change. Overall a change process is a partnership between the leadership, advisers (internal and external) and the members/employees of the organisation. This is reflected in the authorship of this book. Consultants who claim to 'change the culture' do no such thing. If changes occur, it positively involves many people working hard over a long time. Leave the silver bullets for the vampires. The most important platform for change is a coherent, integrated set of concepts which is available to and understood by people involved in the process. This is what we have attempted to provide in this book. This will not be the product of one mind but the product of working relationships. It is imperative that the concepts are internally consistent and make sense. The first test of any articulation of process is whether it can logically be justified or falsified. It must predict its own failures.

For example, in one organisation where we worked the change process chosen was almost entirely based on the Working Together course (the dangerous 'sheep-dip' – the idea that all you need to do is take your people through the course without any other support or systems work). Very little structural or systemic change occurred in parallel. Unsurprisingly, very little positive change occurred and the course itself became a negative symbol only serving to expose the gap between good practice in theory and the evident poor practice in reality. Systems remained that contradicted the teaching, and the leadership handed the process to HR which, as predicted, made things worse, despite some heroic efforts from the HR team.

Although this was a failure in terms of positive outcome, it actually reinforced the conceptual framework by producing the predicted poor results. It was not, however, our proudest moment and Macdonald Associates should have had the courage to withdraw sooner given the conditions.

In another example we worked with an organisation where there was a lack of capability in several key roles in the CEO team, as defined by our capability model. There was a lack of mental processing ability (according to the definitions) and an excess of energy and the use of power. Despite the CEO acknowledging this, it was not possible at the time to remove the individuals, and the change programme faltered because it was implemented in a patchy way. This is *not* to say the CEO was wrong. We must work in partnership, not to a set formula. All we can do is explain and predict that, if it is not judged appropriate to make certain changes, then this will affect the outcome. As was outlined at the beginning of Part 5, there is an ideal process but conditions for an ideal process cannot be created artificially. If the process is to be modified, so should expectations.

The remainder of this chapter examines the four new case studies and then returns to the major case that established Systems Leadership as a highly successful approach and had a significant impact not only on the organisations concerned but society itself.

Case (i): Victoria State County Court Performance 2015–16

EXECUTIVE SUMMARY: TOWARD COURT EXCELLENCE – PRACTICAL APPLICATION OF SYSTEMS LEADERSHIP AT THE COUNTY COURT OF VICTORIA, AUSTRALIA

This executive summary presents the context, process and outcomes of application of systems leadership at the County Court of Victoria. This work began in early 2014 and helped to inform new governance arrangements adopted by the Court in October that year. These principles and models continue to be applied especially in court administration and the performance of the court and the registry in the administration of justice continues to improve.

Context

The County Court of Victoria (the Court) is the principal trial court in Victoria, providing fair, affordable and effective access to justice for the Victorian community. The Court manages over 12,000[1] matters per year. The Court's 65[2] judges (plus the Chief Judge) and its operations are supported by more than 300 staff. In addition to proceedings in Melbourne, judges also hear cases at circuit courts in twelve regional centres. Judges in the Court sit in three divisions: Criminal; Common Law; and Commercial. Circuit operations form a fourth group.

Increasing demand, complexity and other challenges

Sustained increasing demand: as shown in Figure 20.1 the number of matters finalised at the Court from 2009/10 to 2014/15 has increased by 18% (10,377 in 2009/10 and 12,258 in 2014/15), a growth rate of 3.5%.

Increasing complexity of matters heard: an ongoing significant issue for the Court is the growing complexity of the law. This area continues to contribute to increased hearing time for both pre-trial hearings and the average length of a trial. The management of this area is crucial to the Court's ability to meet its obligations to the community and to reduce the negative impact of delay on complainants and accused.

---

1   *County Court Annual Report 2014–15.*
2   Five County Court judges sit in other jurisdictions, including the Magistrates Court, Children's Court, the Coroners Court and the Victorian Civil and Administrative Tribunal.

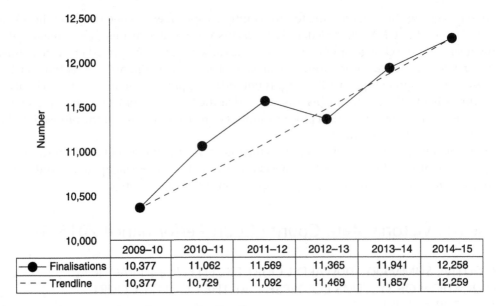

	2009–10	2010–11	2011–12	2012–13	2013–14	2014–15
Finalisations	10,377	11,062	11,569	11,365	11,941	12,258
Trendline	10,377	10,729	11,092	11,469	11,857	12,259

Figure 20.1   Number of Matters finalised[3]

Increasing diversity of court users: there are an increasing number of individuals representing themselves in the Court and these Self-Represented Litigants (SRLs) require greater levels of support and case management. The number of SRL cases finalised in the Court has more than tripled since 2013.

Legacy IT infrastructure: a significant challenge for the Court is the redevelopment of its ageing case management system (the IT system which supports the majority of court processes).

Constrained fiscal environment: the Court operates in an increasingly constrained fiscal environment. Structural funding issues linked to the establishment of CSV need to be resolved to establish a sustainable financial base into the future.

Increasing workload on judges: from 2009/10 to 2014/15 overall judge numbers remained static at 60 (plus the Chief Judge) but the number of matters finalised per judge increased from 169.5 (2009/10) to 201.0 (2014/15).

Listen-Plan-Do: The application of Systems Leadership

Under the sponsorship of the Chief Judge, the CEO (chief court administrator) was supported by an external consultant and together they interviewed more than forty judges using Systems Leadership as the framework for questions and analysis.

The following challenges from a systems and behaviours perspective were identified:

- *Purpose of the Court 'To hear and determine matters in a fair, timely, accountable and efficient manner' was clear but coherent systems of work were lacking as was the court administrative capability to work towards excellence using the International Framework for Court Excellence (IFCE) the Court had adopted.*

---

3   *Report on Government Services, Commonwealth of Australia (2016).*

- *Governance arrangements needed to be established to clarify and strengthen the authorities of the Chief Judge, his ability to delegate authority for judicial administration to Division Heads and to improve the effectiveness of administrative support.*
- *Administration management hierarchy could be better structured to develop, improve and integrate systems of work and change in response to the new operating environment.*

The CEO and a small senior team during 2014 worked closely with the judiciary, supporting the transformation of the governance arrangements for the court. These changes were endorsed by the Chief Judge unanimously accepted by the Council of Judges, the governing body of the County Court in October 2014. The capability gaps to effectively implement improvement underpinned by the principles of the IFCE were also addressed through the redesign, and new appointments to the executive team to reflect different levels of work complexity. The CEO led a programme of change that has encompassed a range of initiatives and improvements based in systems leadership. Work to date has included:

- Developing and implementing a 'Working Together Program' that is being progressively delivered throughout the Court (including some judges who were more involved in the administration of the Court) to build understanding and capability in SLT. More than fifty staff and managers and nine judges have so far participated in the programme. Designed specifically for the Court, this programme is delivering a tailored leadership approach, and aims to strengthen the foundation of capability, foster the desired culture of collaboration and teamwork, and support the implementation of improvements across the Court.
- Adoption of 'team process' as the standard and expected way of working in teams.
- Adoption of 'task assignment' as the standard and expected way of assigning work.
- Role clarity work using SLT principles to redesign roles including clarity of authorities in relation to line management, project management and lateral role relationships.
- Redesign of various systems of work to improve productivity and remove waste.

The redesign of governance structures, is the principle focus of this case as the work was foundational, establishing a system by which the court could be directed, managed and organised to make the 'IFCE work', and through improvement in systems of work, drive with purpose toward court excellence.

Outcomes and benefits

The outcome of the revised governance structure has enabled the Judiciary, Registry and Administration to work together in a system with clearer purpose, boundaries and authorities. The level of work is now appropriate to the complexity of the roles concerned in particular, the capability of the Division Heads has been engaged in order to improve court performance as well as administer justice in individual cases.

The outcomes of judges exercising their newly delegated authorities are evident in the 2014/15 measures of court performance– see Figures 20.5 and 20.8.

Clearance ratio relates the Court's caseload to its capacity. It is the ratio of the number of outgoing matters expressed as a percentage of incoming matters. The clearance ratio is an indicator of whether or not a court is keeping up with the demands for court services in terms of its incoming caseload. The Court has increased its clearance ratio indicating it is getting through the work, meeting demand and that it has capacity to meet its time standards in the future.

The cost per case is measured by dividing the total recurrent expenditure within the court for the year by the total number of finalisations for the same period. It provides a unit measure

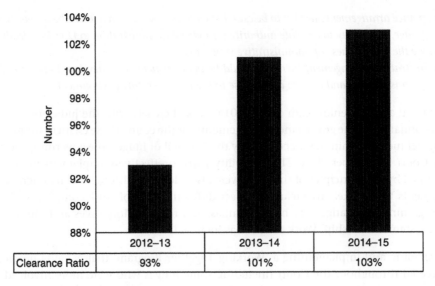

Figure 20.2   Clearance Ratio

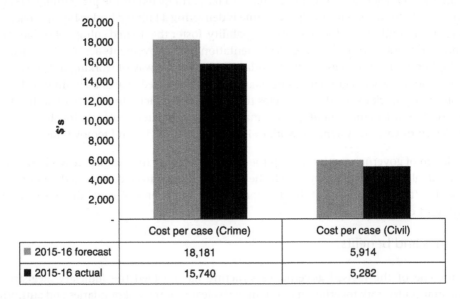

Figure 20.3   Cost per Case

of efficiency. From forecast to actual for 2015/16 there was a 13% reduction in Crime and an 11% reduction in Civil.

The improvements evidenced in the above measures were realised in the face of growing demand and were enabled by the redesigned governance structure.

Judge O'Neill, Head of the Common Law Division was interviewed in the August 2016 Law Institute Journal regarding innovations in the Court. For Judge O'Neill the new authorities as Division Head gave him 'the opportunity to shake up the management of the lists that fall in his division, bringing in innovations to drive efficiencies and slash waiting times'. The effect of the innovations has cut waiting times to 6–8 months and resolution time has also shortened drastically, with 65% of judgements provided within thirty days, and 85% within ninety days. Similar efficiency drives are happening in the other divisions.

Good systems support leadership succession

One of the critical issues identified in planning was *'What if the Chief Judge (who is a champion of this work) leaves the Court?'* The former Chief Judge was due to retire in July 2016, however, following twelve years of outstanding leadership, His Honour Michael Rozenes resigned as Chief Judge of the County Court in June 2015 as a result of illness.

This was an emotional and unsettling time for the Court. But the new governance system allowed the Court to navigate the many and complex issues that arose with the former Chief Judge leaving. A recurrent concern raised in the initial interviews with judges went from a context where 'God knows what is going to happen when the Chief leaves ... It's terrifying' to one where, as challenging as it was, systems were in place to sustain and reinforce change and behaviours. Specifically there was a clear hierarchy of authorities to work with to make decisions and act on the many issues that arose. In addition Division Heads monitoring and improving the delivery of court services in their respective areas.

The most telling evidence of the success of this change was in October 2015 when Chief Judge Peter Kidd was appointed to the Court. He said 'My initial impression was that the court was functioning in a highly organised and structured manner ... it was an ordered, calm but busy environment ...'

Case (ii): Torex Gold – Using the Values Continua as the Cornerstone of External Relationships

FRED STANFORD, CEO TOREX GOLD

Context: I have used Systems Leadership successfully in previous roles in large mining companies that resulted in productivity improvements and better work satisfaction. Moving to a role in a start-up company was a new challenge and provided a new opportunity to use the models in a different setting.

Purpose: The purpose of this case study is to demonstrate the effective use of the Values Continua to address Critical Issues. A fuller account of the project is available on the website.

In 2009/2010, Torex Gold (Torex) raised CDN $300 million on the public markets and used the proceeds to purchase a gold development property in Guerrero State of Mexico. For Torex this purchase transformed the company from 'shell' status to a company with a world-class gold property that could form the basis for building a modern mining company.

That world-class asset, though well-endowed by nature, was not without its challenges. The endowment at the time of purchase was a resource estimate of over 3 million of gold ounces at excellent grades for mining by open pit methods. At 29,000 hectares, the property is large, with significant exploration potential. Together, these two qualities formed the basis for the Company's strategy:

> *Increase the current resource to 5 million ounces and build our first mine. Explore the property to find a resource for a second mine, and then build that.*

An asset of this quality would not have been available to such a small company if it wasn't burdened with a few challenges as well. The foremost of such critical issues was: what if we can't gain access to the ore-body? There had been a two-year blockade, by the local landowners, that had denied access to the previous owner of the mineral rights. The local landowners had negative mythologies about mining companies; in particular they didn't trust them and felt that such companies were unloving and disrespectful towards them. They were also sceptical about the honesty of business leaders.

My experience is that many companies pay a great deal of attention to the Technical and Commercial Domains but underestimate the issues in the Social Domain. Although this is improving there is a need to examine this area in similar if not more detail.

As we looked at the critical issues standing in the path of executing on the strategy, it was clear that there were, as expected, many Technical and Commercial issues that needed to be sorted out, but they were quite manageable. The real uncertainty lay on the Social side, and if the company was going to truly prosper, it would be because of success in solving the social critical issues. The blockade was one such issue, but there were many others associated with integrating a modern industrial operation into an area with little industrial experience and a history that led to the mythologies mentioned above concerning those in authority who often were experienced to resort to power to get their way.

So, using System Leadership principles we designed a social operating strategy that was centred on the following objectives:

1. Create an external experience of the company such that external stakeholders want the company to succeed.
2. Create an internal experience of the company such that team members willingly give their best.
3. Create an organised workplace such that willing team members can be productive.

In the beginning, most of the focus was on creating the external experience of the company. We had very few employees and all of the important relationships were external to the company. These included communities, governments, investors, regulators and contractors. How to create productive external relationships was the key critical issue and with a blockade in place on our only asset, time was of the essence.

Fortunately, Inco Limited had provided fifteen years of experience with Systems Leadership, root cause analysis, and interest-based negotiations. It was in from these models that the essence of our external relationship strategy was drawn. First and foremost was Systems Leadership and in particular the Values Continua model. The model suggests that if you would like others to willingly follow your lead, then at the very least they need to see you as operating from the left side of the values continua. While we were not in a formal leadership role with any of these external stakeholders, the issues at hand were very complex and we were looking to have our leadership to be trusted and accepted. The principle had to be the same: we needed to tailor our actions so as to be received as on the left side of the values continua, in this culture. The tools for doing that had to be the same: management Systems, management Behaviours, and Symbols that are guided by a recognition of where dissonance with existing beliefs is required.

The Values Continua model also provides an excellent end state if one chooses to apply the rigour of root cause analysis to social conflict. Many years of observing and seeking to resolve conflicts in an industrial workplace led to variant on the model that suggests:

Unless the conflict is rooted in ideological differences, the root cause of a dispute is likely to be in a feeling of offense in one or more of the values.

Listening and probing carefully to ascertain which value or values has/have been offended, can lead to the starting point for a mutually agreeable solution. (Interest-based negotiation provides helpful skills for probing past the stated positions to uncover the misaligned value, or interest.)

The decision to 'Get on the left side of the Values Continua and stay there' became a guiding principle in the design of our management systems that interacted with the communities, our management behaviours, and the symbols that helped to define our position on the values continua. This involved a genuine and detailed approach to understand how the local people saw the world. We had to understand what experiences had led them to create negative mythologies and then require leadership behaviours to show that we were different. We needed to design systems that were transparent and open to scrutiny. We needed to be aware of how symbols were interpreted. We were far from perfect in staying to the left side as perceived by local people, but the leaders worked hard at it, we course corrected quickly, and the positive symbols far outweighed the negatives.

The results speak for themselves. The blockade was resolved in four meetings. We found that inconsistency in the commercial relationships between landowners was seen as unfair, so we rectified that. Our genuine, paramount concern for safety and security, demonstrated through our behaviour and systems that we did not put people second. We showed that we were not interested in short-term, apparent commercial gain. Personal contact with leaders, including myself as CEO, demonstrated our serious intent to build mutually beneficial long-term relationships. Permanent land tenure was negotiated on schedule. Environmental permits were achieved on schedule. Over a billion dollars was raised through debt and equity to build the mine and processing plant. Two villages were resettled on schedule, a task seen as almost impossible by others at the outset. Security issues were resolved with the assistance of many stakeholders. The mine and plant were built on budget and ahead of schedule. The first year of operation for the plant has just been completed, and production and cost objectives were achieved.

Looking back, it is hard to overemphasise the positive impact on our business of planning to 'get on the left of the Values Continua and then stay there'. The key word is 'planning' or thinking through in advance as to how actions in the form of decisions and behaviours will be received. In so doing, we were able to tailor our communications to be effective given the listening that was available to us.

For a mining company the available listening is not always charitable. But we can be honest. By definition, what we do has an environmental impact. We have no choice about where we do it, since the mine has to be placed where the ore is. There is also a tendency for many stakeholders to perceive the gold as their gold and they only grudgingly agree to the extraction if they get a 'fair' share. All in all, it is a business environment that has all of the potential ingredients for social conflict.

This business environment makes mining projects increasingly complex to finance, permit, and build. In looking back at the successful build of this one, it is amazing how many people helped along the way. Many of these people were external to the company and they helped at times and in ways that we were not aware of. Without their help, it is doubtful that we would be where we are today with many stakeholders and thousands of families benefiting from the project. It is easy to look at other challenged mining projects, elsewhere in the world, and imagine the same outcome for our project.

Why did some people help when they had no personal stake in the outcome? In many cases it was as simple as people 'doing the right thing'. They could see benefits to the stakeholders that mattered to them and through new experiences they came to trust the management team to do the right thing in balancing outcomes and managing risk. The management team had an advantage: the idea that anyone could do the 'right thing' was elevated from abstract concept to decision friendly clarity by the Values Continua. A comment heard at a recent mining conference sums it up – 'If you want to do that then you have to do it the way that Torex does it.' It turns out that 'it' is elegantly simple, but requires a great deal of ongoing work – Get on the left side of the Values Continua and stay there!

Case (iii): Education Queensland

CONTEXT

Malanda SS (MSS) is set in a rural community with an economy associated with the dairy industry for more than ninety years. It is located 74km south-west of Cairns, in Far North Queensland, Australia, with 335 students from Prep to Year 6. Malanda SS' Index of Community Socio Economic Advantage (ICSEA) is 975. ICSEA values typically range from approximately 500 (representing extremely educationally disadvantaged backgrounds) to about 1,300 (representing schools with students with very educationally advantaged backgrounds). Under 1,000 is considered to be disadvantaged.

The school has had seven Principals from 2012 to 2016, due to complexities associated with a previous Principal (ongoing). Prior to my appointment, the substantive Deputy Principal (DP) for twelve years, did a pleasing job in a difficult situation as Acting Principal.

I discovered on arrival, that the school has an incredibly strong community. The Parents & Citizens' (P&C) committee is focused and passionate about the school, and its connection to the town. The P&C President is the current P&C Area Coordinator. The President is highly active in the school, and led the community's drive to find a replacement Principal with the capability to lead, develop and sustain school improvement.

Forty people staff the school, many of whom have served over twenty years. Of the school's twenty teaching staff, there are four ex-teaching Principals who have the knowledge and understanding of the complexity of the work required to lead a small school and are happy to assist. There are three graduates and the total teaching staff comprises four levels of teacher classification. However, how and to whom they were accountable was unclear. The teaching capability of the teachers was also unclear when I arrived.

I found that the school's Teacher Aides (TA), like the teachers, were dedicated but their work was not clear when I arrived, and a lot of their work was channelled at a minor percentage of the student body.

The Business Services Manager (BSM) role was left vacant in the final week of 2015 due to ill health, which left the school without a person in this critical administrative role for much of the first term. When I sourced someone suitable for the role, she was still attached to a previous school, and operated in both for many weeks. There were constant issues with her access to the MSS computer network as the EQ system continually locked her out. She lost at least five days unable to access the Education Queensland network.

MSS had very little exposure to Systems Leadership (SL) modelling until the commencement of the 2016 school year when I arrived. I discovered that a benefit to our school was the nearby Malanda State High School's (MSHS) long engagement with the modelling, and its application, in all areas of the school's operation. I have no doubt that this long engagement contributed to the successful transition of MSHS in 2016, from the previous Principal to the current incumbent, as that school continues to flourish academically and culturally. I identified some of the systems in place in MSHS, which I thought would benefit us at MSS with minor modifications: enrolment, attendance, IT, innovation via Agriculture Science and student transition, and commenced planning their adoption and implementation in MSS.

Systems Leadership modelling's impact on me has been significant since 2010 when I was first exposed to the material. Life before SLT was hectic, less fulfilling, leaving me feeling overwhelmed regularly, and frustrated with the lack of results and slow progress of projects. I felt like I was letting everyone down. My work wasn't well planned, was reactive and was at times little more than 'event management'. It affected me personally too, as the stress remained with me outside work. Perhaps the greatest epiphany came in the form of learning how to divide my work into 'improving' and 'sustaining', and the scheduling of such tasks which followed has left me in a position where I feel highly effective, and running an organisation which benefits from this. I have now applied this knowledge to other areas of my life, which has been highly beneficial and I'm a better person for it.

Needless to say, my new role provided an excellent opportunity for me to establish a culture where the modelling is not only valued, but is welcomed by staff who have experienced feelings of uncertainty about the work of their roles, and the confusion which spreads to the teams in the absence of consistent high-quality leadership.

PURPOSE

This case study briefly explains my application of SLT material at Malanda SS to demonstrate rapid progress in creating our desired culture.

METHODOLOGY

As Principal, I applied Systems Leadership material in the following ways.

- Improving clarity through the accurate identification of 'What is the work?' in the social, technical and commercial domains of the organisation with an emphasis on the social and technical components.
- Engaging with the Systems Leadership consultant has been of great value re advice about the practical application of the concepts, models and tools to do my work.
- Analysing and revising what was in place, e.g. the Annual Improvement Plan (AIP), resulting in a reduction in the improvement focus from seventeen initiatives to five.
- Identifying and addressing the Critical Issues by:
  - Applying the Tools of Leadership model.
  - Identifying the existing culture by:
    - Analysing and or revising; Teacher Expectations, Classroom Practice, Explicit Teaching.
    - Conducting a detailed analysis of staff mythologies and data to identify an accurate baseline from which we can all move forward.
  - My behaviours have been/are instrumental in the successful culture change at MSS:
    - From the first meeting on the Pupil Free Days, I introduced the Team Leadership and Team Membership Steps and Traps, the Values Continua and our own agreed Staff Meeting Protocols (Be Safe, Be Respectful, Be a Learner) – Behaving in this manner is not just for students.
    - The greetings I use in the mornings and afternoons – Scheduled time in my calendar daily.

- I visited/visit the staffroom most days at 11 a.m. – as scheduled. This is an account-ability of my leadership team members also described in their Specific Role Description's.
- Modelling the Team Leader behaviours/steps – and referring Team Members to behaviours/steps at every meeting/when redirection is required.
  - Implementing key systems – Systems Drive Behaviour:
    - Organisation Chart – Clarifying Authorities.
    - Accurate Specific Role Descriptions – Clarifying Authority and Accountability.
    - Annual Action Plans – demystifying the work.
  - Symbols – symbols are my favourite tool.
- Assigning tasks using the Task Assignment model.
- Creating new mythologies.
- Analysis of the technical component and subsequent clarification of the work to be focused on.
- The Right People in the Right Roles Doing the Right Work – reflected in the allocation of resources.
- Designing essential systems using the 20 Questions.
  - Reading system, Daily Writing system, Students Educationally At Risk system.
- The P&C President and I work continually. We meet in the early hours of the morning which suits his business operations.

RESULTS

Some of the results I have seen as Principal include:

- Excellent productive working relationship with the Parents and Community Committee President. Together we are applying SL material to our P&C organisation.
- The creation of new mythologies with leadership team members – Staff in leadership team experiencing greater clarity in the work of their roles; weekly reporting indicating significant progress; Team Leadership and Membership steps evident in interaction between team, and respect for delegated 'authority' to complete work; my leadership by attending staffroom at 11 a.m. each day to interact with teaching team.
- Delivering on the SL Principle of: the right people in the right roles doing the right work.
- More productivity – progress is highly evident in all areas of the L/Ship team's specific roles – evidenced through rapid transformation of areas relating to the AIP.
- Productive new systems:
  a. Staff have a universal language to apply when engaging in discourse about the social component of their work.
  b. Leadership Team members have engaged with the Task Assignment model, and completed some pleasing work as a result.

'As a Classroom Teacher under Mark's leadership, the school is much calmer because we know the support is there … He has worked with us to design and implement whole school systems like School Wide Positive Behaviour Learning (SWPBL), Sound Waves, Guided Reading and Daily Writing Consolidation systems … With this calmness comes self-assurance for the staff, because we are valued as an individual who is part of a team, creating a network, a community among the school staff … We are comfortable because

there is no 'in crowd' and no 'out crowd'. Everyone is different, but in this culture difference is respected and our tasks are done more efficiently and effectively ... We are able to put forward ideas from our role and know they are considered.'

Writing system

As Head of Curriculum, focusing on the development of a writing system, the application of SLT to my work in 2016, enabled me to operate at a high level of detail effectively for the first time, successfully using social process; to have teachers know the key issues and together develop a targeted response, one where they were the key players. From the first time the data yelled at us to do something, it was thoroughly analysed and planned in detail from the start. It meant that I was able to use knowledge I had been storing away to choose the right people for the right work. I was able to use their skills and their standing in the school to influence the staff in a positive way. Building this effective writing system, easily provided the methodology to maintain and improve it and when I went on leave it was easily trans-ferrable to my replacement. The SLT process I had worked through meant that I had made a sustainable system; a system that is powered by the teachers and is supported by the other systems in the school.

Reading system

The student data above demonstrates the reading systems consistency of purpose and prac-tice, delivering continual, more consistent improvement of reading results in 2016 and 2017 regardless of these students ethnicity, socio-economic status and minor intellectual or behaviour disorders.

As Lead Teacher use of SLT has facilitated ownership of the reading system by all involved through the effective application of social process ... The efficient, successful reading system design has delivered:

- clear understanding of authority and accountability, scripted well-resourced systems, effective training, clear expectations and timelines with accurate data collection.
- a change of the teacher aides role from that of simply reading with students to working at a para professional level – efficient programme delivery, improved skill and knowledge capability and involvement in system innovations.
- analysis of recordable data allowing individual student's achievements to be monitored and alterations made to the system, if necessary, to ensure continual reading growth.
- creating reading goals with students and informing stakeholders of progress has effectively motivated all involved.
- The work of my role as TA team leader and custodian of the reading system, listening to employee's suggestions, ensuring timelines are met, quality assuring the results, continually identifying and implementing innovations is necessary for success.
- This 'relative writing gain' of the MSS students from year 3–5 is demonstrating performance significantly above the 'average gain' of Queensland schools – as a direct result of the Daily Writing Consolidation system, which was implemented in 2015.

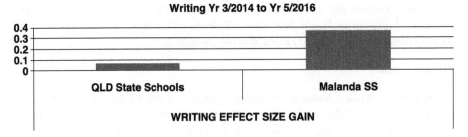

Figure 20.4   Writing Yr 3/2014 to Yr 5/2016

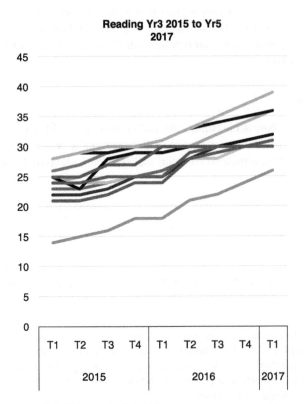

Figure 20.5   Reading Yr3 2015 to Yr 5 2017

SUMMARY: LESSONS LEARNED

The application of the SLT material facilitates identification of 'what is the work' and how as Principal, I can get my work done efficiently, effectively making rapid continual progress as my team becomes more proficient with the material and its application.

Mark Allen, Principal. 30/7/2017

Case (iv): Contrasting Symbols in In-Patient Psychiatric settings in Italy and the UK

Senior leaders from a mental health service in the UK went on a study visit to Trieste to see what could be learned from their services. Mental Health services in Trieste, Italy have become well known for their non-restrictive systems in mental health care. For example, they have no locked wards, no low secure units and use sectioning under their equivalent of the Mental Health Act very rarely. Their ward environments appear less institutionalised than those found in the UK and patients are referred to as 'guests'. Their in-patient suicide rates are markedly lower.

Historically the Trieste services were more institutionalised than their UK equivalents in the early 1970s with more psychiatric beds per head of population. It was the leadership of the psychiatrist Franco Basaglia that made their transition to their current success possible. He defined the work of the organisation as primarily to engage and work with the people it served, rather than to control behaviour according to a set of restrictive rules that assume people will behave badly or unsafely. This created a systems change, with the focus of treatment being on the individual and what they might want or need, and the focus for staff behaviour being how they might go about engaging individuals with the service they had to offer. There was a greater willingness to tolerate uncertainty and risk (and one would assume a less punitive response to adverse incidents when they happened). Thus people were trusted and treated with respect.

In the UK, a common response to in-patient suicide has been to improve 'environmental safety' – to remove any potential environmental feature that could facilitate a suicide attempt. This has mainly focused on the removal of ligature points – anything that can be used for securing a ligature to facilitate a suicide attempt through hanging and has required significant financial investment.

On visiting one of the in-patient wards in Trieste, we were struck by the extensive presence of ligature points throughout the ward environment. In the UK, ligature-free taps, showerheads and door handles all have a distinctive downward sloping design. In the wards in Trieste, the fixtures and fittings were all more consistent with those found in a home environment. This more homely atmosphere was heightened by attractive furniture, pictures and curtains, and in combination more akin to a hotel environment.

In trying to understand the better performance of the service in Trieste in relation to in-patient suicide, it seems possible that one factor may be the prevalence of ligature-free fixtures and fittings. In the UK service the resulting rather clinical and institutional environment may serve to symbolically communicate the message: 'You are very unwell, and such a danger to yourself that you cannot be trusted even with a normal door handle or tap.' This could contribute to someone's sense of fear and hopelessness about their experience of mental illness. We know that in many health conditions, not just mental illness, hope is positively correlated with recovery, and it may be that this powerful symbol denoting an unintended organisational mythology of hopelessness may be actively contributing to poorer outcomes.

Thus we can see that in Trieste the combination of leadership Behaviour (Basaglia) the introduction of new Systems (treatment and environment) and the positive use of Symbols (ligature points) have all contributed to a lowering of suicide rates and the general positive identity of 'guests' as they address their mental health issues.

Benna Waites: Consultant Clinical Psychologist

Case (v): 'Leadership in Combat'

LIEUTENANT COLONEL TOM DE LA RUE AAC (BRITISH ARMY)
COMMANDING OFFICER OF AN APACHE ATTACK HELICOPTER REGIMENT

The purpose of this vignette is to demonstrate in a small way that the facets of 'Systems Leadership Theory' are alive and well in high functioning (military) organisations.

Helmand Province, Afghanistan

A Taliban stronghold had built up one summer at the height of the Afghan campaign at a place called Kunjak Hill just south of the infamous district centre of Sangin on the Helmand River. The enclave was situated on top of a hill complex with commanding views over the river flood plain and the all-important main supply route (611) from Lashkar Gar and Geresk (both forming the central Helmand economic development zone) through Sangin to the towns of Musa Qaleh and Kajaki to the north.

To neutralise the inherent threat posed to this critical supply route, an International Security Assistance Force (ISAF) Brigade plan was put together to conduct an Infantry company group assault onto the strategic position at *first light* one day that summer. Those taking part in the operation were gathered, the orders for the aviation assault were delivered in secrecy – covering the aviation part of the assault and the associated ground manoeuvre operation – and the force then readied itself by conducting final preparations and essential mission rehearsals. Every detail had been considered, contingency plans were in place to mitigate against potential risks and threats, and final assurances were delivered to senior commanders (accountable for achieving operational success) so that 'launch approval' could be granted for the mission.

At this point it is important to note that the aviation part of the assault was to be commanded by an Apache Air Mission Commander (AMC) – a combat seasoned British Army Apache Aircraft Commander with considerable operational flying experience, capable of dealing with complexity, uncertainty and change, and making fine judgements and effective decisions in dynamic and difficult fighting conditions. AMCs were usually highly qualified Army Air Corps Captains (Flight Commanders, sometimes as young as 29 years of age) and Majors (Squadron Commanders) or Lieutenant Colonels (Regimental Commanding Officers) who had reached the pinnacle of flying excellence and unequivocally proven themselves operationally on previous tours of Afghanistan.

Some essential additional context regarding what was expected of AMCs – they held 'mission abort' authority during operations (meaning that as the *on-scene* commanders they alone decided if/when any mission abort criteria had been achieved); were ultimately accountable for the safe infiltration of the assault force onto the ground; for providing command, control and protection capabilities from the air when the assault force was tactically deployed, and for exfiltrating the force once the mission had been achieved. Of note, the ground force elements were often numerous (up to Battalion strength of circa 600 officers and soldiers) and could cover many kilometres as they spread out across the terrain in tactical formation.

Consequently, the analysis, judgements, decisions and actions associated with the role of AMC were very significant indeed, often requiring decisive outcomes to be achieved in dire tactical circumstances, in situations where friendly forces were perhaps pinned down by strong enemy resistance, often at night, having sustained numerous life-threatening casualties; where the distinction between friendly, civilian and enemy was not clear; where radio communications with the ground forces was perhaps intermittent and at times charged with desperation; where contingency plans were potentially not going as well as had been planned or expected; emergency extraction landing sites for the casualty evacuation aircraft were under fire; poor weather prevailed, including terrible dust storms with dramatically reduced visibility (sometimes down to 100 metres or less for prolonged periods of times); where some aircraft had either sustained battle damage or had for other reasons experienced significant mechanical problems necessitating a *pull* on scarce coalition reserves … The list is endless.

In these circumstances, AMCs were required to consistently make effective decisions; clearly articulate the actions to be carried out (i.e. the work); overcome obstacles in the way of achieving mission success, by day and night for months on end, and in the face of considerable long-term fatigue; efficiently manoeuvre aviation assets around the battlefield; adhere absolutely to the Law of Armed Conflict (LOAC) and the Rules of Engagement (ROE) and, in context, deliver accurate and lethal fire onto identified enemy targets, ensuring each time that civilian casualties and damage to civil infrastructure had been avoided. The latter was something which took considerable *moral courage* to get right every time, particularly when under intense pressure from ground commanders in need of urgent fire support to deploy offensive weapons. Importantly, AMCs knew that they would be *fairly held to account* for their decisions and actions, but were content that with appropriate structures and authorities and sufficient resources in place, they had been set up for success.

Returning now to this particular operation. The attack was launched from Camp Bastion at 0430 hours and was made up of British Chinook heavy lift helicopters with the Light Infantry assault force aboard; British Apache Attack Helicopters to provide critical command, control and close combat attack (CCA) to the troops on the ground, and an assortment of supporting air and unmanned air vehicles (UAV drones), including British Tornado, US F–18 and A–10 Warthog ground attack jets, US 'B' class bombers, AC–130 Hercules gunships, Predator and Reaper drones, U2 spy planes and a range of other multinational coalition aircraft on station to support if needed, not least the British Chinook Medical Emergency Response Team (MERT) and US Pedro HH–60G combat rescue aircraft at immediate notice to move.

Interestingly, all of these air and aviation assets were commanded by the Apache AMC whilst the assault force was in the air. Once on the ground, the AMC and Infantry commander worked very closely to ensure that the aircraft were employed efficiently and effectively (much of this was achieved through a qualified Joint Terminal Air Controller (JTAC) who stood shoulder to shoulder with the Infantry commander during any deployment). For some of the larger operations it would not have been unusual for the AMC to direct upwards of thirty aircraft during a mission, stacked and de-conflicted in the air up to 70,000 feet in altitude, whilst maintaining a command and control link with the ground commander to ensure that the latter's *tactical intent* was consistently met (i.e. that the same set of *mission success criteria* were clearly understood by both parties as they worked seamlessly together to achieve a 'unified' outcome).

The infiltration of the assault force was conducted just before first light, into fields to the west and south of Kunjak Hill and overlooked by enemy positions. The heavy lift aircraft quickly extracted into the western desert, leaving the supporting air and aviation assets overhead to provide command and control, surveillance, target acquisition and direct fire as the situation dictated.

The Infantry platoons egressed from the HLSs as soon as they were comfortable that any in-situ improvised explosive device (IED) threat had been neutralised in the immediate vicinity of the HLSs. At that moment 'ICOM chatter' (referring to the insecure hand-held radio communications traffic between Taliban commanders) intercepted by our airborne electronic signals scanning capabilities indicated that the Taliban were rapidly moving their forces into position.

The fighting on the ground over the next few hours slowed the assault force to the extent that their planned HLS extraction time of 0830 hours was put at considerable risk. This became a real concern for the AMC because the operation had been geared around the military tasks to be achieved on the hill, the anticipated enemy resistance expected, and the associated intelligence which suggested that the threat to the Chinook aviation extraction aircraft would rise significantly after that time. Unfortunately, the terrain proved more hostile and difficult to traverse, the IED threat much greater than had been expected, and the insurgent positions in the fortified compounds more difficult to overcome.

As a consequence, the Infantry company commander on the ground notified the AMC that the assault force would not be able to relocate to the HLSs for an extraction at 0830 hours and requested a delay, initially out to 0930 hours, then 1100 hours. More *dynamic* AMC tactical planning was required and ongoing fuel and ammunition sustainment of the aircraft needed to be quickly resolved – against a backdrop of relentless insurgent activity on the hill which necessitated regular engagements with the enemy and a number of aviation MERT casualty evacuations.

The battle became more intense just at the time the assault force finally began its withdrawal to the extraction HLSs. To make matters worse, further casualties were taken by the assault company as they re-positioned which only heightened the sense of urgency to extract them – unsurprisingly, this pressure was felt directly by the AMC.

The Chinooks amassed at very low level in the desert to the west of Kunjak Hill (to dramatically reduce their audible signature), and awaited the AMC's order to ingress. The AMC calculated that the Chinooks had sufficient fuel to make one attempt at the extraction, followed by the journey back to Camp Bastion, with a maximum of five further minutes of *loiter* fuel. AMC direction to the Chinooks to ingress was duly given, confirming at the time that they were 'cleared in', but that the HLSs were 'HOT' (i.e. in contact with the enemy).

The Apaches and supporting 'air fires' platforms stepped up their engagements of identified enemy targets in the hope of suppressing them to buy sufficient time for the extraction to be completed successfully. However, at the moment the first aircraft touched down, enemy fire erupted onto the various HLSs. The northern-most landing site experienced the most hostile enemy reaction, with PKM machine gun fire and rocket-propelled grenades (RPGs) saturating the airspace and ground around the static aircraft. An immediate 'abort' was called by the AMC who directed the Chinooks back out into the desert to check for battle damage and await further orders.

Knowing that the Chinooks and several Apaches were rapidly becoming fuel critical, the AMC decided to undertake a second extraction attempt given that if the aircraft did return to base having not extracted the assault force, the latter would have been stuck on the ground until the following morning which would have been disastrous for them.

The Chinooks were called back in at low level with Apaches flying 'on their wing' firing their 30mm cannons to draw Taliban fire away from the vulnerable Chinooks onto the supporting gunships. The aircraft again touched down on their respective HLSs which, by this point, had wisely been moved to fields slightly further south (away from the Taliban threats to the north). They again took incoming enemy fire but this time remained on the ground whilst frenzied Infantry activity ensued as soldiers and explosives search dogs clambered onto the various aircraft.

The strategic fear during any operation of this nature was that an aircraft would be destroyed on one of the HLSs or, worse still, shot down just after lift-off with forty laden soldiers on board. The reality on this occasion was that although several of the aircraft sustained battle damage (which incidentally increased the complexity of the cockpit work of their respective crews), they all returned under the direction of the AMC to Camp Bastion where the aircraft were rapidly checked and serviced for further deployments, and the crews swapped to allow the next phase of operations to commence. This was also the moment for the AMC to lead his *post-mission debrief,* and for the Apache crews to conduct a comprehensive review of their recorded gun tape to ensure that all engagements had been carried out in accordance with the LOAC and ROE.

Postscript

It is now appropriate to take a step back from this particular operation to consider how human performance can be maximised in a more generic sense. Achieving success through human endeavour in the face of significant adversity or uncertainty is invariably difficult and, ultimately, hard-won. It is not something that can be left to chance; rather, it must be carefully planned and diligently executed (by capable and accountable individuals) from start to finish.

In this context, it should be obvious to the reader how this material relates to Systems Leadership Theory, but it is still worth highlighting a number of common themes which the theory champions and which are also proven characteristics of capable organisations – in this case, the military.

In outline, this vignette demonstrates how individuals and teams working in a productive culture can rise to any challenge if the conditions are favourable (i.e., deliberately designed and *predicted* to be so).

In this operation, the aviators and soldiers were extremely well trained, had an intimate understanding of the purpose and nature of their work (including the associated opportunities, risks and threats), were clear about the organisation structure within which they resided and knew that the structure genuinely reflected the work to be done.

They also had well-thought through and appropriately delegated requisite authorities and defined accountabilities; were fairly held to account for delivery and, in turn, were able to fairly hold their own subordinates (team members) to account.

They acknowledged that the military was broadly meritocratic and that capable and fully tested individuals were therefore in role and could be *trusted* to perform effectively in any situation, no matter how challenging, complex or uncertain – in many cases, lives literally depended upon this requirement.

They operated within appropriate work management and people systems specifically designed to free them up (unconstrained) to work to their full potential.

They were governed by effective leaders who were clear about 'purpose', thoughtful, decisive and committed to seeing things through 'to the finish', whose behaviour was exemplary and who absolutely led by example. They also resided within a team framework where the full potential of the collective was championed, each member playing a full part in planning for and delivering specified outcomes.

All of this was carried out in a *task orientated* working environment where task assignments were clear, resources were matched to the tasks, and contingency plans were in place to mitigate against the specified risks and threats, thereby ensuring that specified objectives could be achieved.

Finally, they existed in a defined and productive culture where good performance was rewarded differentially and the consequences of poor performance were fairly and consistently upheld (the latter requiring considerable *moral courage* on the part of leaders).

On this last point, it is of course acknowledged that organisations (i.e., the people employed within them) do fall short of expectation from time to time, and that military organisations are no exception to the rule. However, the default aspiration should always be to set the 'professional bar' at an appropriate and achievable level of excellence and, through all of the 'people levers' outlined in the paragraphs above, to maintain this bar as high as realistically possible to ensure that people productivity in the pursuit of defined objectives is maximised (commercial or otherwise).

Finally, it is important to note that this particular vignette merely portrayed a day in the life of a British Army Apache AMC. The reality was that these well-trained soldiers were required to perform to the highest of professional military standards, often at the same tempo, for months on end. By the end of the Afghanistan campaign in late 2014, some AMCs had completed as many as five or six tours of Helmand Province, each lasting four to five months. At an individual level this clearly represented an incredible investment of time, focus and energy by these eminently capable people. However, at a more strategic level, this vignette demonstrates the critical interdependence that exists between organisation structure, capability and leadership when it comes to driving effective work performance in demanding circumstances on an enduring basis.

The final cases below have been the subject of television programmes, business magazine articles, newspaper columns and books. It could easily be a book or books in itself. We do not intend to explore all the potential issues. The industrial relations aspect has been well documented in Terry Ludeke's book *A Line in the Sand* (1996). The transcripts of the Australian Industrial Relations Commission (AIRC) case are available publicly. We concentrate here on the relationship between the systems changes and specific outcomes, with the intention of demonstrating a clear link between the two. We also do so because almost all of the material presented here was also presented to the AIRC and accepted as evidence. In other words, this data has literally been exposed to detailed, public examination and found to be valid.

The case studies concern a major change within two companies that were part of CRA in Australia during the 1990s. The companies, Comalco and Hamersley Iron, embarked on a major change programme which eventually led to almost the entire workforce choosing to change their terms of employment, a change that many said could not happen whether or not they were personally in agreement with it in principle. This was generally described as a move to 'all staff' conditions or 'individual contracts' for those in operator or tradesperson roles. Hamersley Iron was a major iron ore mining and rail operation in the Pilbara area of North Western Australia. Comalco was an aluminium mining and smelting operation with sites in Queensland, Tasmania and New Zealand. While much public attention has been paid to the eventual contractual change, the leadership of those organisations did not see the contractual change as the sole purpose. The contractual change was the outcome of a much more detailed plan of action implemented in order to improve the leadership and systems of the organisation which used systems leadership concepts to bring about change. In direct terms, a person's behaviour does not change because they sign a piece of paper; it changes because the leadership and systems have changed.

Comalco

Comalco's smelting business unit consisted of three major aluminium smelters: one in New Zealand (New Zealand Aluminium Smelting or NZAS), one in Tasmania (Bell Bay) and one in Queensland (Boyne Island). The NZAS story is told in detail in the case study reproduced on the website. In more general terms Karl Stewart became managing director of Comalco Smelting in 1987. In his previous roles as head of an organisational development team and vice president – organisational effectiveness, he had been concerned about the quality of leadership and the negative effect of certain systems. Prior to these roles he had spent fifteen years in line management roles, the last four of which were as General Manager of Comalco's bauxite mine. He was acutely aware of the predominant 'them and us' division in employment and specifically linked this to the nature of employment systems.

In effect, Comalco Smelting, like many other traditional industries, appeared to be two parallel organisations: one a 'staff' organisation largely attempting to function as a meritocracy with at least some systems of performance management and pay for performance; the other an 'award' organisation, of 'workers', hourly paid, with a range of role bands, negotiated systems of pay, attendance and overtime. Of course, this is the old 'white collar/blue collar' distinction, a distinction which was simply assumed by most people in leadership and HR roles as if it was some sort of natural order. Essentially the staff were 'management' and primarily identified with the company while the 'hourly' employees were the 'workers' and primarily identified with the union. This was the case right across Comalco, Hamersley and most mining and heavy industry sites in Australia and many other countries.

What was also apparent was that behaviour was very different between the two groups. Two very obvious and symbolic differences were sick leave and time management. In an article in the Business Review Weekly (BRW) (BRW, 31/1/1994) Stewart said, 'the difference between staff and award workers in terms of sick leave is a ratio of one to ten. In other words for every one day of sick leave taken by staff, award workers take ten.' With regard to time management staff generally did not watch the clock and had no punch-clocks (clocking in and out). Workers (under the award) left exactly on time and felt they were 'paid for time, not work'. This was also demonstrated by the very existence of overtime for one group but not the other.

This may seem obvious and is easy to describe; addressing it, however, is not merely a question of putting everyone on salary. How the fundamental supporting systems of this structure are addressed, identified, redesigned and implemented is crucial. The work was done over the three years that preceded the change with major emphasis on improving the quality of the leadership, poor performers in leadership roles were dismissed. In the lead-up to the offer of staff employment being made the entire management team of the NZAS smelter met in Christchurch for several days of intense work. In two days every system was examined in terms of whether it was and should be a system of equalisation or differentiation.

Following this planning period, the work was done to change those systems and symbols that had been identified as needing change. This was not particularly time consuming because over the previous three years a lot of work has been done to improve the systems that applied to the staff workforce. After the event it was interesting to find out (through confidential interview and audit) the comments made by operators and tradespeople. These concentrated upon the more symbolic systems to test whether the company was serious. As a result 'all staff' was tested not simply by the salary system and terms of employment being equalised, but by systems such as the 'staff Christmas party'. Would it now be open to all? The answer was 'yes' – with significant success. The availability of 'biscuits' with coffee and 'beer and cheese' staff briefings were seen as a much more crucial test than even equalising the sick leave system. Car parking, transport, uniforms, canteen facilities and bathroom facilities were others that were carefully watched by those deciding firstly whether to move to staff and whether it really meant they would be 'staff'.

Preparation was meticulous and detailed, using the systems leadership training concepts. Information about change was given to all on an individual basis by their manager-once-removed (M+1). Leaders were assessed as to their capability and removed from role if not up to the new role. As Stewart said in the BRW article, 'You can't expect the troops to take any notice of improved work performance if they have evidence of poor management.'

The Working Together courses were introduced to teach the new requirements of team-work, rather than command and control. Eventually the entire workforce went through this programme. The Working Together courses helped in these specific ways:

- They clarified work expectations with regard to leadership and teamwork.
- They introduced a common language to help in work and communication.
- They built mythologies and a culture based on a shared experience as the course provided stories of success and disasters with rafts, ropes and planks.

So was all this preparation and planning worth it? First, there was a clear measure in simply the number of people who chose to remain with the organisation and to move to staff contracts: 98%. The figures for all of the Comalco plants were not ends in themselves but indicative of a coherent approach, message and leadership. Indeed all the Comalco smelters and Hamersley Iron reached figures in excess of 97%.

It is interesting when considering these figures that the AIRC found specifically that there had been no element of coercion. This can be compared with other organisations that thought they would 'do the same' and only offered the contract with some cash. These operations were fortunate if many more than 50% signed. However signing a contract is *not* an end in itself.

Box 20.2   Comalco Smelters

Tiwai Point (NZAS): 1991–1998

- 30% reduction in hours worked per tonne of saleable material
- Permanent 20% workforce reduction
- Controllable costs down 10%
- High purity metal yield doubled
- Smelter expansion

Bell Bay: 1990–2000

- Absenteeism halved
- Current efficiency up 1.5%
- Workforce 1,500 to 600 over 10 years
- Tonnes per annum 122,000 to 150,000
- Technology change only to reduce physical effort

Boyne Smelters Limited: 1995–2000

- Increase in production from 210 to 350 tonnes/employee at Levels I and II
- Employment 1,300 to 774

What benefits did it produce? The run charts (Figures 20.1 and 20.2) were submitted and accepted as evidence by the AIRC.

These examples of output improvement are clearly linked to the change in leadership and systems. It should be clearly evident when that change occurred. All the graphs show significant change in September 1991 with preparation activity before that. It is interesting to note that the revenue to the smelter from the sale of the additional high purity metal (Figure 20.3) was greater than the cost reduction brought about by having fewer employees.

These changes caused a great deal of debate about the nature of the process, especially whether it was 'anti-union'. This is largely a distraction, even recognising the political significance. The approach was to improve leadership behaviour, appropriately redesign systems and manage symbols including understanding the symbolic significance of specific changes. *The purpose was to improve business performance by realising the capability of the workforce.*

Some months later, however, random interviews were conducted by external consultants about the effect of the changes on work experience. What was evident was the improvement of the work experience itself. Working around furnaces all day is not, for most, an intrinsically satisfying experience, but people reported a step change in the quality of their working lives. Examples included feedback that proved to the operators that they were listened to; they also appreciated that they could use their discretion more and understood the context better. In addition, many reported an improvement in their home life: 'I don't just go home and open the fridge for a beer, I'm spending more time with my children even helping them with homework' (cell-room operator) 'I can't wait to show my kids where I work, I never thought I'd say that, I have real pride in my work now' (tradesman electrician). These were not isolated examples.

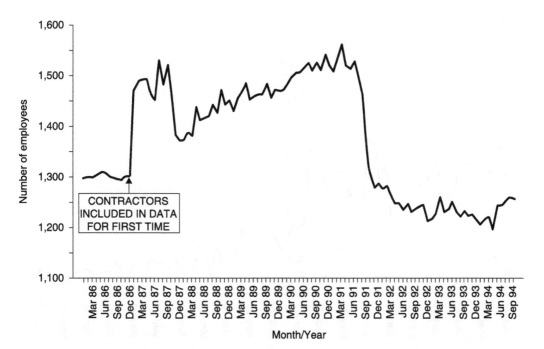

Figure 20.6   New Zealand Aluminium Smelters Employee Numbers

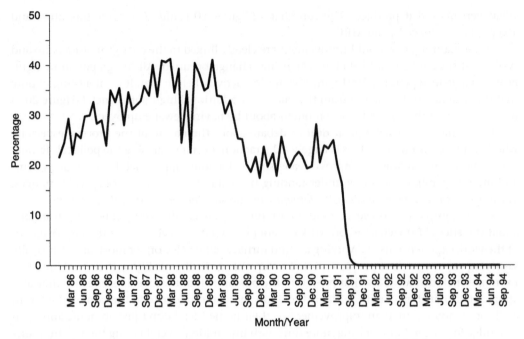

Figure 20.7   New Zealand Aluminium Smelters Overtime Hours Paid (%)

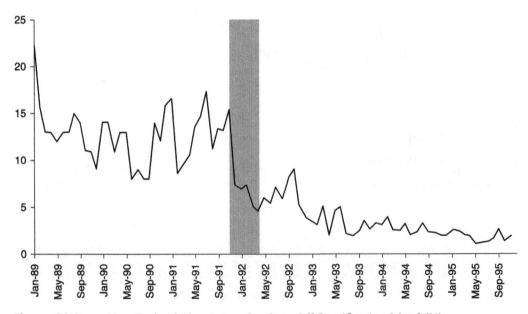

Figure 20.8   New Zealand Aluminium Smelters Off-Specification Metal (%)

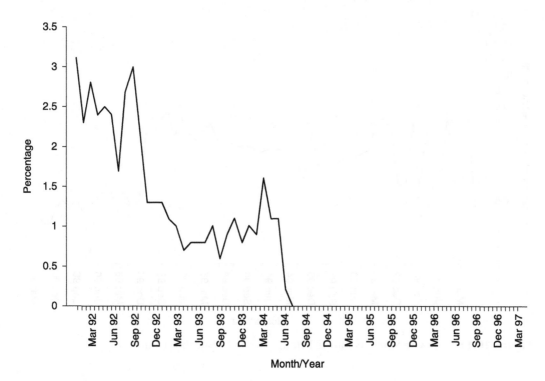

Figure 20.9   Comalco Aluminium (Bell Bay) Limited Overtime Hours Paid (%)

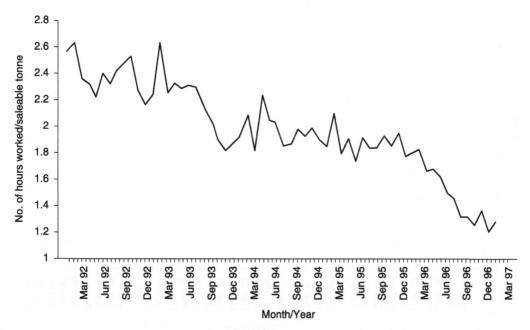

Figure 20.10   Comalco Aluminium (Bell Bay) Limited Metal Products – Hours Worked /
Saleable Tonne

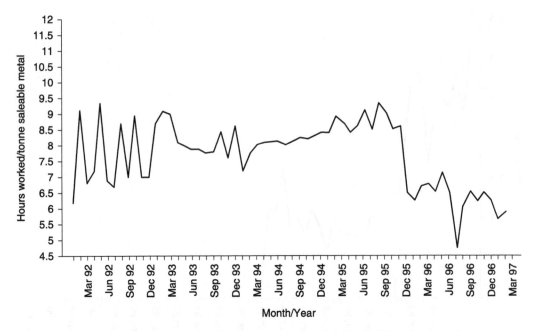

Figure 20.11   Boyne Smelters Limited Hours Worked / Saleable Tonne

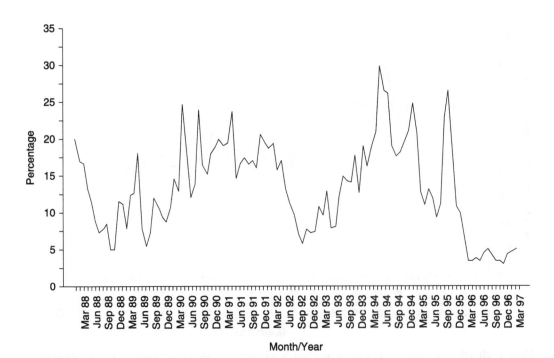

Figure 20.12   Boyne Smelters Limited Off-Specification Metal

The process was applied at the other two smelters with similar results, as shown in Figures 20.4 to 20.12.

Many of these run charts are not directly related to the 'people' systems. They are deliberately chosen to show the effect that changes in leadership and systems can have on operational technical processes.

The overall analysis of Comalco Smelters is summarised in the chart reproduced as Box 20.1, and which was prepared independently.

Hamersley Iron

A full account of this process is contained in a paper by Joel Barolsky (1994) of the Graduate School of Management, University of Melbourne.

The Western Australian iron ore industry was characterised by industrial disputes in the 1980s – see Figure 20.8, which documents the dramatic effect after the change processes were implemented.

In June 1991 Terry Palmer was appointed managing director of Hamersley's operations. He saw the need for change and articulated it as follows:

> The 1980s had been a period of 'winning back the farm'. We wanted to restore management's right to manage and, to a large extent, we were very successful in realising this goal. Through this process, however, we in some ways encouraged the development of a very directive management style; we reinforced the 'us and them' and basically gave the unions a reason to exist. It became apparent that we had gone about as far as we should down that path. If Hamersley wanted to realise its full potential and become a truly great company, management had to effect a dramatic change in the culture of the organisation. We had to bring everyone on board; playing for the same team and by the same rules; all working together. The planning process was started so as to articulate and document this new vision for the company and to develop a coherent strategy around it. Once we had something on paper that managers could talk to, that people could relate to and get excited about, then we could really start leading the change towards a culture of commitment, continuous improvement and shared goals and values.
>
> (Barolsky, 1994)

This was not simply a matter of a general statement. Palmer then embarked on a detailed programme of change. This was largely on three fronts: systems (especially safety and HR systems), capability and team leadership and membership. He and his team outlined key strategies:

- developing a 'customer-focused' culture;
- securing the company's resource base;
- restructuring the product mix;
- consolidating market leadership;
- improving the company's cost position;
- reorienting external affairs (Barolsky, 1994).

Joe Grimmond, who was at the time Hamersley's chief employee relations' consultant, explained that:

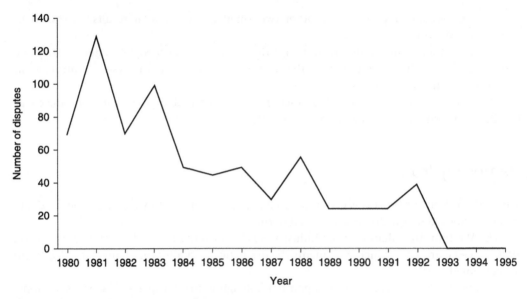

Figure 20.13   Pilbara Industrial Disputation

We recognised that many of these systems had been around for decades and were very much part of the Hamersley way of doing things. While we realised it would be difficult to fight against this momentum of the past, the senior management team had a strong resolve to succeed. This success wouldn't be measured by actual modifications to the systems themselves but rather by what behavioural change resulted from the changes to these systems.

The team identified several key systems that were in box B (authorised but counter-productive – see Chapter 10):

* seniority system of promotion;
* command and control task assignment;
* overtime system used as reward consequently encouraging inefficiency;
* pre-agreed leisure days off and personal days off, sick leave and stop work meetings;
* demarcation between unions and staff, for example, supervisors could not help in hands-on work;
* award pay increases on the basis of qualification not use of skill;
* active encouragement of new employees to join the union.

Palmer studied and learnt from the Comalco work, especially in New Zealand, and sent employees to the NZAS site. He started with key work around safety to build trust and implemented a new safety system. This initiative was led by managers in Level III roles and the general managers.

He then initiated the Working Together programme and, with Macdonald, co-ran courses for his team (roles at Level IV) and all people in Level III roles – thirteen courses in all. He used these to explain what he wanted to achieve and how he intended to achieve it. These courses (as mentioned in Chapter 18) covered all the topics of values, culture and mythologies; work complexity and capability; and the steps and traps of team leadership and membership. He and his team then reviewed the leadership roles and who was suitable.

Then the GMs in Level IV roles presented the plan of work strategy in person to all employees. What was specifically emphasised was the need to be world competitive and 100% reliable in supply, a target some thought was impossible. The use of the systems leadership theory in detail was complemented with business improvement projects including quality initiatives.

In June 1992 there was a major strike over refusal of an employee to join the union, which the company was no longer making compulsory. Despite the fact that enforced closed shop was illegal, the mythologies of the union leadership predicted that Palmer and the leadership at Hamersley Iron would give in. There was huge dissonance created when Palmer backed the individual's rights.

All the details of this strike are not covered here. However, the highly significant and symbolic battle to protect the right of people to work and to prevent harassment created many new mythologies – not least that the 'management' was prepared to be courageous and respectful of the law. The Australian Industrial Relations Commission ordered a return to work on 19 June backed by the prime minister of Australia and the federal minister of industrial relations. The strike continued. On 29 June, workers voted to return to work.

In early 1993, the company was restructured. The workforce reduction of almost 20% was unusual in that proportionally as many 'staff' roles went as roles covered by the 'award'. Voluntary separations were accepted by nearly all to whom they were offered. In fact a greater number left than was intended through the voluntary scheme.

This led to an opportunity to improve many systems, including a new recruitment system using input from shop floor team members. A fair treatment procedure was introduced and the Working Together course rolled out to all employees. Paul Piercy, a GM, commented:

> Using these courses to introduce team concepts also provided us a chance to emphasise to supervisors the importance of their role in the new Hamersley. It was also a chance to start engendering a management style that was more participative and attuned to the needs of team members. For the shop floor employees it was a way for us to communicate Hamersley's vision and strategies and to start building some trust and commitment to them. Most importantly, the courses were the beginning of creating more effective teams on the shopfloor.

(Barolsky, 1994)

Piercy and all the GM operations co-ran these courses as did leaders in Level III roles alongside Macdonald Associates' co-presenters.

Smaller symbolic changes were made, including no preferential parking for staff, and supervisors eating with their crews.

Eventually staff offers of employment were made at the end of 1993. By 1 January 1994, 89% had accepted. The results were similar to those at Comalco – production increased and costs fell (Figure 20.9).

In 1995, there was not as dramatic a change as was seen in the move to staff at the end of 1993 because the new systems had been introduced prior to this change. The staff employment was a consequence of change, not a cause. This demonstrates again that signing a piece of paper does not change behaviour, nor does simply leaving the union-negotiated employment conditions. It is the improved quality of leadership and the underlying work systems that provide real change.

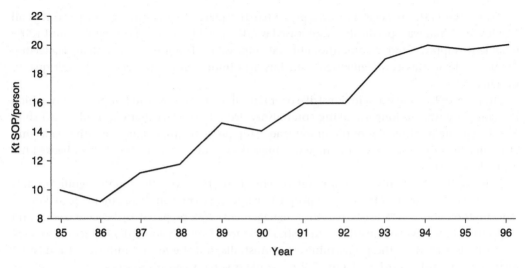

Figure 20.14   Hamersley Iron – Productivity

It was the detailed, hard work of the leadership applied in a thoughtful, disciplined way that led to the change. In turn the new culture provided a platform for other important changes in work practices, quantity, safety and cost reduction. This is detailed in Rio Tinto annual reports from 1994 onwards. These later initiatives were more effective because of the work done in 1992/1993, in the same manner that the systems leadership work was more effective because of the earlier work of restructuring of all CRA operations in the 1980s based on stratified systems theory.

The effect of the cultural change was highlighted by independent reports. In a March 1996 report in *Industrial Relations Magazine*, the following was written:

> *Without doubt, Hamersley Iron is the jewel in CRA's crown. In the six months to June 30, 1995, iron ore contributed $157.6 million to CRA's coffers. This was an 8% increase over the six months in 1994 and was due to increased sales tonnages and marginally higher prices.*
>
> *First half shipments were at a record 26.4 million tonnes – a 9.5% increase over the previous record of 24.1 million tonnes set in the first half of 1993. Total production for 1995 was 52.2 million tonnes and total shipment 54.8 million tonnes. For '95, Hamersley's iron ore production and total shipments were the highest on record, despite the fourth quarter being adversely affected by a cyclone. Shipments to China and Europe were at record levels ... the change in company performance has been nothing short of incredible. Productivity has jumped from an average 15,000 tonnes of ore railed per employee per annum to 24,000 in 1995. The labour force has fallen from 3,000 to 2,500 and labour costs have gone from $186 million to $166 million.*
>
> *Maintenance crews now work 12-hour shifts. There have been zero hours lost to industrial disputes and safety has improved markedly. For every million hours worked, there are now only seven injuries compared with 47 in the past.*
>
> (IRM, March 1996)

The changes were highly public and the subject of press and media attention. Channel 9 in Australia ran a Business Sunday report (on 26 November 1995) on the changes, where in an interview Paul Anderson explained that he was still a union member and stated: 'I have never had anybody even intimate that I had to give the union away … production is through the roof and that's great'.

At no time in either Comalco or Hamersley were people asked, required or told to give up their union membership as part of the deal. They did have to change behaviour, but the biggest change was the behaviour of the leadership. As Geoff Neil, the manager of the rail division, said, 'the ball is in our court now, they have given us their trust, we must not let them down'.

People were not bribed. For many there was not much financial gain, given that there was no overtime and the removal of leisure days off and personal days off. Absenteeism dropped dramatically and people had, for the first time, a guaranteed income. The changes included the opportunity to do different work; one GM's personal assistant trained as a truck driver and many were able to use capabilities they had not been allowed to under old systems.

Finally, the worth to Hamersley was demonstrated when a comparison was made between Hamersley Iron and a competitor organisation's operation. This is as close as like to like in industry and in fact the competitor's resource base is arguably slightly better than that of Hamersley Iron, as can be seen in Table 20.1.

Many commentators in Australia saw this as a CRA conspiracy. In fact, managing directors had significant discretion. In other businesses many of the concepts were introduced without an 'all staff' programme. Macdonald Associates have worked with the Rio Tinto, Anglesey Aluminium smelter in North Wales since 1993 where the leadership has implemented many new systems and gained improvements not only with a unionised workforce of operators and tradespeople – but also with a staff union!

Les Cupper, the CRA vice president of organisational effectiveness, explained the changes at Comalco and Hamersley in the context of the business as a whole:

A key reason is that in all of our industries we don't control the exchange rate (a 1 cent movement in the Australian dollar against the US Dollar means a 22 million change to the bottom line). So what we had to do is concentrate on things we have control over – the work environment.
(Way, *Business Review Weekly*, 31 January 1994, pp. 34–39)

Table 20.1 Comparison of Hamersley Iron and Comparable Iron Ore Company in Australia

	Hamersley Iron	**Comparable Iron Ore Company in Australia**
Tonnes railed (million tonnes)	65	65
Employees/contractors	2090	2485
Productivity (kilotonnes per eemployee)	31	26
		HI costs were 37% lower and return on assets nearly three times more than the comparable iron ore company. Independent, external industrial comparison.

The fear is that discipline can become dogma; that the purpose is lost in the process. This can happen in any initiative, be it organisational, implementing an IT strategy or merging companies. It is a concern that underlies the need for controls, audits and measures on any process. In these case studies our process and the companies output has probably been scrutinised more closely, at least in Australia, than any other. In the article 'The Art of War' in the *Sydney Morning Herald* (8 December 1997), Helen Trinca wrote:

> *By the time Carnegie left in 1986 his impact had been profound. By then, as J.T. Ludeke says in his book The Line in the Sand, Dr Ian Macdonald, a British consultant psychologist who had worked with Jaques at Brunel University in the United Kingdom, had begun working with CRA.*
>
> *He formed an alliance with Karl Stewart, the Managing Director of Comalco Smelting, developing training courses and preparing personnel strategies. Both men were crucial players in the ideas behind the push for contracts at operations in Bell Bay, Boyne Island and Weipa in the 1990s.*

While this was the case, the article also links these processes with earlier work of Jaques and Hilmer, a consultant for McKinsey's. All of this work is connected – as Cupper pointed out in the BRW. It is long-term, hard work and builds upon previous stages, just as new initiatives can build on this work further.

Rio Tinto is an example of a learning organisation. Many years ago Sir Roderick Carnegie expressed the view that gains would only become apparent when operators changed their behaviour. It was only when the systems work was integrated with the structural changes that such obvious changes could be expected and were found.

These case studies have both been from one corporation and a very particular one. This is not to imply that only mining or smelting industries can use these concepts. The breadth of organisations (see the case studies on the website) that have used systems leadership theory demonstrates this clearly. The case studies in the body of this book were chosen because:

- They had a very high public profile at the time.
- Data is available that is already publicly accepted as evidence in law.
- There were no other major changes occurring at the same time (for example, technological process change).
- The case studies come close to meeting the ideal process outlined at the beginning of Part 4.
- The leadership of the companies was fully involved during the process. (The leadership of these companies was actually developing the theory as part of the process.)

When we started working in Comalco and Hamersley, people would ask why theories developed in health and social services at Brunel University were relevant in mining; when we worked in the financial sector people asked us why are we using theories from mining.

Our work in other countries in similar industries is questioned: 'Why do we use 'Western' theories?' We hope to have demonstrated the general applicability of systems leadership theory. It is a theory about people in organised, purposeful activity – not 'just in mining', but in teaching, worshipping, healing, policing, learning, banking, running local councils, providing energy and many other activities. All are concerned with universal human values, culture, mythologies, teamwork and systems, symbols and leadership behaviour that influence all of our behaviour and our willingness to use our capability to the full.

Conclusion

The evidence above clearly demonstrates that Systems Leadership can and does make a significant difference and help to create a positive and productive organisation in any sector. As can be seen, if used in its entirety, it can make a huge difference. However, that does not mean that if you cannot adopt it in its totality it is not of help or it cannot make a difference. Other case studies on the website show how more limited use of Systems Leadership has still been very useful. Even just using it to understand why current practices are not working well can be extremely helpful.

We have been able to help take the unfair pressure from leaders when it is clear they are having to work with counter-productive systems or cannot remove people who are not capable of the work of the role. Just being able to say 'it's not your fault, you can't fix this now' can make a difference.

We have looked at how Systems Leadership can make a difference at an organisational level but we also recognise and enjoy the difference it can make at an individual level. Hearing people say such things as 'I really enjoy going to work now' or 'at least we are working as a team' or 'I now go home feeling I have achieved something' and one person said 'I am proud of my work and I look forward to the open day when I can show my children … I never felt that before in all the years I worked here' is testament to the positive effect these ideas can have for people.

We spend much of our lives at work; these ideas can make that experience enjoyable, challenging, creative, productive and even fun.

Conclusion

21 *Implementation: Discipline or Dogma?*

The word 'guru' always rings alarm bells. Any theory or approach will have its champions, supporters and exponents. Successful change in any field, even the most scientific and technical, needs passion and commitment. It requires an emotional commitment as well as a rational approach. This takes us back to Figure 21.1, the model we started with Figure 1.1.

But passion can become prejudice; debate can be replaced by dogma and what is essentially a set of propositions can become a set of beliefs. Many change processes are experienced or perceived as dogmatic with no opportunity or freedom to question the concepts upon which they seem to be founded or the process by which they are being applied. Principles are not a set of inflexible rules to be applied rigidly with no real opportunity for discussion. Ideas and concepts when poorly explained are experienced as being imposed by people who do not seem to understand what they are talking about. In these circumstances, irrespective of the formal authority relationship, the experience is the exercise of power.

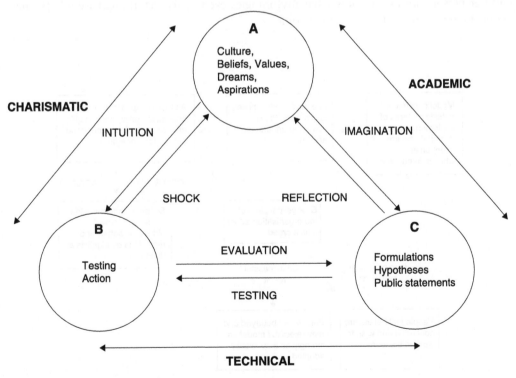

Figure 21.1   Human Decision-Making Model

Where ideas are imposed (or perceived to be imposed due to poor social process) without a full explanation, then two results are common. First, there is a polarisation of the subject group into 'believers' and 'sceptics' and second, subsequent debate and argument shifts from content to process and back again without distinction. We do recognise that in many groups there will be those, usually a small minority, who for their own reasons (mythologies) will not accept the conclusion of a carefully reasoned argument. If the social process and the argument itself are sound, this minority will be marginalised and their counter activity discounted by their fellow group members. In the event of general dissatisfaction, however, it is important to establish whether dissatisfaction with an outcome is due to content or process – or perhaps both. It is also possible to envisage excellent process, enabling the implementation of very poor content. This is often a criticism levelled at management consultants who have a great presentation style and a persuasive manner but no substantial or new ideas.

The model based on a dogmatic approach, Figure 21.2, depicts how the change process can degenerate into a power struggle between believers and sceptics.

It is often the case that the champions of change introduce a new but largely meaningless language, full of jargon, which replaces simple language with much longer phrases. So the 'future' becomes 'moving forward in time'. We 'create new space' (as in 'we need to confront the lack in the motivational space'), which seems to mean means 'people lack application to their work, or energy'.

If 'guru' rings alarm bells, 'disciples', 'acolytes' or 'believers' signal meltdown. We must not invent a new religion. People's beliefs are their own business; beliefs are not a part of a process that must allow real testing of results. As we have discussed, mythologies that people hold do make up part of their beliefs. In these discussions we have sought to be clear that another person can never know what mythologies each of us has, though we all speculate about them as part of life with other people.

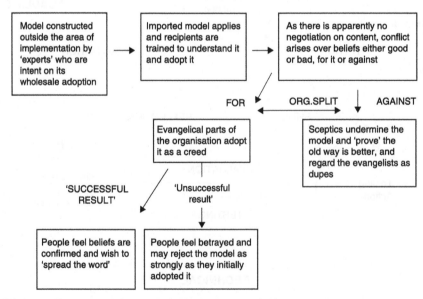

Figure 21.2   Dogmatic Approach to Organisational Change

We make it clear that mythologies cannot be changed, though we do advocate the provision of opportunities for people to form new mythologies. We recommend that leaders seek to develop an understanding of the mythologies held by those whom they lead. We also recommend strongly the measurement of results. We also argue for a disciplined approach to a change programme as that is essential for success. People are not accustomed to a disciplined application of social process and language, so we understand that it can appear, if not done well, to be dogmatic.

As we said earlier in our discussion of social and scientific meaning, people find it hard work to be clear about definitions and meaning. Common language usage includes phrases that go in and out of fashion such as 'like' as in 'it was like, really cool', or 'I was, like sacked'. Well, were you sacked or not? When it comes to our life's work, however, apparently mundane it may appear to others, small, symbolic behaviours matter significantly. 'Yeah, this is sort of like your pay' is not acceptable unless it is my pay, properly calculated.

Being disciplined and precise is not the same as authoritarian. Being clear is not the same as pedantic. Those who are vague have an interesting time in the witness box of a court. Any process must be reviewed with discipline, as should the content.

Reviewing content and process

In reviewing the outcomes of implementation, it is critical to evaluate the process of implementation in detail. If we are to ask, as we should, whether the concepts inherent in the principles that were applied are valid (in other words, the content), we cannot test this just by examining outcomes (the bottom line). The outcomes depend upon how well, or not well, the content was applied (the process). It is in any assessment necessary to examine, in the cases of both failure and success, how projects were carried out. If there is no base theory, only a belief system or set of slogans with no clearly articulated content or process, then this becomes an impossible task. The theory must actually predict failure as well as success. Thus, if people are not capable of carrying out the work of the role, the structure should not work; that is, it should not produce more cost-effective results. If the leadership behaviour does not demonstrate trust, honesty, love, fairness, courage or respect for dignity, then people will not work to their potential, even though these words have been taught on a course. If tasks are not discussed and assigned clearly, we should not expect work to be carried out effectively. Therefore, in considering the effectiveness of the ideas, we must examine also the effectiveness of their implementation. People will find it difficult to assess another's performance fairly if they have received a poor or no assessment themselves. Thus, any evaluation must examine the rigour, of lack of rigour, in implementation. The analysis of both content and process, independent of one another, is required to deliver a clearer comparison of outcomes.

Being precise about the implementation process is not a matter of dogma; it is essential for fair evaluation. Therefore, in discussing whether these ideas are or have been of worth, it is important to evaluate the process. It may be found that the failure is quite predictable; that is, it supports the theory, not falsifies it. Falsification occurs where conditions have not been met and yet the outcome is positive. For example, if increases in productivity have occurred and been sustained in situations of low feedback, random promotion, vague task assignment, low trust and lack of capability in role. This would suggest no link between a particular process and outcome. The 'link' is the theory or content.

Nothing in the discussion above should be taken as proof that there is only one theory or explanation. Many companies have been highly successful without explicitly adopting stratified systems theory or systems leadership theory. However, these theories are attempts to articulate good practice, and, like any valid set of related concepts, have to meet the criterion of internal consistency. We suggest strongly that a careful examination of highly successful organisations would show the application of many of the concepts of Systems Leadership in practice without any need for them to be recognised and articulated.

Theory is not a matter of welding bits of one concept to another. For example, the fact that a car runs on petrol does not mean the driver is dogmatically or ideologically opposed to diesel, nor is it reasonable to assume that, because one vehicle design can run on diesel, all can. It is not a matter of being pragmatic, of just trying it to see by using diesel because there is no petrol. The results are predictable.

It is of absolute importance to appreciate the work of someone. The existence of a violin does not imply that anyone can use it. The fact that I cannot pick up a violin and play Tchaikovsky's violin concerto does not invalidate the instrument or prove that it doesn't work. It depends upon training, practice and undoubtedly some natural talent. The process is similar to leadership: some can play by ear, others only after applying effort and practice – and a few are, sadly, tone deaf to social process. However, we must also consider the purpose and what standard is required. We do not expect the same standard of musical ability from a school concert orchestra as we do from a professional national symphony orchestra. We do not require the same precision of language in social discussion as we do in a scientific debate. In friendships we do not require the same precise outcome as we expect from a product or service. We do not send the steak back at a friend's dinner party when we might send the same steak back at a restaurant. The purpose of a business relationship is to produce a required output, often with very rigorous criteria of quality. Thus, in terms of language, what in one setting may be pedantic is essential precision in another.

In some instances it may be possible to have precise content and process but it may be too costly for our purposes. It may be possible to guarantee a particular outcome but the technical equipment and training required may be beyond our means or simply not cost-effective. These are not questions of whether or not precision has worth per se, but merely a comparison of options. The point is that in comparing options we still need to have clear and common criteria of how to assess content and process in order to make a fair comparison. If another option is proposed, what specific advantages does it have? Does it explain in terms of content and process why these advantages should be expected? Is it internally consistent? What are the comparative data? What is the evidence from elsewhere?

Conclusion

Success with implementation is dependent upon the clear articulation of principles, content and their application through good process. This throws them open to thought, logical analysis, argument and test in practice. They are not a belief system, nor are they dogma. They are not a fad. Fads are merely the replacement of one magic with another. Far from encouraging mystical processes, social science should be in the business of demystifying processes. Power – as opposed to authority – often rests on mysticism because, when dependent on power, the process needs to be kept in the inner circle, hidden from challenge so the results can be maintained through dependency and fear. This does not encourage people willingly to give of their best.

Of course, 'theory' is not sacrosanct. Evidence for or against must be based not only on outcome data but also on an analysis of the process of implementation and a comparison of the implementation processes in relation to outcome. Further, it is important that any alternatives are also examined with equal rigour and evidence sought for their effectiveness, not only in apparent input–output measures, but in the predictive power of their articulated processes. In essence we must all be interested not only in what is done, but how it is done and why the result was achieved.

We are aware that we have raised the bar. We have seen new models adopted as they come into fashion, assuming that other models have an automatic 'sell-by' date. We have invited disciplined critique but we also demand the same analysis of other approaches. When people discuss our 'failures', we need to know if it was a failure of theory or an unproductive business outcome generated through poor process. The former is much more important. If we have a success, was it because of the concepts or despite them? We will discuss this further in Chapter 23.

In short, we ask you not to believe anything without putting it to the test. Test it in terms of internal consistency and predictive ability, and test it with rigour and discipline. Test any other approaches in the same way – that is after all, only fair!

22 *Who is there to Guard the Guards? Essentials of a Positive Organisation*

Checks and Balances

We can design and implement structures, systems and cultures and guide leadership behaviour, but nothing absolutely guarantees that there will not be mistakes. Central to encouraging people to express their capability is the existence of safeguards that operate to correct and redress error or arbitrary judgement. If we proscribe the judgement of people, we lose one of the major advantages of human organisation: human judgement. In attempting to proscribe judgement, we create authorised, counter-productive systems and behaviour that stifles discretion and creativity. There must, however, be checks and balances.

These checks and balances can be provided in many different ways. First, there is the law. Paradoxically, in Western industrialised society, the union movement has been a victim of its own success. Many core, essential issues fought for over many years by the union movement are now actually part of the law. Laws about health and safety, equal opportunity, minimum pay and working conditions have improved workers' lives dramatically in the last century. This does not make unions redundant but means their focus must change if they are to remain relevant. The recent cases concerning 'zero hour contracts' and questionable 'self-employment' are continuing evidence of the need for unions.

The right to belong to a union must remain a fundamental right as a safeguard for employees if they choose to exercise it. Indeed, we regard the freedom to engage in unionised activity as an essential component of a free society and the level of that activity within an organisation as a measure of the trust that employees have in the leadership of the organisation. It is a good indicator of where the employees place leadership behaviour, symbols and the systems of the organisation on the values continua. The more activity and support for a union, in general terms, the more mistrust there is in the leadership and the state of the organisational structure, symbols and systems. The source of the mythologies supporting this behaviour may lie in past leadership behaviour, but an unhelpful mythology may live on if sources of the mythology are not addressed by the current leadership.

We do not regard it inherently sound or advisable that an organisation rely upon third party intervention, actual or threatened, in order that it run well. It does rely upon internal systems that monitor the use of managerial judgement. It is possible to implement systems in such a way that people choose to work in an employment relationship unmediated by a third party. In evidence to the Australian Industrial Relations Commission, Macdonald's statement refers to the key elements of the relationship that have been explained in this book, viz:

> *The essential component of a staff relationship is individual judgement. That is, a person enters a working relationship where he or she is judged on the basis of his or her personal work*

contribution. This judgement is made by a manager. This relationship carries particular accountabilities for the manager and is personally very significant.

Thus, this is a relationship where another individual is accorded the authority (within the law and the policy of the company) to make judgements about another person's work performance and act on those judgements. These acts include a range of forms of recognition from individual feedback in words to salary changes. Work performance has a very specific meaning in this context. It is the pathway that a person builds in order to complete his or her tasks. It is the decision making along the way to achieving a goal. Measuring this by reference only to outputs is to miss what is essentially human, namely, the 'how' of achievement, or as will be described later, the equivalent of a person's signature. Thus work performance is different for each one of us even if our outputs appear the same. If the building of this pathway is ignored by the manager, the person will look elsewhere for recognition.

A staff relationship is central to a meritocracy. A meritocracy is based upon the assumption that any role in a company is filled by the person most capable of doing the work. It is commonly referred to but not very often enacted in its full sense, that is, in relation to all roles. It is the staff relationship in the context of a meritocracy which can allow younger people or new employees to be promoted ahead of longer serving colleagues, or people in apparently the same role to receive different amounts of pay because of judged differences in work performance in that role.

The continuation of a productive staff relationship is dependent on the quality of those judgements. The credibility of a meritocracy and staff relationships rests upon the demonstration of fairness by the manager in these judgements. And in addition, that promotion is based on demonstrated ability not favouritism or nepotism, and that discipline is based on actual negative behaviour not merely victimisation of a person who asks difficult questions.

Given that we are human, it is reasonable to suggest that sometimes mistakes will be made, so it is also essential that there is an avenue of appeal. This avenue must be internal to demonstrate that the company can be fair and just, even if individual managers at times are not. This does not preclude access to the law or external tribunals, but demonstrates that the company does not require that a person appeals outside of the company if they have a concern.

Thus, the staff relationship is founded four-square on trust. Trust in the leadership of the company and its ability to act fairly and with courage. The fear or anxiety aroused by such relationships is that this trust might be betrayed or is dependent on the goodwill or fairness of a particular manager/leader. Thus a person may be quite happy to enter into that relationship with the current manager, but is very concerned as to what might happen when he, or she leaves. In effect the person does not trust the company to replace the manager effectively.

Therefore, this relationship must be underpinned by well designed 'people' systems such as recruitment, selection, task setting and review, performance appraisal, salary review, career assessment, promotions and fair treatment systems. This range of systems must be open and public. It is important to note that such systems do not make the decisions but are the boundaries or limits within which decisions are made and, if necessary, appealed. These systems, and how they are implemented, have a fundamental importance in terms of their effect on employees' feelings of trust and fairness. If a person chooses to enter a staff relationship that person is making a statement of trust. People will make this decision on the basis of:

a.   The personal behaviour of leaders/managers;

b.   The quality of the people systems in operation. Money alone does not buy trust.

Essentially if there is a relationship where one person has the authority to judge another whether that be at work or in any relationship, there is a universal concern as to what reviews, limits, appeals are there to that judgement. One of the features of democratic societies is the separation of the executive and legislature from the judiciary and further the opportunity of appeal within the judiciary. In contrast totalitarian states are characterised by a lack of distinction between the executive and judiciary and rarely offer the opportunity for appeal.

So we could caricature the organisation, especially large multinationals, as having so much more power (and authority) than the individual (employee) so as to be a totalitarian 'judge, jury and executioner'. Indeed, many third parties including trade unions and pressure groups would argue this way.

In our model there are explicit principles and safeguards. As mentioned previously, the controls on executive power are to be found inside the organisation in various forms:

1. There is the role of the M+1. This not only includes the opportunity for access from the person in a reporting role one removed but an active review of the managerial judgements of the intermediate manager.

2. There are also the policies of the company.

3. There are proper and effective 'people systems', as mentioned above, which should mitigate against capricious and arbitrary managerial judgement and decisions. That is a person's health and well-being should not be dependent on the character of any particular manager. Whilst some people will inevitably relate better or personally prefer one manager to another, this should not extend to an option of basic fair and reasonable treatment.

4. In addition as has also been discussed, every organisation should implement a fair treat-ment system which by its nature should expose decisions and behaviour to a wider exam-ination and opportunity for appeal.

5. In addition it must be remembered that organisations exist within the context of the law. They are not free to outline policies and design systems which do not take into account the law of the land. What constitutes unfair dismissal is not solely for the organisation to determine, and the same applies to equal opportunities, racial or sexual discrimination.

Unions

Given all of this, is there a place for unions? If all these safeguards are in place, why would anyone need the protection of an outside organisation? The answer to these questions is quite simple: if the person feels the need for this extra safeguard it is their right to have it and not for anyone else to refuse it. A further feature of open, democratic societies is the right of association. People should be free to form unions and be members if they want to. Again it is a feature of totalitarian regimes that trade unions are banned or severely restricted in their operation ...

... Are the unions still needed? The answer depends upon the members and potential members. If they think so then unions are needed. The key element is coercive power. If people are not free *to join or leave, the whole picture is distorted. The drop in the membership of unions over the last 20–30 years has been influenced by union leadership and counter-productive systems such as 'closed shop', 'compulsory deduction of union dues' and a distancing of the leadership, in terms of full time officials, from the membership. In this way the union organisation and its effectiveness is no different from any other organisation we have discussed. Its continuance has been and will be significantly influenced by its structure, the quality of its leadership and the design and implementation of its systems. It is consequently as difficult to generalise about union organisations as it is with commercial organisations. We have worked in many organisations with active unions both well run and not so well run. We have also worked in situations where employees have either not felt the need for third party representation or have chosen to reject it. Whatever the situation, the key issue is that employees have the right to choose and it is recognised that unions have a potentially significant contribution to make in society. Thus, in a democratic society union membership is and should be another control operated according to the free choice of organisational members and not properly subject to external imposition or denial.*

(Macdonald, 1995)

Given all these safeguards, is this now enough? Our answer would be no, not quite. It was argued earlier (Chapter 10) that the organisation as a social entity also expresses an ethic. That is, through its policies and the work of the board, whether intentionally or not, it creates a social environment which encourages certain behaviours and discourages others. We would argue that as part of that ethic and as a matter of policy there should be an 'employment charter', which states the mutual expectations of the leadership and membership of the organisation.

This is consistent with the continuing need for clarity in other areas such as role descriptions, task assignments, and work performance review and authority. Clarity of expectation is a significant constraint on the use of power since most power is exercised in the context of ambiguity. When a situation is ambiguous it offers the opportunity for exploitation. For example, if you are stopped by the police while driving your car, is there a clear understanding of authority and rights? Are the parties clear about under what circumstances you can be legitimately stopped? What are you required to do and what can you refuse to do?

The Employment Charter

We spend a significant part of our lives in organisations. If we are not clear about expectations and what the boundaries are with regard to authority, then relationships are open to abuse and exploitation. Throughout this book we have argued for clarity in these areas. The final piece is a sample charter that describes what is expected (see Box 22.1).

Box 22.2 shows an example. It may be varied according to the nature of the business but the purpose remains constant.

Box 22.1   Charter Statement Purpose

'To clarify the conditions which each member of the organisation is authorised and entitled to expect so that he or she may experience a constructive, productive and safe environment which encourages people to work to their potential.'

Box 22.2 Employment Charter

For the organisation to achieve its objectives, improve and grow it depends upon the commitment of all employees to give their best. If they are to do so, there are mutual obligations that need to be met and, if in place, should result in mutual benefit. These are described below in the employment charter and explained in the attached statement of principles.

The leadership of the organisation will endeavour to provide for all employees:

- A safe and healthy work environment, free from harassment and discrimination in terms of race, ethnicity, gender or religious belief.
- Behaviour towards all employees based on the core values of honesty, trust, fairness, love, dignity and courage consistent with the culture of the organisation.
- Work that is challenging and appropriate to the capabilities of individuals.

This means that all employees should have:

- Clear role descriptions and work authorities.
- Clear expectation of what is required from each person by setting context, purpose, the quality and quantity of output, the provision of necessary resources and the advice of a desired completion time.
- Feedback and appropriate recognition for work done without favouritism or arbitrary decisions.
- Information about and opportunities for development.

This involves the design and implementation of systems that treat people fairly, specifically:

- Reward and recognition based on the quality of performance at work, disregarding all other factors not related to the work done.
- Promotion based on merit with fair and open opportunity.
- An open authorised and recognised opportunity to appeal internally against any behaviour and/or decision that is perceived to be unfair.

In so far as the leadership endeavours to provide such an environment employees are expected to:

- behave safely and not harass others or act in an unfair or negatively discriminatory way;
- behave towards each other based on the core values of honesty, trust, fairness, dignity, love and courage consistent with the culture of the organisation;
- respond to challenges using their capabilities to the full.

This means that employees should:

- seek to clarify expectations in role and tasks;
- ask for feedback and recognition;
- constructively give feedback to leaders;
- offer ideas for improvement;
- co-operate with other employees;
- seek information with regard to both the business and opportunities for development.

This involves working with and offering ideas for the improvement of systems by:

- using the process (steps) of team leadership and membership;
- working within systems according to their intent;
- using discretion productively;
- using the internal systems to appeal against any perceived unfair treatment;
- contributing to performance review and career assessment by reflecting upon own performance and aspirations;
- accepting that if there is a continuing mismatch between the demonstrated behaviour of the person and the behaviour required by the organisation to meet its purpose the individual will be required to leave the organisation.

The principles upon which this charter is based are founded on some basic assumptions:

- That people are essentially creative and constructive; that they want to work and achieve results.
- That the creation of a productive relationship cannot be coerced but is experienced as a free choice.
- That productive working relationships are critical to a person's sense of self-worth and identity.
- That there must be a demonstrable linkage between intention, action and results whether they are positive or negative.
- That people have a right to work in an environment that is safe and free from harassment and negative discrimination.

Foundations for This Charter

MERITOCRACY

This first principle is that people are assigned to roles on the basis of merit, whether entering an organisation or moving within it. Appointments are made on the basis of the judgement made about suitability of the person to carry out the work of the role, that is, their capability in terms of knowledge, skills (both technical and social), mental processing ability and application. This is in contrast to other systems such as seniority, nepotism or favouritism.

CLARITY OF EXPECTATIONS

The second is that people understand clearly both what they are expected to do and what authorities they have to carry out the work. The work and authority to do it must balance. It is unfair to attempt to hold someone accountable for work when they do not have the authority, which includes resources, to carry it out. Each task must be properly assigned so that the context and purpose, the resources available to achieve a specified output in terms of quality and quantity and a time to completion are all clearly communicated and understood.

FAIRNESS OF JUDGEMENT

Thirdly, people should receive timely feedback and assessment of their work performance. This, in turn, should be demonstrably linked to reward or pay. Such judgements should not simply concentrate on outcome but also the process by which the outcome was achieved (successful or not). The way in which a person approaches work, solves the problems inherent to it, and the complexity of the decisions necessary to achieve an outcome, is an essentially human process which must be central to any understanding and consequential judgement of work performance.

APPEALS

Since work performance is judged by human beings, mistakes may be made. Mistakes are not avoided by ever more specific and detailed measures and constraints on decision-making, which are time consuming and eventually still rest on someone's judgement. Rather, the person whose work is being reviewed must have the opportunity to question such judgement within the organisation and have that appeal heard by someone other than the person who has made the original judgement. The employee should not believe that they need to take matters outside the organisation in order to get a fair hearing, although they may exercise their right to do so.

CHALLENGING WORK

Work that is assigned should be sufficiently challenging to engage fully the mental processing ability of the employee and to provide him or her with the opportunity to use and expand skills and knowledge. While every role has tasks that are routine, the work content of a role should not result in boredom and alienation, nor should it be demanding to the point that it causes anxiety and stress because of its difficulty.

For an employee whose capability is developing rapidly, the work of the role needs to be chosen to promote that development. The absolutely essential requirement of all task assignment is that it does not require work behaviour that is unsafe.

DEVELOPMENT

There should be opportunities for an employee to develop their skills and knowledge as a result of performing assigned work. This may require coaching and training or the provision of opportunities in other roles, but does not imply the necessity of promotion to another level.

SYSTEMS

All of the above require the proper design, implementation and operation of 'people' systems. This is not an easy matter and such systems need to include in their operation the means of system improvement as a result of operational experience and data. Such systems include the structural design of the organisation in terms of levels of work and role descriptions, recruitment, selection, task setting and review, performance appraisal, removal from role, salary review, career assessment, promotion and fair treatment systems. These systems, in the way they are designed and implemented, are fundamentally important in terms of their effect on employees' behaviour and their concurrent judgements about the placement of the systems on the values continua. Whilst information about individuals must be confidential, these systems must be transparent.

BEHAVIOUR

Day-to-day leadership behaviour is also of fundamental importance in whether an employee is likely to give his or her best. The way a person perceives themselves to be treated in relation to the core values, honesty, trust, fairness, dignity, love and courage will profoundly affect their own behaviour. Of critical importance is the behaviour of those in leadership roles who by demonstration create a positive and productive culture and set the standards of how employees' contributions are assessed and given appropriate recognition.

THIRD PARTIES

If a productive work relationship founded on mutual trust and respect for human dignity is achieved, there should not be a need for constant reference to third parties outside the organisation. Third parties include lawyers, union officials and tribunals. An organisation cannot and should not, however, compromise, or appear to compromise, in any way the legal rights of an employee to have access to such third parties. It is a measure of trust in an organisation how far employees feel the need to actually engage third parties on their behalf. The attempt to build a high-trust organisation where people feel free to express their potential is no more anti-union or anti-lawyer than a community health programme is anti- doctor or crime prevention is anti-police. In this way it can be analogous to the felt need for insurance. If people feel insecure or in a dangerous situation, they are more likely to take out significant insurance policies than when they experience a safe environment.

The preparedness of people to give of their best and feel free to work to their potential depends on being in a particular environment. It is an environment where mutual trust and respect for human dignity are the behaviours demonstrated because of good leadership and systems.

Thus, we recommend such a charter as the final piece in the jigsaw. We have said that systems run deeper than individual behaviour because the systems operate continuously; they are the organisation's behaviour, the analogue of leadership behaviour. Systems are a legacy, but left without proper control and audit can atrophy and become counter-productive over time. A high mutual trust organisation will not automatically continue to be so. The charter is an overall reminder of the nature and conditions for a highly productive high mutual trust relationship.

We have been part of the process of building positive organisations in different countries and different sectors. Central to the issue of building a positive organisation is its maintenance over time. Just as systems, symbols and behaviour are used to build the positive organisation they are also potentially part of its dismantling and eventual destruction.

The maintenance of a positive organisation is absolutely dependent upon any changes to the core systems, symbols and leadership behaviour of the organisation being authorised at a level where the capability necessary for the task is available. We recognise this is not a guarantee of sound decision-making if the necessary capability to do the work of system, symbol or behaviour redesign is not in place, because it is not unknown for people to be promoted beyond the limit of their capability. We have seen unfortunate examples of good work undone because these principles are not understood or have been forgotten. We have found many instances of changes being made to systems, symbols and behaviour at relatively low levels and or by people without the capability needed to perform the analysis and synthesis necessary to have the change designed deliberately to improve the organisation. We return to the work of a leader: to create improve and sustain over time.

Thus who is there to guard the guards? We have identified:

- capable people appointed in the first place;
- clarity of role expectation;
- excellent system documentation;
- manager-once-removed (M+1) review;
- controls and audits on all systems;
- fair treatment system;
- an employment charter.

All of this is set in the context of democratic freedoms and legal rights, including the freedom to belong, or not belong, to a union.

23 *SLT and Other Approaches: A Summary*

Throughout this book we have demonstrated how Systems Leadership Theory (SLT), and the derived models and tools, can be applied to a wide range of different organisations: community groups, not-for-profits, public sector organisations and commercial businesses. We should note, though, that it is rare nowadays to encounter a situation where SLT is being introduced into an organisation that is not already implementing, or planning to implement, other organisational change programmes. It is important, therefore, to understand the relationship between SLT and these other approaches. Where implementation is disconnected, people are understandably confused as to how and if these approaches are complementary.

Typically, organisations will implement a change programme for one or more reasons; such as to secure cost reductions, performance improvement, customer satisfaction. Our experience, however, is that these programmes tend to focus heavily on one specific area of work – for example, redesigning a system, or restructuring, or culture change, rather than providing an integrated and comprehensive approach to creating and sustaining change integrated across the organisation. Although the operational changes may be specified in some detail, the impact on the people concerned, and their behaviour, is often underestimated or misunderstood. Since the required improvements will inevitably depend on people changing their behaviour, it is concerning that few initiatives are underpinned by a sound theoretical understanding of social process and human behaviour. A change programme may describe, in some detail, **what** behaviours are required, but it is rare to find an explanation of **why** or how behaviours will actually change.

We consider that SLT can strengthen any implementation by providing an overarching framework which is based on a sound theoretical understanding of human behaviour. This enables an accurate diagnosis to be made of relevant past and current organisational issues. It also provides the opportunity to predict how current behaviours might change in response to changes in organisational strategies, structures, systems, and new leadership behaviours.

We, like others, have noted that this field of organisational effectiveness and design is influenced by current fashion. One year 'leadership' is the answer, the next 'teamwork', the next 'collaboration', the next (and currently) 'innovation'. It is attractive to think that one approach will 'fix the problem'. We are not saying that these ideas have no merit. Clearly all organisations need leadership and innovation, we cannot work together without teamwork and collaboration. However, what these terms actually mean can vary significantly. What actual behaviour is required can be very vague or interpreted in many different, even contrary, ways. Whether such behaviour is encouraged or discouraged by the organisation's structure and systems may not be understood or even analysed.

However, we do need to examine these approaches and consider how and if they are complementary to Systems leadership. In general terms we have found that 'Lean' manufacturing in its various guises; business process re-engineering, Six Sigma and so on can benefit significantly from being integrated with SL. This is because our approach offers a deeper understanding of why people behave as they do and predicts responses to systems changes especially in the technical and commercial domains.

As we have mentioned there is a website associated with this book (ref). We have posted a paper largely written by a colleague Richard Joss with a section by another colleague David Dadswell that examines Systems Leadership in relation to:

a. the related fields of systems and system leadership;
b. Lean Manufacturing including a case study;
c. Innovation;
d. Agile, Scrum and other similar approaches;
e. Big Data.

We are grateful to our colleagues for this work which could easily form a book in itself.

No one has a monopoly on the best way to organise and manage the myriad of institutions that make up advanced industrial and post-industrial societies. Because our work has been applied in businesses, social service agencies, hospitals, city governments, national governments, armies, churches, public utilities and other unique organisations, we find a quote from Drucker particularly apt 'The function of management in a church is to make the church more churchlike, not more businesslike' (Byrne, 2005).

We of course acknowledge that there are many other approaches being used to understand and improve organisations. However, we have argued that many of these approaches concentrate on only a part of the organisation. We would like to say that if anyone is considering any approach they might start off with a few questions (clearly related to the system design questions):

1. Are you clear about your purpose?
2. Why have you chosen this approach? How does it relate to others?
3. Does the approach clearly explain why it should or should not work?
4. Is it based on sound theory? Is it predictive?
5. Where is the evidence?
6. How does it fit with the current systems and structures and what might need to be changed?
7. Do you have the capability and determination to implement?

Many approaches are fads and/or rebadged techniques that are implemented because of 'best practice'; which may mean everyone else is doing this so I suppose we should. Or perhaps it is sold as the silver bullet. We appreciate that creating, sustaining and improving an organisation is hard work. There is no way round that. We would argue it is very much worthwhile spending the time at the beginning working out the desired outcome(s) and why any approach might be expected to deliver these. That is the work of the leadership and we have found that SLT can not only help in that process but also help to understand what other approaches may or may not be complementary.

Conclusion: The Benefit of Foresight

This book is primarily concerned with how people come together to achieve a productive purpose. That can only happen when Productive Social Cohesion can be sustained. Our survival as a species has always depended upon our ability to form and sustain social relationships and build organisations. People have a deep need to be creative and to belong. By creating positive organisations we can fulfil these needs and build a worthwhile society. We spend so much of our lives in organisations of one sort or another. Our lives are hugely impacted by the extent to which such organisations encourage or discourage our creativity. Indeed our mental health is heavily influenced by our experiences of working in organisations. Positive organisations do not happen by chance. In this book we have identified different types of social organisation with different purposes that require different structures and systems if they are to achieve their purposes and support their members and those who interact with them. We have identified sound, general principles of behaviour. We have tried to outline the work necessary to create such organisations and to give examples of these principles in action. We have argued that although we expect to approach the Technical and Commercial Domains with rigour we are often much more cavalier with the Social Domain. It is as if it is all just 'common sense' or should just happen. However, it is hard work to create positive organisations. We are often tempted by the magic of the latest best-selling book revealing the few, simple secrets to guaranteed success. However, understanding the concepts of Systems Leadership, applying them with discipline (not dogma) and creativity, and sustaining and modifying them over time requires persistence and consistency. We have observed and admired what good leaders and team members do and tried to distil the essence of productive, value-based relationships.

We do not claim to be totally original. Clearly we have been in influenced by Jaques in particular, but also by numerous others. We do not believe that creativity is an individual activity. Ideas and efforts are the products of social relationships, which is why we are sceptical of 'gurus'. In the final analysis people are not creative because of a contract, a job title or even pay; we are not, primarily, externally motivated. We believe people are inherently creative, energetic and positive – just observe small children. However, we also have a perverse way, from childhood, of inhibiting, stultifying and depressing that creativity by poor organisational design, inappropriate leadership, capability and the use of power to name but a few.

We have argued that a significant amount of material in the area of organisational behaviour is based on fads and fashion. It is often purely descriptive and is not based on sound theory or propositions that can be tested.

When organisations fail, often spectacularly (for example, Banks in 2008), people will claim how this was only understandable with 'the benefit of hindsight'. We disagree.

By using Systems Leadership to understand how the whole organisation works and interacts with its environment we can make confident predictions of the likely outcomes. Systems

Leadership gives you 'the benefit of foresight'. We can predict what will happen when an unclear structure creates confusion; roles are filled with people unable to do the work; systems are poorly designed and consequently drive counter-productive behaviour and create negative mythologies. We can predict the effects of lack of clarity around work, poor leadership and confusion around teamwork. That is because Systems Leadership is built upon sound theory, tested principles of behaviour and implementation in many companies, cultures and countries around the world. We have included case studies in the book but also refer to cases on the related website. In summary we do not simply say WHAT should be done; 'build trust', 'appoint good leaders', 'innovate' or 'empower' or 'collaborate', 'deal with complexity' but we actually write about HOW to do that. We simply ask that other approaches be critiqued in the same way.

We have offered the principles and practices in this book to help build social organisations that encourage the creative expression of capability. We have had the privilege of working with people who have tried to do just that and if we, through this book, have contributed to that most worthwhile of endeavours; to help build positive organisations and contribute to a just society then we have turned our intention into reality. As for all work, it is for you to judge.

Glossary

Accountability: A component of a work relationship between two people wherein one accepts the requirement to provide an account to the other of the following three questions relating to work.

What did you do?
How did you do it?
Why did you do it that way?

The most common application of the concept of accountability is that which applies as a function of a contract of employment within an organisation and though in our experience this requirement to accept accountability is rarely articulated clearly in the contract; it should be. An effective accountability discussion includes a discussion of the three questions above including how and why the person used particular processes to turn inputs into required outputs.

Accountability is *not* a collective noun for tasks, as in ' your accountabilities are ...'. Too often this is used in employment, contracts and in role descriptions, which confuses work and accountability. A role may describe work but we are still to discover if the person is actually held to account for that work.

Accountability as a concept applying within coherent social groups is brought to the fore for society in general by the process of the courts wherein people in the witness box are required to answer, in public, questions as to what, how and why something was, or was not, done and judgement is passed as an outcome of this process.

Application: The effort, attention and energy that a person puts into applying the other elements of capability to their work (see Kolbe, 1990).

Association: People coming together for a purpose. The purpose is either agreed tacitly or expressed in a written document (Brown, 1971: 48).

Authority: 'The right, given by constitution, law, role description or mutual agreement for one person to require another person to act in a prescribed way (specified in the document or agreement). The likelihood of exercising authority effectively will usually depend upon good Social Process Skills'.

The acceptance of the exercise of authority within a work organisation is a function of the contract of employment.

Is it essential that there is a clear understanding of the difference between authority and power (see below) and that authority is not a one-way process. In a correctly functioning organisation, for example, a manager has the authority to assign tasks to a direct report and the direct report has the authority to require a task performance review by the manager.

Authority and Power: Person A has authority or power in relation to person B when person A is able to have person B behave as A directs.

If person B does not so behave neither authority nor power applies.

Authority applies within the boundary and constraints of the law, policy and rules of the organisation and those of accepted social custom and practice.

Power breaches one or more of these constraints to authority.

Clarity of understanding of the constraints to authority and its correct distribution to the roles within an organisation is essential for speed of reaction to the unexpected.

Within society at large an acceptance of the exercise of authority is essential to maintain social cohesion; however, there is a sharply attuned recognition within societies of the constraints that apply to that authority and an exercise of power by 'appointed authority' is strongly resented.

Authority (resource):   The ability of a role incumbent to apply resources to a task without reference to another person.

Capability:
- knowledge
- technical skills
- social process skills
- mental processing ability
- application – desire, energy and drive applied to work

Chaos: The patterns of complexity and the multiple scales of complexity that are now being studied as part of a general theory of chaos (see Gleick, 1987; 2008; Strogatz, 2014). This is *not* random disorder. Classical science and much theory of organisation has searched for ordered linear patterns that allow prediction: if this, then that.

Chaos theory studies non-linear patterns where the relationships are not simple and linear, prediction of the outcomes with any accuracy becomes more and more difficult over time.

Minute differences in initial conditions have profound effects into the future. Most natural systems are chaotic in their functioning.

Chaos theory forces us to confront the fact that no matter how much experience we have and how well we understand the present, the predictions we make about the future will become progressively less accurate as they extend forward in time. Our mental processing ability is the facility to make order of this chaos, to perceive the universe and to 'discover' or 'create' the patterns (order) which we can then use as we take action.

Constraints (for a task):   Limitations within which a task must be completed. It is the work of the task assigner to articulate these constraints to the task doer and confirm they are understood.

Context (of a task):   The situation in which the task assigner predicts the task will be performed, including the background conditions, the relationship of this task to other tasks and any unusual factors to be taken into account.

When the task performance is being reviewed the actual context needs to be considered in the review.

Critical Issue: Something that if not satisfactorily resolved threatens the achievement of the purpose of the work of an individual, team or organisation. 'What if this happens, how will we address it?'

Culture: A culture is a group of people who share a common set of mythologies.

The group may be very large or relatively small and the strength of the culture will be determined by the number of mythologies that are common to the group.

It is normal for there to be smaller common interest groups within a large cultural group and these are often referred to as sub cultures.

The commonality of the mythologies causes all the members of a culture to ascribe the same value assessment to a system, symbol or behaviour that they experience, be that assessment positive or negative.

The process of changing or creating a culture requires the generation of new mythologies that are common to the group.

Dissonance: A state of mind generated by the clear failure of a prediction that has been based upon a strongly held belief.

Dissonance can be generated by the behaviour of another person or group, the activity of a system or the appearance of a symbol.

Because we need to be able to predict with reasonable accuracy to be and feel safe, dissonance generates anxiety and the need to formulate an explanation. The generation of dissonance is the first step in the process of formation of new mythologies.

Employment Charter: A written document to clarify the conditions and mutual behaviours which each member of the organisation is authorised and entitled to expect so that he or she may experience a constructive, productive and safe work environment which encourages people to work to their potential'.

Employment Hierarchy: The network of employment roles set up by an association of people to carry out work required to achieve the objectives of the association' (Brown, 1971: 49).

Fair Treatment System: A system designed and implemented by the leadership of an organisation that applies to all members of the organisation. The purpose of the system is to provide for a non-biased assessment and judgement on decisions or work place behaviours that are perceived to be unfair by a person who is a member of the organisation.

The fair treatment system functions internally to the organisation and its use is preferred prior to any appeal for judgement from outside the organisation.

Hierarchy: An organisation structure wherein the authority available to a role increases upwards through the structure, increasing as work complexity increases.

The authority structure of the organisation is made visible and accessible by means of role titles. In a correctly structured organisation each role has the authority that is necessary to perform the work assigned to the role and this provides the connection between role authority and work.

Human Decision-Making Model:

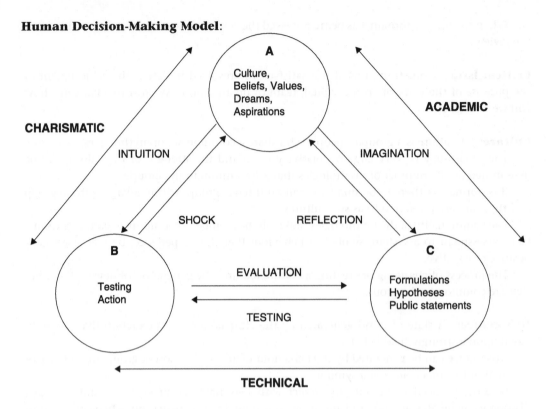

Influence: Activity that attempts to have an effect on the behaviour, or beliefs of another individual or group.

Knowledge: That array of facts and relationships that an individual has available to him or her for the performance of work, it may be part or all of an accepted body of knowledge, or knowledge that has been produced as largely self-generated content by the individual.

Knowledge Field: The knowledge held by an individual about a specific subject. The knowledge will be gained from a range of sources from personal experience to formal study.

    This is the knowledge which a person brings to their work in an endeavour to solve problems that seem to relate to that particular field. Should they appreciate the need to do so, additional knowledge may be sought to resolve a work problem and any knowledge gained then becomes part of that field.

    Each person has unique knowledge fields as they are what he or she has built up through life to date about a particular subject. There will be a core of knowledge in each field that is common to most people in a cultural group with similar educational experiences.

Language – Social and Scientific Meanings:

   Scientific meaning: A precisely defined term with deliberately clear boundaries for the purpose of explaining relationships and testing hypotheses: 'This is what I mean'. An entity or term has a clearly defined meaning by which we can determine whether an entity is 'one of those' or not.

Social meaning: A term which is assumed to provide a similarity of understanding for the purpose of social interaction: 'You know what I mean?' In our everyday lives we approximate and assume an understanding without concern as to whether we mean precisely the same thing.

Leader: A leader is a person who is able to demonstrate the exercise of power or authority, or both, and cause a group of people to act in consort to achieve a purpose.

The objective of a correctly functioning organisation is to have all its leaders clearly identified and exercising authority for the effective and efficient achievement of the purpose of the organisation and where that authority is willingly accepted.

Within an employment hierarchy, all managers are leaders, but not all leaders are managers.

Leader, Work of: The work of a leader is to create, maintain and improve the culture of a group of people so that they achieve objectives and continue to do so over time.

Levels of Work: The sequence of qualitatively different complexity pathways that need to be created to achieve goals when performing work. Depending upon the inherent complexity of a particular task it will only be completed successfully if that complexity is resolved; hence it will fall into a specific level of work.

Management: The work of ordering and sequencing the application of resources to achieve a predetermined purpose. Good management does this effectively and efficiently.

Human capability, in all its aspects, is one of the resources available to a manager that needs to be applied, through a person to person interaction, whereas other resources involve person to object interactions.

Manager: A person who is accountable for his or her own work and the work performance of people reporting to him or her over time. All managers are leaders of people; they have no choice. Their only choice is to be a good or bad leader.

Mental Processing Ability (MPA):   The ability of a person to generate order from the chaos by means of thought. The generation of order, which requires the understanding of relationships, is essential if intention is to be turned into reality, i.e. work is done. The ability to make order out of the chaotic environment in which humans live out their lives and in which they work. It is the ability to pattern and construe the world in terms of scale and time. The level of our MPA will determine the amount and complexity of information that we can process in doing so. (This definition draws in part from I. Macdonald (1984: 2) and also from Jaques (1989: 33)).

Not all people have the same ability to generate order (MPA) and hence the same ability to perform work. Some will be able to resolve more complex problems than others. This distribution of MPA in the human population is discontinuous which leads to differing levels of work complexity or levels of work. There is no evidence that a person's MPA changes in adulthood though the other aspects of capability, and particularly knowledge, are amendable to change over time.

Meritocracy: An organisation wherein people are assigned work, rewarded, promoted and titled based upon their capability to do the work of a role.

Mutual Knowledge Unit (MKU): A structural unit of an organisation made up on a manager and his or her direct reports.

So called because of the need for there to be a reasonable mutual knowledge of the life experience of other members of the MKU if its social processes are to function well in the work environment.

Mutual Recognition Unit (MRU): A structural unit of an organisation made up of a manager, his or her direct reports, some or all of whom are managers, and their direct reports in turn.

An MRU spans three levels of work structure in the organisation.

The need for mutual recognition stems from the authority of the manager-once-removed (M+1) that applies to the direct reports at the lower level of the MRU.

In relation to these MRU members the M+1 has the authority to veto selection, recommend selection, assess potential, review decisions that relate to them and to either dismiss or recommend dismissal from the organisation. The proper exercise of these authorities requires, as a minimum, that the M+1 and the direct reports know one another's work well enough to allow mutual recognition.

Mythology: From Mythos – the story with emotional content: Logos – the explanatory rationale or meaning of the story.

Mythologies are the stories that inform us about what constitutes good and bad behaviour.

We look at systems, symbols and people's behaviour through the lens of our mythologies and assign what we see to a place on one or more of the scales of human values.

Our mythologies are our beliefs about whether what we see strengthens social cohesion in our group or whether it weakens it.

Mythologies are not changed; new ones need to be constructed. Mythologies may lie dormant for years and can be enlivened by an event in the future.

Network: People working towards a common purpose or with common interests where there is no requirement for members of the network to have a work relationship with others, and there is no requirement for mutuality as there is with a team.

Operations Work: Work that is directly connected to the output that an organisation has been established to produce.

Operations work will be directed to developing a product to satisfy the perceived needs of customers, producing a product to satisfy the current needs of customers or directed to the selling of those products to customers.

All three aspects of operations work are essential if a business or service organisation is to remain viable over time (See also Service Work and Support Work).

Organisational level: A band across an organisation in which all the roles have a similar distribution of work complexity (level of work).

Organisational structure: The arrangement of the roles in an organisation that, when correctly done, identifies and matches work complexity and the authority necessary to perform that work so the purpose of the organisation is achieved efficiently and effectively over time.

The structure is the equivalent of the bone structure of the organisation; its form is made visible and accessible by way of its titling system.

Output: The observable result of work having been done. It is assessed in terms of quality and quantity.

Performance (Two Definitions):
1) Output/results (or measures of same)
   The relationship between targeted output and achieved output
   Output or results can, and must, be measured.

2) Work Performance. How well a person has done in producing the results (output) taking into consideration all relevant circumstances. How well has the person carried out the work of the role?
   Work performance cannot be measured; it must be *judged* by a manager based on how well the person has worked to achieve the assigned output, or result, in the situation in which the work was performed.

Policy: A statement that expresses the standards of practice and the criteria required to be demonstrated by the behaviour of people who work for the organisation.
   Policy is the formal expressions of the organisation's ethical framework, it is a statement that expresses the intended ethical and operational standards that the organisation seeks to demonstrate through the application of its systems and the behaviour of its people and the symbols it uses.
   As stated above, the formal expressions of the organisations ethical framework lies in the policies of the organisation. Policies are statements of intent.

Power: See Authority and Power.

Process: The mechanism by which inputs are converted into the specified outputs.

Purpose (of a task assignment):   What is to be achieved by accomplishing a task. For an organisation, policy or system, the objective intended by its action in practice.

Quantity/Quality (of a task assignment):   The expected output of the task and the standard expected. These are treated as a single dimension as one cannot have quantity without quality, nor quality without quantity.

Resources (necessary to complete a task assignment):   Authority, facilities, equipment, money, people, access to information, access to assets, time.

Responsibility: Synonymous with accountability but long use in organisations that failed to hold people responsible for their work has led to its general use as a collective noun for tasks, as in 'your responsibilities are as follows ...' 'the general responsibilities of the role are ...'.

Service Work: Service work is directed towards the efficient and effective performance of those functions that are essential for the continuing activity of the operations functions e.g. accounting and finance: statutory reporting: regulatory compliance: audit: personnel benefits and payroll, etc.

Social Process: Person to person interaction wherein the behaviour of each has a bearing upon the thoughts, emotions and behaviour of the other.

Social Process Skills
Social process skills are those skills that give the ability to observe social behaviour, comprehend the embedded social information and to respond in a way that influences subsequent behaviour in a predictable way. In an organisation this results in behaviour that contributes to the purpose of the organisation.

Staff Relationship: A work relationship wherein a person accepts freely that his or her work performance will be judged on the basis of his or her personal work contribution and recompensed accordingly as opposed to a third party determined requirement such seniority, union nominated classification or externally determined qualification.

Strategy: A military term to do with the disposition and deployment of large military units, such as entire armies, such that the enemy's forces may be defeated.

In business when correctly applied it is a plan for the achievement of the organisation's purpose developed and implemented by the upper levels of the organisation.

Stratum (plural strata): In geology and related fields, a stratum is a layer of sedimentary rock or soil with internally consistent characteristics that distinguish it from other layers. In an organisational sense this term refers to layers in organisations that are internally consistent in work complexity (see Organisational Level).

Stratification on the basis of work complexity is the core of effective organisation structure.

When correctly done it generates a structure that corresponds to the differing capabilities of people to generate order from the chaos and so perform productive work that is required to achieve the purpose of the organisation.

It makes good sense to structure an organisation in a way that is in accord with the thinking patterns of people.

Supervisor: A leadership role in Stratum I, sometimes titled a Crew Leader. A supervisory role does not have the full range of authority that defines a managerial role but is one of the most important leadership roles in an organisation.

Support Work: Sometimes referred to as *improvement work* is that work which is directed towards the improvement of the systems and processes the organisation employs to perform its operations and service activities.

It is a part of the work of each role incumbent to think of ways to improve upon his or her current work, the support roles develop and test these ideas as well taking a wider perspective and seeking to improve the systems and processes that span numerous roles and activities.

Symbol: The outward manifestation of a cultural group, e.g. flags, rituals, medals, posters, slogans.

Symbols are interpreted as representing a position that is strongly positive on the values continua by the culture that employs the symbol and strongly negative by members of counter cultures.

System: A system is a framework that orders and sequences activity within the organisation to achieve a purpose within a band of variance that is acceptable to the owner of the system.

Systems are the organisational equivalent of behaviour in human interaction.

Systems are the means by which organisations put policies into action.

It is the owner of a system who has the authority to change it, hence his or her clear acceptance of the degree of variation generated by the existing system.

System Audit: A periodic review of a system by an external party that examines the system in use to determine whether or not it is being used as designed and intended, whether the control data is valid, whether it is being reported, reviewed and acted upon and whether or not the system is achieving the purpose for which it was designed. System audit is performed on behalf of the system owner.

System Control: A statistically valid sample of data from the system that allows the system custodian to confirm that the system is operating as it was designed to operate or to institute corrective action should it be required to have the system function as designed.

Note the difference between system control and controls as applied in safety systems. In safe work systems controls are activities that form part of the system itself.

System Custodian: The role within the organisation that does the work required to review the control data from a system and to advise the system owner of the state of use of the system and indicators of a system functioning drawn from the control data.

The system custodian may also be the system owner.

System Owner: The role within the organisation that authorises the purpose of the system and its design and implementation to achieve that purpose.

Only the system owner has the authority to change the system.

Systems of Differentiation: Systems that treat people differently, e.g. remuneration systems based on work performance.

All systems of differentiation should be based on the work (to be) done.

Systems of Equalisation: Systems that treat people the same way irrespective of any organisational criteria, e.g. safety systems.

Systems Leadership: An internally coherent and integrated theory of organisational behaviour. It is a body of knowledge that helps not only to understand why people behave the way they do, but also and perhaps more importantly to predict the way that people are likely to behave in organisations.

Systems Leadership is essentially about how to create, improve and sustain successful organisations.

Task: A Statement of intention articulated as an assignment to carry out work within limits that include the context, purpose, quantity and quality of output expected, the resources available and the time by which the objective is to be reached (CPQ/QRT).

Task Assignment Process: The clear articulation to the task doer of Context, Purpose, Quantity/Quality of Output, Resources, Time to Completion.

Task Feedback: Information the task doer receives regarding how well he or she carried out the task. This can come from nature, customers, peers, or the person's leader.

Task Review: An assessment by the task doer's leader of how well the task was performed. Task review provides information that is given to the task doer and comes from the task doer on a regular but random basis. The purpose is for the task doer and the leader to learn from both success and failure so performance may be improved. Note: in a correctly organised work hierarchy a task doer (direct report) has the authority to require a task review and report from his or her leader. Task Review includes all the components of the task: CPQ/QRT.

Team: A team is a group of people, including a leader, with a common purpose who must interact with each other in order to perform their individual tasks and thus achieve their common purpose.

Teamwork: A team member is part of the whole. It is only by active co-operation however, that the whole will be greater than the sum of the parts. The work of interaction that needs to be done by each team member to promote efficient and effective team functioning.

Technical Skills: Proficiency in the use of knowledge. This includes learned routines that improve the efficiency and effectiveness of work required to complete a task.

Time (as a resource): The amount of time available prior to the deadline. This may be expressed as people's work hours available or the sum of hours prior to the deadline.

Time (in a task assignment): The targeted completion time is a boundary condition – a deadline indicating by when the task is to be completed.

Time-span: The targeted completion time of the longest task in a role equals the time-span of the role. It is a measure of one property of a work relationship between a manager and his or her direct report.

Time-span is the elapsed time to disorder, effectively how long a person of a given capability is able to generate order in the chaos in which he or she is working.

Universal Values: A typology of six universal human experiences that rate or judge all behaviours, systems and symbols heuristically. Behaviours, systems and symbols that are demonstrated and rated positively create social cohesion, those that are demonstrated and rated negatively destroy it.

There are six values which are, expressed positively, love: trust: fairness: respect for human dignity: honesty: courage.

As a set they are mutually exclusive and comprehensively exhaustive and apply universally in all human societies.

The mythological lens that is used to position a system, symbol or behaviour on the values continua, either positive or negative, is unique to each person having been developed by their experience of life.

Work: Turning intention into reality.

Work Performance: An assessment made by a leader about how effectively and efficiently a direct report has worked in performing an assigned task taking into consideration the actual context in which the task was done.

Bibliography

Ackoff, R.L. (1999) *Ackoff's Best: His Classic Writings on Management*. New York: John Wiley & Sons.

Addleson, M. (2011) *Beyond Management: Taking Charge at Work*. Basingstoke: Palgrave Macmillan.

Adizes Institute (2017) sourced from http://adizes.com/lifecycle/ Retrieved 25 June 2017.

Arfmann, D. and Barbe, F. (2014) 'The value of lean in the service sector: A critique of theory & practice', *International Journal of Business and Social Science*, Vol. 5, No. 2, pp. 18–24.

Armstrong, M. (2000) *Rewarding Teams*. London: Chartered Institute of Personnel and Development.

Baddeley, A.D. (2000) 'The episodic buffer: A new component of working memory?', *Trends in Cognitive Sciences*, Vol. 4, No. 11, pp. 417–423.

Baddeley, A.D. and Hitch, G. (1974) 'Working Memory', in G.H. Bower (ed.), *The Psychology of Learning and Motivation: Advances in Research and Theory*, Volume 8. New York: Academic Press, pp. 47–89.

Bageant, J. (2008) *Deer Hunting with Jesus: Dispatches from America's Class War*. New York: Broadway Books.

Barnard, C. (1938) *The Functions of the Executive*. Cambridge, MA: Harvard University Press.

Barolsky, J. (1994) *A New Vision for the Company: Hamersley Iron Employee Relations and Change Management*. Perth: Hamersley Iron.

Baron, J. (2007) *Thinking and Deciding* (4th ed.). New York, NY: Cambridge University Press.

Beck, K. et al. (2001) 'Manifesto for Agile Software Development', Agile Alliance, sourced from http://agile-manifesto.org/ Retrieved September 2016.

Becker, C. (1955) 'What is a historical fact?', *The Western Political Quarterly*, Vol. 8, No. 3, pp. 327–340, sourced from www.jstor.org/stable/442890?seq=1#page_scan_tab_contents.

Beedle, M. et al. (2001) 'Twelve Principles of Agile Software', *The Agile Manifesto*, 2001, sourced from http://agilemanifesto.org/ Retrieved 5 July 2015.

Belsky, J.K. (1990) *The Psychology of Aging Theory, Research, and Interventions*. Pacific Grove, CA: Brooks/Cole Publishing Company.

Bennett, J. (1956–66) *The Dramatic Universe*. London: Hodder & Stoughton.

Berkun, S. (2010) *The Myths of Innovation*. O'Reilly Media.

Berkun, S. (2013) 'The Ten Myths of Innovation: The Best Summary.' Posted 26 March 2013, sourced from http://scottberkun.com/2013/ten-myths-of-innnovation/ Retrieved 30 April 2017.

Bernstein, E., Bunch, J., Canner, N. and Lee, M. (2016) 'Beyond the Holacracy Hype', *Harvard Business Review*, July–August, pp. 38–49.

Bishop, W.S. (1989) 'The Exercise of Discretion in the Work of Nursing: Nurses' Perceptions of Their Approach to Work'. D.P.A. Dissertation, University of Southern California, Los Angeles, CA.

Blanchard, K. and Johnson, S. (1982) *The One Minute Manager*. New York: Morrow.

Blau, P.M. (1956) *Bureaucracy in Modern Society*. New York: Random House.

Blau, P.M. and Scott, W.R. (1962) *Formal Organizations*. San Francisco: Chandler.

Bless, H., Fielder, K. and Strack, F. (2004) *Social cognition: How individuals construct social reality*. Hove and New York: Psychology Press.

Bloom, B.S. and Krathwohl, D.R. (1956) *Taxonomy of Educational Objectives: The Classification of Educational Goals Handbook I: Cognitive Domain*. New York: Longmans, Green.

Boals, D.M. (1985) 'Levels of Work and Responsibility in Public Libraries'. PhD Dissertation, University of Southern California, Los Angeles, CA.

Bolles, E.B. (ed.) (1997) *Galileo's Commandment: An Anthology of Great Science Writing*. New York: W.H. Freeman.

Brown, W. (1960) *Exploration in Management*. London: Heinemann.

Brown, W. (1971) *Organization*. London: Heinemann.

Brown, W. and Jaques, E. (1965) *Glacier Project Papers: Some Essays on Organisation and Management from the Glacier Project Research*. London: Heinemann.

Burke, C. and Smith, D. (1992) *Organizing Corporate Computing: A History of the Application of a Theory. Festschrift for Elliott Jaques*. Arlington, VA: Cason Hall & Co.

Burns, T. and Stalker, G.M. (1961; 1966) *The Management of Innovation*. London: Tavistock Publications.

Byrne, J.A. (2005) 'The Man Who Invented Management', *Business Week*, 28 November, p. 104.

Campbell, J. (1949; 1972) *The Hero with a Thousand Faces*. Princeton, NJ: Princeton University Press.

Carrison, D. and Walsh, R. (1999) *Semper Fi: Business Leadership the Marine Corps Way*. New York: AMACOM.

Cattell, R. (1971) *Abilities: Their Structure, Growth, and Action*. Boston, MA: Houghton Mifflin.

Cendrowski, S. (2015) 'What It's Like to Watch Alibaba's Singles Day Spectacle', *Fortune*, 11 November, sourced from http://fortune.com/2015/11/11/alibaba-singles-day-spectacle/.

Chandler, A.D., Jr. (1969; 1980) *Strategy and Structure: Chapters in the History of the Industrial Enterprise*. Cambridge, MA: MIT Press.

Chandler, A.D., Jr. (1990) *Scale and Scope*. Cambridge, MA: Belknap Press of Harvard University.

Chorover, S.L. (1979) *From Genesis to Genocide: The Meaning of Human Nature and the Power of Behavior Control*. Cambridge, MA: MIT Press.

Church, M. (1999) 'Organizing simply for complexity: Beyond metaphor towards theory', *Long Range Planning*, Vol. 32, No. 4, pp. 425–440.

Churchman, C.W. (1979) *The Systems Approach and Its Enemies*. New York: Basic Books.

Collins, J. (2001) *From Good to Great*. New York: Harper Collins.

Collins, J. and Porras, J. (1994) *Built to Last*. New York: Harper Collins.

County Court of Victoria (2014–15) Annual Report, sourced from https://www.countycourt.vic.gov.au/sites/default/files/CCV%20Annual%20Report%202014–15_Single%20Pages.pdf.

Cowan, R.S. (1983) *More Work for Mother: The Ironies of Household Technology from the Open Hearth to the Microwave*. New York: Basic Books.

Cross, R., Rebele, R. and Grant, A. (2016) 'Collaborative Overload', *Harvard Business Review*, January–February, pp. 74–79.

Dahrendorf, R. (1985) 'Work and Life or the New Fear of Freedom', in Boekman (ed.), *Dignity at Work*. Stockholm: Streiffert.

Davenport, T. (1993) *Process Innovation*. Cambridge, MA: Harvard Business School Press.

Dawkins, R. (1976) 'Hierarchical Organization: A Candidate Principle for ethology', in P.P.G. Bateson and R.A. Hinde (eds), *Growing Points Ethology*. Cambridge: Cambridge University Press, pp. 7–54.

De Bono, E. (2008) *Six Thinking Hats* (rev. edn). Harmondsworth: Penguin Books.

Deming, W.E. (1982) *Out of the Crisis*. Boston, MA: MIT Press.

Denning, S. (2011) 'Scrum is a Major Management Discovery', *Forbes Magazine*, 29 April, sourced from https://www.forbes.com/forbes/welcome/?toURL=https://www.forbes.com/sites/stevedenning/2011/04/29/scrum-is-a-major-management-discovery/

Denning, S. (2012) 'The Best Kept Management Secret on the Planet: Agile', *Forbes Magazine*, 9 April, sourcedfromwww.forbes.com/sites/stevedenning/2012/04/09/the-best-kept-management-secret-on-the-planet-agile/.

Denning, S. (2014) 'Making Sense of Zappos and Holocracy', *Forbes Magazine*, 15 January, sourced from www.forbes.com/sites/stevedenning/2014/01/15/making-sense-of-zappos-and-holacracy/#45a2f882121f.

Dingsøyr, T., Nerur, S., Balijepally, V. and Moe, N.B. (2012) 'A decade of agile methodologies: Towards explaining agile software development', *Journal of Systems and Software*, Vol. 85, No. 6, sourced from www.sciencedirect.com/science/article/pii/S0164121212000532.

Donald, M. (1991) *Origins of the Modern Mind: Three Stages in the Evolution of Culture and Cognition*. Cambridge, MA: Harvard University Press.

Drucker, P. (1954; 1969) *The Practice of Management*. New York: Harper.

Drucker, P. (1969) *The Age of Discontinuity*. New York: Harper and Row.

Dubljevic, V. and Ryan, C.J. (2015) 'Cognitive enhancement with methylphenidate and modafinil: Conceptual advances and societal implications', *Neuroscience and Neuro Economics*, Vol. 4, pp. 25–33.

Duhigg, C. (2016a) *Smarter Faster Better: The Secrets of Being Productive in Life and Business*. New York: Random House.

Duhigg, C. (2016b) 'What Google Learned from Its Quest to Build the Perfect Team', *New York Times Magazine*, 25 February.

Dunbar, R. (2010) *How Many Friends Does One Person Need?: Dunbar's Number and Other Evolutionary Quirks*. Cambridge, MA: Harvard University Press.

Dunlop, T. (1999a) 'Missionaries, Mercenaries and Mechanics'. Macdonald Associates Consultancy, internal paper.

Dunlop, T. (1999b) 'Creating a Meritocracy'. Macdonald Associates Paper – unpublished.

Dunlop, T. (2000) 'Core Social Process Skills for Leaders'. Macdonald Associates Paper – unpublished.

Dyer, J.H., Gregerson, H. and Christenson, C. (2009) 'The Innovators DNA', *Harvard Business Review*, December.

Emery, F.E. (ed.) (1969) *Systems Thinking*. Harmondsworth: Penguin Books.

Emery, F.E. (ed.) (1981) *Systems Thinking*, Vol. 2. Harmondsworth: Penguin Books.

Emery, F.E. and Trist, E.L. (1960) 'Socio-Technical Systems', in C.W. Churchman and M. Verhulst (eds), *Management Science, Models and Techniques*. New York: Pergamon, pp. 83–97.

Evans, J.S. (1979) *The Management of Human Capacity*. Bradford: MCB Publications.

Fayol, H. (1930) *Industrial and General Administration* (translated from the French for the International Management Institute by J.A. Coubrough). London: Pitman & Sons.

Festinger, L. (1957) *A Theory of Cognitive Dissonance*. Palo Alto, CA: Stanford University Press.

Freedman, D.H. (2016) 'The War on Stupid People', *The Atlantic Magazine*, July/August.

Freud, S. (1923) *Das Ich und das Es*. Leipzig, Vienna, and Zurich: Internationaler Psycho-analytischer Verlag; English translation, Riviere, J. (trans.) (1927) *The Ego and the Id*. London: Hogarth Press and Institute of Psycho-analysis.

Freud, S. (1930; 2010) *Civilization and Its Discontents* (translated and edited by J. Strachey). New York: W.W. Norton & Co.

Fuller, B. (1969) *Operating Manual for Spaceship Earth*. New York: Simon & Schuster.

Gallup (2015) *State of the American Workplace*.

Gallup (2017) *State of the American Workplace*, sourced from www.gallup.com/services/182216/state-american-manager-report.aspx.

Gerth, H.H. and Mills, C.W. (1946) *From Max Weber: Essays in Sociology* (translated, edited and with an introduction by H.H. Gerth and C. Wright Mills). New York: Oxford University Press.

Gladwell, M. (2005) *Blink: The Power of Thinking without Thinking*. New York: Little, Brown and Co.

Gleick, J. (1987) *Chaos: Making a New Science*. Harmondsworth: Penguin Books.

Goddard, H.H. (1919) *Psychology of the Normal and Subnormal*. New York: Dodd, Mead and Co.

Godin, B. (2015) *Innovation Contested: The Idea of Innovation over the Centuries* (Routledge Studies in Social and Political Thought). Abingdon: Routledge.

Goldman, L.L. (1999) 'Work Strata Selection as a Measurement of Law Enforcement Organizational Leadership'. D.P.A. Dissertation, sourced from https://search-proquest-com.libproxy1.usc.edu/pqdtlocal1006272/docview/304553511/AB4650FF46E149B4PQ/3?accountid=14749.

Goleman, D. (1996) *Emotional Intelligence: And Why It Can Matter More Than IQ*. London: Bloomsbury.

Gould, D.P. (1984) 'An Examination of Levels of Work in Academic Library Technical Services Departments Utilizing Stratified Systems Theory'. PhD Dissertation, University of Southern California, Los Angeles, CA.

Gould, S.J. (1996) *The Mismeasure of Man* (rev. edn). New York: W.W. Norton & Co.

Gray, J.L. (ed.) (1976) *The Glacier Project: Concepts and Critiques*. London: Heinemann.

Grinberg, N. et al. (2013) 'Extracting Diurnal Patterns of Real World Activity from Social Media Association for the Advancement of Artificial Intelligence', sourced from http://sm.rutgers.edu/pubs/Grinberg-SMPatterns-ICWSM2013.pdf.

Gulick, L. (1937) *Papers on the Science of Administration* (edited by L. Gulick and L. Urwick). New York: Institute of Public Administration, Columbia University.

Hall, G., Rosenthal, J. and Wade, J. (1993) 'How to Make Re-engineering Really Work', *Harvard Business Review*, November–December, pp. 119–131.

Hammer, M. and Champy, J. (1993) *Reengineering the Corporation: A Manifesto for Business Revolution*. New York: Harper Business.

Hargreaves, A. and Fink, D. (2005) *Sustainable Leadership* (1st edn). San Francisco, CA: Jossey-Bass.

Harper, B. (1992) *Rivethead*. New York: Warner Books.

Harvey, J. (1999) *How Come Every Time I Get Stabbed in the Back, My Fingerprints Are on the Knife?* San Francisco: Jossey-Bass.

Haselton, M.G., Nettle, D. and Andrews, P.W. (2005). *The evolution of cognitive bias*. In D.M. Buss (Ed.), The Handbook of Evolutionary Psychology: Hoboken, NJ, US: John Wiley & Sons Inc. pp. 724–746.

Innosight (2012) 'Executive Briefing Winter 2012 Creative Destruction Whips through Corporate America', sourcedfromwww.innosight.com/innovation-resources/strategy-innovation/upload/creative-destruction-whips-through-corporate-america_final2015.pdf/ Retrieved August 2016.

Intel IT (2016) www.intel.com/content/www/us/en/it-management/intel-it-best-practices/intel-it-annual-performance-report–2015–16-paper.html/ Retrieved March 2017.

Intel IT (2017) www.intel.com/content/www/us/en/it-management/intel-it-best-practices/best-practices-fast-threat-detection-with-big-data-security-business-intelligence-brief.html/ Retrieved March 2017.

Intel PR (2016) 2016 IDF: 2 Things You Need to Know for Day 2, *Intel Newsroom Website*, sourced from https://newsroom.intel.com/chip-shots/intel-developer-forum-day–2-keynote-highlights/ Retrieved 30 April 2017.

Isaac, D.J. and O'Connor, B.M. (1978) 'A Discontinuity Theory of Psychological Development', in E. Jaques (ed.) with R.O. Gibson D.J. and Isaac, *Levels of Abstraction in Logic and Human Action*. London: Heinemann, pp. 95–120.

Jaques, E. (1951) *The Changing Culture of a Factory*. London: Tavistock Publications.

Jaques, E. (1963) *Equitable Pay*. London: Heinemann Educational Books.

Jaques, E. (1964) *Time-Span Handbook*. London: Heinemann Educational Books.

Jaques, E. (1976) *A General Theory of Bureaucracy*. London: Heinemann.

Jaques, E. (1982) *Free Enterprise, Fair Employment*. London: Heinemann.

Jaques, E. (1989) *Requisite Organization*. Falls Church, VA: Cason Hall and Co.

Jaques, E. (1990) 'In Praise of Hierarchy', *Harvard Business Review*, January, pp. 127–133.

Jaques, E. (2002) *Life and Behaviour of Living Organisms: A General Theory*. Westport, CT: Praeger.

Jaques, E. (ed.) with Gibson, R.O. and Isaac, D.J. (1978) *Levels of Abstraction in Logic and Human Action*. London: Heinemann.

Jaques, E. and Cason, K. (1994) *Human Capability*. London: Gower.

Johnson, J. (1998) *Who Moved My Cheese?* New York: Putnam.

Kahneman, D. and Tversky, A. (1973) 'On the psychology of prediction', *Psychological Review*, Vol. 80, pp. 237–251.

Kautz, K., Johansen, T.H. and Uldahl, A. (2014) 'The perceived impact of the agile development and project management method scrum on information systems and software development productivity', *Australasian Journal of Information Systems*, Vol. 18, No. 3, pp. 303–315.

Kegan, R. (1982) *The Evolving Self*. Boston, MA: Harvard University Press.

Kersten, W., Blecker, T. and Ringle, C.M. (eds) (2015) *Innovations and Strategies for Logistics and Supply Chains: Technologies, Business Models and Risk Management*. Proceedings of the Hamburg International Conference of Logistics (HICL), Vol. 20, sourced from https://hicl.org/publications/2015/20/1.pdf/ Retrieved August 2015.

Kohlberg, L. (1971) 'From is to ought: How to commit the naturalistic fallacy and get away with it in the study of moral development', in T. Mishcel (ed.), *Cognitive Development and Epistemology*. New York: Academic Press, pp. 151–235.

Kolbe, K. (1991) *Conative Connection: Acting on Intent*. Boston, MA: Addison Wesley.

Kotter, J. (1999) 'What Effective General Managers Really Do', *Harvard Business Review*, March–April 1999.

Kwoh, L. (2012) 'You Call That Innovation? Companies Love to Say They Innovate, but the Term Has Begun to Lose Meaning', *Wall Street Journal*, May 2012, sourced from www.wsj.com/articles /SB10001424052702304791704577418250902309914/ retrieved August 2016.

Lane, T.S. and Tripe, P.D. (2006) *Relationships: A Mess Worth Making*. Greensboro, NC: New Growth Press.

Laney, D. (2001) 'Application Delivery Strategies', Meta Group (now part of Garner), unpublished research note, sourced from http://blogs.gartner.com/doug-laney/deja-vvvue-others-claiming-gartners-volume-velocity-variety-construct-for-big-data/.

Lavoisier, A.-L. (1997) 'Preface to *The Elements of Chemistry*', in E.B. Bolles (ed.), *Galileo's Commandment: An Anthology of Great Science Writing*. New York: W.H. Freeman, pp. 379–388.

Lorsch, J.W. and McTague, E. (2016) 'Culture is Not the Culprit', *Harvard Business Review*, April, 96–105.

Ludeke, T. (1996) *The Line in the Sand: The Long Road to Staff Employment at Comalco*. Melbourne: Wilkinson Books.

Lutz, B. (2013) *Car Guys vs. Bean Counters: The Battle for the Soul of American Business*. New York: Penguin, Portfolio.

Macdonald, B. (2001) 'Critical Incidents, Personality and Burn-out in Staff Working in an Intensive Care Unit'. Doctoral Thesis, Department of Clinical Psychology, Cardiff University.

McDonald, G. (2006) 'Better Words, Concepts and Models – Better Safety', Geoff McDonald and Associates Pty.

McDonald, G. (2007) 'Intermediate Measures for Safety', Geoff McDonald and Associates Pty.

McDonald, G. (2016) 'Some Thoughts to Assist Strategic Planning', Prepared for the Safety Institute of Australia, 2008, in K. McDonald, chapter 10, 'Safety Models', unpublished manuscript.

Macdonald, I. (1984) *Stratified Systems Theory: An Outline*. Individual and Organisational Capability Unit, BIOSS, Brunel University.

Macdonald, I. (1988) 'Getting on with the real work', *Journal of the British Institute of Mental Handicap*, Vol. 16, pp. 65–67.

Macdonald, I. (1990) 'Identity Development of People with Learning Difficulties through the Recognition of Work'. PhD Dissertation, Brunel University.

Macdonald, I. (1995) *Statement to the Australian Industrial Relations Commission*. Evidence submitted to Commission.

Macdonald, I. and Couchman, T. (1980) *Chart of Initiative and Independence*. Slough: NFER.

Macdonald, I. and Grimmond, J. (2000) 'Systems and Symbols Audit'. Unpublished paper for Macdonald Associates.

Macdonald, R. (1991) 'Breaking the Frame: The Heart of Leadership'. MA Dissertation, School of Policy, Planning and Development, University of Southern California.

McLeod, S.A. (2012) 'Working Memory'. Retrieved from www.simplypsychology.org/working%20memory.html.

Marcus, G. and Davis, E. (2014) 'Eight (No, Nine!) Problems with Big Data', 6 April, sourced from www.nytimes.com/2014/04/07/opinion/eight-no-nine-problems-with-big-data.html 2016.

Marx, K. (1867; 1987) *Capital: A Critique of Political Economy* (Introduced by Ernest Mandel, translated by B. Fowkes). New York: Vintage Books.

Micklethwait, J. and Wooldridge, A. (1996) *The Witch Doctors: Making Sense of the Management Gurus*. New York: Times Books.

Micklethwait, J. and Wooldridge, A. (2003) *The Company*. London: Modern Library.

Mintzberg, H. (1979) *The Structuring of Organizations*. Englewood Cliffs, NJ: Prentice-Hall.

Mintzberg, H. (1989) *Mintzberg on Management: Inside Our Strange World of Organizations*. New York: Free Press.

Moldaschl, M. (2010), 'Why Innovation Theories Make no Sense', Papers and Preprints of the Department of Innovation Research and Sustainable Resource Management (BWL IX), Chemnitz University of Technology No. 9/2010.

Moldaschl, M., Hallensleben, T., Breßler, J. and Wörlen, M. (2012) 'How to get off innovation capabilities by change programs? Theory and case study', Proceedings of the International Symposium on Innovation Methods and Innovation Management, Chemnitz, Germany, 29–30 March 2012.

Morgan, G. (1986) *Images of Organization*. Beverly Hills, CA: SAGE Publications.

Mosher, F.C. (1982) *Democracy and the Public Service* (2nd edn). New York: Oxford University Press.

Mouzelis, N.P. (1967) *Organization and Bureaucracy: An Analysis of Modern Theories*. London: Routledge.

Mu, D.P. (1993) 'Managing Cross-Cultural Interchange: Interpreting Behavior for Mutual Understanding, the Case of China and the United States'. D.P.A. Dissertation, School of Public Administration, University of Southern California.

Mumford, E. and Hendricks, R. (1996) 'Business process re-engineering RIP', *People Management*, Vol. 2, No. 9, pp. 22–26.

Munz, P. (1985) *Our Knowledge of the Growth of Knowledge: Popper or Wittgenstein?* London: Routledge and Kegan Paul.

Obolensky, N. (2014) *Complex Adaptive Leadership: Embracing Paradox and Uncertainty*, 2nd edition. London: Routledge.

O'Leary, D. and Craig, J. (2007) 'System Leadership: Lessons from the Literature', Nottingham, UK: National College for School Leadership.

Petzinger, T., Jr. (1997) 'Self-Organization Will Free Employees to Act Like Bosses', *Wall Street Journal*, 3 January, p. B1.

Pfeffer, J. (2010) *Power: Why Some People Have it and Others Don't*. New York: Harper Business.

Piaget, J. (1971) 'The Theory of Stages in Cognitive Development', in D.R. Green, M.P. Ford and G.B. Flamer (eds), *Measurement and Piaget*. Columbus, OH: McGraw-Hill.

Piketty, T. (2013) *Le capital au XXIᵉ siècle*. Paris: Éditions du Seuil; English translation, Goldhammer, A. (trans.) (2014) *Capital in the 21st Century*. Cambridge, MA: The Belknap Press of Harvard University Press.

Plsek, P.E. and Wilson, T. (2001) 'Complexity, leadership, and management in Health care organisations', *The British Medical Journal*, Vol. 323, No. 7315, pp. 746–749.

Reason, J. (1997) *Manaaging the Risks of Organizational Accidents*. Burlington, VT: Ashgate.

Report on Government Services, Commonwealth of Australia (2016) Australian Government Productivity Commission, sourced from www.pc.gov.au/research/ongoing/report-on-government-services/2016.

Rigby, D., Sutherland, J. and Takeuchi, H. (2016) 'Embracing Agile', *Harvard Business Review*, May, pp. 40–46.

Ritzer, G. (1993) *The McDonaldization of Society*. Newbury Park, CA: Pine Forge Press.

Robertson, B.J. (2015) *Holacracy: The New Management System for a Rapidly Changing World*. New York: Henry Holt and Co., LLC.

Roethlisberger, F. and Dickson, W. (1939) with the assistance and collaboration of H.A. Wright. *Management and the Worker: An Account of a Research Program Conducted by the Western Electric Company, Hawthorne Works, Chicago*. Cambridge, MA: Harvard University Press.

Rowbottom, R. and Billis, D. (1977) 'Stratification of work and organisational design', *Human Relations*, Vol. 30, No. 1, pp. 53–76.

Rutkin, A. (2015) 'Facebook can recognise you in photos even if you're not looking', *New Scientist*, Vol. 22, June, sourced from: https://www.newscientist.com/article/dn27761-facebook-can-recognise-you-in-photos-even-if-youre-not-looking#.VYlaDBNViko/ Retrieved August 2016.

Schumpeter, J. (1939) *Business Cycles: A Theoretical, Historical and Statistical Analysis of the Capitalist Process*. New York: McGraw-Hill.

Schutz, A. (1972) *The Phenomenology of the Social World*. London: Heinemann Educational Books.

Senge, P.M. (1990) *The Fifth Discipline*. New York: Doubleday/Currency.

Shafritz, J. and Ott, S. (1996) *Classics of Organization Theory*. Fort Worth, TX: Harcourt Brace College Publishers.

Shafritz, J., Ott, S. and Yong Suk Jang (2005) *Classics of Organisational Theory*. Belmont, CA: Thomson/ Wadsworth.

Simon, H. (1962) 'The Architecture of Complexity', *Proceedings of the American Philosophical Society*, Vol. 106, No. 6, pp. 467–482.

Smith, A. (2004) *The Wealth of Nations*. New York: Barnes and Noble.

Sokal, A. and Bricmont, J. (1997) *Impostures Intellectuelles*. Paris: Éditions Odile Jacob.

Sotham, J. (2016) 'Airline Merger Wars: The Battle for the Soul of an Airline', *Air & Space Magazine*, March, 2015, sourced from www.airspacemag.com/flight-today/airline-merger-wars–180953942/?no-ist/ Retrieved 1 October.

Stamp, G. (1978) 'Assessment of individual capacity', in E. Jaques (ed.) with R.O. Gibson and D.J. Isaac, *Levels of Abstraction in Logic and Human Action*. London: Heinemann, 251–270.

Stewart, K. (1994) 'CRA Pulls the Rug from under Unions', *Business Review Weekly*, 31 January, pp. 34–39.

Strogatz, S.H. (2014) *Nonlinear Dynamics and Chaos: With Applications to Physics, Biology, Chemistry, and Engineering* (Studies in Nonlinearity, 2nd edn). Westview Press.

Sutherland, J. and Sutherland, J.J. (2014) *Scrum: The Art of Doing Twice the Work in Half the Time*. New York: Crown Business.

Taylor, C. (2005) *Walking the Talk: Building a Culture for Success*. London: Random House.

Taylor, F.W. (1911; 1972) *Scientific Management; Comprising Shop Management, The Principles of Scientific Management [and] Testimony before the Special House Committee*. With a foreword by Harlow S. Person. Westport, CT: Greenwood Press.

The Standish Group (2012) 'CHAOS MANIFESTO 2012, The Year of the Executive Sponsor', sourced from https://cs.calvin.edu/courses/cs/262/kvlinden/resources/CHAOSManifesto2012.pdf.

The Standish Group Report (2015) 'CHAOS', sourced from https://www.projectsmart.co.uk/white-papers/chaos-report.pdf.

Trinca, H. (1997) 'The Art of War', *Sydney Morning Herald*, 8 December, p. 11.

Trist, E. and Bamforth, K.W. (1948) 'Some Social and Psychological Consequences of the Longwall Method of Coal-getting', *Tavistock Institute of Human Relations*, Doc 506.

Trist, E. and Murray, H. (eds) (1990) *The Social Engagement of Social Science*, Volume 1: *A Tavistock Anthology: The Socio-Psychological Perspective*. Philadelphia, PA: University of Pennsylvania Press.

Trist, E. and Murray, H. (eds) (1948; 1993) *The Social Engagement of Social Science*, Volume 2: *A Tavistock Anthology: The Socio-Technical Perspective (innovations in Organizations Series*. Philadelphia, PA: University of Pennsylvania Press.

Trist, E. and Murray, H. (eds) (1997) *The Social Engagement of Social Science*, Volume3: *A Tavistock Anthology: The Socio-Ecological Perspective*. Philadelphia, PA: University of Pennsylvania Press.

Tuskegee Syphilis Study Legacy Committee (2016) *Final Report of the Tuskegee Syphilis Study Legacy Committee*, May 1996, sourced from http://exhibits.hsl.virginia.edu/badblood/report/ Retrieved 26 September.

Tussman, J. (1960) *Obligation and the Body Politic*. New York: Oxford University Press.

Tversky, A. and Kahneman, D. (1974) 'Judgment under Uncertainty: Heuristics and Biases', *Science*, Vol. 185, pp. 1121–1131.

Van Crevald, M. (1982; 2007) *Fighting Power: German and US Army Performance, 1939–1945*. Westport, CT: Praeger.

Wade, H. (2014) 'Middle Managers as Innovators', *Management Today*, December.

Wall Street Journal (2001) 'Disengaged at Work?', 13 March, p. A1.

Watson, D. (2004) *Watson's Dictionary of Weasel Words, Contemporary Clichés, Cant and Management Jargon*. Milsons Point, NSW: Random House.

Way, N. (1994) 'CRA pulls the rug from under unions', *Business Review Weekly*, Fairfax Media Group, 31 January, pp. 34–39.

Weber, M. (1922a) 'Bureaucracy', in J. Shafritz, S. Ott and Yong Suk Jang (eds) (2016), *Classics of Organisational Theory* (8th edn). Boston, MA: Cengage Learning, pp. 78–83.

Weber, M. (1922b) *Economy and Society: An Outline of Interpretive Sociology* (2 volumes); (translated and edited by G. Roth and C. Wittich). (1978) Berkeley, CA: University of California Press, New Edition. See also Gerth and Mills (1946) where Weber was first translated into English.

Weber, M. (1947) *The Theory of Social and Economic Organization* (translated by A.M. Henderson and T. Parsons). New York: The Free Press.

Wheeler, D.J. (2000) *Understanding Variation: The Key to Managing Chaos* (2nd edn). Knoxville, TN: SPC Press.

Whitehurst, J. (2015) *The Open Organization: Igniting Passion and Performance*. Boston, MA: Harvard Business Review Press.

Whyte, D. (2001) *Crossing the Unknown Sea*. New York: Riverhead Books.

Whyte, L.L., Wilson, A.G. and Wilson, D. (eds) (1969) *Hierarchical Structures*. New York: American Elsevier.

Witzel, M. (2015) *Managing for Success: Spotting Danger Signals – And Fixing Problems before they Happen*. London: Bloomsbury Information.

Woolley, A.W., Chabris, C.F., Pentland, A., Hashmi, N. and Malone, T.W. (2010) 'Evidence for a collective intelligence factor in the performance of human groups', *Science*, Vol. 330, No. 6004, pp. 686–688.

Zimm, A.A. (2003) 'Manifestations of Chaos in an Economic Theory of the Organization'. Doctoral Dissertation, School of Policy Planning and Development, University of Southern California.

Zimmerman, E. 'Jeffrey Pfeffer: Do Workplace Hierarchies Still Matter?' *Insights by Stanford Business*, Stanford Graduate School of Business, 24 April, sourced from www.gsb.stanford.edu/insights/jeffrey-pfeffer-do-workplace-hierarchies-still-matter.

Index

Note: Page references in *italics* refer to figures. Page references in **boldface** refer to tables.